Sunbelt Diaspora

Historia USA

A series edited by Luis Alvarez, Carlos Blanton, and Lorrin Thomas

Sunbelt Diaspora

RACE, CLASS, AND LATINO POLITICS IN PUERTO RICAN ORLANDO

PATRICIA SILVER

University of Texas Press
AUSTIN

Printed in the United States of America
First edition, 2020

Requests for permission to reproduce material from this work should be sent to:
Permissions
University of Texas Press
P.O. Box 7819
Austin, TX 78713-7819
utpress.utexas.edu/rp-form

© The paper used in this book meets the minimum requirements of ANSI/NISO Z39.48-1992 (R1997) (Permanence of Paper).

Library of Congress Cataloging-in-Publication Data

Names: Silver, Patricia, author.
Title: Sunbelt diaspora : race, class, and Latino politics in Puerto Rican Orlando / Patricia Silver.
Other titles: Race, class, and Latino politics in Puerto Rican Orlando
Description: First edition. | Austin : University of Texas Press, 2020. | Series: Historia USA | Includes bibliographical references and index.
Identifiers: LCCN 2019034299
ISBN 978-1-4773-2045-7 (cloth)
ISBN 978-1-4773-2047-1 (ebook)
ISBN 978-1-4773-2048-8 (ebook other)
Subjects: LCSH: Orlando (Fla.)—Politics and government. | Puerto Ricans—Florida—Orlando—Politics and government. | Hispanic Americans—Florida—Orlando—Politcs and government. | Puerto Ricans—Florida—Orlando—Race identity. | Hispanic Americans—Florida—Orlando—Race identity. | Orlando (Fla.)—Race relations.
Classification: LCC F319.O7 S59 2020 | DDC 305.8009759/24—dc23
LC record available at https://lccn.loc.gov/2019034299

doi:10.7560/320457

For Latinos/as/x, Hispanics,
and especially Puerto Ricans in Orlando

CONTENTS

MAPS, TABLES, AND CHARTS

MAPS

TABLES

CHARTS

PREFACE

For Orlando Readers

It is unlikely that this book will fulfill the expectations of all Orlando readers. Judging from conversations over the years, I gather that many are looking for a quantitative rendering of the growth of the Hispanic/Latino community in the Orlando area. Others expect to find *the* history of this community, one that gives the recognition due to individuals whose labors and love have shaped contemporary reality.

There is some of that here, but this book is at best a partial truth. It is not meant to provide a list of great women and men but rather to offer a (and I stress *a*) portrait of a community in ongoing formation. My aim is to tell a story about political community formation amid diverse experiences of race, class, and place of origin.

The story is drawn not from what one person or another may have told me but from the patterns that emerged from what scores of people contributed to my understanding. There are undoubtedly other truths, other stories, to be told. It is my hope that the partial truth presented in these pages can be appreciated for what it is. It stands as an invitation to others for more writing that will attend to what it is not.

A word of explanation is needed about the use of real names and pseudonyms. Ethnography is not history, and it is not journalism. It would not have been possible to learn what people have been willing to teach me without earning and honoring the trust and protecting the *confianza* that so many have given. The people whose real names are used either knowingly participated in oral history collections that were to be made publicly available or were quoted in the media. Political candidates and elected officials in their public capacity are also sometimes mentioned by name. Pseudonyms are used for all others. Many who contributed importantly to the growth of Puerto Rican Orlando are not mentioned at all. I hope that people will recognize the insights they provided even if their names are not given.

The Orlando ground of my fieldwork has shifted under my feet as I have been writing. As this book goes to press, the ripple effects of first Puerto Rico's economic crisis and then Hurricanes Irma and Maria are being felt in Orlando. Events in Venezuela have prompted another group's relocation to Orlando in large numbers. While I have been writing, US history has seen the fiftieth anniversary of the struggles, assassinations, protests, and triumphs from the civil rights era that have had such impact on racial-ethnic relations in this country. The Black Lives Matter movement emerged, the Confederate flag was lowered in South Carolina, the Johnny Reb statue at Orlando's Lake Eola was removed to Greenwood Cemetery, and Orlando began debating how to rename Stonewall Jackson Middle School. The year 2016 saw the massacre at Pulse nightclub in which the majority of victims were of Latin American heritage, as well as the outcome of the presidential elections during which Central Florida bucked the statewide trend in voting. All of this is part of social interaction in Orlando. Indeed, the national imagination in relation to Florida politics has shifted. At the start of my research, the national media equated Florida with Miami and headed there during each election cycle to learn what was on the minds of Latinos. By 2018 they were heading to Orlando. In 2019, Donald Trump chose Orlando to launch his reelection campaign.

Finally, this book has a dual purpose. It is intended for Orlando readers as a partial recording of a story that needs to be told. But it is also for students in Orlando and elsewhere of American studies, anthropology, sociology, political science, Puerto Rican and Latino/a/x studies, and more. Not all parts of the book will be of interest to all readers. I have tried to construct it in a way that allows different readers to read in different ways. After all, the right to be different and to belong is what this book is about.

ACKNOWLEDGMENTS

Little did I know, when I moved from Puerto Rico to Orlando in 2005 for a position at the University of Central Florida (UCF), that I would be sitting in a New York Public Library researcher study room in 2019 composing these acknowledgments for the many individuals and institutions whose support and encouragement sustained me through the years of research and writing for this book. The two institutions that have truly made this book possible by offering much-needed resources to me as an independent scholar during the writing phase are The Reed Foundation through its Ruth Landes Memorial Research Fund and the aforementioned New York Public Library researcher study rooms. Special thanks go to David Latham at The Reed Foundation and to Jay Barksdale and Melanie Locay at the New York Public Library for generously and patiently attending to every question and smoothing every path. The National Coalition of Independent Scholars and Mary Taylor at the Center for Place, Culture, and Politics in the Graduate Center at the City University of New York (CUNY) gave invaluable support as I adjusted to life as an independent scholar.

Generous financial support for earlier phases of research, oral history recordings, and community programming also made this book possible, and these are acknowledged in the appendix. I want especially to thank the individuals whose work made those institutional resources available: Natalie Underberg-Goode, founder and director of the UCF Digital Ethnographies Lab; Susan Lockwood at the Florida Humanities Council; Stella Sung at UCF's Center for Research and Education in Arts, Technology, and Entertainment (CREATE); everyone at the Center for Puerto Rican Studies, Hunter College, CUNY; Cynthia Cardona Meléndez at Orlando's Orange County Regional History Center; Sharon Pesante Williams at the Hart Memorial Central Library in Kissimmee; and Ruth Edwards at the Winter Park Library.

None of the oral history projects would have been possible without the hard work of students and others I met along the way. Emilia Blackwell single-handedly kept the 2008–2009 oral history project on track. Julio Firpo worked tirelessly on that project and later gave valuable feedback on early chapter drafts. Special thanks are due to research assistants Naomi González, Sarah Molinari, Janice Stiglich, and Rachel Torres Zamora. Others providing important assistance include Sherry Cuadrado, Alia Diab, Lisa Cruz, Megan Douglass, Jacquie Marte, Russell Moore, Cyndia Morales Muñiz, Victor Randle, Ricardo Rodríguez, Juan Sánchez, Cheney Swedlow, Miranda Trimmier, Keisha Wiel, and Kate! Weddle.

I also want to thank my fellow anthropologists as well as the historians and other scholars whose input has much improved this book. As my dissertation work was taking shape in Puerto Rico, I was given two names of people I needed to meet. As a result, Eileen Findlay and Arlene Torres came into my life as mentors, and each has continued as a supportive colleague and friend ever since, reading and commenting on endless drafts. Jorge Duany's Orlando work was foundational to my research. He has offered ongoing interest and encouragement, and our work together on a 2010 special edition of the *Centro Journal* on Central Florida taught me more than I can say. Jessica Mulligan and Jimmy Seale Collazo have been with me from our dissertation days in Puerto Rico through the many conversations about the research and writing for this book, and Jimmy lent his critical eye to several chapter drafts. Víctor Vázquez-Hernández and I have shared many fruitful hours of conversation as well as a determination to unearth the hidden Puerto Rican history of Florida. I also want to thank Solsirée Del Moral and Carmen Rivera for their interest in this work and their respective invitations to Amherst College and the State University of New York at Fredonia. Gina Pérez, Carmen Whalen, and Ismael García Colón have offered critical insights, and Ismael introduced me to the New York Public Library's researcher study rooms. I was very fortunate to be able to share thoughts with other scholars engaged with Florida's—especially Central Florida's—growing Puerto Rican and Latino world: René Antrop-González, Elizabeth Aranda, Diana Ariza, Nydia Cabrera Pérez, Annabelle Conroy, José Cruz, Simone Delerme, Zoraida Maldonado, Luis Martínez-Fernández, Estelli Ramos, Fernando Rivera, Michael Rodríguez Muñiz, Julie Torres, Luis Sánchez, Ariana Valle, and William Vélez.

I am grateful to all of my former colleagues in the UCF Department of Anthropology and especially to Rosalind Howard, Leslie Lieberman, Matt McIntyre, Joana Mishtal, and Elayne Zorn. Elayne introduced me to the folklorist and digital media scholar Natalie Underberg-Goode, who became my indefatigable partner in the 2008–2009 oral history and exhibit project that kick-started this book's research. Others whom I first met at UCF and who have lent their encouragement along the way include Barbara Antonisen, Rose Beiler, and Sheryl Cohn.

In New York, I want to thank my former colleagues at the Center for Puerto Rican Studies, especially those at the Library and Archives. I was sorry to see Jorge Matos Valldejuli leave the library as I was arriving; his help and enthusiasm had already been invaluable. Alberto Hernández, Pedro Juan Hernández, and Lindsay Wittwer guided me through Centro's extensive collection as I combed through it for anything and everything I could find about Florida in Puerto Rican history. Special thanks go to Sarah León in the Hunter College Institutional Review Board office. José Camacho worked tirelessly to get me through all my technology issues. Xavier Totti encouraged submissions to the *Centro Journal* and oversaw production of the journal's special edition on Central Florida. Luis Reyes and Carlos Vargas-Ramos shared their lessons learned, and through Carlos I was able to join the Whiteness in America seminar that he organized with Ana Yolanda Ramos-Zayas. Both Carlos and Ana have given wise counsel and warm support over the years, and the members of the Whiteness in America seminar—especially Jillian Báez and Arlene Torres—gave invaluable feedback to an early draft of writing from this research.

New York has afforded me the opportunity to join two other groups of scholars whose members have given important input to this book. Lesley Gill introduced me to the Culture, Power, Boundaries seminar at Columbia University while I was in graduate school at American University. When I moved to New York, Maria-Luisa Achino-Loeb (Mimma) and Pat Antoniello, the seminar's tireless organizers, welcomed me in. I am especially grateful to Sam Bird, Nina Glick Schiller, Louise Lamphere, Antonio Lauria-Perricelli, and Gerald Sider for their comments as I began to pull a book out of mountains of data.

I will be forever grateful to Aldo Lauria Santiago for his careful attention to my work and his generosity as a scholar. Aldo invited me to join his Latinos in US History working group. This talented group of scholars—notably Lilia Fernández, Eileen Findlay, Ismael García Colón, Lara Putnam, Lorrin Thomas, and Carmen Whalen—gave feedback on early drafts. Lorrin Thomas saw this book's value early on and introduced me to Kerry Webb at the University of Texas Press. Lorrin has gone above and beyond her role as series editor, reading individual chapters and giving sage advice. I want to thank everyone I have worked with at UT Press—especially Kerry Webb, Andrew Hnatow, Lynne Ferguson, Cassandra Cisneros, Robert Kimzey, and Joel Pinckney—for their expertise and patient support. I was extremely fortunate to find the cartographers who drew the maps for this book, Dennis McClendon of Chicago CartoGraphics and Molly O'Halloran, and I received invaluable editorial advice from Sheri Englund on my first manuscript draft prior to submission. I also want to thank Luke Torn for proofreading and Scott Smiley for indexing.

In both New York and Orlando, Tony De Jesús, José La Luz, and Naomi González have offered encouragement during those moments when fieldwork became overwhelming. Tony has been a colleague, friend, and research consultant, helping smooth my entry to life in New York and introducing me to Orlando Ricans including his own parents, Elsa and Hector De Jesús. Another New York–Orlando connection is Juan Cartagena, who first noticed my research and invited me into the lawsuit against Orange County that forms a pivotal part of this book. Juan also provided important guidance on the legal nuances of redistricting.

In Orlando, I am also grateful to institutions and individuals who provided documents and maps to complement my fieldwork and interview data. At the Orange County Supervisor of Elections office, Fred Altensee was not only a tremendous help, but he showed great enthusiasm for my research and shared with me his own. Alicia Ramírez and Diana Morales gave me access to the archives for Orlando's Hispanic Office for Local Assistance. The Puerto Rican Federal Affairs Administration in Orlando-Kissimmee had two directors during my fieldwork—Sylvia Cáceres and Betsy Franceschini—both of whom lent encouragement and support from their offices. Tony Suárez and Denise Velázquez made the 2012 Puerto Rican Political Participation and Civic Engagement oral history project possible by lending recording space. I am especially grateful to all the participants in the publicly archived oral history projects, whose names are listed in the appendix. Special thanks go to the members of the community committee who organized the 2012 Cultural Foundations of Puerto Rican Orlando projects at the Asociación Borinqueña and the Casa de Puerto Rico: Elsa and Hector De Jesús, Clara Quiñones, Zoraida Ríos-Andino, Jean Ruiz Sandor, and Nancy Torres.

Friends and family have all found ways to support and encourage this work, even as it seemed it might never end. Although neither of my parents lived to see this book, it is only possible thanks to their love and support as I pushed against the expected and chose other paths. Time away in Pennsylvania with the Vogels, across Central Park with the O'Macs, and at meals with the McNamaras and Allens pulled me out of my writing head and into the world over the past few years in New York. Neighbors Karin Beckett, Marina Fischer, Sharon and Joe Flanagan, Marilyn Silver and Ed Cheng, and Sandy

Washburn have made sure to pull me out as well. Phone calls and visits with Laurie Aguera-Arcas, Daisy Bodón, Karen Chadwick, Carol Coates, Chave Díaz, Naomi González, Carla Hummel, Nicole Levesque, Andrea Matthews, Joyce Nalewajk, Hannah Pickworth, Sue Werthan, and Betty Zara brought laughter and relaxation when it was most needed.

During one Christmas holiday, I arrived from Orlando at my sister Barrie Allen's house in New York, needing to condense more than one hundred hours of oral history recordings into seventeen exhibit panels before early January. Early each morning while others were asleep, I set myself up in an armchair that Barrie and her husband, Peter, began to call my office. Under the tree on Christmas morning was a lap desk, which I still have and use almost every morning in the "office" I now have in a different armchair in my New York apartment.

Careful attention from anonymous reviewers provided insights and greatly improved this book's content. The largest debt of gratitude goes to the many Orlando Puerto Ricans, named and unnamed, whose generosity allowed the stories in this book to be recorded. They gave this gringa who showed up out of seemingly nowhere their time, and even more importantly their trust, sharing their experiences and perspectives as I have tried to see the world through their eyes. Knowing I can never wholly do that, I dedicate this book to them.

Sunbelt Diaspora

INTRODUCTION

Race, Class, Place, and Politics in a New Puerto Rican Diaspora

At 5:30 p.m. on November 6, 2012, I was racing against the clock and an exhausted cell phone battery to meet Rafael Alvarez at a 7-Eleven near his apartment and take him to his polling place in Orlando, Florida.[1] He had to be in line before the polls closed at 7:00 so he could vote, and Rafael was determined to vote. He had tried throughout the early voting period and had met one obstacle after another. The problem was that he had recently moved from Kissimmee, just over the Orange-Osceola County line, to an apartment on Goldenrod Road in East Orlando. He had educated himself about Florida's requirements as the state purged scores of voters if their addresses had changed. He had taken all the necessary steps but had not found a poll worker who would let him vote. Now, on election day, he had been in the hospital all day for an MRI. He was calling me from a city bus that would drop him near the 7-Eleven, but he was not sure where his election-day polling place was. The minutes ticked by as rush-hour traffic crawled through Orlando's East Side, weaving its way around the construction on Colonial Drive.

It was a busy night in Orlando, as in many other places in the United States on the eve of what would become Barack Obama's second election. Things had been especially busy in Orlando because of Central Florida's reputation as the swing part of this important swing state in presidential elections.[2] The pattern has been that North Florida leans Republican, South Florida leans Democratic, and the vote in heavily Latino—and especially Puerto Rican—Central Florida determines the Florida outcome (MacManus et al. 2015).

Not far from where I was sitting in traffic was the headquarters for Mi Familia Vota (My Family Votes). This was just one of several Spanish-language get-out-the-vote organizations that had set up shop in Orlando in the months ahead of the elections. Central Florida Latinos, at somewhere between a quarter and a third of the area's population, were crucial to the election outcome, but how and whether Latinos will vote is hard to predict.[3] Spanish-language radio stations had been urging Latino voters to get out and vote for weeks. That night, ads supporting candidates on both sides of the Democratic-Republican political divide came on the radio every minute or so as I tried to reach Rafael.

Rafael was born in Puerto Rico, which places him among the 50 percent of Orlando-area Latinos who are of Puerto Rican birth or heritage. He and other Puerto Ricans are in the ironic position, as birthright US citizens, of having the potential to determine the US presidency while having no vote at all if they reside in Puerto Rico.[4] For more than a year before November 2012, a steady stream of candidates and their surrogates had visited the Orlando area, among them Puerto Rican elected officials from Puerto Rico and Puerto Rican members of the US Congress from New York and Chicago. Puerto Ricans in Puerto Rico may not vote in federal elections, and of course Central Floridians vote in Florida, not in New York or Illinois. These visits from other places were intended to motivate local Puerto Rican voters, voters like Rafael.

In addition to the political operatives targeting Puerto Ricans, the area was also populated with reporters and researchers like me who wanted to document the activity in this place amid this population that could tip the presidential election one way or another. By the time I found Rafael at the 7-Eleven, I had run into another researcher as my cell phone was on its last bit of battery and used his phone to find the right polling place. Rafael and I headed straight there, arriving at about 6:40. A line of people, mostly speaking Spanish as they waited to vote, wrapped around the church and was at a standstill. The single voting machine in the small room in the back of the church was not working. Poll workers were setting up an old-style locked box in its place. Rafael despaired when he saw the line. His long day at the hospital had left him too weak to stand that long in line.

I had seen the elderly and ill wait their turns in chairs near the front of voting lines all day, so we headed to the front of the line. A poll worker was keeping the line in order, and I served as English interpreter to explain the situation. She asked those in front if Rafael could step in. Although Spanish-language conversation dominated the line, the man whose turn it was to vote next was white, non-Latino—or as is commonly used by Latinos in Orlando, Anglo. He objected to the request. But the couple behind him (also Anglo) said they had been waiting for two hours and had no problem with a couple of minutes more. Rafael stepped in line between the man who objected and the couple who welcomed him in. Once Rafael was inside, I could see him through the window, seated at a table, reading the ballot. The ballot included twelve amendments to the Florida Constitution, four amendments to the Orange County Charter, and a referendum.[5] I guessed that he was carefully considering the full text of each item in order to decide how to vote. It was going to be a while.

Sitting down to wait, I found myself next to an elderly Puerto Rican woman whose daughter was holding their place in line. They had been waiting a couple of hours, and her daughter was not yet in sight. The woman told me she had not voted in a long time, but this time, she said, she had to come out and give her vote to her *negrito*. She sat patiently waiting for her daughter, shivering as the evening grew colder. When Rafael finally emerged smiling at about 8:15, I took my leave of her. As we left, her daughter was just barely visible, rounding the corner to the far side of the church.

On our way to Rafael's home, he talked about each decision he had made as he went over the ballot with care. Later, at one of the election-night parties, I told Joana, a New York Puerto Rican woman, about this man and his determination to vote. "Oh, that must have been Rafael!" she exclaimed. In response to Florida's 2012 purge of voters, activists from the League of Women Voters, the Florida Immigrant Coalition, the National Congress for Puerto Rican Rights, and the Service Employees International Union had been closely monitoring the situation (Bousquet 2014). An active participant in local politics, Joana knew of Rafael's troubles.

My first stop after leaving Rafael at his home was a Colombian restaurant not far from Goldenrod on Orlando's East Side. There I joined the victory party for New Jersey–born Darren Soto, the first Puerto Rican elected to the Florida Senate. Soto would represent District 14, a newly created district stretching across three Central Florida counties. It was all in all a good night for Puerto Ricans in Orlando, a rare moment when they could feel the weight of their political presence in Central Florida and beyond.[6]

Like so much of what happens in Orlando, Rafael's story engages race and class as it brings together people from very different places: Rafael, a working-class Puerto Rican from Puerto Rico; Joana, a retired Puerto Rican cop from New York; researchers and journalists who descend on Orlando during each election cycle; Anglos irritated by what they see as Latino intrusions into their space and others who make room; an elderly Puerto Rican woman from Puerto Rico who speaks little English but wants to vote for her *negrito*; her daughter, a bilingual, professional-looking woman who waits patiently in line for hours; and the celebration of a Puerto Rican electoral win, glossed as a Latino win, at a Colombian restaurant. The story also represents Orlando's racial geography, given that it takes place on the heavily Latino East Side and leaves strikingly absent any representation of Orlando's historically black West Side.

I begin with this story because it is details like these that have pointed me to this book's claim that Puerto Rican political identifications and practices in diaspora are being reworked in important ways as the so-called Latinization of the United States continues and Latinos in Orlando and other spaces in the US South become focal points of national political attention. Rafael's story suggests that this reworking of political identifications and practices, which is under way and under contention in Orlando, is informed by divergent experiences of class, race, and place that Puerto Ricans both bring to and encounter in this new diaspora space in the US Southeast.

Sunbelt Diaspora: Race, Class, and Latino Politics in Puerto Rican Orlando is an ethnographic study of Latino, but especially Puerto Rican, political life in the Orlando area. This means that the stories, observations, and analyses reported in the pages to follow emerge from research methods that privilege locally recorded detail and long-standing relationships with the people who opened their lives to me as a cultural anthropologist trying to know what they know. Key to these methods is participant observation, which is something of a tightrope walk between being an observer and recorder of daily activities and being a fully immersed participant in those activities and the relationships they entail. The data derived from participant observation allow me to draw greater depth of understanding from the more formally structured interviews that also contribute to my analysis.

Latino political participation and voting patterns are often analyzed from a perspective I will call "looking in," by which I mean survey-based and generally focused on a state or national scale.[7] As valuable as this literature is, what ethnographers refer to as "data" are not represented by these research methods. Ethnographic data can be (and most often are) contradictory; they resist any effort to derive regularities that may help predict human behaviors or the outcomes of particular projects. But they also can reveal social realities that would otherwise remain hidden—social realities that by their very invisibility serve to reproduce the social order that gave rise to that invisibility in the first place (Comaroff and Comaroff 1992, Herzfeld 2015). The disappearance of Puerto Ricans into Latinos and the disappearance of Latinos into Orlando's historically black-white racial binary are cases in point that I explore here. This book, then, adds to literature on Latino political life by looking out from one locale to engage questions about Latino politics. I begin with the messy daily interactions that inform how Puerto Ricans and Latinos engage with each other and with others in the larger social arena of the Orlando area.[8]

Although Puerto Ricans are often treated as exceptional among Latinos because of their birthright US citizenship, they share with all Latinos a historical relation to US expansionism and a contemporary experience of being racialized in the United States as not-white in a racial hierarchy with white people at the top (De Genova and Ramos-Zayas 2003:21). "The contiguity created by American imperial expansion," writes Silvio Torres-Saillant (2009:437), "created the historical grounds for the presence of Hispanic communities in the United States." I argue with Juan Flores (2005:200) that Puerto Rican experience offers a "prism through which to scrutinize and interrogate" Latino experience more widely. Looking through the Puerto Rican case, it is clear that "citizenship has never shielded racially marked Latinos from being suspected as 'immigrants'—just as it has never shielded racial minorities from second-class citizenship status" (Dávila 2008:9). I adopt the view that despite their birthright citizenship, Puerto Ricans experience obstacles to equitable socioeconomic and political inclusion in the United States that contribute a more nuanced understanding of public-sphere debates about race, immigration, and belonging.[9]

Despite these overlapping experiences among Latinos with distinct national origins and heritage, divergent experiences of race, class, place of origin, and time spent in diaspora still impact Orlando Latino political identifications and practices. A conversation I had with Eva, a Dominican woman who had spent a good portion of her life in New York and whom I met early on in my research in Orlando, offers a case in point. Holding in her hands a glossy magazine for and about Orlando's Latinos, which sported a cover photo of a perfectly made-up, light-skinned Latina, Eva said to me, "I'm not that kind of Latina." Eva is a military veteran turned working mother of two; at the time of that conversation she was supplementing her full-time weekday clerical job with hourly weekend work. She is married to an Anglo man she met during her military service. With her husband incapacitated by an accident, her time was more than filled with taking care of the family and working two jobs. She objected to the race-class image projected in this consumer-oriented homogenization of a "Latin look" and found the magazine's cover at odds with her own daily, lived experiences.[10]

Rafael's story and Eva's lack of identification with the magazine cover's homogenized image offer an entry point for examining difference and politics in Puerto Rican and Latino Orlando. Given the political volatility of the state of Florida and the centrality of Orlando in that volatility, it is interesting to ponder what a Latino politics that managed to emerge would look like. As Puerto Ricans and other Latinos work to confront marginalization and exclusion and make themselves visible on their own terms, their efforts to form a political community are met by what the political scientist Cristina Beltrán (2010) terms the "incomplete and agonistic 'we'" of those so often lumped together under a homogeneous framing as the "sleeping giant." The question of what might happen if the so-called sleeping giant were to wake up underwrites much of Puerto Rican and Latino political activity in Orlando.

THE FARTHER NORTH YOU GO, THE MORE IN THE SOUTH YOU ARE

The phrase *Sunbelt Diaspora* in this book's title situates Orlando among the US locations that scholars interested in migration and immigration call "new destinations."[11] As the US economic engine shifted during the 1970s from the industrialized Northeast and Midwest to financial, technical, service, and food-production industries in the South and West, these places emerged as magnets for domestic migrants and international immigrants alike. Especially in the US Southeast, where populations have been historically subsumed into a black-white paradigm, these new destinations have experienced rapidly changing demographics. These changes have transformed social dynamics and generated locally specific responses to more widely experienced political and economic processes.[12] Although there is much evidence that the US Southeast has long been a transnational crossroads and a place of diversity, these contemporary changes, which have occurred over the time of a single generation from the 1970s to the turn of the twenty-first century, offer a new challenge to the black-white binary (Holloway 2008, Joshi and Desai 2013, Weise 2012).[13]

In Florida, however, Latino presence—and the power of the Latino vote—are not new. As the Cuban exile community in the Miami area has flexed its muscle over the decades, the importance of Florida's Latino politics has grown. But if Miami is and has been Cuban, Orlando is now Puerto Rican. The Orlando area has become the first destination for Puerto Ricans relocating from Puerto Rico and other diaspora locations. In tension with the historically Republican-leaning political influence of Cuban Americans, the ascendance of the Puerto Rican population, traditionally more aligned with the Democratic Party, is unsettling long-standing political relations in Florida and electoral strategies nationwide.[14] Within two years of the 2012 elections, Florida's Puerto Rican population hit the one million mark. They were projected to outnumber Cubans in Florida by the 2020 Census even before the combined impacts of an economic meltdown and the 2017 hurricane season sent thousands more Puerto Ricans to Florida.

Despite this, during my fieldwork I regularly encountered set ideas about Florida as a place—from the media, among scholars, and in casual conversations with people living anywhere that is not Florida. The assumption was that Florida is Miami. Miami is a gateway city with a diverse population, sometimes called "the capital of Latin America." Therefore, Florida is a place long used to immigration, and although geographically located in the US Southeast, it stands culturally and historically apart from the South. And Orlando is the land of Walt Disney, a relatively recent phenomenon, a never-never land of an eternal present. It's not that there is no truth to these ideas, but they are only part of the story.

Florida is a very large state, stretching over seven hundred miles from Pensacola in the western panhandle to the Everglades in the south and over eight hundred if the Keys are included (map I.1).[15] It is common to speak of three Floridas: South Florida, where Miami is, as the gateway to Latin America and the Caribbean; Central Florida, where Orlando is, as the state's tourist center; and North Florida, where the capital, Tallahassee, is, as "Old

MAP I.1. Florida

Map by Molly O'Halloran.

Florida," a nostalgic reference to a time before Florida's development boom. There's even an expression in Florida that says, "The farther north you go, the more in the South you are."

Nonetheless, it is a common understanding that Florida is not really part of the South, at least not anymore. David Colburn (2007:2) cites southern sociologist John Shelton Reed's claim that because of in-migration and diversification, Florida was no longer part of the South by 1990. Without disputing the impact of in-migration and diversification on Florida history, I argue that the legacy of Florida's Jim Crow racial politics and the civil rights legislation crafted to address African American oppression have left a black-white code embedded in political-legal structures and that these in turn are reinforced by the tenacious idea that southern history is a story in black and white.[16]

The logic that links economic activity and social organization to beliefs and practices situates Central Florida in a mixed cultural legacy grounded in US regional identifications as Deep South and Wild West. Orlando in 1860 was "a tiny settlement sitting in the middle of a huge cotton plantation, with cattle ranging the outskirts" (Bacon 1977:1:19).[17] Following the Civil War, southerners from the ravaged spaces north of Florida moved south to try their hands at growing oranges, while Central Florida cowmen continued to drive herds to the coast for shipping to Cuba. Ranching, oranges, and southern families with deep roots in the area remained at the core of the Central Florida political economy until well into the 1970s.

Other histories also affect the political dynamics of Central Florida and the US Southeast. States' rights politics and anti-union, right-to-work legislation date back to the 1940s.[18] Mega churches dot the landscape, and military bases, with their accompanying veterans' services, inform emergent cultural beliefs and practices. Each of these contributes to the daily dynamics of Orlando's social field. I was reminded of these layers of history in a checkout line at Whole Foods Market when I noticed *Garden and Gun* magazine, advertised as the "soul of the South." In brief, Orlando, with its contemporary reputation as a world-class tourist mecca, sits halfway between the transnational world of South Florida and the Old South of North Florida. It is culturally, geographically, and politically in the center of the state.

TRANSLOCAL TIES AND LOCAL MEANINGS

In this book, I view place-making as both a local and translocal phenomenon. Building from Sharon Zukin's (1991:12) explanation that place "expresses how a spatially connected group of people mediate the demands of cultural identity, state power, and capital accumulation," I look at memories, people, money, and institutions from other Puerto Rican places that underwrite a sense not only of *puertorriqueñidad* generally but of being Puerto Rican in Orlando. I use the term "translocal" rather than "transnational" because it more easily illustrates the local materiality of place, which I will explain and develop further in later chapters.[19]

I also want to stress the impact of Orlando—as a place with a specifically local history—on Puerto Rican and Latino efforts to make a place for themselves. There is no need to mention Disney World for the image of the Magic Kingdom's castle to pop into one's mind as soon as Orlando is mentioned. The equation of Orlando with the idea of Disney as "the happiest place on earth" changed (at least for a while) after the June 2016 shootings at the Pulse nightclub.[20] Although theme-park visitors may never see them, rainbow flags and memorial public artworks have become part of the downtown Orlando landscape. The construction and slow traffic I encountered as I tried to get to Rafael is yet another place description of Orlando as an urban center in the making. The city's racial-ethnic east-west division and Rafael's experience as a voter point to sociopolitical experiences of place. Rafael is determined to vote. He succeeds in that claim to political belonging, to "being in place" in Orlando, but the difficulties he encounters indicate that his is a contested claim.

Rafael's story points to place-making as an abstract, physical, and political process informed by aligning and conflicting social relations. Among these, differences in class relations and racial identifications are often framed as differences of national origin or birthplace. *Sunbelt Diaspora* asks how these and other divergent experiences of race, class, and place affect collective identifications and political practices in the Orlando area.

Race. The social relations informing Rafael's place-making story are embedded in local and national racial histories. Florida's reputation for diversity is about Miami in South Florida, not Orlando in Central Florida. In Orlando and Central Florida, the black-white paradigm has in essence erased from the record all who appear neither black nor white, rendering them at best foreign regardless of their legal status. Indeed, literature from Latino/a/x studies and Asian American studies regularly cites the US framing of those who are neither black nor white as "perpetual foreigners."[21]

In the Orlando area, Latinos and other such perpetual foreigners now include more than 350,000 Puerto Ricans (US Census Bureau, ACS 2017b). Because Puerto Ricans are birthright citizens and therefore permitted to move freely over the geographic border, this book's focus on the Puerto Rican case in Orlando highlights the condition of Latinos generally as people perpetually "out of place." The Puerto Rican case also directs attention to racial categorizations as a social rather than phenotypical or biological phenomenon that is deeply connected to colonial-style relations and the reproduction of US systems of domination and subordination (Rosa and Bonilla 2017).

Amid Orlando's black-white racial history, differently colored Puerto Ricans have often been assigned their separate places as "honorary white" or as part of a "collective black" (Bonilla-Silva 2004). And such distinctions intersect with different ways that Puerto Ricans might identify themselves. Puerto Ricans who have spent much or all of their lives as a US minority in diaspora bring to their relations in Orlando a nonwhite race consciousness that is often at odds with racial perspectives of those who have only ever lived in Puerto Rico and identify as white.[22] An Orlando Puerto Rican from the island put it this way to me: "For the Floridian, any Hispanic, or Spanish speaker, is a useless mix of white and black." Punctuating these observations with an angry-sounding "Hmmm!" the speaker added, "It's a very delicate thing."

Class. In this book I question how emergent twenty-first-century Puerto Rican diaspora spaces, especially in new destinations, may differ from those in the twentieth-century North. Puerto Rican studies scholars have produced a rich and detailed literature that documents the history and analyzes the dynamics of Puerto Rican migration to the US states and the formations of Puerto Rican diaspora communities, particularly during the latter half of the twentieth century.[23] During my years of ethnographic, oral history, and archival research in the Orlando area, however, I have found that the established narrative of working-class Puerto Rican struggle, which has sustained scholarship on and activism in longtime diaspora communities like New York and Chicago, is challenged by the wide range of class relations and interests among Orlando Puerto Ricans and between them and other Latinos.[24] This distinction plays into Puerto Rican and Latino place-making in Orlando and Central Florida, further complicating Latino heterogeneity with differentiated class interests.

Furthermore, in Puerto Rico and elsewhere in Latin America, class relations can carry more social weight than race; the two even become intertwined as education and other class markers have the effect of whitening those who possess them. In the United States, the supposedly color-blind, merit-based myth that social mobility is available to those who work hard enough lends itself to a denial of racial and class oppression and to an explanation for persistent inequality as being about individual and cultural inadequacies rather than white supremacy and structural barriers. Thus, class in the United States is more often equated with racial-ethnic identification than the other way around (Ramos-Zayas 2003:124).[25] In Orlando, distinct US and Latin American perceptions of the relation between race and class encounter a local black-white racial binary, and the tensions of Latino heterogeneity intensify when performances of white Anglo cultural, symbolic, and social capital become part of individual and collective Latino strategies for navigating the social world of this new diaspora space (Delerme 2017).

LATINO HETEROGENEITY AND POLITICAL COMMUNITY

The growth of Orlando's Latino population has paralleled the national emergence of Hispanic/Latino as an identity category. The idea of Latinos as a singular population with common origins outside the United States was so established by the end of the twentieth century "that few Americans [gave] it a second thought" (Beltrán 2010:5). By the twenty-first century, the idea had become so much part of the US cultural landscape that a 2017 Ancestry.com advertisement featured a woman saying that when asked her nationality, she always answered "Hispanic" until she discovered her "true" multinational heritage through her DNA test. The ad uncritically situates Hispanic as a nationality and links cultural heritage to DNA.

Against this assumption that Latinos are naturally bound together by blood and culture, it is important to recognize the approximately thirty-year period in the latter half of the twentieth century during which an umbrella identity category was forged for US citizens or residents who were born in Latin America or who identify with a Latin American heritage. Beginning in the late 1960s, the separate interests of social activists, census officials, and media executives became intertwined as one proved useful to another in something of a snowball effect (Mora 2014). Thus, I understand Hispanic and Latino as referring to a conscious relationship that has emerged from structural and cultural-historical forces rather than as a primordial essence (Comaroff and Comaroff 1992:50–66). By 1990, López and Espiritu (1990:209) were including Latinos in what they describe as a post-1960s "institutionalization of ethnicity."[26] Cristina Mora (2014:155–156) points to that same year, arguing that by 1990 "a viewer could tune into Spanish-language television, brimming with various pan-ethnic entertainment and public affairs programs, to watch census spokespersons and activists comment on the future of the Hispanic community."

Whether seen as fixed or constructed, the umbrella term for a people understood to be distinct from US white and black populations poses questions about what is race and what is ethnicity. The Spanish term *raza* does not have the same meaning as "race" does in English. In Spanish, the term carries connotations of national or cultural origins and thus overlaps with the US use of "ethnicity," defined as a shared cultural and linguistic heritage (Rodríguez

2000:7). The disjuncture between "race" and *raza* presents a conflict for Latinos as they encounter a world in which others give primacy to racial identification and see culture as a consequence rather than the other way around (Rodríguez 1994:141).

Indeed, the terms Hispanic and Latino have taken on a "race-like" quality (Mora 2014:114–115). By 2000, Linda Alcoff (2000:42) asks if "Latina/o" is a racial identity or an ethnicity, and she borrows the term "ethnorace" from David Theo Goldberg to argue that Latinos are racialized without losing their ethnicity as "a product of self-creation."[27] Jorge Duany (2003:266) references the "quasi-racial use of Hispanic/Latino." Silvio Torres-Saillant (2003:147) argues that it is time to recognize the "conceptual fusion" of race and ethnicity. He writes, "Both come from a similar effort to imagine a collective internally or externally. Their reality occurs only as they translate into social, political, and economic advancement or retardation." Torres-Saillant thus positions both race and ethnicity as social constructions rather than as primordial or naturally derived identifications. Aranda and Rebollo-Gil (2004) argue that "ethnoracism" has become a means of maintaining racial order in the United States. I use "racial-ethnic" in this book to recognize the fluid relationship between the two social categories in US public discourse and to emphasize the intertwined histories of race and immigration in the United States.

Many non-Latinos in Orlando and elsewhere indiscriminately use "Spanish," "Hispanic," "Latino," and "Latin" as racialized terms to identify anyone perceived as having Latin American heritage—people who are neither white nor black but simply "foreign." This perspective has been aided by the simultaneous emergence of a nativist discourse that has increasingly framed Mexican immigrants—and by homogeneous extension all Latinos—as a dark and foreboding threat to national unity. In this "Latino threat" narrative, Latinos stand apart from earlier (European) immigrants; they are unassimilable, refuse to learn English, and threaten social norms by their language, religion, fertility, and presumed illegality (Chavez 2013, Dávila 2008).[28] Like the person who described Puerto Rican racial identification in Florida as "delicate," Latinos who identify and are identified as white in their places of origin are startled by this not-white racialization in the United States. In Orlando, Latinos switch between pan-ethnic and national-origin identifications, often selecting them strategically according to situational and political need and race-class interests vis-à-vis non-Latinos.[29]

Following on his argument that Latino experience can be examined through the refracted light of Puerto Rican experience, Flores (2005:200) posits the emergence of a Latino identity category as "history in the making," and he warns against too easily adopting that homogenizing term: "We are standing in the river as it flows by us, and it is made more murky and turbulent because any generalizations about the ethnic or national dimensions of 'Latino' reality are relentlessly qualified by the crosscutting axes of class, gender and race. We should therefore be wary of prematurely fixing on any final or decisive explanatory model."

Among Puerto Ricans in particular, another crosscutting axis is difference in birthplace between island and diaspora. Different responses to the question "¿De dónde eres?" (Where are you from?) engender distinctions among Puerto Ricans that run deep and can be especially divisive for those who may have lived much or all of their lives outside of Puerto Rico but who identify strongly as Puerto Rican. The tensions over being *de acá* (from here) or *de allá* (from there) include perceptions about racial identifications and class relations that mirror common tensions between Chicanos and new immigrants from Mexico. A reader identified as "Puzzled Chicana" poses a question about the tensions in a 2012 blog post in the *Dallas Observer*. She is the US-born daughter of a Chicana and an indigenous Mexican and is married to a Mexican man: "Will I never be seen as an equal by my Mexican in-laws, or will they eventually see that the only difference between us is my mom gave birth to me north of the *frontera*? I can handle discrimination from *gabachos* or any other race but this is really unjust. Why do men and women from Mexico seem to consider themselves superior to Chicanos?" (in Arrellano 2012).

It is hard to miss the parallels in the comment of a New York–born Puerto Rican in Orlando as well as the suggested link between skin color and place of birth: "I'm *trigueño* and my wife is *clara*.[30] She's Puerto Rican right from the island. My mother-in-law loves me now, but in the beginning I was a threat" (PRCF Pérez).[31]

In response to the local conditions that Puerto Ricans and other Latinos encounter, tensions over the question "¿De dónde eres?" intertwine with class relations and racial identifications to form serious challenges to a collective identification for political action. And yet, as scholars of Latino politics note, there is a potential mutuality throughout Latino heterogeneity (Ricourt and Danta 2003, Rocco 2014). Using words that sound very much like Benedict Anderson's (1991) "imagined community," in which a wide spread of members do not actually know each other, an Orlando Puerto Rican once told me that other Hispanics are "just brothers and sisters that I haven't met."

BEYOND BILLIARD BALLS

Rafael's story is one of many that were told and retold in Orlando during the days following the 2012 election. Another that I heard was about the centenarian Gume Ramírez, a Puerto Rican who had voted in every election and was determined that year to cast his vote on election day at the polls. Absentee voting would not do. Reportedly, Ramírez received a standing ovation when someone announced his age, and his photo was featured in the local Spanish-language newspaper. These stories challenge the claims about Latino voter apathy that I heard so often during my fieldwork.

My data show that low Latino voter turnout in Orlando has likely been related to the well-founded belief that non-Latino candidates court Latinos at election time and ignore them afterward. Standing alone, Rafael's story focuses attention on electoral politics, but political actions reach beyond running for office or casting a ballot. Electoral participation is a necessary but insufficient mechanism for a Latino politics that stakes claims to inclusion in the social mechanisms "through which power, resources, and benefits are distributed" (Rocco 2010:43).

For Puerto Ricans, these wider forms of political participation may include engaging in the ongoing need to educate others about Puerto Rico's relation to the United States and their own status as citizens. Political participation may also include street protests against discrimination as well as engagement with organizations working to increase the visibility of Latinos more generally in Orlando's cultural, economic, and political arenas. In a very few cases, it includes constantly addressing meetings of local elected officials to demand inclusion and visibility. In more cases, it includes refusing to engage with either the Democratic or Republican Party, in a statement of protest against the tokenism and marginalization of those seen as foreign by the political machines of both. This refusal to engage may include a focus on maintaining and promoting Puerto Rican and other Latino cultural practices in resistance to pressures for assimilation. And maintaining and promoting cultural practices means teaching youth to identify with those practices as part of their relations with others in the US states.

For this book's purpose, "political" refers to a variety of responses to the exclusion and marginalization that Puerto Ricans and Latinos have so often encountered in the Orlando area. José Sánchez (1996:297) asserts that power "comes to those who are wanted and desired, or can make themselves so." Despite the national attention that Orlando Puerto Ricans and Latinos receive in every presidential election cycle, however, they have struggled to be heard and seen at the local level. Theirs is a form of selective incorporation in which representations such as the one on Eva's magazine cover suggest consumer-oriented recognition and even respect (at least for light-skinned and well-heeled Latinos), while the relations and social structures that would actually allow equitable participation and access have remained closed or at best carefully guarded.

The struggle for equitable inclusion in Orlando is a struggle for what the anthropologist Renato Rosaldo (1994:402) has termed "the right to be different and to belong." As one Puerto Rican activist has told me, "There is a difference between assimilating something and being part of something." This assertion is a claim to participation as Puerto Ricans or as Latinos in terms that recognize the historical impacts of white supremacy on contemporary social, political, and economic structures and relations in the United States.[32] In considering Puerto Rican political participation in diaspora, Sánchez (1994:130) concludes, "Puerto Ricans don't vote, then, for a simple but daunting reason: they have come to think they don't belong in the United States."[33]

Equitable inclusion would mean the end of framing all Latinos, regardless of legal status, as perpetual foreigners; it would mean seeing Puerto Ricans and other Latinos playing political roles reflective of their numbers. It would mean equal opportunities and outcomes for Latinos as for non-Latinos. In that sense, a politics that claims "the right to be different and to belong" recognizes that valuing diversity does not necessarily lead to equal access to political and economic power (Rosa and Bonilla 2017). It is a politics that heeds Dávila's (2008:171) warning to be wary of "public discourse that serves to whitewash Latinos with projects that advance normativity, while creating inequalities among Latinos along lines of citizenship, class, and other variables."[34]

Politics as process. Limits on Puerto Rican and Latino participation in Orlando's social, political, and economic relations and structures are experienced across the diversity that marks those gathered under the Hispanic/Latino umbrella. This reality leads Iris Young (2000b:148) to argue for a "politics of difference" that recognizes the ways in which the groundwork for structural difference can be found in perceptions of cultural difference. Among political philosophers there is a long history of debate around whether an emphasis on difference is divisive and disruptive to a democratic society, whether it is a necessary antidote to inexorable reproduction of existing power relations, or whether it can serve to elucidate existing injustices to the wider public (Pineda 2014, Young 2000a). Scholars in a variety of fields debate these questions using a varied vocabulary—difference, incoherence, heterogeneity, disjuncture.

Such debates can easily slip into referencing difference as either a singular racial-ethnic, gender, national, or class identity or the intersection of any number of these categories. From there, it is a short step to an uncritical glossing of social-group differences as bounded and static notions of internally homogeneous identities that in turn can reproduce marginalization by suppressing differences in favor of a tightly bounded concept of community.[35] Identity politics, when practiced in this way, promotes a notion of difference that lends itself to what the anthropologist Eric Wolf (1982:6) describes as "a model of the world as a global pool hall in which the entities spin off each other like so many hard and round billiard balls."

As a solution to the tension between the need for a unified point of identification and the reality of intersecting lines of difference, Beltrán (2010:157) insists that Latino politics is not a thing but a process through which "new forms of commonality" emerge under shifting conditions. Latino politics, argues Beltrán (73), epitomizes "the inevitable democratic dilemma that no political community is *ever* fully achieved." Ambiguity and contingency, she finds, are constant characteristics of the "inherently incomplete nature of the democratic 'we'" (70).

Moving from this understanding, I agree with the argument that supposedly democratic consensus, when achieved under conditions of inequality, is potentially oppressive if it submerges differences and disagreements into a universalist assumption of commonality that aligns with the particular views of those in power (Pineda 2014). Rather than looking for consensus, this framing embraces dissent and struggle as integral to community, which allows a fluid and dynamic approach to analyses of community formation, political or otherwise. In this view, rather than a problem, conflict becomes a resource (Reyes 2010, Rocco 2014).

Movement in the social field. To avoid projecting images of billiard balls while considering differences of race, class, and place among Orlando Puerto Ricans and other Latinos, I draw a distinction between identification as something people do and identity as a thing people use to various ends. By "identification" I mean a sociocultural process that emerges from historically constructed political and economic conditions (Brubaker and Cooper 2000). The distinction helps to differentiate between political and at times consciously strategic use of a fixed *identity idea*—Latino, Hispanic, American, Puerto Rican, black, white, working class, professional, and so on—and *identification* as an act of individually and collectively intersecting with and responding to a given expression of that idea in relations with others in a particular time and place. This subtle distinction opens the way to analyses that are more responsive to questions about sociocultural phenomena emerging from a constantly shifting social field: Who does what, where, and when? To what end? And with what effect on social relations?

The term "social field" has a long and varied history in anthropology. I borrow from the framing that takes the principles of physics as a conceptual metaphor for the perpetual motion of social relations forming and reforming in histories of power (Schneider and Rapp 1995, Wolf 1982). In this view, societies and other sociocultural phenomena are not things but processes, and their histories cannot be captured by static structural metaphors. Writing specifically about Puerto Rico, Flores (1993:68) suggests a similar critique in saying that cultural history cannot be understood as "the layer-on-layer erection of a multistoried building." By contrast, Wolf's (1982) concept of vectors from physics emphasizes historical relations that take shape in interaction with what Ghani (1995:32) calls "an expanded universe of power." In sum, I use the term "social field" to refer to an intangible and open arena in which social, political, and economic relations form and reform amid vectors of sameness and difference as part of any process of community formation.

In this light, community and the collective identifications that it presumes emerge from sets of relations "whose meanings, structures, and frontiers are continually produced, contested, and reworked in relation to a complex range of sociopolitical attachments and antagonisms" (Gregory 1998:11). Benedict Anderson (1991:7) has referred to the boundaries of the "imagined community" as "elastic," claiming that members share a sense of commonality that prevails despite "actual inequality and exploitation." Raymond Rocco (2006:320) seems to suggest otherwise. He defines the boundaries of "political community" as all who share "a common, linked fate," a claim that suggests a certain equality among community members. When approached in structural-relational-processual terms, however, Anderson and Rocco appear less distant in their views. In this framing, community refers to a collective phenomenon that is continually forming and reforming, as those contesting who belongs and who does not repeatedly push at the elastic boundaries. As the anthropologist William Roseberry (1989:88) puts it, "When we connect these three dimensions—intersecting histories characterized by differentiation, heterogeneous cultural relations and values, and relations of power that encompass contradictions and tensions—we approach a more fruitful and challenging set of understandings." This framing is slippery and at times more difficult to maintain than static and bounded concepts of community and identity, but it more effectively captures the actual complexities of social interaction as Orlando Puerto Ricans and other Latinos navigate divergent racial identifications, class relations, and ideas about place in a historically constructed social field in which their relationships and communities form, disrupt, and reform.

Memory and meaning-making. With this understanding of community as well as the distinction between an identity idea and an act of identification, the question comes up about how Latinos, but Puerto Ricans in particular, have responded to received ideas about them as they navigate daily life in Orlando. What identity ideas have they worked to construct for themselves? Has this changed over time as the numbers have grown? What does this mean for collective identification as Puerto Rican and/or Latino in Orlando? These questions ask how these various ideas have been put to use in the changing dynamics of Orlando's social field and with what effect on Puerto Rican and Latino social, political, and economic relations in Orlando. Who benefits and who is hurt? Along with the institutional and structural relations that emerge from the dynamics of Orlando's open and contested social field, these questions are about the meaning-making that informs how Puerto Ricans and Latinos identify (or not) with each other and with others in that field.

As one vehicle for tracing meaning-making, I turn to collective memory's contribution to feelings of commonality, referencing collective memory as "those parts of the past which remain in the present life of groups or indeed what these groups make of the past" (Hoffman 2002:135n1).[36] In the process of making something of the past, remembering and forgetting underwrite a narrative constructed for present purposes.[37] Simply put, collective memory is about "who wants to remember what, and why" (Confino 1997:1393). As this implies, it is also about who wants to forget what, and why.

Puerto Ricans and other Latinos arriving in Orlando from divergent experiences bring distinct memories that inform how they interact with each other and with others in this new space. But in this new space, new memories also form, and selective processes of remembering and forgetting may help or hinder the development of a collective memory for collective identification in Orlando. Amid tensions of class, race, and place, to what degree can there be any sense of commonality? Or do divided interests hold sway and disrupt the Latino political community imagined by so many politicians and pundits during every national election cycle?

Addressing these questions requires keeping in mind the wider forces that affect daily life in Orlando as well as the local specifics that inform how those wider forces play out in this one location. In other words, William Roseberry asserts, "the local is global in this view, but the global can only be understood as always and necessarily local" (1995:57). In the first two chapters I articulate the local-global dynamics that play out in the particulars of Orlando; suffice it to say here that time and place matter. It matters that the events and relationships described have taken place in the late twentieth and early twenty-first centuries. It matters that they have taken place in a newly emergent and rapidly growing southern city whose economy underwent a transformation from cattle ranches and orange groves to theme parks and aeronautics over the course of a generation.

ETHNOGRAPHIC RESEARCH AND GETTING TO THE HARD QUESTIONS

It is often true in anthropological research that questions find the researcher rather than the other way around. Whatever question or topic we begin with often shifts or changes completely as what we find leads to new questions and more research. I did not set out to study Puerto Rican and Latino political life in Orlando. My process from 2005 to the present has been an organic one, and so it seems that the best way to introduce the data supporting this ethnographic rendering of Puerto Rican and Latino political life in Orlando is to walk the reader through the processes of data collection.

Given my dissertation research in Puerto Rico, the pronounced dominance of Puerto Ricans in Orlando, and the knowledge that Puerto Ricans are often sidelined in Hispanic/Latino research, I initially conducted my research primarily among Puerto Ricans. As the political focus emerged, I increasingly attended pan-Latino political gatherings that were often Puerto Rican–led. Over the years, my contacts have naturally expanded to include Cubans, Mexicans, Colombians, Panamanians, Dominicans, Venezuelans, and others who make up the diversity of Orlando's Latino community, but my focus on Puerto Rican experience has remained.

In the spring of 2005, the Orlando Regional Chamber of Commerce held the first of three annual Hispanic summits, organized by Puerto Rico–born Vilma Quintana. The point was to educate local business owners about the demographic shift that was under way (Martínez-Fernández 2010:38, Ramos 2005a). At the first summit in 2005, Jorge Duany and Félix Matos-Rodríguez presented the first research report about Puerto Ricans in Central Florida (Duany and Matos-Rodríguez 2006). Although Puerto Ricans had been visibly present in Central Florida for some time—including as periodically elected officials in local and state government—the events in 2005 reached a new level of mainstreaming *latinidad* with a Puerto Rican accent into Orlando's social field. In a *Centro Journal* edition focused on Central Florida, Luis Martínez-Fernández (2010:47–50) reviews some of the emergent Puerto Rican and Latino visibility from 2005: the Publix supermarket chain opened Publix Sabor in Osceola County featuring products in demand by Latino consumers; Spanish-language television began broadcasting;

a locally beloved oldies radio station changed to a salsa station; and the Orlando basketball team hired Puerto Rican player Carlos Arroyo.

I knew none of this in the fall of 2005 when, as a freshly minted PhD, I arrived in Orlando to take a four-year visiting position at the University of Central Florida (UCF). I knew very little about Orlando, period. I arrived from San Juan, where I had been living as I wrote my dissertation about a 1990s Puerto Rican school-reform project. The first hint that my experiences in Puerto Rico and the northeastern United States had not prepared me to understand the locally specific dynamics of my new home was when Florida Governor Jeb Bush signed the now-infamous "stand your ground" law.[38] I was also puzzled to learn that the two Central Florida Puerto Ricans in elected positions in 2005 were both Republicans rather than Democrats, as is so often assumed about Puerto Ricans. By the end of my first year of teaching at UCF campuses scattered about Central Florida, I was still not sure how I felt about living in Orlando, but I knew it was too interesting to leave. I was going to stay for a while.

By now I have conducted participant observation at innumerable cultural events, meetings of professional organizations, activist community meetings, public hearings, events hosted by mainstream and ethnic chambers of commerce, Latino church activities, and open and closed political meetings in Orlando. Through these activities I filled some ten notebooks with detailed field notes. I have conducted countless informal interviews with Puerto Ricans, other Latinos, and non-Latino white and black individuals in Orlando. The data also include about 150 interviews and oral histories that I or project team members recorded in Orlando between 2007 and 2012 as well as after Hurricanes Irma and Maria in 2018. Archival research in Puerto Rico, Florida, and Washington, DC, has added other sources, as have reading Orlando's mainstream and Spanish-language papers and listening to Spanish-language radio while driving the endless Central Florida highways. Over the years, I have lived in Puerto Rico, Orlando, and New York, traveling frequently to Orlando when I was not living there full time, and sometimes following people and their memories from Orlando to either Puerto Rico or New York. In Puerto Rico I interviewed former Florida residents and attended a relocation seminar preparing people to move to Central Florida. In New York and Puerto Rico it seemed everyone I met had family in Orlando, and I noted the stories as I heard them.

The bus to Brooksville. As a visiting assistant professor teaching on multiple campuses and supposedly preparing to move on to a tenure-track position somewhere else, my time was at a premium. Fieldwork during my first year in Orlando was limited to casual conversations when the opportunity arose; reading the Orlando edition of Puerto Rico's newspaper *El Nuevo Día*; reading a local weekly, *La Prensa*, which was founded in the early 1980s by Orlando Puerto Ricans; and listening to Spanish-language radio as I drove from campus to campus. Despite my lowly academic position, many of the Puerto Ricans I met insisted on calling me "Doctora." Although I spoke Spanish and had lived in Puerto Rico, the "Doctora" label held me, as a white Anglo, at a distance. Nonetheless, I regularly asked people where they came from, what brought them to Orlando, and how it was for them living there. Although data from Duany and Matos-Rodríguez (2006) clearly indicates that Orlando Puerto Ricans included both diaspora- and island-born, I regularly heard that this was a professional migration from the island. And although many of the Puerto Ricans I was meeting did seem to be living economically stable lives in Orlando, many of those I was reading about in the Puerto Rican papers seemed to be living more precariously. Class relations and birthplace were already emerging as important vectors of difference.

After about a year, I conducted a seed project to help me develop plans for more in-depth ethnographic research.[39] The project added nine recorded interviews and more intentional participant observation to my data collection. I was beginning to frequent Puerto Rican cultural spaces like the Asociación Borinqueña and Café d'Antaño. I had understood that Puerto Rican politics in Orlando was potentially explosive and that I needed to think about how to present myself politically. I was stepping very gently at first as I explored where I was. During an interview for the seed project, one Puerto Rico–born consultant exclaimed to me, "You're not asking the hard questions!" In my efforts to step gently, my questions were oriented toward learning about how and where Puerto Ricans were making *puertorriqueñidad* in Orlando, as though somehow this were happening in an apolitical vacuum. The inquiry remained focused on personal rather than collective experience.

A collective Puerto Rican life continued to emerge more insistently as some people I met along the way began to call me into political activities, both formal and informal, and directed me toward harder questions about Puerto Rican experience as perpetual foreigners in this new diaspora space. By the winter of 2008, with a couple of years at UCF under my belt, I was better able to arrange my time and take advantage when my cell phone rang on February 27 and a woman speaking rapidly and excitedly in Spanish was urging me to get on a bus heading to Brooksville, Florida, early the next morning.

The purpose of the trip on February 28 was to stage a protest outside the offices of Florida Congresswoman Virginia Brown-Waite, who had called on Congress to limit funds for Puerto Ricans in President Bush's stimulus package because of their status as what she called "foreign citizens." Prior to receiving the phone call, I had heard a radio interview in which an island-based Orlando Puerto Rican slammed the protesters as immature Puerto Ricans from New York. Now when I look at photos from the bus ride and protest, I smile because so many of the faces are people I have come to know well. Many of them are indeed New York Puerto Ricans, but not all of them are. Many of them have run for office, and some have since been elected to local and state positions.

Collecting oral histories. At the time of the protest I was working with another UCF professor, Natalie Underberg-Goode, on developing the proposal for an oral history project in an effort to learn more about Puerto Rican history in Central Florida. My interest in the project had grown from the disjuncture between the local narrative that the professional migration had begun in the 1980s and boomed in the 1990s and some chance encounters that suggested a much longer and more varied history. When Puerto Rican musician Roy Brown Jr. announced at an outdoor concert at Café d'Antaño that he was born in Orlando in 1945 and soon after that I met a Puerto Rican man born just north of Orlando in Sanford in 1949, I began to wonder what had been left out of the migration narrative I was hearing.

The 2008–2009 audio oral history collection titled Puerto Ricans in Central Florida 1940s to 1980s: A History (PRCF) resulted from that wondering.[40] "May I meet your mother?" I asked the man from Sanford. His mother, Monserrate Vélez, gave us the first oral history for the proposed project. Roy Brown Jr.'s mother had passed away, but his father, who was at that time living in San Juan, gave his oral history to the project as well.

Stories that pass in silence, as well as those told, inform the historical narratives that contribute to the reproduction of power relations in the present (Trouillot 1995). For an ethnographer interested in recovering the hidden histories needed for this effort, important tools in the toolkit include mining newspapers and reading both US Census data and local histories between the lines as much as possible. But it is oral history's ability to record the histories that people have made for themselves—in the ways that they remember and forget—that best illuminates how people make meaning of the world around them. Oral history helps document difference when social science at times loses sight of the fact "that a culture is made up of individuals different from one another" (Portelli 1991:130). Oral history provides a space where shared experience and individual connection to that experience meet (Yow 2005:284). Between top-down and bottom-up social perspectives, oral history explores the ground in between.

In the press release announcing the project, the only two criteria for participation were identifying as Puerto Rican and having arrived in Central Florida between the 1940s and 1980s. The unexpectedly large number of calls in response to the press release necessitated quickly hiring an office manager and training a team of students to help conduct interviews. Over about four months, project staff conducted sixty interviews, two of which were actually with Cubans and many of which included spouses and other family members of the original contact person. The public exhibit on display at two local libraries for about six weeks used bilingual panels and a series of digital stories to tell what we had learned. Jorge Duany was the featured speaker at the exhibit openings in early March 2009, both of which were standing-room only.

Although geographically the central part of Florida extends from Tampa on the Gulf to the Space Coast on the Atlantic, we narrowed our reach to what would be considered the Orlando area. At the time, the US Census Bureau included Orange, Osceola, Seminole, and Lake Counties in the Orlando Metropolitan Statistical Area; we expanded east from there to include Brevard and Volusia Counties. Brevard County is home to NASA's Kennedy Space Center, and one part of the oral histories focused on the Puerto Rican engineers recruited to Central Florida in the 1970s and 1980s. And we knew Volusia County to be the site of housing developments that had targeted sales to middle-class Puerto Ricans in Puerto Rico and New York. In essence, Disney World to the west and NASA to the east bracketed our project (map I.2).

The interview protocol included a list of topics and guidelines for open-ended questions. Participants were thus free to carry their stories to the things they thought were most important, things we might not have known to ask. We knew that racial perspectives were as volatile as politics. When I had asked about race early on in the research, I had often received answers like "You see me, I'm white!" Thus, despite 2008 being the year of Barack Obama's first presidential campaign, we did not directly include politics or race in the topics. Many participants went there on their own anyway.

Although conducted under less than ideal circumstances, the collection managed to create something where there had been nothing. I was happy to have given something to Orlando-area Puerto Ricans as I continued to ask for time and knowledge from them. There was now something to go on as I developed further questions. Birthplace, race, and class had emerged as fault lines and left me with an open question about those who had *not* participated in the project. Duany and Matos-Rodríguez (2006:19) assert that

MAP 1.2. Central Florida, with Walt Disney World and Kennedy Space Center

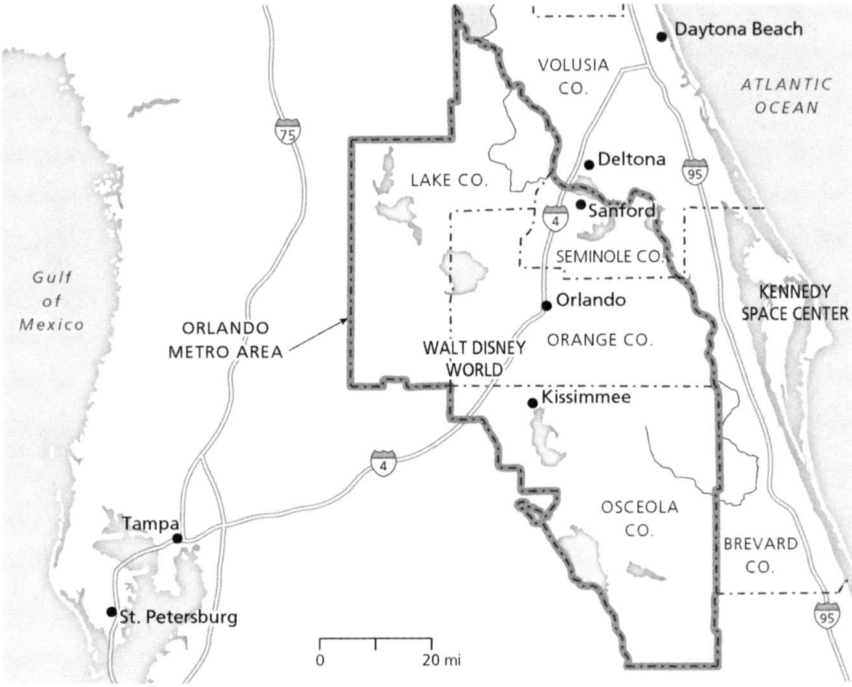

The four Central Florida counties outlined in gray make up the Orlando metro area. Participants in the 2008–2009 oral history project came from the metro area as well as Brevard and Volusia Counties. Map by Molly O'Halloran.

Orlando Puerto Ricans were earning more and had higher education levels than Puerto Ricans in Puerto Rico or in other US states, and participants in the oral history collection by and large seemed to fit that statistic. But the report by Duany and Matos-Rodríguez also indicates that about 44 percent of Orlando Puerto Ricans worked as laborers or in the service industry, and we did not have many stories from them. In addition, very few of the participants identified as being from New York or other diaspora communities, and most of those with diaspora experience had moved to Orlando after having returned to live in Puerto Rico for many years.

On the bus to Brooksville I had met Amy Mercado, a New York–born Puerto Rican. When she ran for local office in 2010 she invited me to follow her campaign. This time, the political emerged again and stayed. The campaign took me canvassing Latino door to Latino door, introduced me to a network of Puerto Rican and Latino political actors, and immersed me in the larger political fields of Orlando and Florida. That same year I moved to New

York as a research associate at the Center for Puerto Rican Studies (Centro). I continued to spend time in Orlando but was never able to stay for long periods or return on any kind of regular schedule. Over the next two years I did manage to conduct thirty-four semistructured interviews, now asking more targeted and harder questions to help me shape an understanding of collective memory and political life among Puerto Ricans and Latinos in the Orlando area. I also worked with a community-based team and three student assistants from Centro on a 2012 project, Cultural Foundations of Puerto Rican Orlando (CFPRO), recording brief oral histories from members of two Orlando Puerto Rican cultural centers: the Asociación Borinqueña and the Casa de Puerto Rico.

Following the 2012 elections I reached out to many in the political community whom I had come to know over the years to ask for their participation in a video oral history project. That collection, Puerto Rican Political Participation and Civic Engagement in Central Florida (PRPPCE), helped me reconstruct Latino and especially Puerto Rican political history in Orlando. The recordings include histories from seven men and fourteen women, ranging in age from their early forties through early seventies. Democratic, Republican, and nonaffiliated voters are represented, as are the pro-statehood, pro-Commonwealth, and independence positions from Puerto Rico's status politics. Participants were Puerto Rican with the exception of one Mexican journalist who had closely followed and documented Puerto Rican and Latino politics in Central Florida for years. The twenty Puerto Ricans included two women who had traveled from Puerto Rico to campaign in Orlando as well as a political organizer who was in Orlando for the election season. Of the seventeen Orlando Puerto Ricans in the collection, eleven had spent some of their lives in the diaspora before moving to Orlando, and five of those had returned to Puerto Rico and moved to Orlando from there. The dates of their arrivals in Central Florida ranged from 1979 to 2009. Together, these oral history projects give a view of Orlando history that is not to be found anywhere else.[41]

Focusing on Orange County. In the meantime, Simone Delerme had come to Central Florida for her dissertation work (Delerme 2013a). During her fieldwork time and afterward in New York, we met to compare notes and talk about our projects. Many of the political actors I was engaged with lived east and north of Orlando, and Simone's work was focusing on the heavily Latino-populated areas in Osceola County and the southern parts of Orange County. After years of trying to do everything and be everywhere at once, I narrowed my focus to Orange County. I was planning on completing fieldwork with the 2012 elections and the PRPPCE oral history project.

My plans changed and my geographic focus on Orange County consolidated when Latino Justice contacted me in 2013 about serving as an academic expert in a lawsuit against Orange County for violating the 1965 Voting Rights Act. Every ten years, voting districts are redrawn by a process known as redistricting or reapportionment.[42] During redistricting, district populations are rebalanced to accommodate demographic changes reflected in the decennial census. Originally mandated by the US Constitution with reference to the US House of Representatives, redistricting has become a highly politicized process at every level of state and local politics. The 2013–2014 *Florida Handbook* explains the "two faces" of redistricting as follows:

> One is the high-minded principle that every person should have equal representation in Congress and state legislatures, so district boundaries need to be redrawn after the census every 10 years to equalize the districts within a state. The other is the political reality that redrawing the districts is done by the political party in the majority in the legislature and is often done in a way that improves the chances of retaining or expanding that majority. (Morris and Morris 2014:261)

During the 2011 Orange County redistricting process, the final map of the county's six voting districts diluted Latino voting power by drawing lines through the East Side. Latino Justice was working with a group of plaintiffs who were challenging Orange County on the outcome. Data from the case, *Ríos-Andino v. Orange County*, including my deposition by opposing counsel and observations from the trial in May 2014, provided a unique opportunity for me to observe and document the play of difference and politics in strategies for Latino containment and struggles for Latino empowerment in Orange County, Florida.

One of the contradictions of ethnographic research with an insistence on process is that at some point it has to stop, while the world of those with whom the anthropologist has been engaged continues. Following the trial in 2014, I continued to visit Orlando but stepped back from full-time fieldwork to focus on writing. But things kept happening—big things like a mass shooting during Latin Night at the Pulse nightclub in which almost half of the victims were Puerto Rican, an economic crisis in Puerto Rico that began to push many more Puerto Ricans to Florida, and the 2017 hurricane season that changed Puerto Rico and Orlando forever. I will have to leave the analysis of those events and their consequences to future scholarship. In what follows here, I offer a perspective on what preceded Puerto Rican Orlando's newest turning point, which arguably began in 2015.

DIFFERENCE AND POLITICS IN A SUNBELT CITY

In this book I point to divergent experiences that Puerto Ricans and Latinos bring to their interactions in this southeastern diaspora space. I assert that whatever emerges from these interactions is also informed by historical trajectories that have drawn political and economic energies as well as new populations to the US Southeast. As Rafael struggled against barriers to his political participation in the 2012 election, his experiences formed an individual memory that no doubt joined with those of others in the days and weeks that followed. His frustrations as he came face to face with representatives of the state power charged with overseeing supposedly free and fair elections in a participatory democracy are one particular case—one example of mechanisms that frame Puerto Ricans and Latinos as perpetual foreigners.

This book is about how such particular cases join (or do not join) other particular cases in forming understandings of collective experience as a basis for the political life of Latinos and especially Puerto Ricans in the Orlando area. It situates the dynamics of Puerto Rican and Latino political community formation in a specific time and place in a social field of pressures that inform how local dynamics around racial-ethnic identifications, class relations, and ideas about place play out in the encounter with myriad differences subsumed under a homogenizing label as Hispanic or Latino. In this introduction I have identified the dilemma of political community formation and Latino heterogeneity in a southern location. I have argued for methods and analyses that emphasize process and contingency in community formation.

Part I serves as a geographic, demographic, political, and historical framing for the ethnographic detail to follow. In "Between Black and White," I locate Orlando Puerto Ricans and other Latinos in the area's social geography, demography, and politics. Then in chapter 2, "Hidden Histories in the New Orlando," I situate Puerto Rican and Latino Orlando as a place where local social relations inform and are informed by the intersections of Puerto Rican migration history, the concurrent rise of neoliberalism and color-blind multiculturalism in the United States, and the particulars of Florida's political history.

Part II is titled "Difference and the Incompleteness of Political Community Formation." In it I use oral histories and ethnographic data to trace the development of Puerto Rican Orlando through invisibility, hypervisibility, and efforts to create a visible presence on Puerto Rican and Latino terms. Part II ends with a historical account of Puerto Rican dispossession and displacement in local government that set the stage for engagement with the 2011 Orange County redistricting process.

Part III takes up the case of the local Orange County redistricting that followed the 2010 decennial census. Using selected ethnographic moments from the redistricting process and the lawsuit that followed, I look through the language of legal, statistical, and mapping technologies to see in concrete detail how local power holders were able to acknowledge the demographic shift in process while still containing its impact on non-Latino white control of local political and economic power.

In the book's conclusion I argue for an approach to social analysis that uses the multiple dimensions of history, heterogeneity, and contradictory relations. A brief epilogue presents events in Orlando from 2015 through 2018 that have informed and been informed by the race, class, and place dynamics of Puerto Rican and Latino Orlando in the twenty-first century.

PART I

PUERTO RICAN ORLANDO

CHAPTER 1

BETWEEN BLACK AND WHITE

Geography, Demography, and Political Place

Landing at the Orlando airport for the first time from Puerto Rico in 2005, I walked off the plane into a new, clean, and efficient space engineered to move people smoothly to their destinations. If I had followed the path that most tourists do, getting into a van or taxi that would take highways running along the south of Orlando itself and heading west to the theme parks, that first impression would likely have lasted. Highways also provide an efficient way to reach Orlando city, which lies due north of the airport. But the most direct route, if not the fastest, follows Semoran Boulevard north from the airport through traffic lights about eighteen miles. This route cuts through the eastern part of Orlando and eventually intersects with the two east-west routes that run through the city center.

Over the years of my fieldwork, Semoran was undergoing changes as powerful business and political interests worked to transform pawnshops and check-cashing outlets into Orlando's "Gateway." A 2011 *Orlando Sentinel* article called Semoran one of Central Florida's "ugliest stretches of road" (Schlueb 2011). By 2012 the newly formed Semoran Business Partnership had worked with the City of Orlando to ban any new "tattoo parlors, pawnshops, bail agencies, methadone clinics, clubs, check-cashing outlets and fortunetellers" (Schlueb 2012). Just a few miles from the airport, Gateway Village now offers an enclave of hotels and upscale chain restaurants. A large billboard directs travelers just up the road to High-Tide Harry's, "where the locals eat." Before High Tide Harry's, traffic passes the Orlando branch of Puerto Rico's Ana G. Mendez University.

Smaller businesses and restaurants—many with Spanish names—appear more frequently as Semoran crosses Curry Ford Road and heads through what is probably the oldest Latino area in Orlando. At Curry Ford on Semoran is an abandoned Kmart plaza across the road from a relatively new and very large Latin market, Sedano's. Beyond that is Oh! Que Bueno restaurant, where Darren Soto celebrated his 2012 win as the first Puerto Rican state senator. Farther north is the large and imposing Orlando Baptist Church, right next to a Denny's that serves as a popular spot for community meetings.

Some refer to this entire area as Azalea Park, from Curry Ford up to Colonial Drive surrounding the portion of Semoran between Colonial and East-West Highway ("the 408") and reaching east to Goldenrod Road. But Azalea Park officially begins just north of the 408 and extends along Semoran's eastern side up to Colonial (map 1.1). Azalea Park Elementary School and Little League field are across the road from La Primera grocery, which has been there about as long as anyone can remember. Just beyond is Lechonera El Barrio, where Barack Obama made a surprise stop during the 2012 elections.[1]

Orlando's contemporary racial-ethnic geography is layered on top of the earlier Jim Crow black-white version. Latinos have settled all around the Orlando area as new housing developments have been built, but Azalea Park and the areas pushing east constitute a principal concentration of Orlando's Latino population. Although not actually within Orlando's city limits, this area is referred to as Orlando's East Side. It is also the area within Orange County with the largest percentage of Puerto Ricans among Latinos, and this was an important element in the 2011 redistricting. As Puerto Ricans and other Latinos eclipsed Anglos in Azalea Park, the non-Latino white population declined from 90 percent in 1980 to 28 percent in 2010. Writing in 2001, Puerto Rican journalist María Padilla (2001a) noted that Azalea Park was called "Little San Juan" and that Hispanics made up more than 40 percent of some sectors in that area.

If the East Side is Latino, the West Side is black. Division Street just to the west of downtown Orlando still marks a racial border only slightly more porous than under Jim Crow segregation.[2] Beginning in the 1970s and increasingly in the 1980s, Orlando's African Americans and newly arriving black residents from elsewhere began moving beyond the earlier legally defined "colored" sections and settling into newer housing just across Colonial Drive in Pine Hills (Kunerth 2006b). As in Azalea Park over the same period, the non-Latino white population in Pine Hills declined from 88 percent in 1980 to 13 percent in 2010.

In between the historically black West Side and the emerging Latino East Side is downtown Orlando, where at almost any time of day the full complexity of Orlando's demography is apparent. The downtown stretch of Colonial Drive is known as "Little Vietnam"; walking through the old brick streets of Orlando just south of Colonial, one will hear multiple languages and see every shade of skin color. In the center of Orlando is Lake Eola Park, populated by joggers, tourists, and the homeless. Images on promotional materials calling Orlando "The City Beautiful" often center around the lake with its fountain and symbolic mix of black and white swans. At one end of the lake stands the Disney Amphitheater, which has been painted in rainbow colors since the attack at the Pulse nightclub. During the years of my fieldwork, the other end of the lake held the statue of a Confederate soldier, known locally as Johnny Reb.

These details point to the local materialities of place that intersect with Puerto Rican and Latino place-making in Orlando and Orange County. By "materiality of place" I refer to two processes under way and under contention in Orlando. The first is the transformation of physical space into an abstracted meaningful place of belonging such as the Latino East Side or Orlando itself as a new place in the Puerto Rican diaspora.[3] The second is the very local struggle for political ground from which Puerto Ricans and other Latinos can insert themselves into Orlando's long-standing socioracial framing in black and white and from there gain equitable access to political and economic resources and social power (Barreto 2007, Cruz 1998, Rocco 2010).

Race and class in Orlando are both local and translocal axes through which social relations are negotiated and navigated as part of local place-making.[4] In other words, a local specificity emerges from particular sets of relationships in this particular place as well as from relations, experiences, and understandings that reach well beyond what is actually perceivable (Massey 1994:154–156). Gastón Gordillo (2004:3) has argued that "places are produced in tension with other geographies" and that the tensions are about memories of these other geographies, which are brought into localized place-making practices. For Puerto Ricans in Orlando, place-specific memories as well as more tangible assets have arrived from Puerto Rico and from Puerto Rican New York, Chicago, Philadelphia, Hartford, and so on. Latino Orlando is similarly in tension with other Latino homelands and with the South, as a place with a particular, historically constructed racial order that Puerto Ricans and other Latinos are challenging as they claim social and physical space. Furthermore, Orlando itself, as a newly emergent Latino space in Florida, is in tension with Miami for statewide influence.

These explanations of place are suggestive of Jacqueline Nassy Brown's assertion (2005:8) that place is an abstraction, a process of meaning-making imbued with power and subjectivity, and that place is linked to "ideologies that rationalize economic inequalities and structure people's material well-being and life chances." Although I embrace Brown's take on place as an abstraction, I do not share her concern that attention to the materiality of places can too easily slip into "the use of place-as-matter to explain the social" (9). As Puerto Ricans and other Latinos struggle to make a place for themselves in Orlando's social field, they are indeed faced with abstracted social and geographic divisions between white and black. But those abstractions refer to a precise physicality that contributes to the reproduction of social inequalities. Redistricting and other mechanisms of state power have historically restrained the ability of Puerto Ricans and other Latinos to make political and economic place for themselves in Orlando. The anthropologist Clifford Geertz notes (1996:262),

> For it is still the case that no one lives in the world in general. Everybody, even the exiled, the drifting, the diasporic, or the perpetually moving, lives in some confined and limited stretch of it—"the world around here." The sense of interconnectedness imposed on us by the mass media, by rapid travel, and by long-distance communication obscures this more than a little. So does the featurelessness and interchangeability of so many of our public spaces, the standardization of so many of our products, and the routinization of so much of our daily existence. The banalities and distractions of the way we live now lead us, often enough, to lose sight of how much it matters just where we are and what it is like to be there.

MAPPING PUERTO RICAN AND LATINO ORLANDO

A first step to situating Puerto Ricans and other Latinos in Orlando's social geography is knowing something about the city and county lines that overlay and interact with that geography. Orlando city is the approximate geographic center of what is commonly called the Orlando metro area, encompassing Lake, Orange, Osceola, and Seminole Counties in their entirety (see map I.2 on page 24). The US Census Bureau labels the area the Orlando-Kissimmee-Sanford Metropolitan Statistical Area. Sanford lies about a thirty-minute drive north of downtown Orlando in Seminole County. Kissimmee lies about a thirty-minute drive south in Osceola County.

By annexation of some areas and not others, the lines demarcating Orlando city from the rest of Orange County (map 1.1) have expanded over time in a piecemeal fashion (Hinton 2001, Lemongello 2017). Indeed, Orlando city has been described as a "municipal patchwork quilt," and at one point on Semoran, it is about one block wide (Brewington 2003a). Although almost all of Semoran Boulevard from the airport to Colonial Drive is itself within the city limits, the areas running along it may not be. Azalea Park lies outside the city limits, and the part described above between Curry Ford

MAP 1.1. Orlando city

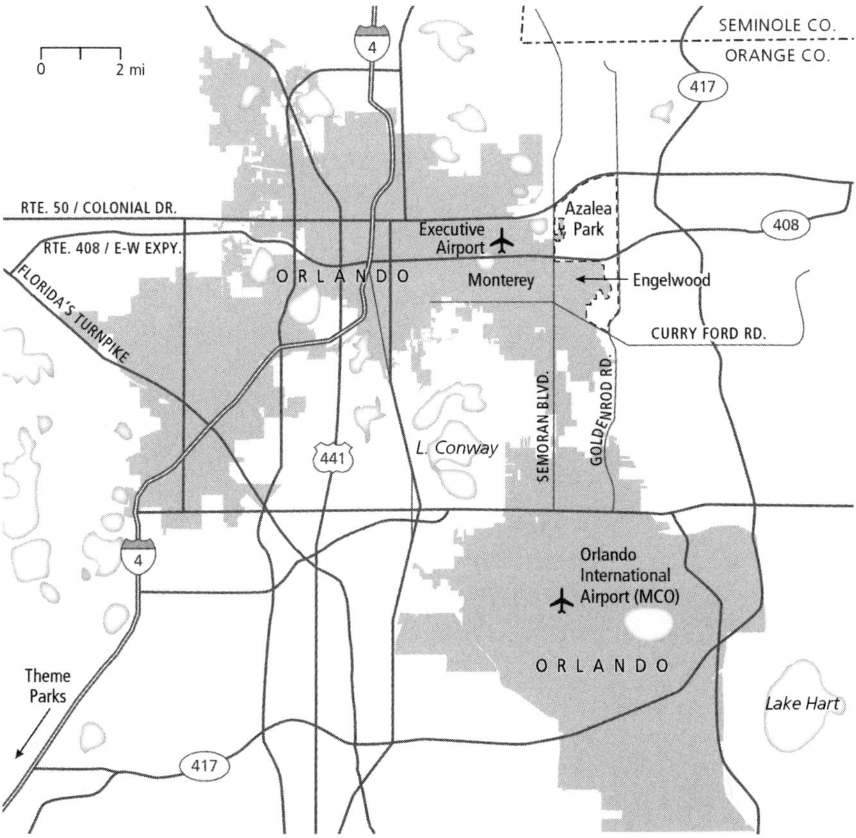

The sprawling, uneven extent of land within Orlando's city limits is indicated by shading. Map by Molly O'Halloran.

and the 408 is actually Orlando's Engelwood and Monterey neighborhoods. Most people who frequent Azalea Park are unaware of entering and leaving the city limits as they go about their daily routines. But the relation to local governments changes from one side of Semoran to another and north and south of the 408 overpass.

Similarly, Orlando commuters regularly cross county lines in the course of a day. Each county has its own political structure and separate history, which together affect how local social, political, and economic relations play out. Orange and Osceola Counties share in the Reedy Creek Improvement District, which is home to Walt Disney World. The economic impact on each county has varied according to Disney's negotiations with the separate county governments (Fogelsong 2001). The counties of the metro area have also responded differently to federal civil rights legislation. Following a collectively resistant response to school desegregation in the 1960s, the counties that include and surround Orlando responded with different time frames to federal requirements for bilingual ballots and English-language assessment and services in public schools in the 1970s. Because the requirements took effect according to the size of the Latino population, some Orlando-area counties chose to stall through the 1980s and into the 1990s rather than accommodate the changing needs of the population.

Where Puerto Ricans and other Latinos are now located in this racial-ethnic and political geography reflects both the location of World War II–era military bases and the expansion of new housing markets that followed Disney World's construction. The first year that an Orlando-area census identified anyone who would now be categorized by the US Census Bureau as "Hispanic or Latino" was 1960. At that time, the Orlando metro area included only Orange and Seminole Counties. The count indicated 471 people who were born in Puerto Rico or had Puerto Rican parents and 171 who were born in Mexico. The 1970 Census added Cuba and "other America" to Latin American birthplace categories. Just under 1 percent of Orlando's metro-area population in 1970 were of Puerto Rican birth or parentage or born in Latin America. Of these, the largest group was Cuba-born, numbering about 35 percent of Orlando's "Spanish" population; those of Puerto Rican birth or heritage were about 20 percent (US Census Bureau 1960, 1970).

Although the numbers are not large, their location is important. The 1960 Census places the greatest concentrations of Puerto Ricans and people born in Mexico next to what was then the Orlando Air Base (now Executive Airport) in the Monterey neighborhood (map 1.1). During World War II, the Orlando Air Base anchored a military presence in the Orlando area (Bacon 1977:2:100–102). Monterey streets all carry Spanish names, and Spanish surnames appear in early property deeds in the subdivision. Historical analysis suggests the probability that Puerto Rican and perhaps other Spanish-speaking servicemen and their families lived in Monterey (Firpo 2012:61–63). Keeping in mind that Orlandoans use "Azalea Park" to refer to the entire area that crosses the city-county limits, it is noteworthy that among the oral history narratives collected for this research, participants pointed to Azalea Park as an area where many Latinos in the US military lived (PRCF Auffant, PRCF Pagán Hill).

Walt Disney World opened in 1971. By 1980 Osceola County's population was expanding rapidly (Foglesong 2001:146). The 1980 Census included that county in the Orlando metro area and added a category for "Spanish Origin." With the expanded geography and the more inclusive category, the count for "Spanish Origin" climbed to almost 26,000, accounting for 4

TABLE 1.1. Orlando metro-area population of "Spanish Origin," 1980

1980 Orlando metro area (Orange + Seminole + Osceola Co.)			
Nationality or descent	**Total**	**Percent of population**	**Percent of Spanish origin**
Spanish origin	25,972	4	100
Puerto Rican	9,158	1	35
Cuban	5,098	1	20
Mexican	4,800	1	18
Other Spanish	6,916	1	27

Source: US Census Bureau 1980

percent of the metro-area population (table 1.1). Puerto Ricans were now the largest single "Spanish Origin" group, numbering just over 9,000; Cubans and Puerto Ricans had traded places. By the 1980 count, Puerto Ricans were 35 percent and Cubans were 20 percent of Orlando metro-area Latinos.

From 1980 onward, the area's Latino population grew exponentially. By the 2010 Census, the Orlando metro area included Lake County. Cubans numbered fewer than Colombians, and Puerto Ricans were almost 50 percent of Orlando Latinos. The second-largest count was Mexican, at a distant 12 percent (US Census Bureau 2010).[5] The 2020 Census will be in process as this book is published. The US Census Bureau's American Community Survey estimates for 2017 (table 1.2) bring the Puerto Rican percentage to 51 percent, and this number is likely to increase as the counts come in from the years following Hurricane Maria.[6]

TABLE 1.2. Orlando metro-area "Hispanic or Latino" population, 2017

Orlando-Kissimmee-Sanford metro area (Orange + Seminole + Osceola + Lake Co.)			
Nationality or descent	**Total**	**Percent of population**	**Percent of all Latinos**
Hispanic or Latino	693,930	29	100
Puerto Rican	354,960	15	51
Mexican	69,537	3	10
Cuban	52,302	2	8
Dominican	47,189	2	7
Colombian	46,087	2	7
Venezuelan	26,939	1	4

Source: US Census Bureau, ACS 2017b

Latino percentages of total population varied (and still vary) significantly from county to county. The 2017 estimates put Orange at 30 percent Latino, Seminole at 20 percent, Osceola at 52 percent, and Lake at 14 percent (US Census Bureau, ACS 2017b). Although the actual numbers are largest in Orange, it is Osceola—a historically non-Latino white county with a very small African American population—that has most felt the impact of this shifting demographic. In Kissimmee city, Latinos are 66 percent of the population. The geographic and demographic details from Orange County are of particular interest here because that county and its 2011 redistricting process are central to this book.

The four images in map 1.2 offer a visual representation of Latino population growth in Orange County from 1980 through 2010, just before redistricting was to begin. Although concentrations of Latinos have grown on the East Side and to the south in the area crossing the Osceola County line, it is clear on the maps that Latinos reside all over the county. The percentages are not as dramatic as in Osceola County, yet for many non-Latinos and especially those for whom Orange County has always been home, this demographic shift has been alarming.

MAP 1.2. Latino population in Orange County, 1980–2010

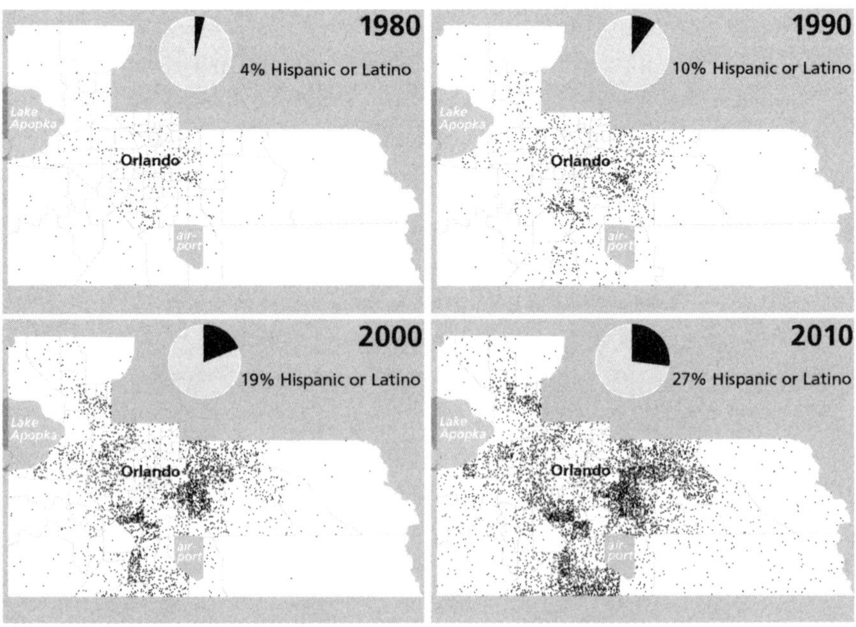

Each dot represents fifty people. The dots are randomly placed within the relevant census tracts. Manson et al. 2018, IPUMS NHGIS. Map by Chicago CartoGraphics.

MAP 1.3. Latino-dominant CDPs in Orange County

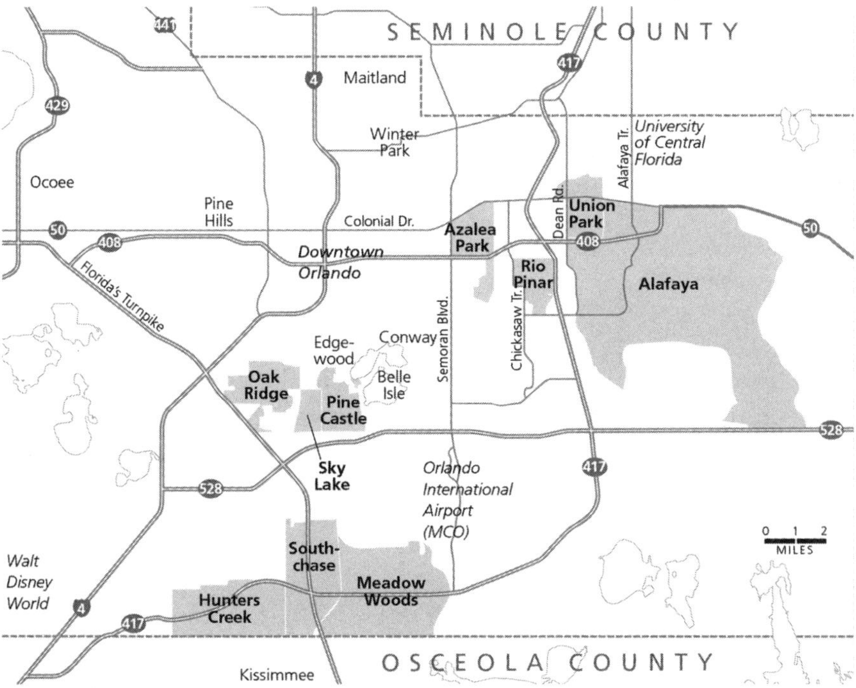

Shading indicates census-designated places (CDPs) in unincorporated Orange County with large Latino populations in 2010. Map by Chicago CartoGraphics.

The largest numbers of Orange County Puerto Ricans and Latinos actually live outside Orlando city or any other incorporated municipality, in unincorporated Orange County. Latinos living in Orlando proper make up less than 25 percent of the total population, while in some areas of unincorporated Orange County the Latino percentage of total population is as high as in Kissimmee city. As part of the decennial census, unincorporated county geographical spaces that have reached a certain degree of population density are assigned a statistical status as census-designated places (CDPs). Map 1.3 locates the nine Orange County CDPs that had the greatest percentages of Latinos in the 2010 Census count that preceded the 2011 redistricting—Alafaya, Azalea Park, Hunters Creek, Meadow Woods, Oak Ridge, Pine Castle, Sky Lake, Southchase, and Union Park—as well as Rio Pinar with its smaller but still significant Latino population.

Clustered in the upper right of map 1.3 are Azalea Park, Union Park, Alafaya, and Rio Pinar. These are the areas referenced as the East Side, which the 2011 redistricting divided. Newer housing developments pushing east from Azalea Park have attracted Puerto Ricans and other Latinos over the decades. During the 1980s the East Side came to be called "Little Puerto Rico" (Delgado 1988a). In the unnamed space between Azalea Park and Union Park CDPs, Chickasaw Trail runs alongside Rio Pinar CDP, with its 25 percent Latino population. Over the years of my fieldwork a new ramp was built from Chickasaw to the 408, and at the intersection with Colonial there is now a Wawa gas station and convenience store. These signs of increasing population indicate that in the 2020 Census a new Orange County CDP named Chickasaw may well join the others shown on map 1.3.

In the middle of the map are Pine Castle, Sky Lake, and Oak Ridge, which (like Azalea Park) are near a former military base (now Orlando International Airport) and figure among the oldest settlements in the county. The 2008–2009 PRCF oral history collection includes evidence of Puerto Ricans attending public school in Oak Ridge and living in Oak Ridge apartments (PRCF Auffant, PRCF Ghigliotty, PRCF A. González). At the southern end of Orange County bordering Osceola are the newer developments of Hunters Creek, Southchase, and Meadow Woods.

Table 1.3 charts Latino percentages of the total population for the nine most concentrated CDPs from 1980 through 2010. The data indicating the 2010 percentages of Puerto Ricans among Latinos show that the East Side CDPs are the most heavily Puerto Rican areas. The Alafaya CDP was not designated until 2010, and the CDPs near the Orange-Osceola County line only got on the Census CDP map in the 2000 count. Heavy marketing of affordable Landstar homes in the area crossing the Orange-Osceola line has more recently attracted buyers to that area as prices in Azalea Park had done in earlier decades.[7] Because Landstar built both Meadow Woods and Buenaventura Lakes just over the county line, the area feels like a continuous community although a county line divides it in two.[8]

Azalea Park and neighboring Union Park, as well as the space in between, are unequivocally Latino areas from the local perspective. The other older neighborhoods of Pine Castle, Sky Lake, and Oak Ridge are less certain. The cities of Belle Isle and Edgewood and the Conway CDP, which are just to the east of Pine Castle, have remained largely white Anglo. But Oak Ridge, Sky Lake, and Pine Castle have moved from being predominantly non-Latino white to a mixed population, close to half of which is Latino.

In Pine Castle, perhaps Orlando's oldest settlement, non-Latino white residents are now only about 20 percent of the population; Latinos number over half of Pine Castle residents (US Census Bureau, ACS 2017b). Pine Castle's relation to Orlando's non-Latino history and its annual Pioneer Days celebration nonetheless lend a non-Latino whiteness to its identification,

TABLE 1.3. Latino and Puerto Rican concentrations in nine Orange County CDPs, 1980–2010

	1980			1990		
CDP	**Total**	**Latino** (%)	**PR to Latino** (%)	**Total**	**Latino** (%)	**PR to Latino** (%)
Azalea Park	8,301	8	38	8,926	18	66
Oak Ridge	15,477	9	37	15,388	24	60
Pine Castle	9,992	7	36	8,726	18	67
Sky Lake	6,692	9	58	6,202	20	61
Union Park	19,175	6	54	6,890	12	55
	2000			**2010**		
CDP	**Total**	**Latino** (%)	**PR to Latino** (%)	**Total**	**Latino** (%)	**PR to Latino** (%)
Azalea Park	11,073	39	64	12,556	59	62
Oak Ridge	22,349	41	46	22,685	44	37
Pine Castle	8,803	36	46	10,805	49	45
Sky Lake	5,651	35	48	6,153	52	42
Union Park	10,191	26	65	9,765	41	63
Hunters Creek	9,369	14	36	14,321	36	41
Meadow Woods	11,286	53	63	25,558	67	52
Southchase	4,633	34	56	15,921	49	45
Alafaya				78,113	33	55

Sources: US Census Bureau 1980, 1990, 2000; US Census Bureau, ACS 2010

and indeed 71 percent of Pine Castle Latinos identified as white in the 2017 American Community Survey five-year estimates. Press coverage of Pioneer Days asserts that most Pine Castle residents are descended from pioneers who came from Alabama and Georgia just after the Civil War (Comas 2002). This may be because before Belle Isle and Edgewood incorporated in the early twentieth century, the name Pine Castle was used to refer to the whole area that surrounds the group of lakes now called the Conway Chain of Lakes. This all mattered in the 2011 Orange County redistricting.

DIFFERENCES OF RACE, CLASS, AND PLACE IN ORLANDO

In a class at the University of Central Florida in 2006, my five students, all Puerto Rican, included Raquel and María, who were born and raised in Puerto

Rico; Daisy and Marguerite, who moved to Central Florida from New York; and Jorge, who was born in Puerto Rico and had lived a life of circular migration between Puerto Rico and many diaspora spaces.[9] One day, as we discussed Puerto Rican migration history and cultural identifications, Daisy pointed to Raquel and said, "I don't know what Puerto Rican is, but I am nothing like her." Daisy's disclaimer highlighted the divisions of island and diaspora behind the question "¿De dónde eres?" and emphasized the intertwining of racial identification, class relations, and birthplace for Puerto Ricans looking for something to identify as a community in Orlando's social field. In Puerto Rico the idea of the New York Puerto Rican is thick with images of blackness and poverty, and the name "Nuyorican" is often applied disparagingly to any diaspora Puerto Rican. But for many from New York, identifying as Nuyorican represents a proud and defiant response to marginalization. In his 2008 oral history, Víctor Alvarado expressed hurt at the disdain shown to New York Puerto Ricans in Orlando by those from the island, saying that is hard to hear for someone who has spent his life fighting for Puerto Rican rights (PRCF Alvarado).

The Puerto Rican birthplace tensions between Daisy and Raquel mirror tensions between Puerto Ricans and other Orlando Latinos more generally. Puerto Rican birthright citizenship, tied as it is to a history of marginalization in the US states, gives other Latinos reason to distance themselves and assert their own national origins. And when Orlando Puerto Ricans see themselves excluded from political and economic relations that some other Latinos enjoy, there is deep resentment. Puerto Ricans tell me that Venezuelans get better coverage in *El Sentinel*, the Spanish-language edition of the *Orlando Sentinel*. A Nicaraguan woman told the *Orlando Sentinel*, "I'm always having to convince people that I'm not Puerto Rican. . . . People don't even ask me what country I'm from; they just assume" (in Kunerth and Brewington 2002). Puerto Ricans and Cubans wrestled back and forth for years over control and direction of a chamber of commerce.

Birthplace alone gives limited information about one's experience of place, but a look at the data for Latinos in the Orlando metro area as well as in the separate counties can suggest different relationships to different places among Orlando Latinos (table 1.4). The data for Florida and other US states lump all Latinos together, but the Puerto Rico– and foreign-born data offer information about residence patterns of island-born Puerto Ricans and other Latinos.[10] Of note is the fact that in the metro area as a whole, approximately the same percentage of Latinos were born in Florida (24 percent), another US state (23 percent), Puerto Rico (25 percent), and in another country (26 percent).

TABLE 1.4. Birthplaces of Latinos in Orlando metro area and by county

Birthplace	Orlando (%)	Orange (%)	Osceola (%)	Seminole (%)	Lake (%)
Florida	24	24	19	27	33
Other US states	23	22	25	27	24
Northeast	17	16	19	18	15
Midwest	3	2	3	3	4
South (not Florida)	2	2	2	3	3
West	2	2	1	2	2
Puerto Rico	25	24	32	21	18
Foreign-born	26	29	23	24	23

Source: US Census Bureau, ACS 2015

Note: The ACS 2015 5-year estimates are the most recent I have been able to access at this level of data.

Like the data for various Orange County CDPs, these data say something at the county level about Puerto Rican and Latino residence patterns in the metro area. Across the counties, with the exception of Osceola, a greater or equal percentage of Latinos was born in Florida as elsewhere in the South or in other regions of the United States. It is also true that in every county close to half and often more than half of Latinos were born outside the US states, either in Puerto Rico or in another country. Of these, the largest percentages of Puerto Rico– and foreign-born are in Orange and Osceola Counties. Latinos born in the Northeast and in Puerto Rico are most likely to live in Osceola and least likely to live in Lake County. Marguerite lived in Osceola and told me one day, laughing, that there were too many Puerto Ricans there and she wanted to move to Lake County. The *Orlando Sentinel* has also taken note of this trend (Unmuth 2002, Shanklin and Minshew 2016).

Racial identifications. In his study of whiteness in Detroit, John Hartigan (1999:14) discusses how racial identifications "are projected onto social space as a means of identifying individuals and positing the significance of their connection to collective orders," demonstrating that both residents and nonresidents of a given area may label it a black area or a white area despite the racial-ethnic diversity of the people who actually live there.[11] One example is Pine Castle's reputation as white. Another is Pine Hills, which was home to enough Puerto Ricans in the 1970s that the 2008–2009 oral history collection from Puerto Ricans in Central Florida includes stories about a Puerto Rican–style Christmas celebration in a Pine Hills home and early meetings of the Asociación Borinqueña in a Catholic church in Pine Hills (PRCF Auffant, PRCF H. and L. Gómez). Although the percentage of Puerto Ricans and other Latinos living in Pine Hills has grown since those early years, the area's racial-ethnic reputation is as non-Latino black and especially West Indian (Brewington 2003b, Gallagher 1991b). When Rosita purchased a Pine Hills home before moving to Orlando under the guidance of a real estate agent who knew the area, it did not take long for her to recognize Orlando's racial dividing line. She soon decided that Pine Hills was not where she wanted to live. She sold her new home and moved to Orlando's East Side. "Pine Hills was not for me," she told me. Besides Pine Hills to the west and Azalea Park to the east, there are also places—like Winter Park, College Park, and Baldwin Park—considered to be white and associated with good schools and a well-educated population. Another reputed white area in the rural, eastern part of Orange County, called Bithlo, is referred to by many as "redneck" although about one quarter of its population is Latino.

The ideas about race that Latinos bring with them, as well as their own racial identifications, affect navigation of Orlando's social and political geography. Latin American racial categories vary from country to country but generally include a continuum that privileges European heritage and lighter skin tones.[12] Nonetheless, in many Latin American places including Puerto Rico a national ethos celebrates its people as a harmonious mix of races; racial distinctions exist but without the stark black-white binary that has historically dominated in the United States.

Among Puerto Ricans, with the mix of Spanish, Taíno Indian, and African claimed by collective national identification, individuals are teased about their "bad hair," and a wide vocabulary exists to describe skin tone and other physical features that place a person closer to or more distant from a European or African heritage (Duany 2002).[13] In a 2017 letter to the editor of the *Orlando Sentinel*, Pura Delgado described her experiences as a dark-skinned Puerto Rican: "I am an 86-year-old Puerto Rican woman, who also happens to be dark skinned. . . . I remember the years of discrimination I faced, not only in this country when I came to New York at the age of 16, but from my own people when I was growing up in Puerto Rico" (Delgado 2017). Delgado goes on to lament that the "rainbow of Puerto Ricans" is largely invisible in Florida leadership and national media.

When the idea of a racial continuum interacts with the US black-white binary, divergent responses may lead to divergent racial-political alliances. Lorrin Thomas (2009) has described efforts by New York Puerto Ricans in the 1930s to be seen as white so as not to be subjected to the social, political, and economic dispossession faced by African Americans. In later decades, Puerto Ricans with diaspora experience made common cause with African Americans, and today many diaspora Puerto Ricans identify as black, or at least not white, no matter how others might read their physical features.

It is important to note that the black-white binary and continuum concepts of race can and do coexist (Findlay 2012, Godreau 2008). When confronted with situations in which a racial identification is either mandatory or useful, Puerto Ricans and other Latinos may draw from either or both the US binary and the Latin American racial continuum according to the needs of the immediate dynamics.[14] For instance, race-place linkages are evident in Latino racial identification choices in the US Census. Chart 1.1 gives state, regional, local, and selected CDP data for Latino racial identification as "White alone," "Black or African American alone," and "some other race alone."[15] The comparative data at the state and regional levels suggest an impact on racial identification in diaspora according to different places. That white identification is dominant across the regions is suggestive of both a distancing from blackness in the US black-white binary and an aligning with European ancestry in a mixed heritage.

Latinos in US regions other than the South show a greater tendency to identify as some other race; that difference may be a response to the special tenacity of the black-white paradigm in the southern region. Similarly, although black identification is lowest across all places, it is highest in the Northeast, where alliances with African Americans have at times historically proven politically advantageous. The findings add weight to the argument that as a former Confederate state, Florida's historically more rigid racial categories may prompt a claim to whiteness among Latinos (Delerme 2014, Rumbaut 2009).

No matter how Latinos identify themselves, they must contend with how non-Latinos see them. Latino scholars argue that in the face of being denied whiteness in US racial schemes, a lack of willingness to clearly identify apart from whiteness can disrupt the potential for an emergent racial-ethnic identification through which to organize politically in opposition to white supremacy and in support of a truly inclusive social agenda. Arlene Dávila (2008:13) points out that "the path toward whitening is not equally open to all Latinos and that those who are white do not face the same level of racial discrimination as Latinos of indigenous and African backgrounds." And Nicholas De Genova (2010:163) contends that the problem with aspiring to "a kind of 'immigrant' would-be-whiteness" is that association with Latinos

CHART 1.1. Latino racial identification

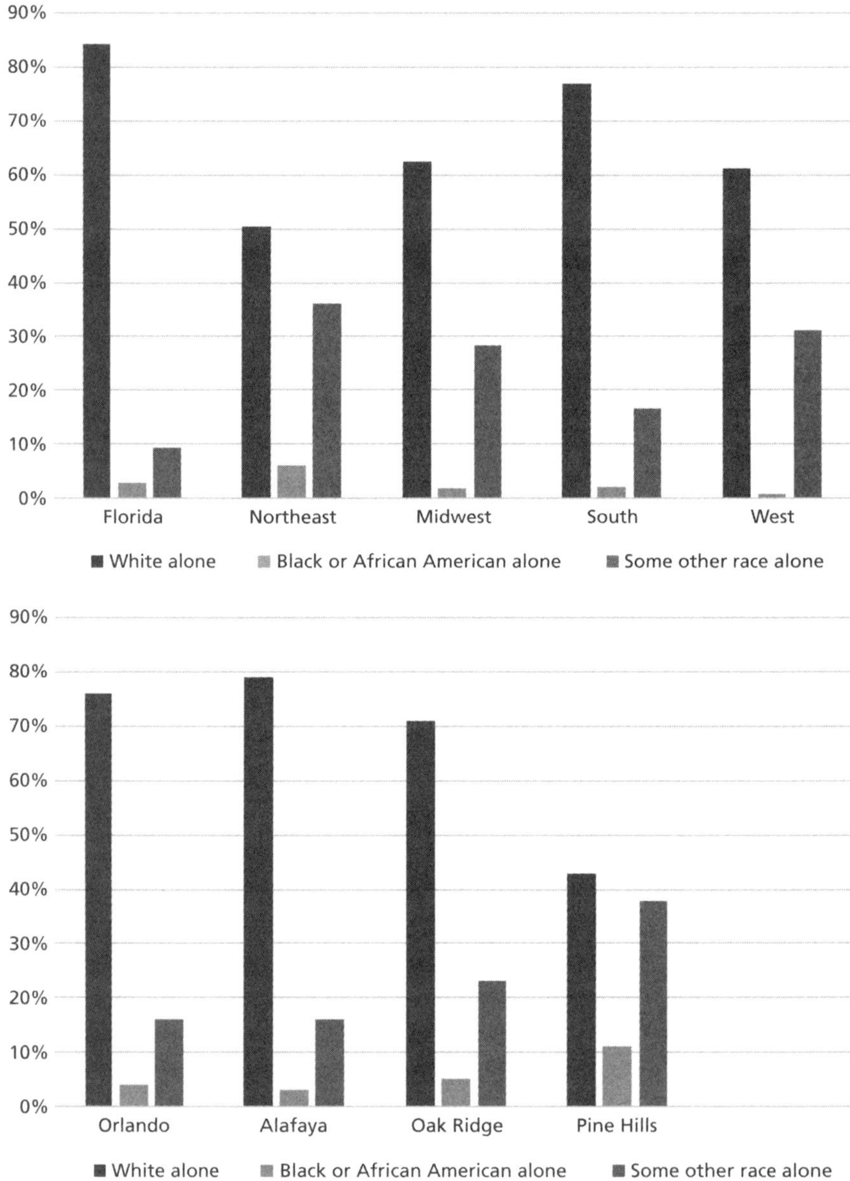

Source: US Census Bureau, ACS 2017b

racialized as not-white then threatens these "tentative and tenuous claims" to whiteness and forces a need to disconnect from other Latinos. Finally, Silvio Torres-Saillant has long argued that Latino "ambivalence regarding their difference from the white majority" has led to "insufficient strides in the quest for full citizenship in American society." Without embracing racial difference, Torres-Saillant argues, dismantling racism becomes impossible, and dismantling racism is "a goal without which no project of social transformation deserves to be taken seriously in the United States" (2003:126).

That Orlando Latinos are not immune to this problem was evident to me during the 2016 elections when I heard a Puerto Rican talk-radio host say to a caller, "Voting for Donald Trump is not going to make you white, you know." It is noteworthy that among Orlando Latinos there is actually a slightly lower tendency than among Florida Latinos generally to identify as white and a greater tendency to identify as some other race (chart 1.1). In the comparative data on the state of Florida and local identifications in the Orlando area, a greater percentage of Latinos in Orlando identify apart from whiteness.

Given Orlando's racial-ethnic geography, Latinos living in different places are more or less likely to have black or white neighbors, which may affect how they identify racially as they either align with or distance themselves from their neighbors. Along with data for the Orlando metro area, the data represented in chart 1.1 use the examples of Alafaya, Oak Ridge, and Pine Hills to consider intersections of race and place within Orlando. Latinos in Alafaya are more likely to have non-Latino white neighbors; Oak Ridge neighbors are mixed; in Pine Hills, Latinos are more likely to have non-Latino black neighbors. Across these three places, there is some increase in identification as black or African American alone, but what is most striking is the increase in identification as some other race. In Pine Hills, this is almost one half of all Latinos. One might ask if and how this informs the reproduction or transformation of race relations in the Orlando area.

Variations in racial identification among Latinos also follow lines of national origin (Rumbaut 2009). Bonilla-Silva (2014:235) finds that Cubans and Argentines are most likely to identify as white, while Dominicans are least likely. In much of the data about variations in racial identification—whether CDP of residence, country of birth, or lived experience in different diaspora spaces—place continually emerges as important to the kinds of racial memories Orlando Latinos bring with them and how they experience self and other in Orlando.

Class relations. Personal stories illustrate that these racialized place identifiers intertwine with socioeconomic status. They suggest that race, class, and place inform Latino political community formation in the Orlando area.[16] Rosita wrinkled her nose a bit when I asked why she had not chosen to relocate to the area surrounding the Orange-Osceola County line. Despite the range of household incomes in the area, a reputation for slumlike conditions marks certain sectors, and so this was another place that she suggested was not for her.[17]

Census data do not indicate the performative and cultural aspects of social class or the impact of inherited wealth or poverty on who has access to which economic resources. The data do not show how the public sphere is constructed to maintain the rules of access and reproduce societal class hierarchies. Indeed, statistical measures of class as a static social position lend themselves to a depoliticized view of class relations (Gregory 1998:140). Nonetheless, it remains useful to situate gradations of some statistical class indicators in relation to different places in the Orlando landscape as part of charting the area's social geography for Latinos as well as for the population at large.

A range of class relations among Orlando Puerto Ricans and other Latinos has contributed to the widespread settlement patterns. Ramón Luis Concepción Torres (2008:109) has found in the Orlando area that "Puerto Ricans with higher socioeconomic status avoided sharing settlement space with other Puerto Ricans with lower socioeconomic status." Among the nine most Latino-concentrated CDPs there is a correspondence between the median Latino household income and the age of the area of residence.[18] In the 2017 American Community Survey five-year estimates, the four areas with the highest household incomes—ranging between $50,000 and $60,000—were the newer developments of Hunters Creek, Meadow Woods, Southchase, and Alafaya. The lowest—ranging from $30,000 to $40,000—were the older areas, Azalea Park and Union Park on the East Side and Oak Ridge, Pine Castle, and Sky Lake to the south. Among the CDPs with lower Latino household incomes, Latino families living below the poverty level could be as high as 38 percent. Even in CDPs with higher incomes, the proportions of Latino families living below the poverty level hovered around 14 percent.

Setting these data into comparison with Orange County areas where the majority are non-Latino white adds to a picture of Orange County's socioeconomic geography. In the same data set from 2017 for the incorporated cities of Winter Park, Edgewood, and Belle Isle, the median household income for all residents of these communities, regardless of race or ethnicity, ranges from $68,000 to $84,000, well beyond the median household incomes for Latinos in the CDPs profiled here. The proportions of families living below the poverty line ranged from only 2 percent to 8 percent. Among Pine Hills residents, by contrast, the median household income across the board was about $38,000, and 25 percent of Pine Hills residents were living below the poverty level.

Orange County sits in a county-based economic hierarchy that aligns geographically from Seminole at the northern end to Osceola at the southern end. In every county of the metro area, Latino median household income was consistently lower than that of non-Latino white households. In the estimates for Orange and Seminole Counties, the gap was as much as $20,000 a year (US Census Bureau, ACS 2017b).

Along with these gradations from CDP to CDP and county to county, aggregated class markers for the Orlando metro area provide a view of Latino class relations with each other and with non-Latino white and black Orlandoans. Breaking down median household income into income ranges makes two points (chart 1.2). One is that Orlando Latino households run the gamut from poverty to wealth, with at least about 10 percent falling into each of the seven income ranges given. The other is that Latino and non-Latino black households are overrepresented in the lower income levels and that non-Latino white households are overrepresented in the higher levels.

This picture of class relations between Latinos and others in Orlando as well as among Latinos is further grounded by data on educational

CHART 1.2. Household income in the Orlando metro area for Latinos and non-Latino white and black populations by percent of households

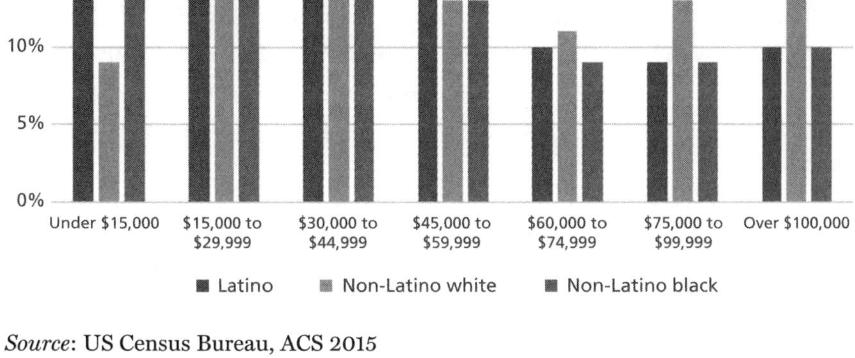

Source: US Census Bureau, ACS 2015

Note: The ACS 2015 5-year estimates are the most recent I have been able to access at this level of data.

TABLE 1.5. Education, work, and economic conditions of Latinos and non-Latino white and black populations in the Orlando metro area

Class Marker	Latino (%)	Non-Latino white (%)	Non-Latino black (%)
High school or higher	85	95	86
Bachelor's or higher	22	39	22
Management work	24	47	28
Service work	23	16	28
Sales / office work	27	25	27
Homeownership	49	70	42
Unemployment	5	4	8
Family poverty	17	6	17

Source: US Census Bureau, ACS 2017a

attainment, unemployment, poverty rates, distribution among employment sectors, and homeownership (table 1.5). While these data indicate that Latinos have graduated high school and earned at least a bachelor's degree in roughly equal percentages to non-Latino black residents, they also show that non-Latino white educational attainment is significantly higher. The gap widens with the employment data, which indicate a 23 percent difference between Latinos and non-Latino white Orlandoans employed in the category represented here as "management."[19] Non-Latino black Orlandoans are also more frequently employed than Latinos in this sector. Despite this difference, Latino households have a slightly higher median household income than non-Latino black households, but again both have much less income than non-Latino white households. The trend is evident as well in the percentages for homeownership and family poverty rates. That the difference is less pronounced in the unemployment rates suggests significantly lower rates of pay for Latinos and non-Latino black Orlandoans.

As this diverse population has arrived in Orlando, bringing equally diverse memories of the places they called home before arriving, they have encountered a new place with its own racial history and collective memories. The economic data give reasons for Latinos to align with black Orlandoans, but the racial identification data suggest a conscious Latino separation from non-Latino black residents that might not happen the same way in another place. Identifications with either a specific national-origin group or a pan-ethnic umbrella may well be disrupted by alliances and oppositions seen through the lenses of class and race.

Yet, under certain conditions in Orlando as in other places, Latinos and non-Latinos use the umbrella term. Cristina Beltrán (2010:8) contends, "Both advocates and adversaries of Latino power make use of a homogenizing logic that portrays Latinos as culturally distinct and engaged in a transformative endeavor capable of reshaping America's political landscape." The idea, empowering for Latinos, may be a source of angst for non-Latinos. There is a compelling argument that the homogenizing pan-ethnic label can depoliticize Latino collective identification (Dávila 2008, 2012). John García (2012:2) poses another view: "The idea of a group of peoples tied together by language, cultural values, and practices, similar histories in the United States, and public policies is clearly visible on the American landscape, and its political ramifications are very dynamic."[20] Indeed, for Latinos, the image of a sleeping giant who might wake up and head to the polls lends power to their presence that no single nationality can command. The real difficulty that remains is uniting the "incomplete and agonistic 'we,'" to again cite Beltrán's term (2010). And the difficulty is complicated by the particular dynamics of Latino politics in this southern place.

"REPUBLICANS DON'T WANT US AND DEMOCRATS TAKE US FOR GRANTED"

Just after the 2010 midterm elections I attended a meeting of Orlando-area Puerto Ricans and Latinos. Central to the meeting's agenda was a discussion about the need to take control of their political future. A reference to "Osceola County in 2006" was enough for everyone to acknowledge that the Latino vote was often a means for others to engineer voting outcomes and maintain their own hold on power.[21]

That year, when a federal court ordered Osceola County to adopt single-member districts in order to increase minority representation in local government, county officials offered a plan that followed the court mandate while still keeping control of local representation.[22] The court refused the plan. In the run-up to a 2007 special election for the newly designated single-member seat, Armando Ramírez, a Puerto Rican Democrat, defeated an Anglo opponent whose argument for his own candidacy had been that it was time "to get over this idea of race" (in Cruz 2010:271). The general election then pitted Ramírez against another Puerto Rican, Republican John Quiñones. In order to run, Quiñones had stepped down from a seat in the Florida legislature that he had won with crossover Democratic Puerto

Rican votes. Rumor had it that Quiñones had been recruited by Osceola's power elite (Cruz 2010:271–272). Whether or not this represented a second effort by non-Latino white stakeholders to get around the federal mandate, it is likely that Quiñones was seen at least as the lesser of two evils in a seat destined for Hispanic representation. Light-skinned Quiñones won the general election standoff in 2007 with darker-skinned Ramírez, and he did so again with crossover Puerto Rican votes. Just days before the 2010 meeting I attended, Ramírez had been reported the winner on election night in a second race against Quiñones, but in the morning the official results again gave the win to Quiñones.[23]

These Puerto Rican versus Puerto Rican campaigns demonstrate the potential power of a Puerto Rican—and by extension Latino—voting bloc and the efforts made to thwart that power. A few years later—again with Quiñones in the spotlight—other Anglo efforts exemplify how the US two-party system itself challenges Latino political power. In that election for another redistricted Hispanic seat, this one in the US Congress, Quiñones was favored to win against two Anglos and another Puerto Rican. Heading into the Republican primaries, the Anglo Democratic candidate ran as though Quiñones were already his opponent and used attack ads against him (Montalvo 2012). Quiñones lost the Republican primary, and the Anglo Democratic candidate won the general election. The seat that had been intended for a Latino had been won in a race between two Anglos.

The 2012 episode points to a tension between ethnicity and party that often marks Latino politics. With Quiñones as the Republican candidate, the election would have forced Puerto Rican Democrats to choose between party and ethnicity (Powers 2012). In a race between two Anglos, it was easier for them to choose along party lines or simply stay home.

This drama had not yet unfolded at the meeting I attended in 2010, but those assembled had already seen Osceola County in 2006 and Ramírez's second loss to Quiñones in the midterms. They knew both parties' tendency to use Puerto Ricans and other Latinos for their votes, and they recognized the need to look out for themselves as Latinos. At the meeting I heard general agreement as one person said, "Republicans don't want us and Democrats take us for granted."

The constant run of Spanish-language ads for Democratic and Republican candidates that I was hearing as I looked for Rafael on election night 2012 would seem to put the lie to that assertion. It seemed clear that night that everyone wanted Latinos. But wanting Latinos does not imply their inclusion *as Latinos*. It is rather inclusion of Latinos as resources to help one party or another achieve its own desired end.

Data from voter registrations appear to bear out claims by non-Latino and Latino political strategists and media that Central Florida Latinos are the swing vote that can determine electoral outcomes. Heading into the 2018 midterm elections, 47 percent of Orange County's Latino voters were registered with the Democratic Party and 14 percent with the Republican Party.[24] That leaves another 39 percent who were neither Democrat nor Republican.

As regards Puerto Ricans in particular, a 2012 report from Florida International University indicates that although 76 percent of US Puerto Rican voters supported Barack Obama in 2008, only 59 percent did so in Florida (PIR-SIPA 2012). From the same data set, a comparison of Puerto Rican political identifications in the United States and in Florida in 2012 offers an interesting view into reworkings of Puerto Rican political identifications that may be happening in other new diaspora spaces (table 1.6). The 22-point difference in "no party affiliation" between US Puerto Ricans generally and Florida Puerto Ricans in particular explains away the otherwise surprising statistic indicating a greater percentage of Republican Puerto Ricans in the United States as a whole than in Florida.

A further factor making it hard to place Central Florida Latinos in Florida politics is the mix of those arriving from other US states and those arriving directly from Puerto Rico and other countries with distinct political dynamics. In Puerto Rico, political parties are organized around preferences for what Puerto Rico's status should be vis-à-vis the United States. Those in favor of some version of the current relationship—known in English as a Commonwealth and in Spanish as Estado Libre Asociado (Free Associated State)—group together in the Partido Popular Democrático (PPD, Popular Democratic Party). Those who want statehood for Puerto Rico belong to the Partido Nuevo Progresista (PNP, New Progressive Party). As the name implies, the Partido Independentista Puertorriqueña (PIP, Puerto Rican Independence Party) advocates for Puerto Rican independence. The word "democratic" is embedded in the PPD party name, and historically many

TABLE 1.6. Puerto Rican political identification in the United States and Florida, 2012

Political party	**Florida** (%)	**United States** (%)
Democratic	55	71
Republican	14	23
No party affiliation	27.5	5

Source: PIR-SIPA 2012

mainland Puerto Ricans have registered and voted with the Democratic Party. Statehood supporters are sometimes referred to in Puerto Rico as *republicanos*, and several pro-statehood supporters in Orlando have told me that when first registering to vote in Florida they selected Republican for that reason. A further confusion is that the PPD in Puerto Rico is symbolized by red and the PNP by blue, while in the United States Democrats are symbolically represented by blue and Republicans by red.

Although the dominant group, Puerto Ricans are only one group of Latinos in Central Florida. Latino politics reaches beyond local concerns to engage different homelands and their respective relations with the United States. Cuban politics in Florida has long been affiliated with the Republican Party, and for decades the Cuban-exile community lobbied successfully for the United States to maintain pressure on the Castro regime through travel bans and an embargo on imports from Cuba. In assessing the meaning and direction of Florida Latino politics, it is important to remember that conditions in the separate countries whose diasporas are so often lumped together as one in US discourses will affect positions taken by many US Latino voters.[25]

A brief history of Central Florida firsts for Puerto Ricans in the 1990s illustrates that Puerto Rican and Latino political affiliations in Central Florida are less about ideology than political expedience in a system where neither major party gives more than lip service to Latino issues.[26] In 1995 José "Joe" Pérez, a Republican, was elected to the Deltona City Council. Citing lack of support from the Republican Party in a later run for Deltona mayor, Pérez switched to the Democratic ticket (Kassab 2001). In 1996 Robert Guevara, a Democrat, was elected to the Osceola County Commission (Cruz 2010). Eddie Martínez, a Republican, won a seat on the Winter Springs City Commission in Seminole County in 1997. In 1999 Anthony Suárez was elected as a Democrat to Florida House District 35, which included parts of Orange and Seminole Counties. Angry at being sidelined and railroaded by Democrats, Suárez later switched to the Republican Party. Following the 2016 elections, Suárez made front-page news when he dropped his membership in the Republican Party and became independent. In a manner not unlike the practice of strategically adopting pan-ethnic and national-origin identifications according to situational or political need and race-class interests vis-à-vis non-Latinos, Puerto Rican and Latino candidates in local politics often strategically select and switch party affiliations.

Amid localized responses to manipulation by both the Democratic and Republican Parties, scholars and political strategists on the national level argue for the weight of Latinos voting for Latinos (Barreto 2007, Cruz 2010). And in the particular dynamics of needing to navigate the historical black-white binary of the Orlando area, the extension of the Voting Rights Act to language minorities does offer the opportunity to claim political territory as Latinos. But divergent race, class, and place memories and interests continue to intersect with the US two-party system, catching Latinos in a dilemma between party and ethnicity as Latino candidates switch back and forth. Beltrán (2010:119) describes Latino nonpartisanship as a strategy for maintaining political relevance and influence while simultaneously being a potential cause of political paralysis if Latino heterogeneity remains unexamined and unarticulated in appeals to "Latino interests." In other words, Latinos' position as the swing vote can speak to their empowered political relevance or to their containment through treatment as political and economic resources to serve the interests of more powerful others.

CHAPTER 2

HIDDEN HISTORIES IN THE NEW ORLANDO

Colonial Migrations, Color-Blind Multiculturalism, and Natural Neoliberalism

The Orlando International Airport, the code for which would logically be OIA, is instead identified as MCO. This is because it was not always the Orlando International Airport. Originally the Pinecastle Airfield, the base was renamed for Colonel Michael McCoy, who died in a crash near the base in the 1950s. When McCoy Air Base was converted to an international airport in the 1970s, MCO remained, much like the *pentimento* of a previous image in revisions to a painting. To the casual air passenger moving through on the way to the theme parks or to a business meeting downtown, this history is not evident. The only clue to the airport's location is in the shops selling memorabilia from Disney, Universal, and NASA and the lines of children waiting to board flights home with Mickey Mouse hats perched on their heads or Tinker Bell dolls tucked under their arms.

My own first impression of this modern, efficient airport was reiterated in my introduction to Orlando as an emergent city with construction cranes everywhere, tearing down the old and erecting the new. With time, I learned why the airport code is MCO, and I learned to see the traces of other histories just below the surface of Orlando's social and political landscape. Orlando seems to me now a place where history is being selectively erased from much of the built environment, validating Michel-Rolph Trouillot's (1995:xix) claim that "we are never as steeped in history as when we pretend not to be."

Soon after my arrival the *Orlando Sentinel* began publishing an occasional series on "the New Orlando." The first article opened with the description of a 1971 luncheon on the top floor of the Citrus Center building downtown, which was still under construction. That floor would house a private club, and the luncheon was an opportunity for the invited guests from Orlando's business elite to see the view from Orlando's tallest building: "What they could see to the southwest was the faint silhouette of Walt Disney World under construction. What they couldn't see—what no one could imagine—is how people flooding in from throughout the country and around the world would completely transform Orlando during the next 34 years" (Kunerth and Tracy 2005).

Although the Orlando elite attending the luncheon were looking to the southwest and the construction of Walt Disney World, Orlando had already seen other changes during World War II and its aftermath. During the war, Orlando became home to the largest aircraft manufacturing industry in the world (Bacon 1977:2:123). Orlando's population doubled between 1950 and 1960 (US Census 1960). In the 1950s the Martin Company (later Martin Marietta and eventually Lockheed Martin), Minute Maid, and Tupperware each chose sites just south of Orlando for their headquarters (Bacon 1977:2:198, 204). These economic developments entailed building new housing and better roads and expanding the school system and access to water and electricity. It became clear that Orlando needed a university to provide an educational pipeline for the growing city (Foglesong 2001:87). When the local newspaper's owner, Martin Andersen, organized a motorcade for Lyndon Johnson in the 1964 presidential campaign and Johnson offered his thanks, Andersen replied that he wanted a military base (Foglesong 2001:87). The US Navy soon transformed the Orlando Air Base near Colonial Drive into an extensive Naval Training Center, which remained a key feature of the landscape until it was closed in the 1990s and converted into the upscale, new-urban housing development Baldwin Park. A portion of the former air base lying between Colonial Drive and the 408 became Executive Airport, near where I was sitting in traffic on election night 2012. It was in the middle of all that had preceded the Citrus Center luncheon that Walt Disney flew over Central Florida in 1963, looked down at the intersection of two highways in Orlando, and said, "That's it" (Foglesong 2001:15).

Orlando's transformation would challenge the legacy of Jim Crow segregation statutes that were only repealed a few years before the 1971 luncheon. Indeed, arguing that his business could not function amid racial unrest, Walt Disney had had to strong-arm Florida officials in the mid-1960s into complying with civil rights legislation (Colburn 2007:53). With the business elite convinced that Orlando's tourist future required desegregation, the 1960s in Orlando were not as openly violent as in other places (Porter 2003). Not long before, however, cross burnings, voter intimidation, and lynchings left deep marks in local African American memory (Brotemarkle 2005).[1] In 1951, an ice cream stand was dynamited for selling to white and black people from the same window (Beatty 2002:54–55). In 1962, eight black families sued the Orange County school system to end segregation (Kunerth 2008a). But still in 1971, as Walt Disney World was opening, the Orange County School Board members voted to go to jail rather than allow students to be bused for racial balance in schools (Hobbs 2009b). This was a world with a racial hierarchy clearly written in black and white.

A mere generation later, a vocabulary was in place for the newspaper's New Orlando series to use in its celebration of the city as a multicultural, color-blind place. This may seem like a contradiction in terms since "multicultural" refers to a recognition of differences and "color-blind" suggests that people are seen as fundamentally the same. The combined term, "color-blind multiculturalism," refers to a recognition of difference incorporated into a universalist view of human sameness that normalizes the particular perspective of those in power (Rocco 2014:116).[2] As the area was experiencing transformative changes in its racial-ethnic makeup, this language worked its way into the public discourse that underwrote development strategies and construction projects in the New Orlando.

The opening article of the *Sentinel*'s New Orlando series positions the city as a place of novelty and innovation rather than static tradition (Kunerth and Tracy 2005). Another article describes Orlando as a youthful space where millennials do not see color as the previous generation did (Joe Newman 2006). Yet another is about the transformation of Pine Hills from a segregated white to a mostly black neighborhood, observing that it was becoming an immigrant neighborhood (Kunerth 2006a). An article calling Buenaventura Lakes in Osceola County "Little Puerto Rico" notes, "Many still come from the island, and others are New York transplants. But more now are native Floridians" (Ramos 2006a). One by one, the articles in the series celebrate Orlando's diversity as part of a harmonious whole.

For the casual observer—driving past the Islamic center on Goldenrod or the huge Buddha statue in Kissimmee, or listening to Spanish-speaking customers in one of Orlando's many Vietnamese restaurants and seeing a range of skin colors at the tables—it is easy to conclude that multiculturalism is the new face of Orlando. With time, living away from the theme parks and teaching at campuses of the University of Central Florida across the region, I began to see that the histories beneath the newly fashioned skyscrapers and housing developments were still felt in the New Orlando's contemporary racial-ethnic and sociopolitical dynamics.

As reference points for the stories and analyses to come, I use this chapter to situate Orlando's contemporary social field in interaction with a confluence of histories during which Orlando's transformation from small southern town to world-destination city has occurred. Vectors of sameness and difference emerge from these intertwined histories, which inform how newer arrivals and longtime Orlandoans experience self and other and how collective memories and identifications may form (or not) around those understandings and interactions. Puerto Rican relocations to the Orlando area are only the next chapter in a long history of diaspora-building and political practices that have emerged from US colonialism in Puerto Rico. Many have brought memories from struggles in other Puerto Rican places to Orlando. Other Orlando Latinos are part of the simultaneous and intertwined histories of the global spread of neoliberalism and the rapid growth of Latino populations around the United States.[3] The color-blind multicultural language of the New Orlando series is a local manifestation of "how the post–civil rights synergy of color-blindness and neoliberalism has shaped public debates about Latinos" (Dávila 2008:3). And as these histories inform and are informed by Orlando's social field, they are joined by Florida's political history. In the confluence of these state, national, and global histories, Orlando offers a specific site in which neoliberalism, the rise of the Sunbelt, and a post–civil rights conservatism claiming to be color-blind combine to inform the social field that Puerto Ricans and other Latinos must navigate as they work to make a place for themselves.

Ethnography is not an objectified translation of the ethnographer's notes; it is rather "a historically situated mode of understanding historically situated contexts" (Comaroff and Comaroff 1992:9–10). Looking historically at political and economic forces, it is easy to lose sight of how communities, identifications, memories, and forgetfulness all emerge from human action (Schneider 1995:4). But with attention focused on individual or collective subjectivities, it is just as easy to lose sight of the histories involving people in nets of relationships that then link individuals to those wider forces and influence the conditions in which they choose to act one way or another (Schneider 1995:7). This ethnographic rendering of political questions is an effort to examine the movements and contingencies of the space in between.

The histories related here affect but do not determine Puerto Rican and Latino political choices and strategies as they engage with each other and with others in Orlando's social field. They inform contestations about race, class, place, and belonging for political community formation. Orlando's particular place in Florida's sociopolitical field, Florida's racial-ethnic and political history, the post–civil rights emergence of multicultural neoliberalism in the United States, and the impacts of globalized neoliberalism on Latin America all inform Orlando Puerto Rican and Latino political life. The City Beautiful, with its constant construction and color-blind rhetoric, is promoted as a multicultural place of innovation and openness. What is less immediately visible are the historically entrenched power structures under the veneer of the new.

COLONIAL MIGRATIONS AND PUERTO RICAN DIASPORA

In the same way that "¿De dónde eres?" holds significance for Puerto Ricans, the conflicted trajectories of Puerto Rican history inform what it means to say "I am Puerto Rican" (Duany 2002, Flores 1993, Rivera 2007). Different ideas about Puerto Rico as a place as well as identifications with Puerto Rican New York, Chicago, or some other Puerto Rican diaspora space in the US states intertwine with tensions of race and class and play out in daily lived experience in Orlando. In increasing and somewhat balanced numbers, Puerto Ricans from island and diaspora have arrived for decades in this Central Florida space that is new to both. With reference to US interventions in Latin America, Juan González (2000) has referred to the growing Latino population in the United States as the "harvest of empire."[4] The point is that while each nationally identified Latino group has its own history of relations to the United States, all have experienced similar vectors of US imperialist expansion, with locally specific results. Because of its direct colonial relation to the United States and because Orlando Latinos are overwhelmingly Puerto Rican, it is useful to understand the particular harvest of empire that is Puerto Rican migration history.

Puerto Rican citizenship and migration. Puerto Rican migration to the US states, before and after the United States took possession of the island nation, has been well documented.[5] In the 1800s, Puerto Ricans joined with Cubans in New York, Tampa, and Key West in resistance to Spanish colonialism. These three locations were also centers of the cigar-making industry that drew Puerto Rican and Cuban workers to the mainland. After the 1898 Spanish-American War, the United States maintained some control over Cuba but annexed Puerto Rico completely.

In 1901 the US Supreme Court ruled that unlike earlier territorial acquisitions, Puerto Rico was "foreign to the United States in a domestic sense"; rather than being fully incorporated, it remained "appurtenant thereto as a possession."[6] Subsequent US legislation, including the 1917 act of Congress that made Puerto Ricans US citizens, rested on this distinction (Cabranes 1978; Trías Monge 1997; Venator-Santiago 2013, 2015). Indeed, Puerto Rican citizenship makes clear the contradictions of citizenship as a system of equality that emerged historically in tandem with capitalism as a system of inequality (Marshall 1950:29). By World War II, Puerto Ricans in Puerto Rico had been living under US-appointed governors for decades. Following the war, Puerto Ricans' push for autonomy and Cold War Washington's interest in showing the world what the capitalist model could do produced a political-economic project centered on modernity and democracy.

In the late 1940s, the US government in Puerto Rico began Operation Bootstrap, an industrialization program focused on attracting US corporations to Puerto Rico through tax breaks and wages that were simultaneously lower than in the US states and higher than the existing needlework, sugar, and tobacco industries in Puerto Rico (Ayala and Bernabe 2007:179).[7] As agricultural employment in rural areas disappeared, Puerto Ricans migrated from rural to urban centers and later to the US states. Many of these migrants were initially part of a farm-labor program, traveling seasonally to the US states and then returning (or not) to Puerto Rico. The Puerto Rican Department of Labor's Migration Division, headquartered in New York, offered social services to smooth Puerto Rican adaptation to this new environment.

By 1970, 27 percent of the island's 1950 population had left as part of the "Puerto Rican Great Migration" (Ayala and Bernabe 2007:194–195). More than thirty US cities had Puerto Rican populations of at least 10,000, with the greatest concentrations in the Northeast and Midwest (Ayala and Bernabe 2007:180–181). The Migration Division morphed into the Puerto Rican Federal Affairs Administration (PRFAA), originally headquartered in New York and then in Washington, DC, with offices at various times in Chicago, Philadelphia, Orlando city, and Kissimmee. By the 2010 Census, Puerto Rico's population was 3.7 million, while 4.5 million Puerto Ricans lived in the US states. Over the decades, out-migration, return migration, and circular migration have become familiar Puerto Rican patterns (Duany 2002). Elizabeth Aranda (2008:452) has argued that some Puerto Ricans have been able to use their "colonial migrant" status for access to resources for social and economic advancement in island and diaspora.[8]

The Puerto Rican problem. Puerto Rican migration's impact on New York and other northern US spaces was dramatic. From a population of about 60,000 in 1940, the Puerto Rican population of New York City grew to more than 600,000 by 1960 (Sánchez Korrol 1994:213). Although earlier New York Puerto Ricans had included shop owners and doctors, the Puerto Rican Great Migration mostly brought laborers, and many ended up crowded into New York tenements (Thomas 2010). New York Puerto Ricans were increasingly depicted in the media as a problem, dependent as individuals on New York welfare rolls and as a people on the United States.

The identity idea of Puerto Ricans as a problem was further entrenched by *West Side Story*'s enduring images of Puerto Ricans as knife-wielding gang members. Lorrin Thomas (2010:137) has argued that this representation of New York Puerto Ricans "captured their identity as problematic strangers, presenting it in a political vacuum that made the colonial context of Puerto Rico disappear completely." This argument follows Otto Santa Ana's insight (2002:8–9) that public discourses draw on the very human process of image- and metaphor-making as part of reproducing the social order. Discourse alone does not reproduce Puerto Rican marginality, but it contributes images like that of knife-wielding gang members to the rhetorical justifications for political and economic policies that reproduce social inequality.

The term "culture of poverty" exemplifies how the idea of "the American nation as a [white] meritocracy" reproduces class and race subordination in the United States (Ramos-Zayas 2003:9). The phrase was first coined by Oscar Lewis (1966) to help explain the cycle of poverty in which Puerto Ricans found themselves. Although Lewis attributes Puerto Rican poverty to a flawed capitalist system, journalistic and other academic uses of culture of poverty often point to supposedly pathological behaviors rather than the structured relations of colonialism and capitalism (Harvey and Reed 1992).[9] The combination of media-generated images of the so-called Puerto Rican problem and social scientific analyses grounded in culture-of-poverty theories cemented the notion that conditions of Puerto Rican life were "a problem of migrants themselves rather than a political problem resulting from US imperial policy" (Thomas 2010:146).

The mid-twentieth-century idea of Puerto Ricans as a problem has proven tenacious and still contributes to Puerto Rican marginalization in twenty-first-century US society. Through this identity idea, Puerto Ricans from island and diaspora are homogenized as at best a problem of dependency and at worst a danger. This identity idea is widely available to non–Puerto Ricans with little to no historical consciousness of US actions and inactions in Puerto Rico and the Puerto Rican diaspora.

Cultural nationalism. In conjunction with Operation Bootstrap in Puerto Rico and a burgeoning Puerto Rican population in the US North, a political shift was under way on the island. In 1948 Puerto Ricans chose their own governor for the first time, and in 1952 Puerto Rico's current ambiguous status as a commonwealth of the United States was created. Puerto Rico has its own constitution and representative government selected by popular vote, but the United States retains control over its commercial and foreign relations as well as any proposed changes to its constitution (Ayala and Bernabe 2007). A nonvoting Puerto Rican resident commissioner is elected to sit in the US Congress.[10] As US citizens, Puerto Ricans may be drafted into the US military when there is a draft, but they may only vote in federal elections if they reside in a US state.

The Puerto Rican Nationalist Party put up a stiff fight against this so-called commonwealth form of government. The resistance was repressed through coercion and persuasion. Besides violent suppression and systematic tracking of anyone supporting independence for Puerto Rico, the Puerto Rican government deployed a cultural corollary to Operation Bootstrap called Operation Serenity, which promoted educational programs to help move Puerto Ricans into "modern times" (Marsh Kennerley 2003). These programs worked to replace political nationalism with cultural nationalism. Despite economic modernization, a series of government initiatives promoted nostalgic images of rural Puerto Rico as emblematic of the Puerto Rican soul or spirit (Dávila 1997).

The Instituto de Cultura Puertorriqueña (ICP), founded in 1955, became the arbiter of Puerto Rican cultural authenticity. Puerto Rican anthropologists and other public intellectuals of the 1950s helped the ruling Popular Democratic Party (PPD) craft a reified notion of a culture unique to the Puerto Rican people and in opposition to American culture (Ayala and Bernabe 2007, Dávila 1997, Duany 2002). This objectification of Puerto Rican culture as a thing or a product rather than as a way of life has enabled a cultural politics guided by what is "deemed more or less likely to provide the 'content' of Puerto Rican identity" (Dávila 1997:4–5). In light of the distinction between an identity idea as a thing used to a particular end and identification as an act of connecting with such an idea through social relations, it is important to note that this reified idea of Puerto Rican culture has across time served as a point of commonality for Puerto Ricans across race, class, and birthplace.

Diaspora politics. When police opened fire on a peaceful Nationalist Party march in Ponce, Puerto Rico, on Palm Sunday in 1937, the repercussions in New York politics demonstrated the potential power of Puerto Rican political action in diaspora communities well before the 1950s Puerto Rican Great Migration. The tragedy in Ponce galvanized New York Puerto Ricans and contributed to the victory that year of the first Puerto Rican elected to a US state office (Thomas 2010:125). With a crossover vote by Puerto Rican Democrats and backing from the American Labor Party, Oscar García Rivera won on a Republican ticket against a non-Hispanic Democrat (Ayala and Bernabe 2007:114).[11] This was a case of Puerto Ricans voting as Puerto Ricans rather than as members of a US political party.

As migration continued apace in the 1950s, Puerto Rican activism in New York quieted. Scholars debate why and how Puerto Ricans "allowed" a silencing of their voices by the 1950s.[12] Was it due to the influx of newcomers, who were unaware of New York's history and saw themselves living there only temporarily? Edgardo Meléndez (2003:18) argues instead that this demobilization of New York Puerto Ricans was actually a response to the history of Puerto Rican political activism and their growing political clout in New York. The view of Puerto Ricans as a problem intensified in the 1950s when Puerto Rican Nationalist Party members carried out attacks on the island and against President Truman and Congress. Stereotypes about Puerto Rican poverty, disease, and crime expanded as those threatened by Puerto Rican activism pointed to links with revolutionary communism and framed Puerto Ricans generally as "a dangerous addition to the citizenry" and "an anti-American political force" (Thomas 2010:137).[13] The PPD in Puerto Rico and the Democratic Party machine in New York had reason for working together to depoliticize Puerto Ricans in the metropolis (Meléndez 2003).

As Operations Bootstrap and Serenity unfolded in Puerto Rico, Puerto Ricans in New York were subject to another form of social engineering in a "battle between reform liberals and revolutionary activists for pre-eminence among barrio hearts and minds" (Guzmán 1980:145). Lorrin Thomas (2010:202) describes a push for middle-class assimilation:

> Adult migrants were barraged with messages from the Migration Division and other social service agencies about voting and learning English, as well as about comportment in the workplace and proper standards of dress and housekeeping, and younger Puerto Ricans were targeted by liberal educators who hoped to provide the most promising students with the tools to embark on middle-class lives.

Even as Puerto Ricans in New York experienced these pressures toward assimilation, they formed organizations that celebrated Puerto Rican culture and offered social services to mitigate economic deprivation and political subordination. Puerto Rican hometown clubs that predated the Puerto Rican Great Migration continued to proliferate, combining social, cultural, and political work in their services. Many organizations that formed during the 1950s and early 1960s—among them, community-based social service organizations such as the Puerto Rican Family Institute, the Puerto Rican Forum, and Aspira—continue to this day.[14]

Several of these organizations grew out of the work and inspiration of a group of college-educated New York Puerto Ricans led by Puerto Rico–born Antonia Pantoja, who simultaneously challenged and worked within the existing power structures to improve conditions for Puerto Ricans (Ayala and Bernabe 2007:239, History Task Force 1979:152–153). Pantoja pushed against the conservative and accommodationist policies of Commonwealth officials operating in New York in those decades, arguing that a community development approach was best for educating and empowering Puerto Ricans and preventing future problems (Pantoja 2002:74). "The leadership of the office," Pantoja wrote in her memoir (2002:77), "espoused integration and assimilation, but I knew that only those of us who were white-skinned had any hope of this kind of acceptance." Racial-ethnic identifications and class relations thus figured into Puerto Ricans' navigation of New York's social field at that time.

Puerto Rican grassroots activism in New York and elsewhere surged in the later 1960s and 1970s. Young Puerto Ricans of a new generation who had come of age in US urban environments began protesting displacements caused by urban renewal and took to the streets demanding social justice for island and diaspora (Morales 1998, Thomas 2010, Whalen 1998). In many places they forged alliances with African Americans.[15] The radical Puerto Rican activism that emerged at this time combined and incorporated class relations and racial-ethnic identifications with anti-imperialist analyses of Puerto Rican subordination.[16] The Puerto Rican Legal Defense and Education Fund (PRLDEF), which was renamed Latino Justice PRLDEF in 2008, was founded in 1972 in response to outrage at New York's lack of responsiveness to the needs of Puerto Rican and Latino children in schools. PRLDEF represented the service organization Aspira in a lawsuit against New York City's Board of Education, which led to a 1974 consent decree requiring bilingual education (Reyes 2006).

In 1977, Puerto Rican activists hung a Puerto Rican flag across the brow of the Statue of Liberty as an attention-getting tactic in the struggle to free Puerto Ricans held in federal prisons following the attacks on Congress and the president (Thomas 2010:246). Despite such tactics for Puerto Rican visibility, much of civil rights history—especially in the Northeast and Midwest—is recorded in black and white (Mora 2014:22–23). Thomas (2010:246) reports, for instance, that press coverage of the Puerto Rican flag on the Statue of Liberty was buried deep in the papers.

Much of the renewed activism in the 1960s and 1970s was inspired by a militant youth movement called the Young Lords. Following a 1966 Chicago uprising sparked by the police shooting of a Puerto Rican youth, a group that had been a Puerto Rican street gang since the 1950s began a transformation into a politically conscious community activist organization (Fernández 2012). The Chicago Young Lords used disruptive tactics to push for a housing project on an urban renewal site (Padilla 1987:120–123). Soon afterward, the Young Lords emerged in New York and Philadelphia (Baver 1993, Whalen 2001). The New York Young Lords conducted streetwise, direct-action campaigns such as setting fire to mounds of garbage in the street to draw attention to the city's neglect of the Bronx and taking over a local church to provide free lunches (Ayala and Bernabe 2007:241–242; Sánchez 2007:129).[17] In Philadelphia, the Young Lords decided that the existing Aspira chapter was too conservative; as a direct-action alternative, they ran clothing drives and served free breakfast with lessons to the recipients about the connection between their poverty and the capitalist system (Whalen 2001:231–238). The Young Lords also made their presence felt in Boston, Bridgeport, Buffalo, Cleveland, Detroit, Hartford, Hoboken, Newark, Rochester, and Detroit (Sánchez 1994:118).

The renewed drive for self-determination and social justice challenged the mainstream academic underwriting of the Puerto Rican problem (Whalen 2009). In New York, students fought for a Puerto Rican–centered college campus and curriculum (Ayala and Bernabe 2007:264). The field of Puerto Rican studies and the Center for Puerto Rican Studies (Centro) at the City University of New York emerged (Hernández 2012, Pérez 2009, Whalen 2009). Oral history became a Puerto Rican methodology for recording diaspora history through Puerto Rican voices and memories (García Colón 2006).[18] Centro's Oral History Task Force helped Puerto Ricans take control of their stories and upend the ongoing attribution of Puerto Rican poverty to cultural pathologies (Whalen 2009).

Rejecting the culture-of-poverty theory, Félix Padilla (1987) describes Puerto Rican subordination in Chicago as "internal colonialism," which transfers the stigma and practice of colonial relations in Puerto Rico to migrants in the metropolis. Grosfoguel and Georas (2000) have taken the idea further by connecting colonial histories to contemporary racial-ethnic hierarchies. Puerto Ricans, the authors assert, are "racial/colonial subjects" who have long been subject to racist stereotypes (90); as other newly arriving Latinos seek to distance themselves from these stereotypes, their relationships with Puerto Ricans are made more difficult.

Along with the more radical 1960s activism, a push continued for political representation inside the power structure. Following García Rivera's term in the New York state assembly (1938–1940), only one other Puerto Rican, Felipe Torres, had been elected to state government in the 1950s (Thomas 2010:183). In 1966 Hermán Badillo became the Bronx Borough president and in 1971 a US congressman, the first Puerto Rican in each of these positions (Ayala and Bernabe 2007:240). José Sánchez (2007:131) has argued that the Young Lords' radicalism made Badillo's more moderate stance attractive to voters. Robert García, who later replaced Badillo in Congress, was elected to the New York state legislature in 1965.

As President Lyndon Johnson's War on Poverty programs made federal funds available in the 1960s, a report by the Puerto Rican Forum helped establish programs targeting and staffed by Puerto Ricans (Ayala and Bernabe 2007:240). Gilberto Gerena Valentín and Ramón Vélez gained political clout through organizational networks in antipoverty programs (Sánchez Korrol 1994:233–235). Several Orlando Puerto Ricans of the late twentieth and early twenty-first centuries came of age during this time in New York. Their oral histories show that they have carried those memories to Florida.

Broken memory. The pejorative label "Nuyorican" was born in Puerto Rico during the 1960s and 1970s as return migration became a new pattern. Ironically, island-based narratives about the Nuyorican reflect the mid-century US framing of the Puerto Rican problem that was initially applied to island and diaspora. Juan Flores (1993) calls the distance between island and diaspora Puerto Ricans "divided borders." In Puerto Rico, diaspora Puerto Ricans are seldom included in accounts of twentieth-century Puerto Rican history. Arcadio Díaz Quiñones (1993) calls this historical silence Puerto Rico's "broken memory."

In pushback against islanders, diaspora Puerto Ricans argue that their "exile" from Puerto Rico facilitated Operation Bootstrap by reducing the island's population. They contend that their struggles in the US states have given them a deeper identification with Puerto Rico.[19] During the 1970s a New York arts movement reappropriated the term "Nuyorican" and wove class and race together with place, lending a diaspora-based tone to Puerto Rican cultural nationalism (E. López 2005, Thomas 2010). The Nuyorican Poets Café provided a space for new voices reclaiming the pejorative label and infusing it with expressions of resistance. This reframing of Puerto Rican experience has spawned a series of "diasporican" identifications that continue to incorporate a translocal feeling of *puertorriqueñidad* with place-specific references like Chicago Rican, Orlando Rican, and so on.

Darío González came to Central Florida from Puerto Rico, but he had also spent much of his life in New York. One day he pulled out his wallet and showed me a laminated clipping from a 1958 New York paper that named him as the first to register for the New York Puerto Rican Day Parade. For him, identifying with New York was as much a point of pride as his equally strong identification with Puerto Rico. In his 2008 oral history, González switched to English as he described his young years in New York and switched back to Spanish to continue talking about the dynamics among Puerto Ricans from different places:

> Puerto Ricans who came from the island or who lived in Puerto Rico when they met a, a Nuyorican, well, they considered him strange, different. Of course, the culture of a boy raised, a boy or a girl, raised in New York, with the influence of the American culture was more American than Hispanic. Because that's natural. And that one would have an accent when speaking and that made him different. All these things. But it wasn't a hatred or anything like that. It was more, "He's one of those from over there; he's not one of us from here." (PRCF D. González)[20]

As island-born and diaspora-born have met in Orlando, disparaging remarks about Nuyoricans can be heard, countered by New York Puerto Rican claims to a special savvy in the ways of navigating and resisting Anglo domination as something much needed in Orlando. Luis Sánchez (2009:80) has argued that island-born disdain for New York Puerto Ricans in Orlando is "not as much to exclude 'Nuyoricans' from their community as to exclude themselves and their offspring from becoming the 'other,' the Nuyorican." The trope of professional migration plays into this distinction as Puerto Ricans from diaspora and island try to detach themselves in the Anglo gaze from associations with so-called Nuyorican ways and in the Puerto Rican gaze from the poor, less educated, rural Puerto Rican migrants of the mid-twentieth century.

For several years during my fieldwork, Tony Suárez held an annual Nuyorican Night that reframed the term and celebrated Orlando's Nuyorican diaspora. Jorge Duany has observed, "The two groups have some differences. But they clearly talk among themselves. Still they marry each other and they hang around and they dance salsa and put together parades and so forth" (in Brown 2002). Orlando is where Suárez said he learned to honor the "cultural encounter between the Nuyorican and *los puertorriqueños puros de la isla*" (the pure Puerto Ricans from the island):

> I learned how to be Puerto Rican and be happy within this new role that I had, which was a Puerto Rican New Yorker, without being embarrassed by not being a Puerto Rican from the island. And not taking second class. I wasn't going to take second-class citizenship in New York. I wasn't going to take second-class citizenship here. And now a second-class Puerto Rican. . . . I'm culturally different than the Puerto Ricans. But I'm proud of it. From that came Sonia Sotomayor.[21] (PRPPCE Suárez)

In Orlando, family members separated for decades have unexpectedly found each other again. Childhood friends, out of touch for most of their adult lives, have bumped into each other at the Asociación Borinqueña and elsewhere in Puerto Rican Orlando. Although the diaspora has formed and reformed its own place-based cultural representations, ICP-certified images still provide translocal references for common identification. Orlando Rican artist Amaury Díaz smiled as he told me that everyone sees their own grandmother in his painting *Abuelita*. At gatherings in Orlando, a roomful of Puerto Ricans—from New York, Chicago, Puerto Rico, and elsewhere; Republican, Democrat, and nonaffiliated; pro-statehood, pro-Commonwealth, and pro-independence—join to sing "En mi viejo San Juan" (In my old San Juan). Despite Puerto Rican Orlando's differences, at times I wonder if it may be the place that reconnects Puerto Rico's broken memory.

FROM SOUTHERN STRATEGY TO MULTICULTURAL NEOLIBERALISM

The so-called harvest of empire that has brought so many from Latin America to the United States has been the consequence of free-trade practices promoted by the United States and by international trade and financial organizations during the last quarter of the twentieth century. But the origins of these practices are to be found decades earlier in the incentives to US corporations that formed the basis to Operation Bootstrap. As US citizens, Puerto Rican workers were protected by US labor laws, and so eventually the search began for other places interested in receiving US capital investments (González 2000:232–233). The development of what has come to be called "neoliberalism" intertwines with other histories that also inform Orlando's contemporary social field.

Understanding how the confluence of histories is formative to the social field in Orlando that Puerto Ricans and Latinos need to navigate requires going back to the racial politics of the post–civil rights era in the United States. During the first half of the twentieth century, white southern Democrats, dominated by segregationist Dixiecrats, made up essentially the only political party in the South (Dye 1998:12). Because of segregationist Dixiecrats in Washington, it was Republicans who gave the edge to passing civil rights legislation (Nichols 2014). As he signed the 1964 Civil Rights Act, Democratic President Lyndon Johnson famously predicted that Democrats would lose the South for a generation. Soon after the signing, South Carolina Democrat Strom Thurmond became a Republican and began recruiting others to join him (Nichols 2014). Republican Barry Goldwater, who had voted against the Civil Rights Act, lost the 1964 presidential election, but he won the states of the Deep South running along Florida's northern border and lost Florida by very little. Republicans looking toward future elections took note, and by Richard Nixon's 1968 run, a "southern strategy" was in place (Cobb 2011, Crespino 2012).[22]

Nixon needed to walk a fine line between calming the fears of white voters and avoiding the overtly race-centered strategy pursued by the third-party candidate and segregationist George Wallace (Cobb 2011, Colburn 2007). Lee Atwater, a Republican strategist and adviser to Ronald Reagan and George H. W. Bush, described the evolution of Republican language in an interview conducted during Reagan's first year as president in 1981. According to Atwater, while talking about something other than race, Republicans were promoting policies by which "blacks will get hurt worse than whites." Atwater elaborated,

> You start out in 1954 by saying, "Nigger, nigger, nigger." By 1968 you can't say "nigger"—that hurts you, backfires. So you say stuff like, uh, forced busing, states' rights, and all that stuff, and you're getting so abstract. Now, you're talking about cutting taxes, and all these things you're talking about are totally economic things and a byproduct of them is, blacks get hurt worse than whites. . . . "We want to cut this," is much more abstract than even the busing thing, uh, and a hell of a lot more abstract than "Nigger, nigger." (In Perlstein 2009)[23]

Talk about "liberal, free-spending Democrats" and the problems of "big government" entered the discourse of the 1966 and 1968 campaigns (Colburn and deHaven-Smith 1999:52). Asserting that "the accent is on freedom," the 1968 Republican platform called for creating public-private partnerships to resolve social problems, creating tax incentives for development corporations to stimulate urban renewal, giving states greater control over federal resources, "liberating" the poor from "dependency," promoting individual freedoms within the rule of law, and giving local governments responsibility to "quell civil disorder" (Republican Party 1968). In the following years, the linguistic trajectory described by Atwater, combined with the emerging Republican coalition, helped to remake Republican politics "rooted in the politics of Goldwater and Nixon but presented with Reagan's more appealing language and charm" (Colburn 2007:114). By the 1980s the basic tenets of the southern strategy underwrote a supposedly color-blind conservatism with the bootstraps argument that social mobility is available to those who work hard and that persistent racial-ethnic inequalities are attributable to individual and cultural failings rather than to white supremacy and systemically reproduced structural inequality.[24]

Amid the shifting sociopolitical rhetoric, a 1973 oil embargo by Arab nations protesting US support for Israel sent the US economy into a tailspin and New York City to the brink of bankruptcy. As deindustrialization clobbered the economies of northern US cities, new economies emerged in the Sunbelt from Florida across the Southeast and Southwest to California (Fairbanks and Lloyd 2011, Nickerson and Dochuk 2011). Resistance to federal regulations and anti-union politics already had a long history in the South. Those factors, together with the economic shift and the post–civil rights supposedly color-blind conservatism, gave new power to southern states in a neoliberal-neoconservative economic and political alliance of North and South (Cobb 2011; MacLean 2008, 2010). In brief, the Sunbelt promoters engaged in a North-South collaboration that "planted the seeds of American neoliberalism" by promising an environment unfettered by regulations and taxes and one that kept workers' rights in check (Needham 2011:246).[25]

Neoliberalism and Latinization. Conservative scholars describe neoliberalism as a project aiming to situate market principles as "the guarantor of individual freedoms," and those on the left see it as a project aiming to thwart redistributive social justice and restore class power to the elite (Fairbanks and Lloyd 2011:4). I use the term as shorthand for a global system of political-economic policies that have promoted market- over state-based solutions to social problems through deregulation and privatization, international free trade, domestic consumerism, and tax cuts, especially for corporations.

Neoliberalism came to Latin America through a political and economic project grounded in structural adjustment programs mandated by the World Bank and International Monetary Fund in exchange for loans (Gledhill 2007). Structural adjustment program requirements to privatize government services and implement social and political reforms produced economic retrenchment and prompted grassroots social protests in response to the austerity measures that fed the reproduction of social inequalities. Together with a pull to the north by the 1965 Immigration and Naturalization Act in the United States—removing national-origin quotas and focusing on bringing in skilled labor—the push away from Latin American economic conditions converted that region from a world immigrant destination to an exporter of populations (González 2000:250).

The combined use of coercion and consent to break resistance to neoliberalism has been an important achievement of those promoting this social vision. Regarding consent, the United Kingdom's Prime Minister Thatcher famously stated in 1981, "Economics are the method, but the object is to change the soul" (Harvey 2005:23). Indeed, the neoliberal economic method has been accompanied by political and sociocultural corollaries that have shifted public-sphere attention toward a depoliticized, merit-based individualism expressed through consumption patterns. The incorporation of color-blind multiculturalism into market-based neoliberal principles has contributed to a commodification of *latinidad* in the whitewashed, well-heeled, "Latin look" of the magazine cover that sparked Eva's comment that she was "not that kind of Latina."[26]

Using framings such as neoliberal personhood, neoliberal subjectivity, neoliberal citizen-subject, and neoliberalization of consciousness, scholars have documented how new ways of being emerged over the last quarter of the twentieth century that embrace individualism, personal responsibility, the positive value of change, and skillful flexibility.[27] The erasure of historical consciousness in favor of reasoning according to market principles and a turn from collective and public to individual and private have flattened and depoliticized the public sphere. The new "neoliberal person" is a "solitary achiever, able to succeed without the intervention of the state" (Ramos-Zayas 2012:27). In the absence of an alternative vision from either Democrats or Republicans, Raymond Rocco (2014:10) argues, Latino politics needs to promote changes "that would make an alternative possible."

Using the term "neoliberal multiculturalism," Charles Hale (2005) explains the irony that collective recognition of a group's historical disadvantage underwrites the neoliberal emphasis on the individual.[28] Twentieth-century purported corrections to this historically grounded problem supposedly cleared the way for individual merit to be the barometer for achievements and failures. The phrase "neoliberal multiculturalism" captures the tension between the universal and the particular in a system that privileges the individual while resting on a set of values and practices that assume human sameness but actually work to reproduce structural inequality.[29] In this, "the primacy of the particular rests not in particularity per se, but in that which is particularized" (Flores 2005:202). Which particular position aligns with the perspective of those in power and which does not? This is the tension apparent in the color-blind multicultural discourse of the *Sentinel*'s New Orlando series, as well as in language used during Orange County's 2011 redistricting.

This is not to say that these combined economic, political, and sociocultural trajectories determine social interactions and individual perceptions of self and other. I argue that the simultaneous histories of neoliberal multiculturalism and Latinization render it all the more difficult to disentangle the intersecting histories of race and immigration in Latino experience. In brief, Latinization has occurred in tandem with the spread of a social ethos that claims color-blindness and privileges individualism, and a political-economic regime that promotes privatization and values competition. The dynamics of the individual and the collective in Latino political community formation in the Orlando area since the late twentieth century respond to but are not necessarily determined by the supposedly color-blind privileging of the self-regulating individual over the collective race-class actions that have marked Latino political histories.

Orlando's natural neoliberalism. In the Orlando area, the tenets of neoliberalism resonate with the *pentimento* of entrepreneurial activities of ranchers and grove owners. In Central Florida, privileging the self-regulating and entrepreneurial individual did not need to change the soul. In this book, I refer to Orlando's "natural neoliberalism" because it is easy enough to imagine a depoliticized social response to late twentieth-century neoliberalism in Orlando as a seemingly natural progression from Central Florida's economic history.

Politically, Orlando's twentieth-century history demonstrates the public-private partnerships that mark the neoliberal state. An early example is the Orlando Utilities Commission, founded in 1923 as a publicly owned venture under the control of "a self-perpetuating business elite" that Richard Foglesong (2001:88) has dubbed Orlando's "informal private governance." When the Martin Company wanted to relocate to Central Florida, for instance, the president of Orlando's First National Bank used his political influence and his own money to option land and get approval from the state for two access roads and a special sewer district (Foglesong 2001:87).[30] Given this history, it is not surprising that Walt Disney was able to engineer the creation of a special district on land that straddles Orange and Osceola Counties. Via the Reedy Creek Improvement District, the Disney Corporation has been able to form its own government and essentially remove its theme parks from state control.[31]

Although the self-regulating entrepreneur has long been part of Orlando, the claim to a multicultural color-blindness has emerged since the civil rights era. Before the birth of the southern strategy, defendants in the 1962 lawsuit against Orange County schools argued that it was up to individual families to change the system, even as the system relied on a 1955 law engineered to maintain school desegregation in defiance of the 1954 Supreme Court decision in *Brown v. Board of Education* determining such practices to be unconstitutional (Kunerth 2008a). And as the political language of white supremacy was shifting in the 1960s, Walt Disney pushed for color-blind multiculturalism in the name of profit.

For this reason, I reverse Hale's wording and refer to "multicultural neoliberalism" to describe the phenomenon of appearing inclusive while reinscribing racial-ethnic and class hierarchies. The term captures how the tension between the universal and particular in color-blind multiculturalism normalizes whiteness in Orlando and elsewhere, shaping "notions of normal while [also making] invisible the work that normal does to obscure racism, discrimination, and prejudice" (Shankar 2015:5).[32]

The New Orlando is touted as a multicultural and color-blind place where hard-working individuals have found opportunities for self-improvement. The impact, much as Lee Atwater suggested in 1981, is to use "the logic of economic and civil rights" to entrench racial-ethnic inequality (Nickerson and Dochuk 2011:18). Puerto Ricans and Latinos arriving in Orlando find a locally specific manifestation of multicultural neoliberalism in a place where a flattened and depoliticized neoliberal personhood has long since worked against collective political struggle for social equality.

RACE, PLACE, AND POLITICAL POWER IN CENTRAL FLORIDA

The growth of the Orlando-area Latino population has paralleled a historic realignment of political ideologies and affiliations in Florida that correspond to national-level changes. The long-standing institution of the Democratic Party's white voters' primary, which by definition excluded black voter participation, was in effect the general election in the US South. The Supreme Court was forcing change in the 1940s; by 1950 Orlando was the only Florida city still conducting a white voters' primary. Following a lawsuit by a Jacksonville-based black law firm, Orlando's mayor finally did away with the practice and opened the vote to all (Bacon 1977:2:165).

Florida's NAACP was at work registering black voters in the 1940s. As heirs to the party of Lincoln, Republicans had traditionally attracted southern black loyalties. In Orange County in 1946, more than three times as many black voters were registered as Republicans (about 1,100) than as Democrats (about 340). Among white voters at that time, some 23,000 were registered as Democrats and only about 2,700 as Republicans.[33] Prior to that time, Florida Democrats, as in other southern states, were called "Yellow Dog Democrats" because they claimed that that dog would get their vote before a Republican would (Colburn 2007).

Nonetheless, in the post–civil rights era, many white voters eventually moved into the Republican Party, while black voters were shifting to the Democratic Party. By the end of the twentieth century, more than 90 percent of Florida's registered black voters were Democrats; white voters were divided 45 to 49 percent, slightly favoring the Republican Party (Dye 1998:14). As the state's Latino population grew throughout the second half of the twentieth century, the Florida House and Senate went from neither chamber having a single Republican member to Republican majorities in both (Colburn 2007:105). While northern Democratic transplants in South Florida struggled with Old South Democrats in North Florida, Republicans gained votes from disaffected white Democrats, the growing Cuban exile community, and a new wave of Republican retirees from the Midwest (Colburn 2007).

As individuals responded to the southern strategy and switched parties, the ability to determine the shape and content of voting districts became a new way to embed racial-ethnic and political relations in physical space. Since the 1920s, North Florida had dominated the state economically, demographically, and politically. As Florida's population growth shifted southward to metropolitan areas in the postwar years, little changed in how Floridians were represented in Tallahassee (MacManus et al. 2015:9). In the 1950s, barely one fifth of Floridians were electing the majority of the legislative members (Morris and Morris 2014:254).

A series of US Supreme Court decisions in the 1960s required Florida to revise its political districts. New state legislative districts balanced the numbers and contributed to Republicans' ability to break up the Old South Democratic power in North Florida (MacManus et al. 2015:186–187, Morris and Morris 2014:255). Nonetheless, multiple-member districts continued to marginalize minority voters in urban areas and helped maintain control in white Democratic hands (Tauber 2005:46).

The 1965 Voting Rights Act (VRA) extended protections to voters from practices or policies restricting the ability to vote based on "race or color," and a 1975 amendment extended the same protections to "language minorities." During state-level redistricting in 1982 and 1992, black Floridians and Republicans forged an alliance, pressed for single-member districts, and sought to pack black voters into majority-minority districts that gave them greater representation in accordance with the VRA, while leaving increasing concentrations of white Republicans in other districts (Colburn 2007:141, Morris and Morris 2014:266, Tauber 2005:45–49). Although Democrat Lawton Chiles retained the governorship through most of the 1990s, Republicans had gained a legislative majority in both houses of the state legislature for the first time by 1996 (MacManus et al. 2015:146).

Florida Democrats had tried to talk black voters out of the deal with Republicans but were not willing to create more than one majority-minority district (Colburn 2007:141). Ultimately, then, the refusal by Florida's white Democrats to share power in substance and not merely in word helped Republicans gain the upper hand.[34] Thus, as black voters and former

Dixiecrats switched parties respectively from Republican to Democratic and Democratic to Republican, white Floridians stayed in power regardless. Some Latino districts were created in 1982 and 1992, but these went to South Florida Cubans. The growing Central Florida Latino population remained largely invisible in the political landscape.

Jeb Bush's election as governor in 1998 and 2002 consolidated Republican influence in Florida. While working on his father's presidential campaign in 1988, Bush connected with key Republican strategists including Lee Atwater (Colburn 2007:159). Bush's wife, Columba, was born and raised in Mexico and proved a valuable asset for him with Latino voters (Nolin 1998, Silva 2001). Jeb Bush also demonstrated awareness of the growing Central Florida Puerto Rican population. Orlando Puerto Rican and military veteran Dennis Freytes served on the transition team (Montanez 1998).[35] By Bush's second campaign, Puerto Rico–born Waldemar Serrano was running his Orlando-based Central Florida office (Silva 2001).[36] During that year, Bush also appointed Cuban American Raoul Cantero to the Florida Supreme Court. By his second term, his approval rating among Latinos was at 58 percent, higher than among Florida's white and black populations (McDonald 2004). An assessment from the *Orlando Sentinel* sums up what I have heard from Orlando Puerto Ricans who remember those years: "Jeb has cracked the code in romancing the Hispanic population" (Lush 2004).

With Republicans in control during the 2002 redistricting, packing white Democrats into districts again served to protect black representation in compliance with the VRA, while maintaining a Republican majority (MacManus et al. 2015:188–189). Additional Hispanic districts in the 2002 redistricting were again located in South Florida despite growing pressure from Central Florida Latinos. Neither black nor white and often without party affiliation, Orlando-area Latinos were not really on the redistricting radar at either the state or local levels until after the 2010 Census. Political wrangling over voting districts was mostly about white and black, Democratic and Republican. The creation of majority-minority districts did benefit Latinos, but only Cuban Republicans from Miami-Dade. During the 2011 redistricting process, I heard determination from Orlando Puerto Ricans that this time would be different. Although there were gains at the state level, at the Orange County level the outcome diluted Latino voting power rather than protecting it.

By 2015, non-Latino white Floridians were about 56 percent of the state's population but 67 percent of the Florida House members and 75 percent of the Senate. Non-Latino black Floridians were about 17 percent of the state's population; they held 18 percent of the Florida House seats and 15 percent of the Senate. Even with new South Florida districts, Latinos, who were about 24 percent of Floridians, had only 15 percent representation in the House and 10 percent in the Senate (MacManus et al. 2015:193). By 2019, seven Florida Latinos had been elected to the US Congress; all but one were Cuban American, five from the Miami area. The other two were from the Orlando area; Mel Martinez, born in Cuba, was elected to the US Senate in 2004, and in 2016 Darren Soto became the first Florida Puerto Rican to serve in the US House of Representatives.

The combination of Central Florida Latino voting practices, Jeb Bush's popularity among Florida Latinos, and steadily growing Republican power locally and in the state help explain the Puerto Rican political landscape I encountered in 2005. At that time, Martinez was in his Senate seat and John Quiñones represented Florida House District 49. Puerto Rico–born Republican Mildred Fernández was in the nonpartisan position of Orange County commissioner for District 3; she was the only Hispanic representative on any city or county governing body in the Orlando metro area at that time. Martinez, Quiñones, and Fernández had all been supported by Puerto Ricans and other Latinos across party lines, including crossing votes for these Republicans with a presidential vote for Democrat John Kerry in 2004.

In the middle of this political transformation, Latinos arrived in increasing numbers in Florida and in Orlando, bringing with them their own ideas about politics, place, and race. In a place where a historic black-white political frame had defined political affiliation and where Latino politics was about Cuban Republicans in South Florida, Puerto Ricans and other Latinos arriving in Orlando have not easily found their place in the political field. In a 2012 oral history, New York Democratic activist Carmen Torres described the political world she found when she moved to Central Florida in 1993: "Then when we left New York and came to Florida, it was really interesting because politics . . . of Florida, of the South, period, is a different animal. Of course, you have to learn how it works. Right? So there was a learning process."

THE NEXT CHAPTER IN THE PUERTO RICAN MIGRATION STORY

As Sunbelt boosters were promoting new economic opportunities and Orlando was feeling the impact of Walt Disney World's opening, Puerto Ricans from island and northern diaspora communities began to arrive in larger numbers in Central Florida. In this new place, which itself was unaccustomed to newcomers, neither islanders nor those from other diaspora spaces had a deeper history than the other. Puerto Ricans had been among those hardest hit by the economic devastation of US industrial centers during the 1970s, and Puerto Rico's newly industrialized economy, largely dependent on US investments, was pulled into that same vortex (Rodríguez 1979:207, Whalen 2009:226). Rising crime rates in Puerto Rico and New York, combined with the imploding economy and the loss of manufacturing jobs, pushed Puerto Ricans from both places to relocate.

Orlando's economy, climate, and proximity to Puerto Rico proved attractive to Puerto Ricans from everywhere. An added pull for those from the urban diaspora were the affordable low-rise developments. So distant from the highrises and housing projects in northern spaces, these developments are reminiscent for many of the Puerto Rico that they either remember from direct experience or have learned about from the memories of others. Another pull was the network of Puerto Ricans already settled in the Orlando area. Narratives from oral histories collected in 2008–2009 about experiences as far back as the 1940s include frequent mentions of Puerto Ricans who were already in the Orlando area. Each new arrival established another connection between Orlando and the sending community. Translocal networks grew among (at least) Orlando, Puerto Rico, New York, Chicago, and Miami.

By the post–Cold War 1990s, Puerto Rico's strategic military position and privileged location for US capital investments was less important to the United States (Cabán 2018). Puerto Rico's relations with the US tax code and therefore with US corporations protected it from neoliberal restructuring longer than its Latin American neighbors. Beginning with the 1994 North American Free Trade Agreement (NAFTA), however, globalized agreements removed the US need for offshore production in Puerto Rico. A ten-year phase-out of the tax breaks that had kept US corporations in Puerto Rico began in 1996. In the wake of those changes, the US territory experienced the full force of what others around Latin America had experienced for decades.

As Latinization in the US states progressed in response to the push-pull, Puerto Ricans as US citizens, many with bilingual skills, were increasingly recruited as teachers and medical personnel to Orlando and other newly emerging Latino communities. Just ahead of the bursting of the US housing bubble and the consequent recession, the ten-year phase-out of tax breaks to US corporations in Puerto Rico came to its completion in 2006, and a new wave of Puerto Rican out-migration was under way. With Orlando's translocal networks well established, increasing numbers followed their connections to this new diaspora space. In the middle of my fieldwork, Orlando replaced New York as the primary Puerto Rican destination. Ironically, Puerto Ricans and other Orlando Latinos are arriving in a place where the same neoliberal political and economic practices that disrupted their economic lives and pushed them from their places of origin find a comfortable fit in and much political support from Orlando's particular history and its contemporary natural neoliberalism.

In a reassessment of the long history of Puerto Rican struggle for their right to belong in the US states, the historians Lorrin Thomas and Aldo Lauria Santiago (2019) stress the importance of noting changes in motivations and strategies according to changing contexts of time and place. In their summation of that history (194), I see an apt description for approaching a study of Orlando:

> [T]he motivations that guided them and the strategies they developed to meet the challenges at hand were constantly changing, partly in response to changing context. Economic opportunities shifted, alliances formed and broke apart, political winds blew in multiple directions, and racism and ethnic prejudice blocked opportunity in different ways in different settings.

PART II

DIFFERENCE AND THE INCOMPLETENESS OF POLITICAL COMMUNITY FORMATION

CHAPTER 3

"YOU DON'T LOOK PUERTO RICAN"

Race, Class, and Memories of Place in Orlando

There is a road in Lake County named Soto Road for the schoolteacher Gilbert Soto Torres. Born in Puerto Rico, Soto Torres joined the Seventh-Day Adventist Church when he was sixteen, went to New York soon after completing high school in 1958, and left New York to attend a Seventh-Day Adventist college in Tennessee. There he met and married an Anglo woman from Lake County, Florida, and the couple moved there in the late 1960s, just as legally sanctioned Jim Crow segregation was ending. Soto Torres taught Spanish in local schools for thirty-five years. He remembered teaching black and white students separately; he remembered by the 1980s teaching the children of Mexican orange pickers (PRCF Soto Torres).

This story is absent from the historical narrative summarized earlier. In fact, the established narrative of Puerto Rican migration only mentions Florida because it has become the primary destination. Similar silences also pertain to Orlando's and Florida's historical narratives. From the *Orlando Sentinel* and oral histories, I know that in downtown Orlando in the early 1960s there was a Cuban grocery called El Refugio (Delgado 1988a, PRCF González Durocher). Newly arriving Cubans were directed from there down the street to the home of Puerto Rico–born Patricia González Durocher, who was collecting clothing and furniture for them (PRCF González Durocher). Another market, owned and run by Cuba-born Rafael and Luisa Medina, opened in 1970 and quickly became a gathering place for Orlando Latinos (Firpo 2012:66–67, PRCF Medina). La Primera grocery on Semoran opened in 1974, along with a nearby Puerto Rican restaurant El Bohío (Padilla 1999a). Although a two-volume history of Orlando (Bacon 1977) lists events large and small in the city's history year by year from 1821 through 1975, it makes no mention of any of these places. Puerto Ricans are not much present anywhere in documents about Florida history until they become hypervisible as the main driver of the Latinization of Orlando.

Scattered sources do give hints of a Florida chapter to Puerto Rican history and a Puerto Rican chapter to Florida history. Víctor Vázquez-Hernández (2015) has traced a "Boricua Triangle" that developed historically, with concentrations of Puerto Ricans first emerging in Tampa, then Miami, and now Orlando.[1] He found evidence of Puerto Ricans in Orlando as far back as the 1920s. Florida Puerto Ricans in the first half of the twentieth century apparently included a cross-class range of workers, small-business owners, and investors. Although my data include stories of Puerto Rican farmworkers in all three parts of this triangle, much of the recorded farmworker history is drawn from the archives of the Migration Division, which leaves the privately managed practice of recruiting Puerto Rican farmworkers to Florida largely unrecognized.[2]

Duany and Matos-Rodríguez (2006:12) assert that a small group of Puerto Ricans bought land in South Florida in the 1940s for a sugarcane refinery. During the 1950s the *Miami Herald* described Puerto Ricans as the largest and fastest-growing group of Spanish speakers in Miami (Shell-Weiss 2009:168). In an oral history at the Center for Puerto Rican Studies in 2010, former Miami mayor Maurice Ferré described two Puerto Rican Miamis in the 1950s, divided between workers and owners (Ferré 2010).[3]

Scores of Puerto Rican soldiers likely passed through bases in Florida and around the South from at least the 1940s onward, but those stories have not yet contributed a chapter to Puerto Rican histories. Ernesto Peña Roque was stationed at Orlando Air Base in 1957. He witnessed the crash of Colonel McCoy's plane, which led to the renaming of the base and eventually to MCO for identifying the Orlando airport (PRCF Peña Roque). José Santana, a US Air Force pilot, patrolled the waters between Cuba and Florida in the 1960s. He recalled,

> Maybe because of my bilingual capability, I was one of the chosen ones to be transferred permanently to McCoy Air Force Base. . . . Cubans were trying to leave the island, some in rubber boats, some in innertubes, truck innertubes. . . . We might have saved a few lives. . . . Our missions were flown about 50 feet off the water. . . . We had to elevate the plane to make a turn, otherwise the wingtip would hit the water. (PRCF Santana)

And even before Walt Disney was quietly buying up the property needed for his new East Coast location in the mid-1960s, developers were promoting Florida to a middle-class market as an affordable paradise. While workers were leaving Puerto Rico for northern US spaces, Operation Bootstrap and the Commonwealth's expanding state apparatus were contributing to a growing Puerto Rican middle class on the island. Those marketing new Florida properties took note (Alden 1960). Among other populations targeted by developers, Puerto Ricans from island and diaspora as well as in the military were a focus of the marketing campaigns (Silver 2010).[4]

As Orlando's shifting demographics pushed at the boundaries of white and black during the second half of the twentieth century, supposedly colorblind discourses were emerging in response to calls to balance the playing field for the historically oppressed and marginalized. In this chapter, I use oral histories and other data from historical ethnography to examine how class relations, racial-ethnic identifications, and ideas about place informed how Orlandoans have viewed Puerto Ricans as a group and how Puerto Ricans who participated in the 2008–2009 PRCF oral history collection navigated those expectations. The data suggest that prevailing race- and class-based stereotypes about New York Puerto Ricans rendered middle-class, lighter-skinned Orlando Puerto Ricans, including those from New York, practically invisible for a good while. As the growing numbers shifted Latino Orlando from invisibility to hypervisibility, the intersections of Orlando's racial history, Puerto Rican racial codes and class interests, and the encounter of island and diaspora informed how Orlando Puerto Ricans worked to identify themselves to others.[5]

HIDDEN IN PLAIN SIGHT

Following a move to single-member districts in 1980, Orlando voters made history by electing a city council that included two black men and two women. The women are not identified racially in the *Orlando Sentinel Star* coverage; presumably normalized as white, they are simply described as "housewives" (Ziffer 1980). Although not mentioned, the election of one of the women, Mary I. Johnson, also made history because she was the first "Latin" elected to public office in Central Florida.[6] Her birth name was María Ignacia Cristina Pérez; her parents were Cuban and Puerto Rican. She grew up in Miami and married an Anglo serving in the US Navy. Upon his retirement, they moved to Orlando in 1968 because of the community of Navy personnel there and the benefits available at the new Naval Training Center. It seems likely that given the slight southern lilt to Johnson's voice and her Anglo name, non-Latino white voters in 1980 never questioned where she fit into Orlando's racial field.

In a 2008 oral history Johnson tells of knocking on Cubans' and Puerto Ricans' doors during the 1980 campaign, but her campaign literature projected her solid position in Orlando's mainstream white social order.[7] The flyers listed her credentials as the wife of a naval officer and mother of three sons, a community volunteer for Scouts and Little League, regional president of the Navy Wives of America, and precinct election official. A reference in campaign materials to Johnson as bilingual was immediately followed by mention of her marriage to "Naval Chief" Bob Johnson. After the election, an article suggested a distant Latin connection with a passing mention that her grandfather had been the mayor of a town in Cuba. That reference was immediately followed by the information that she was born in New York and grew up in Miami (Wadsworth 1981).

The dichotomy of knocking on Cubans' and Puerto Ricans' doors while conducting a campaign that makes almost no mention of her Cuban–Puerto Rican heritage speaks to the general invisibility of Latinos in Orlando's social field before 1980 and the potentially adverse impact that visibility might bring. The numbers were strong enough that those who were aware of Orlando's Latino population knew where to knock on doors. But until the media seized on the numbers from the 1980 Census, the non-Latino public seemed unaware that a demographic shift was already under way.

One simple explanation is geography. Despite the eventual East Side reputation as a Latino place, in 1980 there was no one neighborhood where Latinos were settling. Among the Orange County census-designated places (CDPs) with the highest concentrations of Latinos in 1980 (table 1.3), the largest proportion of Latinos to the total population was only 9 percent, in Sky Lake and Oak Ridge. In the Union Park CDP, where the second-largest number of Orange County Latinos resided, more than 1,000 Latinos were still only 6 percent of the total population. Seminole and Osceola Counties also saw some Latino settlement.

In her 2008 oral history, Dora Casanova de Toro remembered that in the early 1980s whenever she heard anyone speaking Spanish, she would ask right away where that person was from. The second question, she said, was always "Where are you living?" (PRCF Casanova de Toro). This must have occurred even more often in earlier decades. Before Disney and even for a good while after 1971, Central Florida was rural. Orlando Puerto Rican memories as late as the mid-1980s continually reference orange groves where there now stand housing developments.

Darío González, who arrived in Orlando the year Mary Johnson was elected, compared his experiences in New York with life in Orlando. As so often happens in Orlando, González first used "we" in seeming reference to the umbrella term "Hispanic" but then identified the central place of Puerto Ricans:

> A funny thing is that when we, the Puerto Ricans especially, went to New York, we went to live in certain areas. Those who went to Brooklyn lived in that area; those who went to the Bronx did the same thing; those who went to New York [Manhattan], also with the Hispanic barrio. But we Puerto Ricans who came here, to Central Florida, we didn't go to a specific place. In other words, we went to live all over the place, all over. There was no place called the "Latin barrio." (PRCF D. González)[8]

Medina's grocery had been a gathering spot for Latinos living all over the place for a decade already by the year of Mary Johnson's first election. Yvonne Milligan, who came to Rollins College in Winter Park in 1951 and stayed, remembered that in 1970 Medina's was so small that people had to wait outside for their turn to go in (PRCF Milligan). While waiting, they would argue about politics, she said. Within a short time, Medina's expanded and added a cafeteria in the adjacent space that offered more room for social interaction. In his interview Rafael Medina recalled, "Here, when we started, sometimes I'd say to people, 'When you leave, turn out the lights.' Because it was 11 at night. . . . To get together on the weekends, there was no other gathering place" (PRCF Medina).[9]

A Cuban-owned Spanish-language radio station, La Mágica, was broadcasting from Kissimmee in those days, although by all accounts its signal was barely strong enough to reach Orlando. By 1978 an outdoor Latin music festival had taken place and continued as the annual Hispanic Latin Fiesta (Firpo 2012:94, McFaul 1985, PRCF Auffant). The Asociación Borinqueña started up that same year. James Auffant, who was president of the association in 1980, remembered buying the group's first property:

> The first clubhouse was in Goldenrod. I bought that property; it was two acres for $13,000. Paid it off cash. We had $14,000, paid it off, because we couldn't get a loan as a group. So we paid it off. Left the association with a piece of land and with $1,000 in the bank. Now, we used to meet in different places. . . . We used to do dances at least once a month. We'd make 800, 900 bucks and that's how we built up our pot. We'd make our monthly assemblies [in the Pine Hills church] too, until we grew up to that we could have a place. (PRCF Auffant)[10]

Along with the Pine Hills church where members of the Asociación Borinqueña met, Good Shepherd Catholic Church in the heart of Azalea Park was and is an important gathering place. Other churches scattered around the area also provided gathering points. One of these was a Seventh-Day

Adventist church in Seminole County's Forest City that continues to draw many Puerto Ricans to that area.

It may be because these venues were in various locations around metro Orlando rather than in one place that the activities went largely unnoticed. It may also be that the invisibility that initially cloaked Mary Johnson's Latin roots was due to the racialized equation of Latin with Cuban and Cuban with honorary white among many Floridians at that point in time. The argument that Puerto Ricans are racial/colonial subjects whose experiences highlight the ties between colonial histories and contemporary racial-ethnic hierarchies proposes that images of and ideas about distinct groups of Latinos are framed according to the conditions of their entry to the United States (Grosfoguel and Goeras 2000). Cubans, who were granted special privileges via the 1966 Cuban Adjustment Act, are not "Puerto Ricanized" as other groups have been (Grosfoguel and Goeras 2000:111).[11] In this light, it is noteworthy that the brief mention of Johnson's Latin connection in the 1980 campaign was to Cuba but not Puerto Rico.

Perhaps the first public evidence of a specifically Puerto Rican presence in the Orlando area was the surprisingly successful Noche de San Juan organized in 1980 by Amaury Díaz. Díaz convinced the Wet 'n Wild water park to experiment with a traditional Puerto Rican festival every June 23 in which falling backward into the water multiple times clears one of all past adversities and prepares one for the year ahead. Central Florida does not have an ocean, and the many lakes are full of alligators. What better substitute than a water theme park? Díaz explained,

> If it was a weekday, we couldn't do it because everybody's working. So it had to be close to the date but on a Saturday night. Wet 'n Wild agreed, and the requirement was that I had to guarantee 600 people in the park that night or pay $10,000 . . . [*laughs*], which I didn't have, but anyway, you know, you take chances in life. . . . And that night, instead of 600 people showing up we had 1,200 people. . . . As of today, Wet 'n Wild does the fiesta.[12] (PRCF A. Díaz)

That events like Noche de San Juan could take everyone by surprise again suggests little notice given to Puerto Ricans living around the Orlando area at the time. I contend that this was due in part to a disconnect between the prevalent race- and class-based idea about Puerto Ricans and the actual Puerto Ricans in Orlando. In brief, these Puerto Ricans did not fit the idea of the colonial migrant that was emanating from both the island and northern diaspora spaces during the decades of the 1950s through the

1970s.[13] If mid-century Orlandoans knew anything about Puerto Rico and Puerto Ricans, most likely their impressions included poor farmworkers, the so-called New York Puerto Rican problem, and gun-wielding nationalists presumed to be communists. And the Puerto Ricans in Orlando did not square with those images.

The collected PRCF narratives reveal the common experience of being told in one way or another, "You don't look Puerto Rican." Puerto Rico–born Hank de Arrigoitia is a dermatologist who came to the Naval Training Center in its earliest days; he was likely the first Puerto Rican doctor in Orlando. He and his wife, Tere, recalled the disbelief they encountered when they said where they were from. "You're white," they heard. "How can you be Puerto Ricans?" (PRCF De Arrigoitia). Yvonne Milligan was a friend of the De Arrigoitia family, and she had similar experiences. Although her attendance at the elite Rollins College and her marriage to a prominent Anglo Orlandoan put her firmly in white Anglo social circles, she was questioned about her racial background: "Nobody ever hurt me or anything like that, but they'd ask me, 'Do you have any colored people in your family?' or 'Oh, I thought all Puerto Ricans, they were blacks'" (PRCF Milligan).

Also of note in Milligan's narrative are the ways she was internationalized. A local newspaper sought her out with two other women and staged a photo for an article celebrating that Orlando was becoming "international." Milligan recalled, "It was the front page. There were three of us—a Japanese lady, a Cuban lady, and myself. And they had us walking down Orange Avenue on the sidewalk. The headline says 'International Flavor Comes to Orlando.' That goes to show you how small Orlando was. . . . It must have been '56, '57, '58, had to be around there" (PRCF Milligan).

Over the years, Milligan found that people would confuse Costa Rica and Puerto Rico and question how to exchange her Puerto Rican dollars. This internationalization of Milligan as a Puerto Rican simultaneously removed her from the stigma of the racial/colonial subject and denied her inclusion as a full member of Orlando's social field.

The black-white-foreign categorization reflects what Bonilla-Silva (2004) describes as an emergent tripartite US racial order with an honorary white category situated between white and collective black. Despite their lives on the white side of the black-white color line, the individual Puerto Ricans in the collection often implied that they did not feel the Anglos around them saw them as equals. The sometimes subtly contested place of this in-between honorary status is reflected in the experiences of Monserrate Vélez's son Glenn in Central Florida schools in the 1950s. Vélez was born and grew up in Sanford. Despite having two Puerto Rican parents, he recalled that as a child he did not think of himself as Puerto Rican. He did think of himself as somehow different, though, and he recalled comments from his schoolmates about his "tan" skin (PRCF Vélez).[14]

Sheila Durocher Alexander is the daughter of Patricia González Durocher, the Puerto Rican woman who collected items to pass on to Cubans in the 1960s. The family name, Durocher, along with the girl's blond hair and fair skin meant that she probably did not receive comments from her classmates like those directed at Glenn Vélez, but then there was her mother. People had trouble understanding González Durocher, and her daughter had to translate for her even when she was speaking English. Alexander remembered feeling embarrassed as a child about the race- and class-based associations with Puerto Ricans in New York. Although by about age twelve she came to identify strongly as Puerto Rican, before that she was trying as much as possible to belong in her white world:

> When we first came here, that was I'm sure part of my embarrassment, at first, . . . of that, "Oh, well, you're one of those no good Puerto Ricans. You're going to be somebody who's going to need welfare." Or whatever the perception was that Puerto Ricans were in New York. That was part of what we maybe—or I certainly did—dealt with when I was younger. I think that was also perhaps the embarrassment of saying my mom was Puerto Rican. I didn't say that for many years. I said she was, her family was from Spain for many years. (PRCF González Durocher)

Taken together, the stories suggest that these mid-century Orlando Puerto Ricans lived in a contradictory tension between the invisibility of honorary white status and the hypervisibility of Puerto Ricans as outsiders, a problem, a threat. For these early Orlando Puerto Ricans, there were consequences to being seen or unseen. One Orlando Puerto Rican told me about Ku Klux Klan marches on Dean Road in Union Park in the early 1980s. And although he did not mention the Klan activity of the time and asserted that he did not feel unsafe, one of the Kennedy Space Center engineers recruited from Puerto Rico in the 1970s talked in his oral history about the concern of driving back to Orlando late at night through the desolate stretch of road in eastern Orange County around Bithlo (PRCF Gelpi).

Being unseen could both serve and challenge Puerto Ricans in their day-to-day living in Orlando. Their condition seems a direct reflection of Donald Carter's (2010:6) observation that invisibility is "a flexible phenomenon that can be generalized, normalized, and deployed in multiple contexts, allowing it to be invoked like a discursive shroud in one decade only to disappear in the next or reappear elsewhere to freeze another group of people in a zone where public discourse is afraid to visualize and acknowledge their presence." For these earliest of Orlando Puerto Ricans, invisibility was a kind of protection, but the potential hazards of hypervisibility as nonwhite and foreign in Jim Crow Florida were what made this ability to be unseen desirable in the first place.

TIPPING POINT

A cab driver taking me to catch a flight to Puerto Rico from Orlando one day showed me a route to the airport that avoids the highways, heads south through shortcuts and residential streets, and ends up on Semoran just a couple of miles north of the airport. He asked where I was going, and as we drove along, he said, "This area turned Puerto Rican overnight." He was unsure about exactly when that was, but it seemed to him like sometime in the 1980s. Although his comment showed no sign of anything but welcome to this new demographic, it nonetheless reflected a moment when many Orlandoans felt they woke up one day to a new reality.

Because the oral history narratives in the PRCF collection rely on memories at least thirty years old, the dates as remembered may not be exact. Nonetheless, the narratives point to the period from about 1978 through the mid-1980s as a time of increasingly visible Puerto Rican and Latino presence in Orlando. Soon after the 1980 Census made the Orlando area's "Spanish Origin" population numerically visible, newspaper reports used the numbers to inform non-Latino Orlandoans about the change.[15] Latinos were a population out of place that the mainstream media were trying to situate in relation to Orlando's black-white social field.

In the racial confusion, efforts to locate Latinos used racial-ethnic language in talk that was actually about class relations, as well as class references that appeared color-blind while talking about racial-ethnic identity ideas.[16] A newspaper reporter in 1981 observed, "The Latins are everywhere, yet they are almost invisible. Being mostly professional or white-collar workers, they blend into the fibers of Orlando society" (Santos-Berry 1981). In this case, professional status suggests color-blind criteria for inclusion in Orlando society. At about the same time, another reporter framed "Latins" as a whole in competition with black workers for low-wage jobs (Sabulis 1981).

The racial confusion also suggests that there was already a range of class relations among Orlando Puerto Ricans and other Latinos and that longtime Orlandoans were perhaps assigning racialized class status according to the Latinos they encountered. Kennedy Space Center began recruiting Puerto

FIGURE 3.1. Medina's grocery and cafeteria, circa 1985. Courtesy of Rafael Medina, to "Puerto Ricans in Central Florida 1940s-1980s: A History." Used with permission. Copyright 2011, University of Central Florida.

Rican engineers in 1977. Disney's EPCOT theme park opened in 1982, adding another attraction for tourists and job seekers. In a random search of a Puerto Rican newspaper I found five advertisements for Disney in one day in 1985, and my data are full of people telling me that they came for a Disney vacation and stayed. It is telling that most of those who participated in the PRCF collection did not come for Disney employment, and many spoke of their professional credentials.

Perhaps because Latinos were living all over the place, the now more visible Latino activities may well have appeared to non-Latino Orlandoans as suddenly happening all around them. Puerto Ricans and Latinos were forming their own spaces where they could gather as Puerto Ricans, as Cubans, and sometimes as Hispanics. The first edition of the weekly Spanish-language paper *La Prensa*, founded in Orlando by Puerto Rico–born Manuel Toro and Dora Casanova de Toro, came out in 1981. In its pages was a list of churches offering services in Spanish and advertisements from six Latino grocery stores scattered from Seminole to Osceola County. The members of the young Asociación Borinqueña were soon holding fund-raisers outdoors in the empty lot they now owned in East Orlando.

Around this same time, a group of Latino students was forming on the campus of what is now the University of Central Florida (PRCF Caldero, PRCF V. Díaz, PRCF Gamache, PRCF I. Gómez).[17] They made their presence felt through a protest in front of the Naval Training Center against US interference in Latin America and in a cultural parade on campus (PRCF V. Díaz, PRCF I. Gómez). By the mid-1980s Orlando had a new radio station with the same frequency (1140 AM) and name as the popular 11Q in Puerto Rico (PRCF Gamache). A Cuban social club was founded in 1985 (Salazar 2015).[18] The Casa de Puerto Rico opened its doors in 1991, and the Centro de Cultura Puertorriqueña—which I have been told was the first outside Puerto Rico to be certified by the Institute for Puerto Rican Culture—was started later in the 1990s. A Puerto Rican folkloric dance group, Grupo Batey, emerged in 1986 from those gathered at the Asociación Borinqueña; among other venues, the group held performances at Valencia Community College and in the park around Lake Eola (PRCF Auffant, PRCF H. and L. Gómez). One of the group members was Haydée Gómez; her husband, Luis Gómez, was a New York Puerto Rican who had a law office in Azalea Park at the corner of Semoran and Curry Ford. His office was known as "the *alcaldía*" (city hall), and he began to refer to the area as "El Barrio" (PRCF H. and L. Gómez).[19]

Latin music became increasingly easy to find. Amaury Díaz met his Uruguayan wife at a dance in the early 1980s. By 1984 Rafael Rosado had his own big-band group, the Orquesta Nueva Sensación (PRCF A. Díaz, PRCF R. and Y. Rosado). The engineer Angel Martínez's reputation as a musician preceded him when he arrived in Orlando in 1985, and before long he was performing and teaching in his spare time (Martínez 2018). His students performed all over Florida as La Rondalla de Orlando, and eventually he started Orlando's Latin Music Institute. From 1986 to 1988 the Puerto Rican tradition of *viernes social* (Friday happy hour) was a popular occasion at Victor and Carmen Julia Dávila's San Juan Restaurant near Forest City in Seminole County. Throughout the week, in addition to the members of the area's Seventh-Day Adventist church, the Dávilas said the restaurant was frequented by military personnel and their families (PRCF Dávila).

Commissioner Johnson by then was identified as Hispanic in the papers. Within a year of Johnson's election, Orlando Mayor Bill Frederick, also elected in 1980, created a Hispanic Advisory Committee. By the 1984 election, Johnson and others were bringing a voter-registration campaign to Latinos. An article covering the effort identified Azalea Park and another area near Oak Ridge as areas of Hispanic settlement (Johnson 1984). Despite the greater proportion of Puerto Ricans among Orlando Latinos, the article skipped any reference to Central Florida and identified Cubans as the largest Hispanic group in Florida. And despite Johnson's being a Democrat, the article told readers that Hispanics in the Orlando area were "tending Republican."

This journalistic sleight of hand suggests an emerging anxiety among Orlando's longtime stakeholders, and the oral histories add weight to this supposition. Although the earlier narratives among the oral histories relate awkward individual encounters, the narratives from those who arrived from the late 1970s onward suggest that Puerto Ricans and Latinos as a group increasingly experienced a homogenizing hypervisibility that set them apart from the Orlando mainstream. As the population grew and became more visible, the kind of white, middle-class Latino invisibility of earlier decades gave way to an intensifying hypervisibility, through which Puerto Ricans and Latinos were racialized by the receiving society as something apart from black and white, a foreign population, speaking another language (Cobas et al. 2009, Vaquera et al. 2014).

As the Puerto Rican proportion of Orlando Latinos continued to grow, it is easy to imagine a transition in the minds of non-Latinos in Orlando from the mid-century idea of the Puerto Rican problem to the emergent nativist discourse about a so-called Latino threat. Indeed, a narrative from the 2012 Puerto Rican Political Participation and Civic Engagement in Central Florida (PRPPCE) oral history collection describes a bumper sticker on many cars during the 1990s that read, "I'm native. What are you?" (PRPPCE Ramírez). Puerto Ricans and Latinos were perpetual foreigners in a black-white space. Those whose accents may not have been as strong, having grown up in New York or Chicago, were also northerners in a southern space.

Stories from the oral histories about looking for work in the 1980s reflect the kinds of abstractions that Lee Atwater described, in his 1981 interview, as vehicles that paved the way for policies in which "blacks get hurt worse than whites." Being asked for Florida experience or being told "You're overqualified" were frequent occurrences for those from Puerto Rico and northern diaspora communities. Coming from Puerto Rico in 1989, the social worker Ana González eventually took her level of education off her resume and still had trouble getting work. Although González understood English very well, someone told her at one point that her accent was too strong; she finally landed her first Central Florida job typing information into a computer at Burger King (PRCF A. González).

Similar stories emerge from the narratives of those who had no language barrier. Betsy Franceschini had lived half her life in Chicago and half in Puerto Rico when she and her husband followed her parents to the Orlando area in 1985. Given her level of education and fluency in English, finding a job would be easy, she thought. She recalled,

> I have a master's degree in counseling and I started looking for work. . . . Because since I didn't have any experience here in the United States, wherever I went they would say to me, "Well, you don't have experience here." I would say, "Well, I have in Puerto Rico. I have already seven years

in Puerto Rico, of experience. I have my preparation." But it was extremely difficult. (PRCF Franceschini)[20]

Like Franceschini, Amaury Díaz moved to Orlando from Puerto Rico but had spent his childhood in the diaspora. In his case, it was New York, where he lived from age six through the end of high school, when he was drafted into the military. In Puerto Rico he had been a civil servant, but in Orlando he had trouble finding work. His description of looking for work in 1979 and 1980 Orlando sounds very much like Ana González's experiences nearly a decade later:

> I was a federal employee. I had a career status and there was an opening here at the IRS office in downtown Orlando. When I applied, I mean, I never got a reply and everything. It . . . was just that they weren't hiring any Hispanics. We had the qualifications, but their excuse for not hiring us was that they used to tell us, "You're too qualified." . . . So what did we end up doing? Working at the hotels. Washing dishes. But even back at that time it was very hard for Hispanics to get a job. (PRCF A. Díaz)

Less abstract was when a coworker told Eddie Heinzman he had taken a job from an American. In his oral history, he described his response:

> When I was going through college in 1967, I got a letter in English. . . . I had to put my life on hold and go to fight for this country in Vietnam. And my words were, "If I'm good enough to put my ass on the line for this country, I think I can come here and do whatever the hell I like doing." Like maybe getting a job in this company. Like maybe buying a house in this city. (PRCF Heinzman)

More than one person told me that the challenges to securing employment are what pushed them to start their own business.

Even before the tipping point of the 1980s, those Puerto Rican families with members in various shades from white to black apparently drew unwelcome attention from non-Latinos. Margarita Coll Cermeño came to Orlando from Puerto Rico in 1975 with her husband, their two children, and her husband's parents. She remembered the stares:

> Unfortunately, hardly anybody wanted to talk to me because of my color. And it was very strange for me to, to see that. And my husband is Puerto Rican white, so, and my father-in-law. But he also faced the same thing

> because my mother-in-law was Indian. So when we used to go in the street and everything, people used to stare at me. They didn't look; they stared. (PRCF Coll Cermeño)

Increased use of Spanish in public spaces also raised Latino visibility. That, along with Spanish surnames, set Puerto Ricans and Latinos apart from the mainstream racial binary. Where earlier arrivals like Monserrate Vélez and Yvonne Milligan heard that their accents were "cute," language now became a form of racialization.[21] In 1986 an amendment to make English the official language of the state was included in the Florida Constitution.

Hank De Arrigoitia remembered that non-Latino Orlandoans could not (and still sometimes will not) understand him: "So everybody, to many people, it was shocking to the point that they could not listen to what you were saying, you see. . . . Many people will listen to you, will hear you talk, and immediately they would close their ears. You know?" (PRCF De Arrigoitia). The narratives are full of anecdotes about being out with family and friends, speaking Spanish, and being told, "Speak English," by random passersby.[22]

As Puerto Ricans and Latinos gained visibility over the course of the 1980s and onward, individual experiences of feeling out of place began to be sensed as a collective vulnerability. In this tightrope walk between invisibility and hypervisibility, one has to wonder how these Puerto Ricans sought to locate themselves in the Orlando social landscape. As greater numbers of Puerto Ricans and other Latinos were trying to make Orlando their home and Jim Crow was morphing into a supposedly color-blind conservatism, how did the newcomers identify racially, and how did their racial identifications combine with their class relations? How did their understandings of social categories from other places intersect with those they found in this new location?

NAVIGATING RACE, CLASS, AND PLACE

Luis Martínez-Fernández (2010:43) describes Orlando as a social and political frontier where many Puerto Ricans and Latinos have been able to remake themselves apart from the more entrenched social hierarchies of Puerto Rico and other Latin American societies and where many others have moved away from the equally entrenched marginalization of New York's barrios. Orlando, he argues, has offered political and economic opportunities that would likely have been closed in the more established hierarchies in their places of origin (Martínez-Fernández 2010:44).

For Puerto Ricans in particular, historical ethnography suggests that Martínez-Fernández's observation applies to Florida more widely, reaching back to at least the 1940s. Florida and most likely other nontraditional destinations seem to have offered the possibility for Puerto Ricans to distance themselves from the tenaciously disparaging race- and class-based idea of the Puerto Rican. In 2008 I interviewed a middle-class family in San Juan who explained their move to Florida during the mid-twentieth century as a decision "to do something different." When Puerto Rican investors opened a sugar refinery, they made a point of telling the Miami papers that they would be bringing engineers but not day laborers to Florida (Duany and Matos-Rodríguez 2006:12). Nonetheless, workers did come, and Puerto Rican Miami in mid-century had a cross-class population.[23] A 1960 article in the Puerto Rican paper *El Mundo* acknowledges the hardships faced by Puerto Rican workers in Miami but also points to efforts among workers, merchants, and professionals to pull together as a community. The writer then asserts that in Miami "it cannot be said, as in other places, that 'there is a Puerto Rican problem'" (Negroni 1960).[24]

As new economic opportunities during the 1970s and 1980s were arising in tandem with the shifting sociopolitical field of the post–civil rights era, many Latinos—especially those among the rapidly growing Puerto Rican population—were in Orlando for that reason. Maybe the Orlando Puerto Ricans who did not "look Puerto Rican" had the opportunity to rewrite the idea of the Puerto Rican and finally open doors to full inclusion in the United States. For Betsy Franceschini, Orlando represented uncharted territory. She explained,

> It was new. It wasn't like saying you were going to move to New York or Chicago, which was already a longtime, established city. Here this was growing. So, there were better opportunities. To have your own property. To develop yourself in the field that you wanted. As long as you focused and overcame the obstacles that could present themselves to your achieving your goal. (PRCF Franceschini)[25]

The oral history record indicates that Puerto Ricans and other Latinos did indeed face obstacles. And along with the obstacles there were the inherent tensions between the individualist ethos of Orlando's entrepreneurial history and the related and contradictory tendency to apply judgment about an individual to the group as a whole (Cruz 2010:253). Distinctions among Latino groups were and often still are a mystery to many non-Latinos. In an oral history interview in 2008, Kennedy Space Center engineer Heriberto Soto, who came in 1990, pointed to the ongoing tendency to lump all Spanish speakers together under a single label: "Just because we're speaking Spanish, we're Mexicans. They assume. Because that's the biggest group before us. . . . Or Cubans when I go down to Miami or whatever. . . . As human beings, they try to put you in the bracket that they know" (PRCF Soto).

Whether as separate nationally identified groups or collectively as Latinos, the struggle in Orlando to shift the invisible-hypervisible dynamic to a visibility created on their own terms has presented a möbius strip of opportunity and danger. James Auffant talked about the challenges:

> So it's kind of difficult for me to explain this, but I think a lot of our youth does not understand that what they have today was done by other people who came into this town and realized, "I cannot screw up. I'm the first Hispanic who's going to work in this company; I'm the first Hispanic attorney who is going to be arguing a case; I'm the first Hispanic doctor in this town," and so on and so on. And the pressure that meant on a lot of us. (PRCF Auffant)

Even before activists were promoting the idea of a pan-ethnic category for political identification in the 1980s, Puerto Rican and Chicano political organizing had begun making a shift from working-class solidarity to a view of racial-ethnic identification as an "essential component of political community" in the 1960s and 1970s (Beltrán 2010:37). Although the majority of Puerto Ricans in US diaspora communities remained working-class, there is evidence in Antonia Pantoja's 2002 memoir of a middle-class turn away from class solidarity and toward organizing along racial-ethnic lines that involved an assertion of *puertorriqueñidad*. After civil rights legislation was extended to language minorities in 1975, the availability of that identification lent weight to reaching beyond Puerto Rican or Chicano to a pan-ethnic identity idea. Writing about *latinismo* in 1980s Chicago, Félix Padilla (1985:1) notes that "the concept of Latino or Hispanic . . . is being drawn more and more to the attention of increasing numbers of people in the United States," and from there he points to a growing awareness of the political strength to be gained by a pan-ethnic identification. As more Orlando Latinos are born and raised in Florida, evidence suggests that new generations will be more likely to identify pan-ethnically.

A counterclaim from Puerto Rican history—that greater sociopolitical power has not translated into better economic conditions for the majority of Puerto Ricans—can extend to Latinos more widely as well (Cruz 1998:49, Meléndez 2003:28, Sánchez 1996:285). Silvio Torres-Saillant (2003:127) has warned not to mistake wider media visibility for greater social power and improved material conditions. It is a tug of war over the relative powers of sociocultural recognition and socioeconomic equity as organizing principles behind solidarity, political strategy, and social justice (Alcoff 2005, 2007; Alcoff et al. 2006; Fraser et al. 2004). In a biting critique, David Harvey (2003:240) refers to recognition as a "fetish mask that hides social relations beneath the ferment of representational politics." On the ground in between is the understanding that exclusionary racial-ethnic practices have underwritten socioeconomic inequality in the first place (Thomas 2010). Raymond Rocco (2014:44) contends that what is now called identity politics would not even exist if there had been no "history of exclusionary practices based on 'identities.'" It seems clear that class conflict is often referenced and played out through other social categories (Gupta et al. 2015).

As the umbrella term has become an available vehicle for legitimizing Latino claims to political and economic resources, identification with this emergent social category has presented Latinos with the tension between opportunity and danger reflected in Torres-Saillant's warnings. Media representations often commodify "Latin culture" and homogenize Latinos as family-oriented, hard-working, and religious consumers (Báez 2018, Dávila 2001). The danger of this portrayal is that it can flatten and depoliticize Latinos in a whitewashed, middle-class image (Dávila 2008). As one Orlando Latino activist told me, "You want our money as consumers, but when it comes to including us, you say we have to assimilate." Turning this idea of the passive citizen-consumer on its head, some Latinos actively combat depoliticization by using media representations and Latino buying power as the grounds for claims to the right to be different and to belong in the United States (Báez 2018).

Another specifically Puerto Rican tension is about the opportunity afforded, by greater numbers and collective identification, against the danger of disappearing into a homogenized Latino politics. Extending the argument that "Republicans don't want us and Democrats take us for granted" to Puerto Ricans in particular, Orlando Puerto Ricans have pointed out to me that they have little to no power in the local two-party system, in which Republicans "have" Cubans and Democrats "have" African Americans. For Orlando Puerto Ricans in the 1980s, was it politically more advantageous to focus on reclaiming and reforming *puertorriqueñidad*, or to risk a new form of erasure by disappearing into the emergent and potentially politically more powerful notion of *latinidad*? One fallout from a collective Latino politics has been that the separate histories of and lessons learned from Puerto Rican and Chicano struggles in the 1960s and 1970s are often overlooked as those two nationally identified groups are merged "into a newly created 'ethnic group' with a new notion of its heritage and identity" (Oboler 1995:83).

The conflict over Puerto Ricans' racial-ethnic identifications in Orlando's political-economic field is evident in the history of the chambers of commerce.[26] James Auffant started a Hispanic committee as part of the mainstream chamber, but in time separate Cuban and Puerto Rican chambers formed (PRCF Auffant). In 1982 these separate Cuban and Puerto Rican chambers merged as the Latin Chamber of Commerce (PRCF J. P. Rivera).[27] For a decade or more, Puerto Ricans alternately merged with Cubans in a single chamber using an umbrella identity idea and broke off again when they felt sidelined. Sometime in the 1990s Manuel Toro started another separate Puerto Rican chamber. In 2019 iterations of both chambers were in operation: the Hispanic Chamber of Commerce of Metro Orlando and the Puerto Rican Chamber of Commerce of Central Florida.

Around the Orlando area today—in addition to organizations specifically identified as Puerto Rican, Cuban, Colombian, Venezuelan, Dominican, and so on—the physical, social, and social media landscape is dotted by organizations with names like Hispanic Achievers, Latino Leadership, and Trabajando Juntos (Working Together), all situating a Puerto Rican presence at the core of a pan-Latino expression. The Hispanic-American Business and Professional Women's Association began in the mid-1990s; it and several other organizations were facilitated by Gladys Casteleiro, the first director of the Orlando office of the Puerto Rican Federal Affairs Administration (PRFAA). In 2000 Lizette Valarino founded the Hispanic Heritage Scholarship Fund, which has helped scores of Latino youth obtain college degrees. When Josephine Mercado was unable to gather health statistics on Latinas in Central Florida for a national report, she addressed this form of invisibility by founding Hispanic Health Initiatives in 2000 (PRPPCE Mercado). The Hispanic Office for Local Assistance (HOLA) began in 2004 as a partnership between the City of Orlando and the Puerto Rican–run organization Latino Leadership. In 2006 it was moved into the city administration, and Puerto Rican Alicia Ramírez ran it until her retirement in 2016. In 2007 Palmira Ubiñas founded the Asociación Internacional de Poetas y Escritores Hispanos (AIPEH). Throughout this history, racial-ethnic identifications, class relations, and place of origin have worked sometimes in conflict and sometimes in concert to stake claims to belonging in the face of ongoing marginalization and dispossession.

Merry-go-round of identity. I borrow the phrase "merry-go-round of identity" from another anthropologist to think about different identity ideas in relation to Puerto Rican and Latino claims to political, economic, and sociocultural ground. In Odile Hoffman's analysis (2002:123), the merry-go-round is about the link between identity and territory. I use this understanding to consider how it might facilitate Orlando Puerto Ricans' and other Latinos' ability to establish visibility on their own terms and stake claims to equitable access to power and resources. Hoffman's research in Colombia centers on a remaking of local socioracial identifications prompted by national-level legislation in 1993 that granted new physical property rights to one racially identified group. As a consequence, a conscious and strategic shift in social identification played out locally under the national-level impetus of new access to territory.

In the Colombian case, the people in question lived in scattered settlements along the Pacific coast and shared an Afro-Caribbean heritage. Although the Colombian state viewed these scattered peoples as black, locally significant identifications had emerged over time that did not necessarily coincide with a single, static idea of blackness as embodied in the national legislation. While blackness was recognized, the concept of a black community was new. In response to the new legislation, a merry-go-round of identities ensued among the coastal inhabitants as the externally imposed definition of what would constitute that community vied with local ideas about belonging that were embedded in collective memories of past associations. Different parties to the question had distinct priorities and aims, but all were embarked on the "same quest for legitimacy" (Hoffman 2002:123–124).

Similar tensions and negotiations are evident in questions about what Hispanic is. Is it Cuban? Mexican? Puerto Rican? What color is Hispanic? Is Hispanic a race or an ethnicity? Are Hispanics taking from welfare rolls or are they a potential new market? The questions apply to efforts by non-Latinos to place Latinos in Orlando's social landscape and by Latinos themselves to figure out how to identify racially and in class terms. Hoffman asks (2002:126), "What is the situation of those . . . who fall outside the categories currently officially recognized and those who do not think of themselves as others might classify them?" Given Florida's dynamics and the tightrope between opportunity and danger that Orlando Latinos regularly experience, one might also wonder what the result could be of pan-Latino identification with the umbrella category. Would non-Latinos draw a racialized line of association to a perceived Latino threat or to the honorary white category enjoyed by so many Florida Cubans? And how might the distinct racial perspectives and experiences among Latinos from different places affect their choices about sociopolitical alliances?

To consider these questions, it is worth noting a trend among Latinos toward increasing white identification in the Orlando area from 1980 to the present that goes against the grain of the national trend. Nationally there has been a steady increase of Latinos identifying as some other race (Dávila 2008:11). Chart 3.1 takes the 2017 numbers about Latino racial

CHART 3.1. Orlando metro-area racial identifications among Latinos, 1980 and 2017

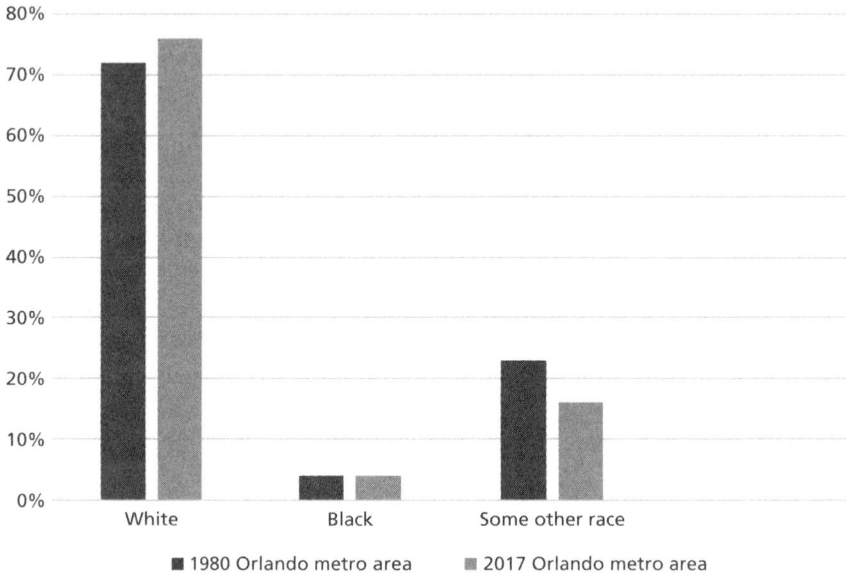

Source: US Census Bureau 1980; US Census Bureau, ACS 2017b

identification from chart 1.1 and sets them against similar data from 1980. In this comparison, Orlando-area Latinos from a range of nationally identified groups were more likely in 2017 to identify as white alone than they were in 1980. While the later data may point to a defensive response to the movement from Latino invisibility to hypervisibility, the 1980 data suggest an awareness among earlier Orlando Puerto Ricans of falling outside the categories currently officially recognized.

In 1984 Orange County Latinos registering to vote still selected white or black on the registration form. By 1988 Orange County had added a Hispanic category to voter registration, but other counties took longer. In Volusia County, John Hernández confronted the supervisor of elections in 1991 to push for Hispanic visibility in voter-registration numbers (PRCF Hernández). Many narrators in the PRCF oral history collection emphasize their families' European descent while still clearly drawing a distinction from Anglos by identifying as either Puerto Rican or more generally as Hispanic. Reina Rubert, a light-skinned, New York–born Puerto Rican who came to Orlando in 1979, said in her oral history that in her Orlando life she has always insisted, "I'm not white, I'm Hispanic" (PRCF Rubert).

Under the supposedly color-blind conditions of multicultural neoliberalism, class talk is another way to reference racial-ethnic identifications. As oral history participants took pains to remove themselves from the idea of being a problem or a threat, they sometimes joined their Hispanic identification to the professional migration discourse:

> Many professionals have moved here. You know, they've awakened a Hispanic consciousness that changes the image that those who come from Puerto Rico simply come here to live off the government and to live off the system. It's a new culture of professionals who come to advance themselves and to bring, to contribute to the society of Central Florida. (PRCF Conville)[28]

Among the oral history participants from New York, there were church pastors, lawyers, engineers, and real estate brokers who also rejected the stereotype of New York Puerto Ricans as a problem and positioned themselves among Orlando's professionals.

If the claim to being part of a professional migration works to overcome racialized ideas about Puerto Ricans and fears of the Latino threat among non-Latino white people, it also glosses over class divisions among not only Puerto Ricans but Latinos more generally. Latino identification as professional members of a whitewashed middle class may mitigate some of the stereotypes and work to change public perception, but it does so at the possible cost of the ability to form a large and inclusive collective identification for a Latino political community. Dávila (2008) observes that although an individual may be white, the group remains not-white in the social order. This presents another möbius strip of opportunity and danger in which gaining status as honorary white in the black-white binary can create what John Comaroff and Jean Comaroff (1992:63) frame as "the contradiction of being a member of a group whose primary class position is different" from that of most Latinos.[29]

Before leaping from that observation to conclusions about racial-ethnic and class politics behind any collective voice that might emerge, it is important to stop and consider the hidden histories at play as Orlando's color-blind multiculturalism intertwines with the area's Latinization and the merry-go-round of identity ideas. The oral histories that frequently refer to Orlando Puerto Ricans as professionals were recorded during the same period that Latino scholars were writing about the growing Latino middle class in the United States (Dávila 2008, Rocco 2010). The question emerges as to what effect the idea of a professional migration has on transformative social justice for Puerto Ricans and Latinos in Orlando. In other words, what is important is not the identity idea itself but how it is used and with what effect on social relations and equitable access to power and resources. Rocco (2010:42) has pointed to a "small but significant professional class" among Latinos that may use its position to bring better recognition of conditions facing Latinos into mainstream institutions and consciousness. On the other hand, Dávila (2008:25–26)—in alignment with the issue about recognition and socioeconomic equity—has expressed alarm about juxtaposing the view of "upwardly mobile" Latinos with a "lack of debate about the social and political consequences of such positive projections." Her concern is that the rise of this middle-class Latino identity idea depoliticizes *latinidad* and removes from the political radar the issues that so many Latinos face around housing, health care, schools, employment, and so on.

In the Colombian case, Hoffman raises another question about the challenges to collective identification for political claims to territory that I again find pertinent to Puerto Ricans in particular and Latinos in general in Orlando. Hoffman asks (2002:120), "With such a fluid and mobile memory as a starting point, scattered into a myriad of juxtaposed space/time elements, how can the unified whole, which has been made necessary by the changing political and social landscape, be constructed?"

The question references challenges to collective identification emergent from living all over the place and coming from the diverse places of origin of Orlando Puerto Ricans and other Latinos. For Puerto Ricans alone, the merry-go-round of identity ideas is a topic replete with claims and contestations as individuals situationally and strategically adopt labels as Puerto Rican, Hispanic, or Latino. For the wider question of Latino political community formation, myriad and juxtaposed racial perspectives and class interests—all the more complicated by national differences—are a clear challenge.

LEARNING TO DEAL WITH WHAT'S HERE

In 2004, on the occasion of the fiftieth anniversary of *Brown v. Board of Education*, the *Orlando Sentinel* ran a nine-part series titled "50 Years of Integration," exploring the legacy of school desegregation in the Orlando area. Most of the articles focus on black-white issues, perspectives, and memories, but one article discusses the growth of the Latino population, zeroing in on Engelwood Elementary in Azalea Park as an example of school resegregation (Pacheco 2004). The article explains that the school opened as an almost entirely white school in 1958. By 2004 it had again become segregated, with Latinos making up 71 percent of students in the school. The article also brings to light Latino contributions to civil rights struggles by reference to a 1940s California case predating the *Brown* decision, in which a Puerto Rican–Mexican couple successfully challenged a public school's denial of entry to their child (McCormick and Ayala 2007).[30]

In keeping with color-blind discourses of the late twentieth and early twenty-first centuries, the writer states that "although the segregation of old was a result of discrimination, today Hispanics are separated by housing patterns, poverty and language" (Pacheco 2004). Thus, even while deflecting a racial-ethnic reason for segregation, the article still projects a homogenized image of Latinos as poor and foreign. While presumably seeking to put Latinos into the historic discussion of Orlando's racial order, the article unfortunately reflects prevailing public discourses that have alternately rendered Orlando Puerto Ricans and Latinos invisible and hypervisible. The former reaffirms the black-white binary of Orlando recorded history. The latter sets Latinos apart, as a one-dimensional, collective black population in a racialized paradigm.

School desegregation was again the topic of another *Orlando Sentinel* series, published during Black History Month in 2008. The first article in the eight-day series celebrates the eight African American families who participated in the 1962 lawsuit that ended legal segregation in Orange County schools (Kunerth 2008a). The article ends by assessing the contemporary situation: Orange County remained one of sixteen Florida school districts that the courts still monitored for signs of segregation. In Central Florida, Orange County stood alone as the only one without federal recognition that "all vestiges of the segregated system have been abolished" (Kunerth 2008a).

The issue surfaced yet again in April 2009 when an *Orlando Sentinel* reporter learned that a slate of school closings in predominantly black areas had been approved by a single white member of the system's ten-member biracial committee (Hobbs 2009a). Further investigation revealed that the biracial committee was created by court order in 1970 to act as a local volunteer body charged with oversight of the 1964 federal mandates regarding school desegregation and that the committee had not been fully functional for at least five years (Hobbs 2009c). As school officials scrambled to reassemble the committee and convince the public that the situation was merely a "technical glitch" (Hobbs 2009b), the question arose about how and whether to include Latinos and others who fall outside the categories currently officially recognized.

Soon a small but vocal Puerto Rican–led protest emerged, spearheaded by an activist group called Frente Unido 436, which had formed on the East Side and taken its name, meaning United Front 436, from the state road number for Semoran Boulevard. Gathering outside the school board offices, protesters demanded representation that more accurately reflected the demographics in the schools (Ramos 2009a). The episode offers an example of a collective Latino embrace of the umbrella term to back the demand of a seat at the table. In their protest, Latinos claimed visibility on their own terms as the parents of about one-third of Orange County's schoolchildren. In Hoffman's terms (2002), they used the idea of a collective identity, in this case Hispanic, to back a local claim to territory.

The *Orlando Sentinel* reported that the Orange County NAACP president expressed understanding of the Latino demand but held the position that Latinos had their own school advisory group and that the issue had "deep historical roots" that did not include them. A school district spokesperson told the *Sentinel* that to join the committee, Latinos would need to choose to be either black or white (Ramos 2009a). Being told in 2009 to choose whiteness or blackness is akin to disappearing into Orlando's black-white public record in earlier decades. Although invisibility was not altogether unwelcome by individual Puerto Ricans managing their lives on the white side of the color line in the Jim Crow era, by the twenty-first century Puerto Ricans and Latinos were experiencing another version of being hidden in plain sight. In the former, invisibility provided a kind of protection; in the latter, invisibility became a form of erasure. In the eyes of local stakeholders, Latinos had no historically legitimate place in Orlando's social field from which to lay claim to territory.

This failed Latino effort to gain ground in Orlando came to be known as "the biracial issue" among Puerto Rican and Latino activists in Orlando and contributed one moment to a locally forming collective memory from which to "legitimize current positions by founding them on a shared experience" (Hoffman 2002:119).[31] In this process, locally situated memories can become vehicles for navigating intragroup differences and intergroup political and economic relations (Jenks 2008:235). As later political battles unfolded during the years of my fieldwork, the biracial issue would come up as a point of comparison about the ways that Latinos and often specifically Puerto Ricans are marginalized in the Orlando area.

Other moments of being denied full membership in Orlando's social field—by having to identify oneself using categories not of one's own making or being told in a job interview that Florida experience is required or being told not to speak the language in which one best knows how to express oneself—have also become a collective experience among Puerto Ricans and Latinos across race and class in Orlando. A seasoned New York Puerto Rican activist, Víctor Alvarado, emphasized the importance of the local as he urged Orlando Puerto Ricans to forget about other places and learn to be in Orlando:

> The Puerto Rican community here is now learning, even the ones from New York and the ones from the island, that they have to live here. Forget about how you did it in New York. Forget about how you did it in Puerto Rico. You live here now. You gotta deal with what's here. And that was a major issue. (PRCF Alvarado)

As they deal with what's here, Puerto Ricans are staking claims to territory in Orlando amid divergent ideas about place and race that they bring with them from across the socioeconomic spectrum. And they do so in concert and sometimes in conflict not only with each other but also with other Orlando Latinos as well as with non-Latino white and black Orlandoans.

But "what's here" can also cut across class and birthplace differences and lump all together into the Latino threat. More recent arrivals who have not lived the history when supposedly there was no one there sometimes criticize those who came before for not having made more progress politically; it is a dynamic similar to that of New York in the 1960s and 1970s (Thomas 2010). Social field vectors from capitalism, colonialism, and white supremacy have exerted pressures in Orlando similar to those elsewhere in the diaspora, and there are parallels between Orlando and the dynamics of an emergent Puerto Rican and Latino political presence in New York City in earlier decades. But twenty-first-century Orlando is also a new time and place in which specifically local histories combine with other national and global histories and inform how Puerto Ricans and other Latinos deal with what's here.

CHAPTER 4

ENOUGH IS ENOUGH

Memory, Political Formations, and Participatory Citizenship

Dear Honorable Congressman,

Please consider my views when you are voting and representing voters. I believe we must close the doors to all foreigners for awhile until we get this economy and the schools back on their feet. As a classroom teacher in Florida for 28 years, I know that foreigners are the largest users of our taxpayers' money. Foreigners are taking all of the jobs that poor and little-educated Americans could have. Many people are being paid under the table, and therefore they are not paying their fair share of taxes. Schools are dealing with too many problems with language differences, and time is lost to our American children who have parents who pay taxes. I'm seeing money going to local charities going to Mexican, Haitian and Mid Eastern immigrants instead of to the poorer people of American descent. Our school at Sadler Elementary where I teach is 92% Puerto Rican. Please consider changing the laws and keeping these people home in Puerto Rico. They are trashing Orlando daily. These P.R. children are holding American children back academically, and Puerto Rican teachers can keep getting extensions on their temporary certificates so that they are allowed to teach without proper training. I can truthfully say that Puerto Rican teachers at my school ask me continually for help with math, as they do not get but the equivalent of a fifth grade education in Puerto Rico. They almost always can do no algebra and rely on the system to get by. I find that Haitian children are more aggressive in the classroom and have not been to school regularly. Their poor conduct is yet another real problem. In Winter Haven, Fl., a large orange grove area with Mexican migrants to do the work, jobs that poor Blacks and poor whites used to take are filled by Mexicans, who I am told bring in drugs and diseases such as incurable TB, for the most part. I know that the solution is difficult, but other countries

> protect their borders and do not allow foreigners to take citizens' jobs. Please do not allow criminals to stay, as they are filling the jails in Fl. It is time to get our troops home! (In Shanklin 2005)

On August 17, 2005, the Orlando edition of the Puerto Rican newspaper *El Nuevo Día* printed a Spanish translation of the above letter that an Orlando schoolteacher sent to members of the Florida congressional delegation (Guzmán 2005). The letter ignited a firestorm in the Orlando media. Arguments about the dangers of racism and bigotry in the classroom were countered with defensive claims about the First Amendment right to free speech. According to one news report, at the Orange County School Board meeting after the letter's publication, applause from "minorities in the audience" alternated with that of "free-speech advocates" depending on whether a speaker talked about racism or constitutional rights (Shanklin 2005). A Puerto Rican reporter for the *Orlando Sentinel*, Victor Ramos (2005c), identified the moment as "the latest flash point to divide Central Florida." Summarizing a flood of "calls, e-mails, letters and online postings," Ramos writes, "Hispanics were horrified at the letter's hurtful words, while non-Hispanic voices rose not only to support the First Amendment right of free speech but also, in many cases, to agree with the letter's divisive contents."[1]

The letter and its impact reflect a long history of talk about national belonging in the United States, with debates around who is deserving of membership that have engaged race, class, gender, sexuality, ethnicity, and religion (Oboler 1995:15). Rather than using an umbrella term for Latinos, the letter specified Mexicans and Puerto Ricans. The historical experience of these two groups includes their respective incorporation into the United States through conquest and colonialism and the subsequent assignment of an "exclusionary inclusion" that has been foundational to the racialization of Latinos more widely (Rocco 2014).[2] Mexicans and Puerto Ricans have been subjects of protracted debates about who is deserving and who is undeserving of US citizenship (De Genova and Ramos-Zayas 2003, Pérez 2015, Ramos-Zayas 2004).

As in the case of the biracial committee for Orange County schools that blocked Latinos from participation, the letter writer uses a black-white-foreign frame for determining membership and belonging. The gap between foreign and American is cemented by the word "citizen" in the letter's final lines, with explicit reference to black and white. Before naming those deemed undeserving of membership—Mexicans, Haitians, Middle Easterners, and Puerto Ricans—the writer uses voting and paying taxes to distinguish between those considered foreign and American. The fact that many individuals among the groups singled out are citizens who pay taxes and vote underscores that the letter writer's definition of citizenship is not only about legal status but also about a substantive measure of belonging.[3]

In the days following the letter's publication, some opinion writers criticized its author for not knowing that Puerto Ricans are US citizens, but the request to change the laws and keep Puerto Ricans from moving to the US states implies knowledge of the particular form of Puerto Rican citizenship (Venator-Santiago 2013, 2015). Because Puerto Rican citizenship was created by an act of Congress, it is something that the US Congress can dismantle (Rocco 2014:80). At the very least, the letter writer takes it as a given that Puerto Ricans hold a more tenuous claim to belonging in the United States than that of black and white "American children."

As the US Congress grappled in 1900 with how to consider the residents of the newly acquired colonial territory of Puerto Rico, the words of Senator Foraker recorded in the Congressional Record assert that the term "citizen" was expressly not intended to give Puerto Ricans "any rights that the American people do not want them to have" (in Cabranes 1978:428). Venator-Santiago (2013:60) argues that US citizenship for Puerto Ricans was designed to incorporate Puerto Rico politically "while simultaneously excluding the island from an equal status within the polity." This form of exclusionary inclusion assigned to Puerto Ricans as colonial citizens serves as a mechanism for circumscribing Puerto Rican participation in US social, political, and economic arenas while simultaneously keeping Puerto Rico and its residents under US control (Rocco 2014:80).

In reporting on the letter, Ramos (2005c) matches the writer's use of essentialized, homogenized identity ideas with equally essentialized but more inclusive terms. He zeroes in on Hispanics as the driving force behind Orlando's changing demographics and points to their economic participation as a "vibrant Hispanic market." Other responses in the print media reference a collective "Hispanic community" and further challenge the letter writer's assumption about the lack of political and economic belonging. In *El Nuevo Día* Sylvia Cáceres uses her political position as director of the regional office of the Puerto Rican Federal Affairs Administration (PRFAA) to demand a public apology, and Jaime Paz y Puente, the Mexican consul, points to Mexicans' economic contributions to the United States (Molina 2005, Osorio 2005).

The publication of the schoolteacher's letter produced a moment of emergent collective identification for a political response to Latino marginalization in Orlando. Evidence shows that practices of exclusion and dispossession by the ruling group give rise to collective identification for political mobilization among the dispossessed.[4] Although differential incorporation of Mexicans, Puerto Ricans, and other Latinos according to national origin can feed conflict among them, the common experience of racialization can also foster a sense of commonality (De Genova and Ramos-Zayas 2003). Chicanos as Chicanos, Puerto Ricans as Puerto Ricans, and more recently a mix of differently identified national origins as Latinos/as or Hispanics or Latinx have claimed membership in US society through their fights for bilingual education and ballots and against police brutality and discrimination in housing, health care, and employment. These are moments "when diverse and even disparate subjects claim identification with one another" (Beltrán 2010:168).

The schoolteacher's letter, the biracial issue, and other such happenings begin to build a collective memory of place-specific experiences lived as Puerto Ricans or as Latinos in Orlando. They begin to build the Orlando chapter of a longer history of Puerto Rican and Latino politics in the United States. In the move from invisibility to hypervisibility, Puerto Rican and Latino responses to exclusion from full participation in Orlando's social, political, and economic relations have been informed by prior histories in other places and by the particulars of Orlando's social field. For Puerto Ricans, individual and collective responses draw on their long history as colonial citizens, which references colonialism in Puerto Rico and the exclusionary inclusion of colonial migrants in the United States. It is a history of struggle that combines rather than separates "citizenship rights, economic justice, antidiscrimination, and anti-imperialism" as fundamental to full citizenship (Thomas 2010:252). Situated into earlier histories of what may now be called Latino politics, Puerto Rican politics highlights the entanglement of formal, legally defined citizenship with a kind of exclusionary inclusion embedded in the historical construction of what constitutes membership in the United States.

In this chapter, I examine how Orlando Puerto Ricans have struggled to move beyond invisibility and hypervisibility by establishing a visibility on their own terms. It is their demand for the right to be different and to belong. The de facto exclusion that marks Puerto Rican citizenship extends to Latinos more generally as perpetually foreign to the "public self image of the 'American people'" (Oboler 1995:32).

Orlando Puerto Ricans use their birthright citizenship to back their claims to belonging and to extend them to Latinos more widely. In the process, many bring their memories from other times and places to bear on the conditions encountered in Orlando's supposedly color-blind and multicultural meritocracy. And these join with a growing, locally specific collective memory of the exclusionary inclusion they have experienced in Orlando. The distinct political styles that have emerged—from quiet, behind-the-scenes negotiations to a loud street politics of presence and protest—mark the early formations of Puerto Rican and Latino politics in Orlando.

DIASPORA POLITICS AND PUERTO RICAN REMEMBERING

As we were winding up an oral history interview in November 2012, Zoraida Ríos-Andino said she wanted to show me some T-shirts she had saved from her political work in East Chicago, Indiana, and then Orlando over the years. One by one, she held them up and explained their importance, connecting each T-shirt to significant events and organizations in those Puerto Rican places. First was the National Conference of Puerto Rican Women in East Chicago and the Orlando chapter she started soon after her arrival in 2000. The collection also commemorated the first Puerto Rican mayor of East Chicago and campaigns in Indiana and Orlando for non-Latino candidates who had proven to be solid allies. There was a telethon from Indiana for Puerto Rico after Hurricane Georges in 1998 and a newly formed Orlando group adding their efforts to the campaign to release Puerto Rican political prisoner Oscar López Rivera. There was the Orlando piece of a national voter-registration campaign of 2002–2004 dubbed Que Nada Nos Detenga (Let Nothing Hold Us Back). Local to Orlando, there was the Casa de Puerto Rico, the Asociación Borinqueña, and Frente Unido 436.

Along with other oral histories I have conducted or consulted, the 2012 collection Puerto Rican Political Participation and Civic Engagement in Central Florida (PRPPCE) helps stitch together separate memories that Orlando Puerto Ricans draw on to frame individual understandings about what it means to be political in response to colonial controls and exclusionary inclusion. Cristina Beltrán (2010:96) has argued that memories of "emotive encounters" sustain "political actors through the tedious, frustrating, and disillusioning aspects of political involvement." And, yes, Ríos-Andino's narrative includes stories about tedium and frustration. But throughout this final portion of the recording, she smiled as she remembered successes long past as well as others from the weeks immediately preceding our interview. She continued smiling as she ended the show-and-tell by looking toward future achievements.

As Ríos-Andino's narrative makes clear, memories are embedded in relationships and places (Epele 2010:28). Remembering and forgetting shape historical narratives, and they become what the anthropologist Carole McGranahan (2010:19) has called "social practices with a politics," which is as much about the future as about the past or present. The following are excerpts from oral histories by Orlando Puerto Ricans Anthony Suárez, Betsy Franceschini, Ana González, and James Auffant. As they remembered key moments from their pasts, their individual memories linked to a continuum of Puerto Rican experience in multiple places.

> *New York, 1950s*: I have a picture . . . of me in the first Puerto Rican Day parade. I was three years old, and I was in my softball uniform. Because that was how it was. The parade was put together with all these teams, you know, the social teams and the [hometown] clubs, the social clubs. (100PR_OHP Anthony Suárez #3)[5]

> *Chicago, 1960s*: I remember that my father, one day we went looking for an apartment and when they saw we were Puerto Rican, they shut the door in our faces. You know. That we had some previous experience. (PRCF Franceschini)[6]

> *Puerto Rico, 1970s*: Someone from—I don't remember whether it was from the CIA or the FBI—appeared at my house . . . and he said to me, "I need you to give me information about your boss." . . . And I refused. . . . And I paid for it because they followed me for a year. . . . They were making a *carpeta roja* on me because I was an associate to my boss. (PRPPCE A. González)[7]

> *Orlando, 1970s*: One of the things I learned quick is that Cubans and Puerto Ricans think that they're US citizens and that most people who are Anglo Saxon make that distinction. They don't. You speak Spanish, you're a spic. . . . That was my experience. Coming to a town that was not receptive to us. Not at all. (PRCF Auffant)

These and other memories I have heard from Orlando Puerto Ricans bring Puerto Rican political history into the fabric of Latino political mobilization in contemporary Orlando. Individual memories of collective histories lived in different times and places converge and conflict as they inform how someone chooses to act in response to discrimination and marginalization in Orlando. They indicate that although Orlando is a new site for Puerto Rican and Latino politics, many of the actors there are not new to the struggle. Whether or not directly involved in other places, Orlando Puerto Ricans from island and diaspora have indicated to me, "I've seen this before."

This remembering adds personal details to broad-strokes accounts of Puerto Rican histories. Ana González talked about her participation in a protest in Puerto Rico to keep a mental health center open. And in doing so, she referenced the 1978 execution of two young *independentistas* in a sting operation in a mountain area of Puerto Rico called Cerro Maravilla: "It was just a few years after the thing at Maravilla had happened, so things were really heated. And anyone who got engaged in a thing like that was targeted. They opened a file on you" (PRPPCE A. González).[8]

Other memories give life to the New York Puerto Rican story. Evelyn Rivera worked first at the Puerto Rican Forum and later for the City University of New York: "And there I was involved in the movement . . . to establish Hostos College and Boricua College. And we worked very hard to establish the Puerto Rican Studies Program. And it was very, it was a hard fight, but we did it" (100PR_OHP Evelyn Rivera #9).

As New York's reputation for the so-called Puerto Rican problem prompted efforts to redirect Puerto Rican migrants to the Midwest, Chicago became another Puerto Rican diaspora space.[9] From her childhood there, Betsy Franceschini remembered the deep and lasting impression that the 1966 Chicago uprising made on her contemporary social practices with a politics. She remembered a ride with her father through Humboldt Park, the heart of Chicago's Puerto Rican barrio, where the uprising had begun:

> My father would sit my brother and me down . . . and he talked about the importance of being proud of our roots. And he took us to where there had been some riots for racial issues. It was the time when Martin Luther King's movement, there was a lot of discrimination. . . . He talked to us a lot about the importance of the struggle for people's rights because there was a lot of abuse. (PRPPCE Franceschini)[10]

During those years in Chicago and elsewhere, arson fires in low-income areas populated by Latinos and African Americans were how landlords succeeded in simultaneously removing unwanted tenants and making money from property damage. Anthony Suárez remembered when the Bronx was burning: "I lived in a purely Puerto Rican community. I lived in the South Bronx, Hunts Point area of the Bronx. . . . That's when the Bronx was burning down. It's got to be the worst history of the Bronx was when I was there as a young man" (100PR_OHP Anthony Suárez #2).

Along with place-specific struggles, the T-shirt that Ríos-Andino had from the Orlando chapter of the effort to free Oscar López Rivera points to translocal Puerto Rican struggles. During the 1970s López Rivera joined Puerto Rican militants who organized bombings of federal buildings and multinational corporations, and by the early 1980s he and other Chicago *independentistas* were in federal prison. All but López Rivera left prison in the 1990s. During my fieldwork in Orlando the group pushing to "free Oscar" was making the issue visible at local events and on the internet.[11]

Other evidence of translocal Puerto Rican remembering is apparent in Orlando's physical landscape. Café d'Antaño over the years has closed and opened again in different spaces. The little house that was home to Café d'Antaño when I first arrived in Orlando was full of artwork referencing a collective memory of rural Puerto Rico. A colorfully painted building out back evoked the practices in New York and other places where Puerto Ricans took over empty lots and turned them into urban gardens. The lots were marked by *casitas*, reminiscent of rural housing in Puerto Rico. Decorated with Puerto Rican flags, these reclaimed spaces became centers of cultural activity and political organizing.[12] In Orlando the flags that decorated the *casita* were from other Latin American countries as well.

Broken memory in Orlando. Despite the balanced mix of island and diaspora experience among Orlando Puerto Ricans, direct island affiliation carries serious weight. Drawing the contrast, Anthony Suárez said, "In New York, you're Puerto Rican because you say it" (100PR_OHP Anthony Suárez #5). His Orlando life story includes an embarrassing moment when he called the Bronx his hometown and the roomful of people burst out laughing (Padilla 1998). Although reportedly hundreds came over the years to Suárez's Nuyorican Night, the impact of Puerto Rican broken memory is still apparent in the disdain for what many see as New York–style brashness. The protest in Brooksville that first drew me into this project serves as a case. The island-born man who criticized the protesters on the radio used Puerto Rican citizenship to assert belonging at the same time that he diminished New York political experience and infantilized Nuyoricans: "We have to mature. We're citizens. We're part of this country. . . . Many of the organizers of that protest are Nuyoricans . . . that means that they come with the New York attitude of marching and protesting and unions and this and that."[13]

Like other diaspora-based Puerto Ricans before them, Orlando Puerto Ricans with diaspora political experience claim to be more knowledgeable about how to push back. Víctor Alvarado put it this way:

> The New Yorker feels, or has felt, the discrimination because they've been exposed to it a lot more. Whereas in Puerto Rico you're not exposed to it that much. . . . The problem is that New Yorkers, we develop a, an attitude, a thick skin, . . . whereas the ones from the island do not have that, that protective coating. All right? Because you've had to fight. (PRCF Alvarado)

In an *Orlando Sentinel* article, Puerto Rican journalist María Padilla (1998)—who has herself lived on the island and in diaspora—explores these differences: "To say that stateside Puerto Ricans are more worldly implies that islanders are hicks or jibaros, a stereotype about islanders that many flatly reject." She quotes a pushback from Magín López to the claim that New Yorkers are tougher: "Islanders know how to climb a mountain. We know how to walk through difficulties. Everything is not as easy as it is in the states. The person here cannot visualize life in Puerto Rico." The many examples of islander ingenuity and perseverance in the wake of Hurricanes Irma and Maria give added weight to this argument. Still others assert that being *independentista* in Puerto Rico also requires a thick skin.

These Orlando Puerto Ricans with their direct memories of Puerto Rican and diaspora histories were in their mid-forties and older during my fieldwork. Some of the next generation nostalgically remember their parents' stories of resistance and struggle, but younger Orlando Puerto Ricans and Latinos, especially the growing number of those born in Central Florida, have had a different experience. The decades that saw the rise and disruption of Puerto Rican organizing on the island and in the diaspora are also those during which Walt Disney selected Central Florida for his new park, the southern strategy emerged as a core component of the US political field, and the stepping-stones leading to a color-blind multiculturalism privileging individual merit took hold in Florida and elsewhere.

With the rise of the umbrella identifier, the critical edge of Chicano and Puerto Rican resistance to US imperialism became blunted (Beltrán 2010, Mora 2014). Simultaneously, as the market came to be seen as the solution to social problems in the neoliberal era, decreased availability of government and private foundation moneys was met by corporate sponsorships (Dávila 2008:28). The accompanying emphasis on corporatization and professionalization pressured activist organizations away from participatory mobilizations and toward "electoral politics and questions of representation" (Beltrán 2010:99). In brief, corporatization prioritizes the necessary chase after money and often diverts a project's energies away from those it is intended to serve. In a veiled reference to how the corporatization of social-justice work undermines grassroots activism, Orlando activist Nancy Rosado told me during an oral history interview, "There's always these secondary gains issues that never really serve the community, that just don't let the full service arrive at the community" (Rosado 2018).

Furthermore, for younger Orlando Puerto Ricans the pace of a twenty-first-century work life, demands of a young family, geographic sprawl, and time spent in cars have combined with a cynicism toward the political that is endemic to the neoliberal era, producing a significant challenge to sustained collective political activity. Remembering her father's union activities, Francheschini stressed the importance of the collective and said that the younger generation does not understand that what they have was gained through hard-fought campaigns for social justice; she knows urgently that the rights now taken for granted can be lost (PRPPCE Franceschini).

An Azalea Park family with members from Puerto Rico and New York talked to me about how personalization and individualism work to disrupt a sense of the collective.[14] Despite their combined memories of and family lore about political activism in Puerto Rico and New York, there was agreement around this description from a twenty-seven-year-old family member about Latino political involvement in Orlando: "Their priority here is work, increase their standard of living. I think politics isn't on the agenda for them. They don't see that as a way of improving their life. . . . I think it's more of that individualism when you come here. You're going to get yours; you're going to do everything on your own."

So it is that remembering and forgetting of other times and places along with an emergent local collective memory intersect with Orlando's historically market-based ethos and supposedly color-blind multiculturalism to form different social practices with a politics. And all of this affects what a Latino politics, which works to resist colonial-style efforts to control the degree and level of Puerto Rican and Latino participation, might look like.

MAKING VISIBILITY IN THE 1990S

The 1990 Census informed Orlandoans that the Latino population, led by explosive growth of the Puerto Rican population, had more than tripled in the 1980s, and soon it would be clear that the Orlando Hispanic market was growing faster than anywhere else in the United States (Stutzman 1994). With the growing population came more discrimination and outright abuses from longtime Orlandoans who did not welcome the change. Stories from the 1990s tell of profiling by police and uphill struggles to bring bilingual teachers into the schools and Hispanic officers into the police department. To smooth transitions for the growing Central Florida Puerto Rican population, a regional PRFAA office opened in Orlando city hall in the mid-1990s. People often point to the 1990s as the decade when the "Puertoricanization" of Orlando began. Much history preceded the 1990s, but that decade marks the time when Puerto Ricans began organizing for collective political actions to craft a certain visibility on their own terms and from there to push against exclusionary inclusion and assert their rights to full citizenship.

In November 1996, two Orlando-area events were especially important to an emergent awareness of the potential political power of Puerto Ricans and by extension Latinos in Central Florida. In each of these events, Puerto Ricans made themselves visible as they took to the streets and the airwaves to mobilize area Latinos and stake claims to territory. Both events drew on Puerto Rican memories of political actions in other places to engage participation in Orlando. Together they claimed legal and substantive belonging, building from a reactive sense of *puertorriqueñidad* and *latinidad* to promote a collective racial-ethnic identification apart from white and black from which to underwrite a new power awareness.[15]

One of these events figured among the firsts in the string of Puerto Rican electoral wins that followed the Deltona election of Joe Pérez in 1995. This was Robert Guevara's election as the first Hispanic commissioner in Osceola County, in November 1996. The campaign and electoral victory were the direct consequence of Osceola's switch to single-member districts, and they pointed to the growing electoral power of Latino voters (Bonner 1996, Montanez 1996). In an oral history recorded almost twenty years later, Zulma Vélez Estrada remembered how the Guevara campaign worked to evoke island-based political traditions to engage Puerto Rican voters:

> We did what no one had done. We did politics Puerto Rican–style. We did the first political *caravanas* in Osceola County, we did it in this political campaign. It was extraordinary. We went with convertibles. We went with music. . . . Inviting people to vote. . . . We did voter registrations like you can't imagine. (100PR_OHP Zulma Vélez Estrada #13)[16]

Vélez Estrada also said the campaign used radio for an educational program about political processes and structures in Florida and Osceola County. That too was part of making a Latino visibility in Orlando. Visibility, writes the anthropologist Donald Carter (2010:15), "implies a claim to a kind of truth; it is not a matter of what is seen as much as what it means to be seen or unseen." In the Guevara campaign, Latino visibility was an assertion of their presence and potential power in Central Florida.

During my fieldwork Puerto Rico's political tradition of the *caravana* became institutionalized. In a *caravana*, a long line of cars makes its way through the streets with people waving Puerto Rican flags and honking horns and inviting others to join in. It is a noisy affair, and people come out of their houses to watch. Some laugh and wave back, shouting the recognizable Puerto Rican "Wepa!" Like the reactions to Rafael's cutting the line to vote in 2012, the non-Latino reactions to *caravanas* in Orlando are mixed. Some observers look perplexed, some annoyed, some entertained.

The March for Dignity. The second event was a collective mobilization in Orlando called the March for Dignity. In October 1996, articles in the *Orlando Sentinel* had been detailing a drug pipeline from Colombia through Puerto Rico to Orlando. Other reporting was about Puerto Rican drug dealers being dumped in Orlando as part of the witness protection program.[17] Despite the *Sentinel*'s occasional references to Orlando Puerto Ricans' professional respectability, the combined impact of the reporting was to fuel an already-present anti-Latino sentiment (Feigenbaum 1996, Marquez 1996a).[18] For Orlando Puerto Ricans this was a breaking point.

In the middle of this, Rico Piccard was tinkering in his garage one day and listening to *Quédate con Miguel* (Stay with Miguel) on the radio. The topic was the destructive impact of the articles. In a 2012 oral history, Piccard described his response this way:

> So I started to circle around to see what Mr. Miguel Angel Negrón, may he rest in peace, a radio announcer whom we listened to carefully, I listened to him, and he would bring consciousness to the people. So then he called his friend Tony Suárez . . . and as soon as they said "Let's go out to protest," it was like something in me came back again to get into politics and demonstrations and things that were to defend the Puerto Rican people. (PRPPCE Piccard)[19]

The call to protest triggered Piccard's memories of struggle from a poor San Juan neighborhood; from New York during the time of Badillo, Vélez, and Gerena Valentín; and from Vietnam. "I consider myself a fighting man because since I was very young I've had to struggle for everything I have," he said (PRPPCE Piccard).[20] Piccard was the founder of Frente Unido 436. He will be remembered for the call to action "¡Arriba los de abajo!" with which he often closed his "people's column" in the *Nuevo Día* and which was printed on the T-shirt he wore to protests.[21]

Tony Suárez also brought memories to Orlando from New York. Along with remembering the Bronx burning down, his political remembering included "the tail end of the movement with Hermán Badillo and Ramón Vélez" and the "early stages of Bob García" (100PR_OHP Anthony Suárez #12). Remembering his own political path, in which he pushed against both the Democratic and Republican Parties, Suárez said in a 2012 oral history, "Somebody has got to teach these people that's not how this game is going to be played in Central Florida" (PRPPCE Suárez). He pointed to how his New York experience influenced his response to the *Orlando Sentinel* articles:

> I saw the whole thing all over again. . . . Oh, my God! This is what's going to happen. The banks will start writing off and redlining the districts where Puerto Ricans are. . . . When the insurance companies redlined the South Bronx, what would landlords do? They couldn't replace a boiler because a boiler is $40,000. You can't get the insurance to cover it. Phsst! Just burn the building down and take the insurance and go home. . . . And when I saw it happening here, all of a sudden the newspapers saying, "Puerto Ricans this and Puerto Ricans that." And the next step, . . . you can't buy a house in that location because we're not going to insure it. . . . I was able to see the exact connection between those negative headlines and what would happen eventually to our neighborhoods if this went unchallenged. (100PR_OHP Anthony Suárez #12)

On November 3, 1996, Piccard and thousands of others joined Suárez and Negrón in the first-ever Latino mobilization in the streets of Orlando. Leadership in the Asociación Borinqueña mobilized the membership and marched with the rallying cry, "¡Basta ya! We are here to stay!" The event marked a turning point and was a frequent topic in the 2012 PRPPCE oral history collection. Alicia and Samuel Ramírez were among those who talked about it:

> **ALICIA:** That was the first time that we realized our strength. . . . It was, I believe, in my opinion, like the beginning of a mass movement. Where the Puerto Ricans realized for the first time, what is strength when we all come out and unite with the same effort.
>
> **SAMUEL:** And people began to take notice of a vibrant, powerful, minority—and especially organized by Puerto Ricans. (PRPPCE Ramírez)

They asserted that respect for the community began with this march. "It was a culminating moment," said Alicia, "when . . . we said, 'basta, ya.'" I have translated their words from the Spanish, but as Alicia went on naming Puerto Rican institutions such as the Asociación Borinqueña, Spanish-language radio, and PRFAA, she switched to English and said, "We're here to work. We're part of the community. We're not going anywhere."

The March for Dignity organizers made a conscious appeal beyond Puerto Ricans for wider Latino participation. Orlando Colombians, implicated as drug traffickers in the news, were a natural ally. Mary Johnson, who by then was serving as Orange County commissioner for District 3, observed, "It's not only Puerto Ricans who are affected. It's all Hispanics, and we all need to work together" (in Jackson 1996). Manuel Toro lent *La Prensa*'s collection of Latin American flags to the effort. Dora Toro recalled, "We marched with all the flags of all the countries in an act of solidarity" (100PR_OHP Dora Casanova de Toro #33).[22] In a flashback to when activists put a Puerto Rican flag across the brow of the Statue of Liberty in the 1970s—now with reference to Latinos more broadly—the march route circled an Orlando replica of the Statue of Liberty. "Immigrants helped build this country. And we are helping build this community" is how Suárez explained this symbolic gesture of belonging and refusal of foreignness (in Jackson 1996).

The march was a clear claim to Puerto Rican and by extension Latino belonging and specifically to belonging in Orlando. For many with no prior diaspora history, the experience of being maligned and marginalized in this place was shockingly new. For those who had lived as a racialized minority in other US places, this was something they had seen before and were now experiencing all over again in this new time and place. The March for Dignity thus inserted itself into Puerto Rican and Latino political history in the US states and made a visible statement to Orlandoans that Latinos deserved and demanded respect. If Noche de San Juan in 1980 showed Orlando that Puerto Ricans were a sizable consumer group, the March for Dignity—followed two days later by Guevara's electoral victory—demonstrated their potential political power: "People started seeing, 'wow! we can put this many people in the street?' Attention started coming to the Puerto Rican community in 1996" (PRPPCE Suárez).

Where uprisings marked the limits of forbearance in the inner cities of the 1960s, in the color-blind multiculturalism of 1990s Orlando it was this March for Dignity. Although remembered today as a protest march, the public expressions about the march at the time in the news coverage and by the march promoters themselves used depoliticized language to describe a march for unity in the fight against drugs.[23] In the debates among political activists between the goals of recognition and socioeconomic equity, the March for Dignity, which made no demands about better housing, jobs, or education, weighs in on the side of recognition. As its name implies, however, it was a demand for a kind of recognition "that promises not just formal equality within the state but also the 'respect' and 'dignity' that come from real equality" (Thomas 2010:250).

The march was a demand for substantive citizenship, grounded in the understanding that racial-ethnic and class-based politics are not mutually exclusive but rather two interwoven logics (Harvey 2003:183). Indeed, Suárez saw the connection between misrecognition of Puerto Ricans and a process of discrimination leading to the inability to find safe and sure housing.[24] The march was a participatory political action that through the energetic and collective presence in the streets of Orlando was "not merely a tactical maneuver . . . but an all-out assault on marginality" of all kinds (Carter 2010:23). It was an expression of "festive anger" in which protesters show themselves to be peaceful participants in the social field while at the same time engaging in a disruptive display of defiance (Beltrán 2010:143–144).

Beyond momentary visibility. The Guevara election and the March for Dignity were moments in which a collective identification emerged not as a "*thing* that social groups possess" but as "an activity in which subjects engage" (Beltrán 2010:164). These events asked for and received Latino participation, and they marked the beginnings of a collective memory about the turning point for locally grounded Latino political consciousness. Even Puerto Ricans who have come to Orlando decades after these moments of visibility know of them because they are told and retold in Orlando by those who lived them. During the 2011 redistricting process fifteen years after the March for Dignity, a Puerto Rican man who was among those giving testimony at the public hearings in support of a majority Latino voting district recalled the march: "We had a big march, and I remember Manuel Toro at that time was alive, from *La Prensa*. We marched that time. We marched from the Statue of Liberty all the way down to the *Sentinel* and said, 'Enough is enough'" (RAC May 25, 2011).[25]

These moments punctuated the emergence in the Orlando landscape of more enduring and recurring markers of Puerto Rican and Latino presence, which drew from other places to make a local *puertorriqueñidad* and *latinidad*. At the time of the 1996 March for Dignity, the Puerto Rican parade in Orlando was already in its sixth year. In New York the parade has long been an important vehicle for advancing Puerto Rican interests, social and political (Meléndez 2003:32, Sánchez 1994). The first Orlando parade took place in 1990, organized by Puerto Rico–born Laura Mullenhoff (Jiménez 1990, Patrizio 1990). "We all went," a woman from Chicago told me. Within a couple of years and for twenty years after that, the parade came under the direction of Mildred Zapata, who brought her New York parade experience to Orlando. Along with translocal participation from politicians and youth from Puerto Rican towns and representatives from other parades around the diaspora as well as the ever-present Goya and MacDonald's floats, the

Orlando parade is grounded in the local community. During my fieldwork, the Asociación Borinqueña and the Casa de Puerto Rico were regular parade participants, as were churches, cheerleaders and marching bands from local high schools, and local elected officials. The annual participation by Bolivian and Mexican groups also gave witness to a wider Latino community.

Three Kings Day on January 6 marks another important Puerto Rican–inspired, pan-Latino, and very visible moment of the year in Orlando. Christian teaching says that January 6 is the day the three kings arrived bearing gifts for the baby Jesus. Traditionally, Latin American children put grass and water by their beds the night before so that the camels can eat and the kings will leave a present. Because it is not a holiday recognized in the United States, when the date falls during the week adjustments need to be made. Individual families may hold onto the actual day, but community celebrations come on the weekend. Oral history narratives locate the first Three Kings celebration in the mid-1990s at the Sociedad Cubana (PRCF Auffant). María Padilla (2000a) notes increasing observation of Three Kings Day and describes an outdoor event in 2000 at Downey Park, which is located in the middle of the East Side along Colonial Drive at Dean Road.

In a reverse strategy for inclusion, non-Latino politicians have increasingly weighed in on what it means to be seen, making themselves hypervisible at these and other events in order to argue for their own belonging as political representatives for Puerto Ricans and Latinos. By 2012 if not before, non-Latino candidates were joining the *caravanas*. In an oral history right after the 2012 elections, Democratic activist Vivian Rodríguez, who had led the Hispanic outreach effort for a non-Latino candidate, talked about the importance of Latino cultural events for visibility. At my mention of the *caravanas*, her eyes lit up as she remembered the overwhelming reception they received as they went through Hispanic neighborhoods: "They were waiting and laughing and jumping, and with their flags waving" (PRPPCE V. Rodríguez).

Another annual event marking Puerto Rican visibility and connecting directly with elected officials is the homegrown Puerto Rico Day observed every year in Tallahassee. Chartered buses leave Orlando and other parts of Florida at the crack of dawn and head to the Florida capitol building. It is a full day of meeting with Florida legislators amid the sounds of Puerto Rican music and the smells of Puerto Rican food.

Radio programs are another assertion—this one daily—of Puerto Rican and Latino presence in Florida. Spanish-language and sometimes bilingual radio fills the time that people spend driving the Central Florida highways.[26]

Radio hosts and callers speak with each other in a manner that suggests long acquaintance. Even I recognize certain voices as people call in, and at times I have felt I was listening in on a private conversation. Ana González explained:

> I listen to the radio a lot because my work is in part to travel from one place to another. So, I take advantage. . . . I put it on when I go from one house to another, from one office to another, from one school to another. I put on my Spanish station and listen to the political programs on the radio. (PRPPCE A. González)[27]

To the best of my knowledge, the longest-standing of these programs is *Quédate con Miguel*, the broadcast that Piccard credited with reawakening his political sensibilities in 1996. The program that Miguel Angel Negrón began in 1991 continued beyond his death in 2006, with his son Fernando as host. Hispanic radio in Central Florida exploded in the 1990s. Programs hosted by Maritza Beltrán, Sandra Carrasquillo, Lucymar Rivera, Magda Yvette Torres, and others have provided venues that inform people about community events and create a space for public political discussions across the Orlando area. Still others like *Voces y Guitarras* with Mike Rivera and Sammy Ramírez and *Domingo Internacional* with Juan and Millie Díaz have provided cultural programming that promotes a collective sense of *puertorriqueñidad* and *latinidad*.

In this age of internet and social media, non-Latinos holding the purse strings to campaign funding have not always paid attention to radio's importance in motivating Orlando-area Latinos to vote, and this has been a matter of some frustration to those working hard to increase Latino political participation in the face of all the obstacles. But as I experienced in my car on election night 2012, stations with different political leanings all call on Latinos to go out and vote. The radio programming that Vélez Estrada employed during the Guevara campaign is now part of a well-established practice. James Auffant remembered as far back as 1992 using Spanish radio in his work for the Clinton campaign in Central Florida. According to Auffant, there were only four stations, all on AM frequency. He recalled, "Back then, I could buy for $75 an hour and have every afternoon from 5 to 6—driving time—we had what we called *La Hora Democrática* and we just bombarded our community" (PRCF Auffant). Sixteen years later, while talking about the 2008 Obama campaign, Zulma Vélez Estrada again mentioned daily use of the radio, adding, "because Puerto Ricans listen a lot to the radio" (100PR_OHP Vélez Estrada #22).[28]

DUST AND DIPLOMACY IN ORLANDO LATINO POLITICS

In March 2011 a visiting delegation from the National Congress for Puerto Rican Rights (NCPRR) held a meeting at Ana G. Mendez University on Semoran for the purpose of urging Orlando Puerto Ricans to start a local chapter. The NCPRR was founded in New York by a former Young Lord with the mission of ending discrimination and advancing human and civil rights for Puerto Ricans (Torres 1998:19). Like many of the organizations I have seen come and go in Orlando, this one is no longer active, but my field notes from the meetings I attended point to distinctions among the different social practices with a politics at play in Puerto Rican Orlando.

Although later meetings attracted a wider representation, the dominance of diaspora experience among those attending the first one was noticeable. Attendees had lived in at least Philadelphia, New York, Indiana, Miami, Chicago, Hartford, and with the US military around the world. There were some who had lived for years in Puerto Rico, but none to my knowledge had come directly to Orlando from a life lived entirely in Puerto Rico. Also present were a few non–Puerto Rican Orlando Latinos. The conversation included a reference to being supportive of Hispanic "brothers and sisters" without letting immigration questions sidetrack work on issues like jobs, education, and political empowerment.

A rumor was circulating that an island-born Orlando Rican had been telling people not to go. Expressing a caution I had often heard, some who did not attend at first told me they were watching to see what came of it. There were concerns that it tipped too far toward protest politics and in-the-street assertions of collective rights. The *Sentinel* columnist Myriam Marquez (2001) offers an explanation for this sort of hesitance when she writes that many Hispanic business and civic leaders do not speak up publicly because "they don't want to be stereotyped as those 'loud Latinos.'" Despite tensions, however, there is a certain respect for those willing to be loud. At the second NCPRR meeting I attended, one of the quieter and more circumspect attendees pointed to the "tough people" who speak out and acknowledged that "people are listening" to the issues being raised.[29] As one of those tough people put it, "We kick up the dust and they come behind us with the diplomacy." This dust-and-diplomacy frame is also evident in other Puerto Rican histories, as when Badillo's appeal to New Yorkers increased in comparison to the Young Lords' radical politics (Sánchez 2007:131).

Quieter yet persistent individual efforts to deal with what's here are illustrated in the choices made by Nydia, Sarah, and Linda. They represent those Marquez said were trying to avoid identification as loud Latinos. Yet I saw repeatedly that each holds fiercely to her identification as Puerto Rican and her keen awareness of the tactics that keep Puerto Ricans and other Latinos in a condition of exclusionary inclusion in Orlando.

Nydia came to Orlando from Puerto Rico in the 1980s. Her earliest years were spent as a military child, but the family soon returned to Puerto Rico to stay. Nydia is a Republican. She said she is not a typical Republican and that many of her friends are Democrats. She said she votes for the person, not the party. In reference to the loud ones, she said, "My heart is with them." But for Nydia, a political act is going to places where Puerto Ricans do not usually go and taking the opportunity to confront and disrupt stereotypes when people tell her, "You're not like the others."

Although I have spent a good deal of interview time with Sarah, I do not know what if any political affiliation she has. Others have assumed out loud to me that she is a Republican; one person said Sarah is a Democrat. By all accounts, she is known as a socially engaged, professional Puerto Rican who is dedicated to serving Orlando's Hispanics. She tells the dust kickers not to back down, and she lends them her support in ways unseen by others. To me she identified Puerto Rican and Latino marginalization in Orlando with a whisper: "Some people just don't like us very much."

Linda's pre-Orlando experiences include living in multiple locations during her childhood in a military family, but she spent her adult life before coming to Orlando in Puerto Rico. Her children were born there. In Orlando she walks softly. Perfectly bilingual, she moves easily among different worlds. She now has no party affiliation, but for more than a decade she was a registered Republican, and some people assume she still is. She attributes her choice to register as a Republican less to the platform and more to getting by in Orlando. Quietly she said she questions the merits of the capitalist system and that others share her perspective as long as the conversations remain private and behind closed doors. No names were mentioned, but I know her circle to include many who work within the system, pushing persistently for social justice and Puerto Rican visibility.

During my fieldwork I have been told in confidence about collective, behind-the-scenes efforts to meet with non-Latino power holders and pry open targeted spaces for greater Puerto Rican and Latino access and participation. Loud confrontation, individual acts of resistance, and quiet collective lobbying are all part of Puerto Rican and Latino politics in Orlando. Each of these strategies represents efforts to reject both invisibility and hypervisibility and to create visibility as full and equal participants in Orlando's social field. Despite differences in political styles, there is nonetheless a common understanding that Puerto Rican and Latino claims to belonging in Orlando are constantly contested and that an exclusionary inclusion is offered at best.

An anecdote from one NCPRR meeting offers support to the argument that Puerto Rican citizenship is about US control and not Puerto Rican rights and freedoms. The group stressed nonpartisanship and included Democrats, Republicans, and people not affiliated with any party. At this particular meeting, a politically active Anglo Republican repeatedly and insistently voiced his suspicions that the organization was a front for Democrats using Puerto Ricans. When others in attendance questioned who he was and why he was there, he said he was attending and speaking for "conservative Puerto Rican Republicans." I do not have information about what kinds of conversations this man may have been having with Puerto Ricans or why those voters did not just attend the meeting themselves. What I did see was a paternalistic, non-Latino white person attempting to control the proceedings in a manner that reiterated the exclusionary inclusion of Puerto Rican colonial citizenship. And this is something that all of those involved in Orlando's NCPRR—Republican, Democrat, and nonaffiliated—understood because it was something they had all seen before.

PARTICIPATORY CLAIMS TO CITIZENSHIP AND BELONGING

The dynamics at the NCPRR meeting point to the fine line between the opportunity and danger of what it means to be seen. The Anglo man's efforts to dominate the meeting illustrate a common non-Latino response to Puerto Rican and Latino practices staking claim to their right to be different and to belong. It is a response that appears to recognize and accommodate Latino political issues while incorporating that recognition into an agenda that instead marginalizes Latino interests in service to either the marketplace or non-Latino political gains. This political and economic objectification of Latinos is the very definition of exclusionary inclusion as "a type of belonging that regulates and restricts the degree and nature of participation in the primary institutions of society" (Rocco 2014:xxx).

In resistance to this colonial-style control, participation itself can become a political tactic for a nonrestrictive claim to collective belonging. Participatory citizenship, writes Carol Hardy-Fanta (1993:120), means "being active in determining the policies that affect life within the community." In this view, community, citizenship, and participation are inextricably linked. A sense of community emerges from collective participation, and collective participation is an expression of citizenship (Hardy-Fanta 1993:100).

FIGURE 4.1. Protest sign from action in Brooksville, Florida, 2008. Photo by the author.

An example of this tactic is evident in Wanda Ramos's 2012 oral history. One facet of Ramos's Orlando activism is urging Puerto Ricans and Latino citizens to participate in electoral processes. In this way, she argued, they take steps to speak for themselves and for the larger Latino community. Ramos expressed her joy at having seen her "Hispanic brothers and sisters" at the polls. Slowly saying each word and using her hands to emphasize her point, she asserted, "It—counts—you—in." And she continued, "You're important not just because it's an election and . . . you should go to vote. But also because you're part of the equation. You're part of all this. And this is going to affect you. Don't let other people decide for you. You decide what you want" (PRPPCE Ramos). In this framing, it is the act of conscious participation that makes a person part of the equation. It is a claim to citizenship in the making through participatory action that stresses the collective over the individual.

Insistence on participation as a claim to citizenship is something that Orlando Puerto Ricans often extend to a broader view of Latinos as a community deserving of substantive belonging as societal members, whether or not that includes legal documentation. In his oral history for the 100 Puerto Ricans Oral History Project (100PR_OHP) at the Center for Puerto Rican Studies, Orlando Puerto Rican Carlos Guzmán talked about Latino

Leadership's achievements, saying, "Anything we achieve doesn't come with the Puerto Rican label on it" (100PR_OHP Carlos Guzmán #17). Comments from non–Puerto Ricans suggest the same. A steady voice in Latino Orlando is that of Ecuadorian Trini Quiroz, who often asserts the importance of Puerto Ricans in gaining civil rights for Latinos "up north." And Mexico-born journalist Roxana de la Riva credits what Puerto Rican experience brings to Orlando Latino politics: "They are the ones who open the way for us to have access to bettering the life of Hispanics in the region. . . . The majority are Puerto Rican. They are the ones who guide us other Hispanics" (PRPPCE de la Riva).[30]

The schoolteacher's letter cited earlier identifies the kinds of participation that set Americans apart from foreigners as voting, paying taxes, and serving in the military. These are, of course, all activities in which Puerto Ricans engage. They also frequently form the basis of Puerto Rican demands for moving beyond exclusionary inclusion to full citizenship. This is all part of the "politics of worthiness" that has emerged from the continual need for Puerto Ricans to prove themselves deserving of the rights and benefits of US citizenship (Delerme 2011, Ramos-Zayas 2004). Orlando Puerto Ricans regularly counter denials of their worthiness by naming their political, economic, and military participation. And by extension, they help other Orlando Latinos to be part of the equation.

Political citizenship. Wanda Ramos's voice is among those making constant calls to Puerto Ricans in Central Florida to use their votes as a vehicle for political access to all Latinos. In a 2015 oral history interview, Dora Casanova de Toro asserted,

> As American citizens, we have an advantage that no other Latin American country has. We are going to use it. We are going to make a difference. . . . And that the numbers that are reflected then make a difference in getting politicians who are aligned with or who respond to our particular interests. (100PR_OHP Dora Casanova de Toro #14)[31]

Voter-registration drives have been an important first step, as Mary Johnson's work in the 1984 campaigns suggests. Also in the 1980s, a group of Orlando-area Puerto Ricans started the Hispanic-American Voters League.[32] During the 1990 midterms, Víctor Alvarado was the league's president, and he confirmed that "the community is organizing on every single level" (in Tracy 1990). The advocacy group Latino Leadership actually began as a voter-registration group in 1999.

When Governor Jeb Bush's brother George won the 2000 presidential election in a close call in Florida—where minority voters were disproportionately denied their right to vote—the state took center stage in national political attention. Efforts from outside Florida increasingly partnered with local groups to protect minority voters (Padilla 2000b). During the 2002 midterms, Latino Leadership was among a group of local Latino advocacy groups who joined with the national organization People for the American Way to form the Orlando Tu Voto Es Tu Voz Alliance (Your Vote is Your Voice Alliance) for educating Latino voters about their rights (Brewington 2002). Que Nada Nos Detenga, the subject of one of Ríos-Andino's T-shirts, was a voter-registration drive run through the PRFAA offices around the US states from 2001 to 2004. Another campaign was Vamos a Votar (Let's Go Vote), which came out of the combined efforts of Democracia USA and the League of Women Voters (100PR_OHP Casanova de Toro #14, Ramos 2008). During the years of my fieldwork, national organizations such as the National Council of La Raza, Mi Familia Vota, and the Hispanic Federation established their presence each election cycle. Toward the end of my fieldwork, a new group called Boricua Vota was working year-round to educate and motivate Puerto Rican and other Latino voters.

Heading into the 2016 election cycle, it was no longer the case that Republicans did not want Puerto Ricans and that Democrats took them for granted. Central Florida Latinos and especially Puerto Ricans were being sought after by moneyed interests representing competing political ideologies. Union money was becoming increasingly visible in the effort to counter the corporate funding that entered politics in Florida and elsewhere after the 2010 *Citizens United* Supreme Court decision. At about the same time I began to hear about a group called Libre Iniciativa that was offering social services and registering voters. I soon learned that Libre Iniciativa was bankrolled by the ultraconservative Koch brothers, whose money had entered Florida politics some years before.[33] By 2016 there was pushback from the left with outside funds specifically targeting Central Florida Puerto Ricans (Rohrer 2016). Amid all this activity, the tripwire between opportunity and danger remains. Like the identity idea of the sleeping giant, new resources for political formation can both empower and contain.

Economic citizenship. Noting the lack of Latino representation on the Orange County School Board in 2001, María Padilla (2001) writes in the *Orlando Sentinel*, "Hispanics also pay sales and property taxes, and they buy lottery tickets—all of which help fund our schools." Her framing extends claims to the rights of the taxpaying citizen to other forms of economic participation. As the 1990s were beginning, Víctor Alvarado was arguing,

"If we continue to contribute millions of dollars to the community (in business and taxes), we have to have a voice in the community" (in Gallagher 1991a). And about fifteen years later, Victor Ramos's response (2005c) to the schoolteacher's letter used the marketplace to assert Hispanic belonging in Orlando. Likewise, Cuba-born René Plasencia used economic participation to point to another path through which Puerto Ricans open the way:

> If it hadn't been for the Puerto Rican people, this town would be, there would be nothing. There would be nothing. Because they came to work, to start businesses, to buy properties, to spend in Hispanic stores, to spend in American stores. So the flow of Puerto Ricans has been a benefit to this community, for all of Central Florida. (PRCF Plasencia)[34]

In these claims to economic citizenship there is an appropriation of the neoliberal idea of the passive citizen-consumer, reframed in support of activist claims to rights of participation (Báez 2018). Claims to economic participation are an example of resistance to social incorporation as a depoliticized Hispanic market of individual consumers. They are a demand to be counted as equal contributors to the local economy who deserve equal benefits from it.

Soldier citizens. A key component of claims to worthiness is military service (Ramos-Zayas 2004).[35] One of the first pathways bringing Puerto Ricans to Central Florida, the military is an agent of middle-class assimilation in a color-blind and multicultural United States, and it is once again both an opportunity and a danger for Latinos claiming the right to be different and to belong.[36] Gina Pérez (2015) has found in Lorain, Ohio, that Puerto Rican, other Latino, and African American youth participating in Junior Reserve Officer Training Corps (JROTC) programs in their schools expressed pride in this association with the military. Using a substantive view of citizenship that Pérez describes as "anyone who chooses to actively participate," these youth saw the performance of citizenship, such as cleaning up a park or helping a person in need, as a deeply local act that expressed both solidarity and belonging (157). Rather than a vehicle of assimilation, JROTC was a means to assert participation and belonging in a manner that created "a space of affirmation for communities that are otherwise defined as deficient and as 'takers' rather than 'makers'" (196).

In Orlando there is ample evidence of using individual military service to claim collective belonging on Puerto Rican terms. I have heard the most conservative to the most radical of Puerto Ricans talk about their military service in this way. When Eddie Heinzman asserted his rights in response to the coworker who accused him of taking a job from an American, he used military service as a measure of belonging (PRCF Heinzman). Simone Delerme (2011, 2020) has documented this very Puerto Rican claim as it played out locally in dramatic fashion when Commissioner John Quiñones proposed that a new park in Kissimmee be named in honor of the all–Puerto Rican regiment known as the Borinqueneers. A version of the debate in Kissimmee was also playing out at that time on the national level through a protracted campaign to award the Congressional Gold Medal to the entire regiment. In a Veterans Day appeal well before 2011, Orlando Puerto Rican veteran Dennis Freytes highlights the Borinqueneers as he also opens the way to Hispanics as a whole: "Even before this regiment, Hispanics participated in most every major U.S. military conflict. From the American Revolution . . . to the present-day world war on terrorism, Hispanics have served bravely" (Freytes 2007).

Although the park was dedicated and the medal bestowed, the entrenched opposition points again to the restricted access that Puerto Ricans and other Latinos have to the political structures that affect the recognition of Latinos as a group deserving of equitable inclusion. Much like Beltrán's notion (2010) that *latinidad* is a verb, the Borinqueneers example posits these enactments of citizenship as active and participatory. Honoring the Borinqueneers makes a symbolic extension of belonging to all Latinos and offers this substantive form of citizenship as a strategy of Latino politics. It counts them in.

VISIBILITY, PARTICIPATION, CITIZENSHIP

The Guevara election, the March for Dignity, and all the ways in which Orlando Puerto Ricans and Latinos have made themselves visible are expressions of citizenship defined as "a collectively lived sense of belonging . . . born primarily from daily life participation in the public sphere" (Oboler 2014:xiii). Given their numeric dominance in Orlando, Puerto Ricans' ability to push their formal citizenship front and center opens the way to a Latino politics that, although full of contradictions and controversies, is at times collectively reactive to non-Latino efforts to contain and control their social, political, and economic participation. Exercising their voting rights in the Guevara election, Puerto Ricans used their citizenship as a vehicle for Latino empowerment. In the March for Dignity, citizenship became a symbolic and cultural rejection of foreignness for all Latinos. In both, citizenship—like collective identification—was an activity rather than a thing; it was the active rejection of an imposed identity idea through participation in new forms of identification. And all of these were happening locally at the same time that national recognition of Hispanic/Latino as a unified and homogeneous category was taking root.

Despite these participatory expressions of community and citizenship, the many lines of difference among Orlando Latinos remain, and the legal fact of Puerto Ricans' birthright US citizenship is a significant one.[37] Non–Puerto Rican Latinos who do not necessarily understand the exclusionary inclusion at the root of colonial citizenship can be judgmental, thinking that Puerto Ricans should be more successful economically and politically. Similarly, Puerto Ricans can be slow to embrace immigration rights as a core issue, focusing their political energies instead on improving material conditions for themselves and other Latinos. The statement at the NCPRR meeting about trying to recognize the immigration question without getting sidetracked is an example of how Puerto Rican activists may try to maneuver around this thorny issue. A longtime Orlando Puerto Rican told me that when people say he does not have to worry about the immigration issue, he expresses his opposition to US immigration practice with a simple statement of solidarity: "But it's wrong."

Despite comments that immigration "is not our issue," many Puerto Ricans recognize that they too are subject to being profiled as undocumented. In the 1970s Miriam DaCosta was working with migrant Mexican families when she was stopped by immigration officials. She said, "I was trying to explain—I was so nervous—that I'm Puerto Rican. And the person from Immigration didn't understand that we Puerto Ricans are American citizens. And that I was born an American citizen" (PRCF DaCosta).[38]

In 2015, as director of the PRFAA offices in Kissimmee, Betsy Franceschini took part in a meeting for immigrants about how to navigate the process of gaining temporary legal status under Deferred Action for Childhood Arrivals (DACA).[39] She talked about her own father's Chicago experience in 1963 when he was stopped and asked for papers. When he explained he had no papers because he was Puerto Rican, he was still jailed for hours until the police finally confirmed his status. Decades after this 1960s Chicago arrest, in the lead-up to the divisive 2016 elections, a National Public Radio program host had to explain to a caller why Puerto Ricans were not being "vetted" as Puerto Rico's economic crisis was pushing many from the island to better prospects in the US states (Abbey-Lambertz 2016). Looking at the broad strokes of overlapping experiences among Latinos coming from places with unequal histories with the United States and being uprooted from that place, Silvio Torres-Saillant (2009:438–439) argues, "The feeling that ours is a contested terrain—that we do not inherit our social space but must carve it out for ourselves in the face of adversity—leads us to lift the banner of our oneness despite differences in the circumstances under which each of our distinct groups became part of the United States."

A decade after the events of 1996 and within a year of the schoolteacher's letter, another Latino march came to Orlando as part of a nationwide Day without an Immigrant. Once again, the motivation was not the ongoing need to improve material conditions but the affront to dignity effected by the criminalization of immigrants in a bill passed by the US House of Representatives (Oboler 2014:xiii). The extension of this criminalization to a specifically anti-Latino political agenda regardless of legal status worked to mobilize Latinos around the United States across a multitude of lines of division (Rocco 2014:176).

On May 1, 2006, some 20,000 marchers filled the streets of Orlando; the next day the *Orlando Sentinel* reported that it was the city's largest-ever political march (Stratton and Ramos 2006). Reports on the national scale indicate solid Puerto Rican support for the nationwide protest (Barreto et al. 2009). Locally, reports were mixed. Luis Martínez-Fernández (2010:49) laments the absence of many Hispanic leaders and blames the depoliticized atmosphere and the impact of "disneyfication" on Orlando's social field. The *Orlando Sentinel* cites Puerto Rico–born Nereida Liciaga's belief that Puerto Ricans could also be targeted: "The political situation on the island is very unstable right now, and things here have turned very anti-Hispanic. Today, I'm marching with the Mexicans, but who knows if I'd need them to march for me tomorrow" (in Stratton and Ramos 2006).

Throughout this and the many activities detailed earlier, Puerto Ricans rejected the exclusionary inclusion of colonial citizenship and together with other Latinos made themselves visible on their own terms. Whether addressing the blatant racism in the schoolteacher's letter or the more subtle effort at the NCPRR meeting to serve Latinos by controlling them, Puerto Ricans and Latinos were saying, "Enough is enough. We're here and we're not going anywhere."

CHAPTER 5

"THIS BUILDING IS OUR ISLAND"

Seen and Unseen in Orlando

Colonial Drive, where I was as I tried to get to Rafael on election night 2012, is one of Orlando's major east-west corridors. That night, I sat in traffic near the headquarters for Mi Familia Vota, which has since moved to Semoran Boulevard near Ana G. Mendez University. The space it held in 2012, in the back of an office park near Executive Airport, later was occupied by two other Latino organizations, Domino USA and the Casa de Puerto Rico. Executive Airport, near Azalea Park, marks the approximate beginning of the East Side. Driving from there east along Colonial, one may not know that many of the small storefronts with signs in English are Latino-owned. About one mile east of Semoran, as Colonial runs along the northern edge of Azalea Park, it is easy to miss the newest location for the Café d'Antaño tucked away on a side road just off Colonial. More visible is the restaurant Mi Viejo San Juan, just before the intersection at Goldenrod, where I turned to go get Rafael. The next intersection is Chickasaw Trail, where the new Wawa is.

Beyond Chickasaw at Dean Road, a sign identifies the beginning of Union Park. On the far corner is Downey Park, where the Three Kings event continued to be held after 2000. On the near corner is Lechonera Latina, a popular eating spot with a very large parking lot. In 2018, that parking lot was the site for a rally and voter-registration drive that was featured in Samantha Bee's *Full Frontal* episode "The Great American Puerto Rico." Bee teamed up with Puerto Rican star and Central Florida resident Olga Tañón to further motivate the crowd. Steps away from Lechonera Latina is a barbershop where years ago someone told me "everybody goes." It too appears in "The Great American Puerto Rico" episode.

Before getting to that visibly Latino space at Dean and Colonial, one would have crossed Econlockhatchee Trail, its name commonly shortened to "Econ Trail." Off to the left on Econ Trail, it would have been hard to miss the imposing building topped with a replica of the emblematic *garita* (watchtower) that graces the Spanish-colonial fort El Morro in Old San Juan. Built in 2003, this building was home to the Asociación Borinqueña during most of my fieldwork. Lillian Auffant, one of the first presidents, called the organization a "home away from home" (PRCF Auffant). Dora Casanova de Toro called it "a pioneer of the Puerto Rican community" in Orlando and likewise emphasized the idea of home, saying that it had been important to have that place as a "home in good times and in bad times" (100PR_OHP Dora Casanova de Toro #28).[1]

The various locales that housed the Asociación Borinqueña over the decades witnessed events large and small, and the building on Econ Trail, with its grand reminder to those crossing the threshold that they are stepping into a piece of Puerto Rico, has continued to do so. As the place where Tony Suárez held Nuyorican Night, where politicians from across the spectrum have come to make their pitches for Puerto Rican votes, where Orlando Ricans have gathered to dance and celebrate as well as to struggle with each other over competing plans for the future, as the place where all these activities and more have occurred, the building on Econ Trail is very much a place of shared memory.[2] It is a physical location in Orlando where a local sense of *puertorriqueñidad* has been and still is being contested and constructed. And the construction of this large and imposing building represented a statement to Orlando that Puerto Ricans are making themselves visible on their own terms. Remembering back to the decision to add the *garita*, Betsy Franceschini attested to the need for a "signature that anybody that passes there knows that this is a Puerto Rican facility" (CFPRO Franceschini-AB).[3]

As a place of shared memory, the Asociación Borinqueña building illustrates that place-making is an achievement gained through active and ongoing participation in a "complex web of social and affective relations and attachments" (Raffaeta and Duff 2013:331). Emphasizing this aspect of place-making, Casanova de Toro talked about the work it took to have a place for the Asociación Borinqueña and quoted Orlando Puerto Rican Harry Pecunia: "We made this possible *bacalaíto* by *bacalaíto*, *alcapurria* by *alcapurria*" (100PR_OHP Dora Casanova de Toro #30).[4] With a nostalgic smile, Casanova de Toro continued, "That was, I remember, as if it were today."

Some of the bad times that Casanova de Toro referenced were the several years during which the Asociación Borinqueña struggled with debt, caused in part by the *garita*'s expense and exacerbated by the economic crash that followed the bursting of the housing bubble in 2008. The situation caused bad blood among different factions of the organization, and several members were expelled. During a moment of optimism for a peaceful outcome in 2012, Amaury Díaz composed and painted a mural titled *En mi viejo San Juan*, which he gifted to the Asociación Borinqueña for the wall of the main room. At the mural's dedication just months before the 2012 presidential election, I recorded Díaz's words as he called the organization a home for "all of the Latino community." He went on to say, "We have to unite and become a force here in Central Florida. And so, I dedicate this mural not only to the Asociación Borinqueña but to all Latinos in Central Florida."[5]

After years of uncertainty and constant rumors, a Puerto Rican–owned and New York–based group of Latino agencies called the Acacia Network bought the building and resolved the debt in 2015. Tony Suárez had worked his New York connections to facilitate the deal. Within a short time following the Acacia Network's purchase of the building, it was renamed the Centro Borinqueño, but people most often just call it "Acacia." The degree to which Orlando Puerto Ricans had come to see themselves as Puerto Ricans *in Orlando* was evident when the news of new ownership by outsiders had many worried about the fate of the *garita* and the Díaz mural. In April 2015, the building's new owners hosted an open town hall to introduce themselves and dispel any rumors. Again, I recorded the program in which they let it be known that as long as the Acacia Network was around, the *garita* and the mural would stay. At the meeting's end, the new Orlando-based director of the Centro Borinqueño told all in attendance, "This building is our island in Orlando."

Although the fate of the former Asociación Borinqueña building has been resolved for the foreseeable future, during much of my fieldwork the uncertainty about what would happen to the building was matched by a changing landscape of Puerto Rican organizations all around the Orlando area. Several times when I had to leave Orlando and return to New York, before being able to visit one location or another, I would tell myself that the missed location would be among the first stops during my next fieldwork trip. But when I next returned to Orlando, as often as not the organization I had meant to visit was no longer where it had been when I left. Either it had relocated, as happened several times with the Casa de Puerto Rico and Café d'Antaño, or it had closed completely. With time I came to think about this constantly changing physical landscape in which Puerto Ricans moved about in efforts to make a place for themselves as a metaphor for efforts to claim social, political, and economic belonging in Orlando. During an interview with Puerto Rico–born Desmaris in 2010 I learned of her daily commute from Lake County to work in Orlando. She referred to the geographic spread of Orlando Puerto Ricans and said to me, "We haven't found an anchor, you know?"

For some time, there was a branch of the Puerto Rican Banco Popular at the intersection of Orange Avenue and Central Boulevard, the dead center of Orlando city. The bank's wall held a mural painted by the Colombian artist Alberto Gómez that depicted the intersecting worlds of Latino traditions and Orlando's actuality (Silver 2015). At some point on a return trip to Orlando, I found that both the bank and the mural were gone. The Puerto Rican Federal Affairs Administration (PRFAA) office closed and reopened twice from about 2008 to 2018, moving from Orlando city hall to Kissimmee and then to a place near the Florida Mall in Sky Lake. Some organizations have never had physical locations; members meet up instead in someone's home or rent a place from time to time for an event.

The 2008 crisis of neoliberal capitalism and the recession that followed were part of what produced this shifting landscape of Puerto Rican Orlando. Home foreclosures dispossessed legions of families nationwide. In Orlando, following what an *Orlando Sentinel* reporter called "the 2003–07 homebuying frenzy" (Shanklin 2011), Puerto Ricans and other Latinos were among those hardest hit.[6] Those who were able to keep their homes saw property values drop precipitously. The Banco Popular branch that vanished from downtown was not alone; there are no branches of the bank left in Central Florida. Another business familiar to Puerto Ricans from the island was the insurance company Seguros Multiples; that too was shutting its Orlando doors by 2010 (de la Riva 2010c).

Parallel with these displacements were challenges to the political ground that Puerto Ricans and other Latinos had achieved during the 1990s and early 2000s as they had countered invisibility and hypervisibility by making visibility on their own terms in the streets, on the airwaves, and at the ballot box. In various ways, much of what happened in the decade or so leading up to the 2011 redistricting process undid the hard-won gains that Puerto Ricans and other Latinos had achieved. In a manner similar to what Rafael was experiencing in his efforts to vote in 2012, this shifting physical and political ground reflects how the Orlando Latino claim of belonging is a contested one. In contrast to the achievements that contributed to being seen on their own terms, a process of dispossession during the first decade of the twenty-first century left Puerto Ricans and other Latinos again feeling invisible in the Orlando area.

In the face of this dispossession, the inside spaces of places like the Asociación Borinqueña offer another version of being unseen—a protective intimacy in which there is no need to concern oneself with how things might look to non-Latinos. Jacqueline Centeno described the Casa de Puerto Rico as providing that kind of a safe space. There, she said, "I feel at home. I feel protected." She continued, "We, as a community, you look for places to call home because we come from different places" (CFPRO Centeno-CPR). Casanova de Toro recalled that her husband, Manuel, would say about their house, "From the door in is Puerto Rico, from the door out is Central Florida" (PRCF Casanova de Toro). And at the 2005 Puerto Rican parade in downtown Orlando, a Puerto Rican woman referenced a more private experience of that very public event when she told an *Orlando Sentinel* reporter, "This makes me feel like I'm at home" (in Pedicini 2005).

In the previous chapter I discuss citizenship as an activity, using Suzanne Oboler's words to define citizenship as "a collectively lived sense of belonging" (2014:xiii). Oboler's definition further connects citizenship and belonging to "a sense of being 'home,' a sense of one's place" (xiii). The former Asociación Borinqueña building—the abstraction of its physical space into a meaningful place that feels like home to Orlando Puerto Ricans and its rescue by networks to and resources in Puerto Rican New York—encompasses the local and the translocal that have informed Puerto Rican place-making in Orlando. And its positioning as a Puerto Rican and Latino island in Orlando emphasizes the importance of spaces, unseen by most non-Latinos, where relationships of trust and mutuality are formed that are needed for even brief moments of collective political action (Rocco 2014).

In this chapter I tie collective and participatory forms of citizenship and belonging to the idea of place-making at home, which is itself a claim to belonging. Tying this idea of home to the rights of Puerto Ricans as US citizens, I return once more to Casanova de Toro. In a 2015 oral history, she expanded her idea of home from the Asociación Borinqueña to Orlando itself, as she called on other Puerto Ricans to stake a claim to what is theirs: "This is our home. Our family is here. We must plant our flag" (100PR_OHP Dora Casanova de Toro #14).[7] Her comments imply a twofold process that encompasses both the intimacy of home and family and the public face of participatory citizenship.

COMFORTS OF HOME

While getting to know Orlando, I would conduct windshield surveys, which simply means driving around an area to get a sense of the sociocultural landscape. Some of the obvious Latino presence in Azalea Park was at restaurants like Oh! Que Bueno and Lechonera El Barrio and other businesses with Spanish-language signs, even one displaying flags of Puerto Rico, Cuba, Mexico, and the Dominican Republic. Driving up and down Semoran Boulevard or on Orange Avenue en route to Kissimmee, I would see cars with

Puerto Rican flags dangling from the rearview mirrors or sporting bumper stickers expressing Puerto Rican pride or license plates naming Puerto Rican towns. Sometimes small handwritten signs advertising *pasteles* and other Puerto Rican foods are visible on street corners on Semoran, especially near Curry Ford. A large Latin grocery anchors each of the areas that have been called Little Puerto Rico—Sedano's in Azalea Park and the Publix Sabor in Buenaventura Lakes.

I also found that Puerto Rican and Latino places were not always as evident as I thought they would be. Like the small storefronts along Colonial, a good deal of Puerto Rican and Latino presence in Orlando's East Side is only visible to those who know where and how to look. Although more Latinos live in Orange County than in Osceola, they are less concentrated and less visible.[8] For instance, Orlando Bakery, founded in 1977, was reported in 1997 to be located in the back of a shopping center on Semoran, but the owner at that time told a reporter that no one outside the Hispanic community knew about it (Koenig 1997). And despite some visibility on Semoran, Azalea Park has been home to many other less visible islands in Orlando. In 2018 I had trouble finding Azalea Park's Iglesia Episcopal Jesús de Nazaret, where I was going to attend a meeting. I drove past the church on my first try; the large sign out front in English identified Christ the King Episcopal Church. As I was parking once I was sure I was at the right address, I met up with someone I had met years before on the bus to Brooksville. She was also coming to the meeting, and she was as uncertain as I was. Eventually, we saw a small plaque by a door off the parking lot indicating that a Spanish-speaking congregation also worships there.

A 2002 *Orlando Sentinel* article about Puerto Ricans moving to Orlando describes a grocery store on Semoran in a way that I recognize from my early windshield surveys: "You generally have to go inside to see it. The sign outside the local Winn-Dixie, the Sunbelt grocer, says 'The Beef People' like any other store in the chain. . . . But inside, a singer croons in Spanish on the intercom" (Swift 2002).[9] The article describes the Spanish signs inside the store and "shelves of Puerto Rican coffee, and . . . Latino dishes at the deli counter." During my interview with Laura, who came to Orlando from Puerto Rico in 1989, she recalled tables immediately inside the Winn-Dixie for coffee and conversation. Next door was Mary Lou Records, she said, with every bit of Latin music one could want. Because of construction in 2012, I kept missing the turn for Good Shepherd Catholic Church. I finally turned into a gas station to get my bearings. My field notes describe what I found when I went inside: "Inside the Quick Mart, the wall was covered with a variety of license plates with town names from Puerto Rico, Dominican

Republic, and Venezuela. One plate said 'Pide su pueblo' [ask for your town]. I picked up *El Venezolano* newspaper."

Similarly, in much of Orlando and Orange County there is nothing that visibly identifies a Puerto Rican home from the outside.[10] But entering a house either in one of the newer developments in Alafaya and Southchase or older ones in Azalea Park and Sky Lake, one may well see walls covered with nostalgic images of Puerto Rico. Out back, there may be a *flamboyán* tree and other plants grown from seeds brought back from a trip to Puerto Rico. The Centro de Cultura Puertorriqueña is one of the organizations that has not had its own physical space; during my fieldwork years the president, Judith Magali Rojas, used her own home in Buenaventura Lakes for teaching traditional dances to Puerto Rican children as part of a group called Sembrando Raíces (Putting Down Roots) (Ramos 2006a).[11]

In the following pages, I name and locate some of the places in the Orlando area that feel like home to Puerto Ricans, places where connections are made across the disconnected spaces of Puerto Rican and Latino Orlando. Much of what I describe is in Orlando's East Side (map 5.1), which has the densest Puerto Rican population in Orange County and was divided up during the 2011 redistricting process. But grocery stores, churches, and restaurants in other places also draw people from around the area, offering spaces where mutuality can grow. As one Orlando Puerto Rican told me, "Once you find the places, you make the connections."

Places that make connections. Besides Sedano's and Publix Sabor, other grocery stores that draw people from around the area are the Bravo at Semoran and Colonial, Compare on Goldenrod, and Las Americas in Seminole County not far over the Orange County line. Desmaris likes the Bravo because she can get meat cut the way she had it in Puerto Rico. Medina's downtown closed its doors during my fieldwork, but La Primera in Azalea Park remains. The larger markets have room for café areas inside, where the kinds of interactions, political and otherwise, that marked Medina's in earlier years continue.

A popular Puerto Rican restaurant is El Jibarito near the Bravo on Semoran at Colonial. A huge Puerto Rican flag is painted on the roof that can be seen from the Colonial Drive overpass.[12] An early discovery for me was Guavate, which was on Colonial near Semoran but has since moved to Alafaya. The name references the town in the Puerto Rican mountains where a collection of *lechoneras* attracts families who come to enjoy roasted pig and music on Sundays. Lechonera Latina has done well and opened two other locations, one on Curry Ford Road near Conway Road south of Executive Airport and the other on Colonial Drive in Alafaya.

Bakeries are also popular gathering spots. People will travel to go to their favorite places for the right kind of breakfast sandwich on bread that tastes like Puerto Rico. Many also serve up rice, beans, roast chicken or pork, and other food from home. Early on in my fieldwork I frequented a small bakery on the East Side in the unnamed space between Azalea Park and Union Park. The owner, María, lived a short walk away. Her daughters helped at the bakery after school. Inside there were two chairs at a counter and about seven or eight tables. Above the pastry display was a clock with the image of a Puerto Rican flag on its face. Spanish and English flowed back and forth easily.

In these and any number of Puerto Rican and other Latino food spaces around the area, patrons are likely to run into people they know. In 2018 at Valisa, a bakery a good bit past the Bravo on Semoran north of Colonial, I met up with a family coming from mass at St. James in downtown Orlando. While we were there, others I knew from different parts of Orange County arrived. One day in 2010 I was at Guavate in Alafaya with an Orlando Puerto Rican activist. As she saw a man go by wearing a cap with "Korea" and "Vietnam" patches, she stopped him and asked if he had been part of the Puerto Rican Borinqueneer regiment in Korea. He had been; this and other conversations kept us there for hours.

At María's bakery, customers' talk often centered around God's power to heal. María and her family attended a small church that met in a private house, an unseen space where they were finding the connections for making Orlando feel like home. The number of churches large and small with Spanish services has mushroomed since the 1980s.[13] During my windshield surveys it was unusual *not* to find churches. Along with Catholic churches, Latinos also attend mainstream Protestant and nondenominational churches. Small shopping plazas often house *botánicas* selling religious candles and other products that serve the spiritual needs of those who follow Afro-Caribbean religious practices. Several Puerto Ricans I know attend Jewish synagogues, and in Pine Castle there is even a branch of the Mita congregation that originated in Puerto Rico in mid-twentieth century.

Diana, a Puerto Rican woman from the Bronx, found her church community in Orlando by asking around for a Catholic church in the area where she lived. She described how she found it: "So I went and I checked it out. And I saw a lot of Puerto Ricans. And that I liked. I said, 'Oh, this is home,' you know. And there were a lot of Puerto Ricans from the island. And I knew that because a lot of their cars had license plates from the different towns. And I said, 'Oh, this is home.'"

The church that Diana found was St. John Vianney in Sky Lake. It has both Spanish- and English-speaking congregations. Nearby in Oak Ridge is the nondenominational Iglesia El Calvario, which formed as a spinoff of Calvary Assembly's English-speaking congregation in Winter Park. Spanish-speaking members of Calvary Assembly began to meet together in 1975, and with time they outgrew the space available to them (Banks 1990). The congregation eventually bought its own land and moved Iglesia El Calvario to Oak Ridge.

Like the family I met up with at Valisa, some people travel a distance across the Orlando area to attend the church where they feel at home. One family I know travels every Sunday to an Episcopal church in Kissimmee. Although there is a church near her home, Laura drives about thirty minutes to Azalea Park to attend mass at Good Shepherd, which she and most others call Buen Pastor, not far from where she used to frequent the Winn-Dixie and Mary Lou Records. Several of her friends attend there, so for her, church is a social time. Resistance from churches to offer mass in Spanish is another reason for traveling to another neighborhood.[14]

Also in Azalea Park, Christ the King Episcopal Church, which houses the Iglesia Episcopal Jesús de Nazaret that I had trouble finding, dates back to the 1950s. The large sign out front is in English, but Latinos make up a significant and energetic part of the congregation. Together with the Episcopal church in Kissimmee, the Iglesia Episcopal Jesús de Nazaret was a crucial contributor to helping Hurricane Maria evacuees. Marking the change in the Azalea Park neighborhood by 2012, the 9:30 a.m. English-language service on Sunday held about "50 mostly elderly white worshippers," and the 11 a.m. service was in Spanish with "hymns to the beat of bongo drums and acoustic guitars" (Kunerth 2012).

Buen Pastor in Azalea Park also has a large and vibrant Spanish-speaking congregation that attends the 9:30 mass on Sunday mornings, while the church's Anglo congregation attends the more traditional 11 a.m. mass. During my fieldwork, Yaya's Café was a favorite spot after mass at Buen Pastor. Eggs and *quesitos* were served up amid a cacophony of English and Spanish. Yaya's was another of those more intimate spaces, tucked away next door to the church but not really visible from Semoran. And it is another place that I realized was gone on one of my return trips to Orlando from New York. Apparently, the construction that surrounded Buen Pastor made it difficult to keep Yaya's open. Renamed Zaza New Cuban Diner, it left Azalea Park and moved to three new, more visible locations in Alafaya, in Seminole County, and on Curry Ford Road. I am told that after church at Buen Pastor, people now go off in their own directions.

There are nondenominational churches with Spanish-language signs on alternating sides of Chickasaw Trail between Colonial and the 408, and I was once told that their pastors' political leanings alternate sides as well. One of these is Discípulos de Cristo, which started in 1979 as a Latino subset of the local Disciples of Christ Evangelical Church (Banks 1990). The Discípulos de Cristo Facebook page in 2017 gave evidence of the networks of places that make connections; there was a suggestion to "like" Zaza New Cuban Diner along with Lechonera Latina on Dean and Colonial and the Old Cuban Café on Colonial in Alafaya. Across the street from Discípulos de Cristo is the Centro Cristiano Restauración, which for a long time was known simply as the Tommy Moya church, after the name of its pastor. It is common to refer to a church by the name of its pastor, and this is another indication of the mutuality that is nurtured in these spaces. Much farther south on Chickasaw is St. Isaac Jogues Catholic Church, where in 2010 I attended a traditional Puerto Rican *misa de aguinaldo*, a predawn service of Christmas songs.

The places that feed body and soul also become places for talking about social concerns and sponsoring political gatherings. During my fieldwork, at any 9:30 Sunday service at Buen Pastor, Peruvian American Gonzalo Capristán was passing out political literature. St. John Vianney was the site of a meeting in 2003 of the grassroots Federation of Churches United to Serve (FOCUS) that brought parents and school leaders together in a space where Latino parents could feel more at home than in their children's schools; at the schools parents sometimes could not find anyone who spoke the language they best understood (Pacheco 2003). That same group pushed Orange County in 2002 to give more attention to making park spaces in areas like Azalea Park, where there were none (Kunerth 2008b). In 2011 I was invited to listen in on a meeting at Orlando Baptist Church to coordinate efforts for pushing the state of Florida to expand Medicaid. The group included pastors and laypeople from different places on the political spectrum. Churches also often serve as voting centers, like the one where I took Rafael in 2012.

In the church services, political messages can be subtle. The pro-life argument is persuasive for many, but there may also be a disconnect between that Republican-leaning stand and a position on immigration that aligns more with the Democratic Party. When the immigration debate heated up approaching the 2008 election, El Calvario's Pastor Nino was reportedly shocked to see Anglo and African American leaders in other evangelical churches arguing against legalizing undocumented workers; according to an *Orlando Sentinel* article, this "propelled him into the political arena" (Pinsky and Rivera-Lyles 2008). In 2012 I attended a kickoff to the campaign season at El Calvario. The event was organized by the National Latino Evangelical Coalition, a group that works to raise awareness of "the growing number of Latino Evangelicals who are not captive to partisan politics."[15]

In other spaces, political talk is more open. As in the days of Medina's grocery and café, the conversations that happen inside the larger markets, at restaurants, or while customers are waiting in line for *quesitos* at a bakery may well revolve around one political question or another. More visible are the outside spaces of Latino groceries and eateries; they have been and are the sites of choice for voter-registration and voter-education drives. As I waited to meet up for an interview outside the Taíno Bakery in Azalea Park in 2018, a young woman with a clipboard asked me in Spanish if I was registered to vote. This is a common sight in the lead-up to election seasons.

On a Friday in April 2012, the parking lot of Sedano's in Azalea Park was particularly busy. The Puerto Rican mayor of Hartford had come to stump for the Orlando mayor's reelection. There was some fanfare in the parking lot about this event, and over to the side was another group mounting a protest. At the same time, supporters of a Puerto Rican candidate for city council were standing on the busy corner of Semoran and Curry Ford waving signs and cheering the cars that honked their approval as they passed.

For many, however, the political grandstanding does little to reach their daily lives. With all of that going on at Sedano's that day, shoppers came and went. Some were curious and hung around, and others got what they needed and left. To the repeated explanation that low Latino voter turnout is due to voter apathy, Luis Martínez-Fernández (2006) has responded, "Many Hispanics follow politics closely, not just locally but in their nations of origin. Their low voting rates are not the result of ignorance or apathy but of a feeling of alienation regarding the two political parties, whose leaders show up to utter a poorly pronounced 'Hola Amigos' every two or four years." That sentiment was echoed by a shopper at Las Americas supermarket: "They wait two weeks before the election and start plastering their photos everywhere, but nobody knows who they are, and the smiling photo won't tell you" (in Ramos 2006c). Latino Leadership President Marytza Sanz asserted, "We want them to come and talk to us" (in Ramos 2006c).

This is a vicious circle in which candidates give only superficial attention to Latinos because they supposedly do not vote, and Latinos often do not vote because they feel ignored. It is why Wanda Ramos was so adamant about being counted in and making oneself part of the equation. She proposed that part of the solution is not about the uphill task of convincing non-Latinos to behave differently but rather for politically active Latinos themselves to practice a "politics in rice and beans" (PRPPCE Ramos). By that she means talking with everyday people about everyday things. Similarly, another Orlando Puerto Rican activist pointed out in response to the economic crisis on the island that talking about hedge-fund debts as the source of the crisis gets little response, but talking about a family member's pension disappearing goes to the heart. Ramos argues that the politics of rice and beans brings people together. Raymond Rocco (2014:181) defines this kind of mutuality as "having similar concerns, experiences, struggles," and he takes that a step further to a "trust in trust" itself.[16] In contrast to the individualist ethos so prevalent in Orlando, Ramos says, "Standing alone is hard. Coming together is better" (PRPPCE Ramos).

Analys Cruz has taken Ramos's words to heart.[17] She maintains that those intimate spaces that one has to go inside to see are where she can most effectively inspire participation and help Puerto Ricans and other Latinos "plant a flag" in Orlando's political field. She takes up opportunities in the grocery line or at the Laundromat to engage people in conversations about how exercising their right to vote can affect their children's education, their access to transportation and a secure home, their place as Latinos in Orlando. She works to build relations of trust and mutuality with individuals as part of an effort to establish collective claims that push against exclusionary inclusion.[18] She is known in her neighborhood for this, and at election time neighbors with absentee ballots in hand stop by her home with questions. Who are these judges on the ballot? How much postage do I need? Maybe it's better to just hand my ballot in personally? Where can I do that?

Analys at home in the East Side. Analys and her husband, Juan, are both deeply connected to Puerto Rico, having spent their full childhoods there, but they have also lived in various places in the diaspora. After many years of moving around "up north," they missed Puerto Rico and returned there to live and raise their daughter. But their return paralleled the beginning of the end of the tax breaks to corporations in Puerto Rico. As the Puerto Rican economy went from bad to worse, things were getting hard for Analys and Juan. Like so many others, they moved to Orlando in the late 1990s.

Although Analys identifies her home area as Union Park, neither of the two places where she and her family have lived have actually been in the Union Park census-designated place (CDP). They first moved to an apartment just to the east of Dean Road and south of the 408. In 2003 they bought a house just west of Econ Trail and north of the 408. For Analys, Dean Road is not the dividing line between Union Park CDP and an unnamed part of unincorporated Orange County. It is the center of her geographic world, which extends from about a mile or so west of Semoran through Alafaya. Her daily life takes her across Dean Road multiple times as she takes her daughter to school, goes to work downtown, and stops to pick up groceries on the way home. Because Union Park will figure importantly in the 2011 redistricting, I take a moment here to situate Analys and her family in that space (map 5.1).

MAP 5.1. Orlando's East Side

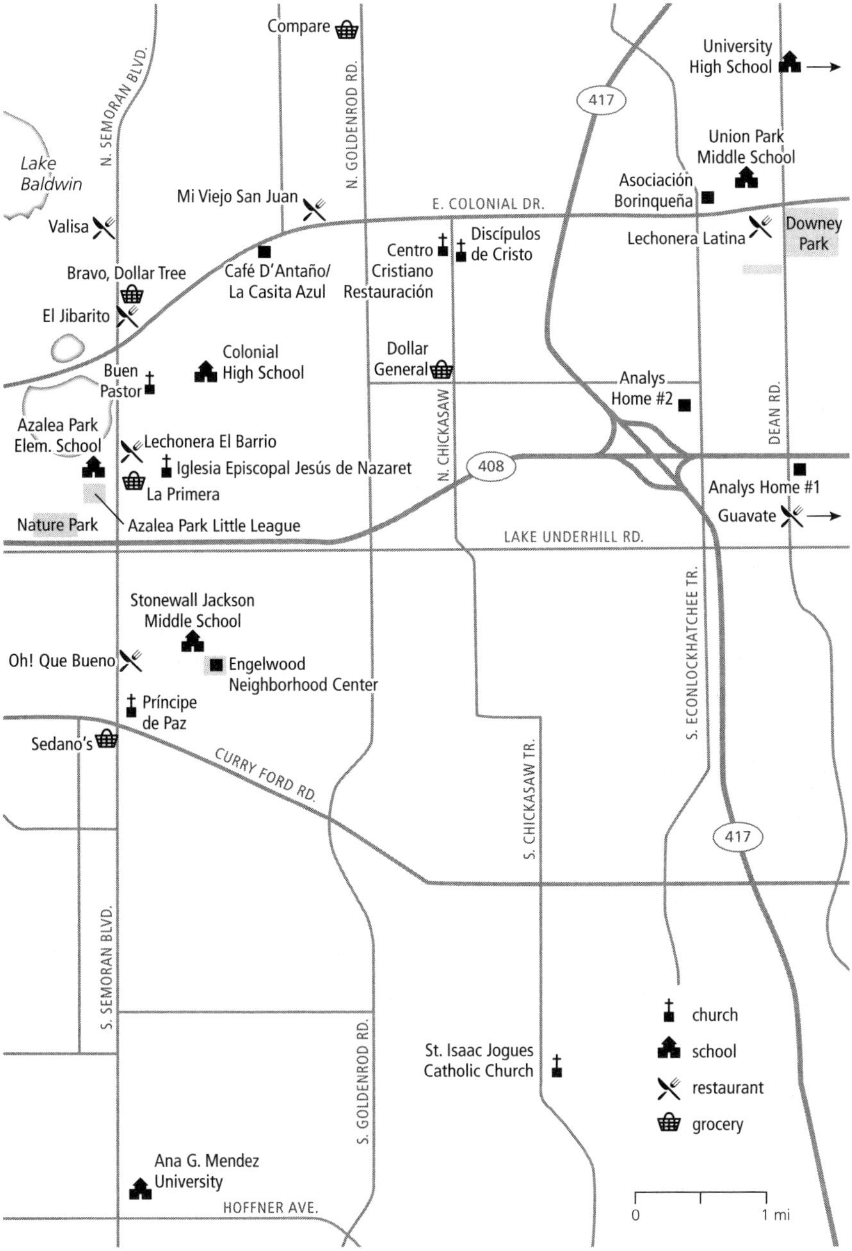

The East Side, between Semoran Boulevard and Dean Road, is shown with selected markings for important places for Orlando Latinos. Map by Molly O'Halloran.

Analys's daughter went to Union Park Middle School, on the northern side of Colonial about a mile and a half from their house. Later, she attended University High School. The best way for Analys to get there is to take Econ Trail up to Colonial and head east crossing Dean Road before cutting north again.

Analys asserted that church provided a place "where you feel like you can breathe" as she adjusted to her new life in Orlando. She used to attend mass at Buen Pastor, but now she prefers Prince of Peace (Príncipe de Paz) Lutheran Church. It is across from Sedano's, but she does not shop there. She prefers Bravo for some items and Las Americas for others. Until Medina's closed, every once in a while she would shop there if she was in that area of downtown. When I asked what restaurant she liked, she immediately said Guavate. Restaurants are not in the budget these days, though. Analys and her husband managed to keep their home in the mortgage crisis, but they had to take out a second mortgage to pay for a surgery that their daughter needed. Since then, Analys goes to the Dollar General for some things that she says are too expensive in the Spanish groceries.

After many years in Orlando, Analys sees a great deal through the rice-and-beans political lens. She has learned about the structures of the Orlando area's local governments through her own efforts. At first she and Juan were more grounded in Puerto Rico's political landscape. They had lived and voted in other diaspora spaces, but every state has different structures and rules for local government. It took a while to learn about Florida. Soon after they arrived, Analys heard about the voter-registration drive being conducted by Latino Leadership, and she was inspired to know that it was a Puerto Rican woman, Marytza Sanz, who was running it.

That voter-registration drive was ahead of what turned out to be the controversial 2000 presidential election, in which 537 votes in Florida determined the outcome. It was the first election for Analys and Juan in their new home. Their county commissioner was Mary Johnson, and she was running for her third and final term in District 3. Tony Suárez had been their Florida House representative for District 35 when they arrived, and James Auffant was running to replace Suárez as he stepped down. They did not know much about any of this, but they did want to vote for president. As happened to so many in that contested election, they were turned away because their names were not on the voter list at their polling place. They were more successful in 2002, and although they are Democrats, they voted for by-then Republican Tony Suárez for the Florida Senate. For Analys, this was a case of ethnicity over party. Although it was not to be in this election, she had hoped to have a Puerto Rican represent her.

Analys sometimes listens to *Quédate con Miguel*. It was through the radio that she began to learn about local issues. She was especially interested in the effort to get park space for underserved communities. She and Juan had taken their daughter to the 2000 Three Kings celebration in Downey Park, and they were glad to have that resource nearby. Analys learned that Herndon Nature Park, west of Semoran just north of the 408, had been created after years of pressure from Mary Johnson about dedicating part of Executive Airport's land for park space (*Orlando Sentinel* 1988). The park was closed in the late 1990s as drug problems in the area grew, but a local community-based cleanup effort, with support from the PRFAA office, convinced city officials to reopen the park in May 2002. When the city suddenly canceled the park's opening, claiming that permits were not in place for the event, Puerto Ricans and other Latinos in and beyond Azalea Park were furious (Brewington and Pacheco 2002). A year later, Herndon Nature Park was still closed (Padilla 2003). Even if the city resolved to reopen it, the children on the east side of Semoran, which is under county jurisdiction, still would have no park access without crossing major roadways. Analys was glad to learn that Johnson had promised a county park for the Azalea Park area during a community meeting at Buen Pastor (Mathers 2002).

In the following years, Analys had experiences that pushed her to reevaluate her Puerto Rico–based political views. As an hourly worker in Florida she was surprised to learn how few protections the law in this right-to-work state afforded her and her coworkers, some of whom she saw lose their jobs with no recourse to protect themselves. Eventually, she was one of those workers. She had not seen this degree of vulnerability in Puerto Rico or in the northern US diaspora spaces where she had lived. In Puerto Rico her political affiliations were about status for the island, but in Florida—and now as a displaced worker and the mother of a child in school—she began to see that what mattered was how effectively her local government protected workers and addressed access to education, health care, and housing.

Analys felt somewhat intimidated by the school system. She completed her own high school years in Puerto Rico, and so her daughter's school environment felt foreign to her. Eventually she learned about the Parent Leadership Council (PLC) for parents of students whose first language was not English. Her own daughter was fully bilingual, but Analys had to fight to keep her from being assigned to an English as a Second Language (ESOL) class because of her last name. Analys joined the PLC and through it became more proactive in her daughter's education. Her involvement with local issues grew, and she began to call into radio programs to voice her opinions.

Analys and Juan were more acclimated by the 2004 elections. James Auffant had lost the 2000 election for Florida House District 35. They were happy to see another Puerto Rican, Mike Deliz, running for that district, but the district lines had been pushed west in the 2001 redistricting. District 35 now included largely white and affluent Winter Park. The new district lines made a Latino win improbable, and that turned out to be the case. Mary Johnson was also on that ballot for the position of clerk of courts. They liked Johnson's work for the East Side children, but this at-large race required countywide support, and she did not win. Their pick for their District 3 county commissioner, Mildred Fernández, did win. Fernández had stumped hard in their neighborhood and attended Buen Pastor church.

When their subdivision was experiencing the impact of new construction accompanying the growing housing bubble, Analys began attending community meetings and then contacted Commissioner Fernández about the issue. Her enthusiasm for Fernández waned as the commissioner seemed more interested in protecting the developers than in addressing residents' concerns. As their economic situation deteriorated post–2008, Analys and her husband felt entirely abandoned by their Florida House District 35 representative, Dean Cannon. Analys was disheartened as she did so much civic engagement and still felt such little response from elected officials. And she was not alone, although often many others were responding by not engaging in the first place.

When Amy Mercado challenged Cannon for the District 35 seat during the 2010 midterms, Analys was excited. The 2008 Obama campaign had energized her political activities, and she remembered that Mercado and her mother, Carmen Torres, had been instrumental in the 2008 Orlando4Obama campaign. Mercado's anger at the number of foreclosed East Side homes and her argument that Cannon had largely ignored her community in both his campaigns and his representation in Tallahassee struck home with Analys and many others. Analys decided to get involved and went out canvassing for Mercado, which took her from the manicured lawns of palatial homes in Anglo-dominated Winter Park and Baldwin Park to houses on postage-stamp lots in some of the Latino-concentrated parts of the East Side. The contrast could not have been more stark. Although Analys knew this, her time on the street knocking on doors drove it home in new ways.

Cannon billboards suddenly started going up in places where Analys had never seen them before, and he managed to be one of the Three Kings in that year's event. In her growing enthusiasm from her door-knocking, Analys reasoned that Cannon must be seeing the potential for a Latino upset. For a brief moment she felt proud to think that a Puerto Rican woman might represent her and her family in Tallahassee. In the end, she was again disappointed as she saw Orlando's Democratic mayor as well as an influential group of Puerto Ricans give their support to Cannon because of projects they had before the legislature that needed his support. It was another case of the secondary gains issues that emerge from giving priority to following the money over serving the people; neither racial-ethnic identification nor political party had held sway.

Another disappointment that Analys experienced in the 2010 elections was to see the Orange County School Board remain without Latino representation. In that absence, Mildred Fernández had become something of a de facto Hispanic representative for parents (Marquez 2005). Due to her disillusionment with Fernández, Analys was glad to see Jacqueline Centeno step up to run against the incumbent school board member in District 1. Analys did not live in that district, but she knew about Centeno's work in bilingual education because of her involvement in the PLC, and she had been at the Casa de Puerto Rico's annual fund-raiser that year when Centeno had won an award for her work in education. In the August primaries, however, Centeno lost to the Anglo incumbent. Analys knew that Latino voter turnout during primary elections is especially low, so her disappointment was that much deeper that Centeno did not even have the chance to be on the November ballot.

During the 1990s, Orlando Puerto Ricans and Latinos had struggled hard against discrimination and marginalization, and through those efforts they had managed to plant flags in the social, political, and economic fields of their new home. Analys's family had arrived in Orlando as that decade was coming to a close. During her family's first decade in Orlando, Analys saw those gains challenged by local practices that continually thwarted Latino participation. That story is next, and it actually begins the year before Analys and her family arrived in Orlando.

CHALLENGES TO POLITICAL GROUND FOR ORLANDO LATINOS

In spring 1998, Medina's grocery was abuzz with political talk (Maxwell 1998b). Orange County Commissioner Mary Johnson and Mel Martinez were both running for Orange County chair.[19] There were others in the race, but Johnson's and Martinez's campaigns meant that two Latinos were running. Martinez had supported Johnson when she launched her political career in 1980, and the two had been friends for years (Maxwell 1998a,b). One *Orlando Sentinel* report quotes Martinez's memories from Johnson's 1980 campaign: "I remember hugging her and telling everyone: 'Let's go get 'em, Mary!'" (in Maxwell 1998b).

Martinez had never held an elected position, but through his connection to Orlando Mayor Bill Frederick, he had served as chair of the Hispanic Advisory Committee, the Orlando Housing Authority, and the Orlando Utilities Commission.[20] He was thus well integrated with Orlando's Anglo elite, who approached him in 1996 at an exclusive all-male club to recruit him to run for county chair (Foglesong 2011:99). Martinez's initial effort to raise money was hugely successful; from there, his campaign followed the lead of winning Orlando mayoral races, focusing fund-raising on the downtown business elite and making it difficult for a viable alternative candidate to compete (Foglesong 2011:103).

Mary Johnson was very much a viable alternative. After serving through the 1980s as the District 2 representative for Orlando, she had been elected to the Orange County Board of County Commissioners (BCC) District 3 seat in 1992. Johnson's Orange County district encompassed some of the areas with the greater proportions of Latino population, running east from I-4 along Colonial Drive and the 408 to a short way past where the Asociación Borinqueña building stands. The district's north and south boundaries zigged and zagged but managed to encompass Azalea Park and Union Park. She entered the county chair race in spring 1998 with strong support from minority groups, activists, and unions (Spear 1998).

The Medinas had endorsed Martinez early on, but they also had always supported Johnson and had her image displayed prominently above the cash register at their grocery store (Maxwell 1998b). Johnson's argument that she was the one with the right experience was a strong one, but her entry into the race caused confusion about loyalties. One Spanish-language talk-radio host framed it this way: "It's like if I had a brother and sister running for the same office. . . . I would love them both. But I could only support one of them" (in Maxwell 1998b). Under some pressure, the Medinas took down Johnson's photo; Johnson withdrew in the summer, citing the financial strain against Martinez's larger funding base and saying, "This should be an election, not an auction" (in Maxwell 1998a).

Orange County had switched to nonpartisan elections for its commissioners in 1992, but it was no secret that Johnson was a Democrat and Martinez was a Republican. When Johnson stepped aside in the Latino versus Latino race, Latino Democrats had to choose between party affiliation and racial-ethnic identification. James Auffant and Evelyn Rivera, two well-known Puerto Rican Democratic activists, both supported Martinez despite their differences in party ideology and nationality (Foglesong 2011:107). As Johnson had done before him, Martinez won with Latino crossover votes.

Johnson remained in her county commission seat until she termed out in 2004. Coming just two years after the March for Dignity and Guevara's Osceola election, the 1998 election left Johnson as the only woman but one of now two Latinos on the Orange County BCC. Both Johnson and Martinez had grown up in Florida and were married to Anglos. Together with the likelihood that non-Latino voters in 1980 did not know of Johnson's Cuban–Puerto Rican heritage, it is equally arguable that the powerful, all-male elite that recruited Martinez knew that he was Cuban but did not really think of him as Hispanic.

The Orlando elite was beginning to count Cubans and a few well-heeled Puerto Ricans in the honorary white category, but this was not the same thing as opening the door to Puerto Rican and Latino political participation *as Latinos*. As Analys would observe over the next decade, Puerto Ricans and other Latinos—as an identifiable racial-ethnic group deserving of equitable participation in Orlando's social, political, and economic fields—faced a variety of structural and procedural mechanisms that converged in a supposedly color-blind way and contributed to a dispossession from the gains made in the 1990s. In the following sections I explain how some of this has worked.

Nonpartisan primaries and election schedules. Low Latino voter turnout in the Orlando area was the subject of a presentation by the local Anglo activist Doug Head in January 2012 at a seminar organized by Frente Unido 436 at Ana G. Mendez University. Head's presentation explained the combined impact of election schedules and nonpartisan races as a key element in the problem of low voter turnout. For those coming from Puerto Rico and elsewhere, where elections happen on one day every several years for all elected positions, the structure and scheduling of elections in Florida can be extremely confusing. The inclusion of nonpartisan races on partisan primary ballots is another problem.

In nonpartisan elections, any number of qualifying candidates, regardless of party affiliation, compete in the primaries. If none receives a majority, the top two go on to the general election. If one candidate receives the majority, the election is won and there is no general election for that seat. Latinos who are not registered with either major party may not realize they can participate at all when nonpartisan seats are included on partisan primary ballots. Decisions can be made in the primaries with very little Latino participation, as Analys saw in Jacqueline Centeno's run for the District 1 seat on the Orange County School Board in 2010. Only 10 percent of registered Latino voters in District 1 voted in those primaries, and the Latino vote in the district was only 8 percent of the total.[21]

The day after Head's presentation, a series of eight 2012 elections affecting all or parts of Orange County began with the 2012 presidential primary. Turnout was overwhelmingly Republican because President Obama was the Democratic nominee and there was no Democratic presidential primary. The ballot included a referendum on granting tax exemptions to businesses in the county, which passed with 62 percent of the vote. Along with the presidential primary and the November general election, a series of five municipal elections around Orange County took place on different dates during the spring. In the Orlando election in April, the mayor and four city commissioners were elected with only 8 percent of Orlando Latino voters participating.[22]

On August 14, 2012, more primaries were held, this time for selecting state and federal legislative candidates to be on the November general-election ballot; just 9 percent of Latino voters participated. That year, as part of the partisan primary ballots, nonpartisan races on the August ballot were won outright for five judges, three Orange County School Board seats, and the Orange County BCC District 5 seat.[23] Orange County BCC District 3, where Latino voting strength was diluted in the 2011 redistricting, was also on the August 14 ballot. Latino contenders for District 3 were all eliminated in that primary. Foreshadowing this result at the January 2012 seminar, Head had commented, "August elections are where Hispanics go to die."

The November 2012 election was when I took Rafael to the polls and sat with the elderly Puerto Rican woman waiting for her turn to vote. Latino turnout that November was 59 percent, still less than that of non-Latino white and black voters but dramatically up from the other elections that year. Indeed, because of Latino participation nationwide in the 2012 presidential elections, that year is considered by many to be the year that the so-called sleeping giant woke up (Affigne et al. 2014).

English-only versus language minority. Although voting-rights protections were extended to language minorities in 1975, Orlando Latinos have had their share of difficulties in voting. The 2000 presidential elections, when multiple complaints statewide came from African Americans and Latinos turned away at the polls, offer a case in point (McKay 2000, Shenot 2000). At the request of Orlando Latinos, the Puerto Rican Legal Defense and Education Fund (PRLDEF) began an investigation into complaints that Latinos in Central Florida were not able to get the language assistance required by law, that their names were missing from voter rolls, and that they were told a single form of identification was insufficient to vote (Padilla 2000b). It was in this election that James Auffant lost his bid to replace Tony Suárez in Florida House District 35. Orange and Osceola Counties were cited by the US Department of Justice, resulting in a separate consent decree for each county in 2002 (Newman 2007). More complaints surfaced in 2004 that Orange County had not provided bilingual poll workers at early voting sites as required (Stratton 2004).

Resistance to other laws requiring language assistance for nonnative speakers also contributes to Latino marginalization. Orange County Public Schools in particular has repeatedly been at the center of grievances. Bilingual education in Orange County dates back to 1976 (Kunerth 1976). Nonetheless, complaints that the school system has failed to meet the needs of limited English proficient students stretch across the decades. In 1990 the state of Florida signed a consent decree with the League of United Latin American Citizens that addressed equal rights for language minorities according to federal civil rights legislation.[24] One part of the consent decree was the creation of Parent Leadership Councils like the one Analys joined after her bilingual daughter was almost placed in an ESOL class. More than a decade later, concerns about soaring Latino dropout rates in Orange County indicated a lack of compliance with the 1990 requirements (Marquez 2000). After years of repeated citations of the schools, three elected leaders of the district PLC—Evelyn Rivera, José A. Fernández, and Radhames Reyes—created a nonprofit organization by the same name in order to be able to turn to the courts as needed (Horvitz 2001b). The good news is that by 2010, Orange County schools were running a bilingual-education program that was a model for others, but that same year the school district made plans for drastic cutbacks to the program (Hobbs 2010a). By 2013, as more students needing ESOL continued to enter the schools, Tomasita Ortíz, who had headed the program from 1998 to 2009 just before the cutbacks, observed that Orange County was "moving backwards instead of forwards" (in Roth 2013).

Political districts and racial-ethnic representation. Gerrymandering political districts is a well-acknowledged means to maintain power. Separate issues during the 2001 redistricting for the Orlando area help to illustrate that point. The City of Orlando's 2001 process simultaneously diluted West Orlando black voting power and undercut the growing power of the East Orlando Latino vote; Doug Head accurately predicted that there would not be another Latino on the city council before 2008 (Schlueb 2001). Before being forced to change its plan, the Orange County School Board decided to conduct the redistricting process itself rather than appoint a demographically representative redistricting committee. One of the school board members defended the decision, saying to a reporter, "We have always treated the public in a colorblind way" (in Horvitz 2001a). As for the Orange County BCC process, all public proposals offered were rejected—at least one of which would have increased black and Latino voting power—and in the final map only small adjustments were made to the existing lines (Steinman 2001). At the state level, the 2002 Florida Senate map put Latinos into an African American district rather than creating a Latino seat.[25] In effect, this identified Latinos as part of a collective black population and left the non-Latino white population with greater representation. This was also the redistricting cycle that put Winter Park into Florida House District 35.

Local representation also turns on choices about at-large or single-member district elections. At-large voting is a common strategy for racial manipulation of voting power (Buchman 2003, JoNel Newman 2006). The Orange County BCC switched from five at-large to six single-member districts and one at-large seat in 1988 (Griffin 1991). It is no coincidence that Orange County's first black commissioner was elected in 1990 (Villarreal 1994). Mary Johnson won her seat on the Orange County BCC in 1992. As Analys witnessed, though, Johnson was unable to win the at-large race for clerk of courts despite her twenty-four years in local government. Voters in Osceola County chose to reverse the decision to have single-member districts and return to at-large elections in 1996. Ironically, the proposal to return to an at-large system was on the same ballot on which voters elected Robert Guevara to one of the new single-member districts (Cruz 2010, JoNel Newman 2006, Marquez 1996b).[26]

Co-opting Latino resources. While Orange County public offices have openly resisted compliance with laws protecting Latinos, the City of Orlando has projected a more welcoming image as it has nonetheless brought Latino advances and resources under its control. The story of the Hispanic Office for Local Assistance (HOLA) is an example of how local power holders have maintained political and economic control while appearing to accommodate the growing Latino population. When Latino Leadership and the City of Orlando began a two-year public-private partnership in 2004, the idea was that the financially struggling nonprofit would be able to leverage the partnership to attract more grant money for HOLA (Marquez 2004). The offices were housed in that same space behind Executive Airport that has since been home to Mi Familia Vota, Domino USA, and the Casa de Puerto Rico.

In a sarcastic critique of the need for private funding, Myriam Marquez notes (2004), "It's hard to come up with $60,000 for an office to serve almost one in five of city residents when you've squeezed the city budget dry with multimillion-dollar giveaways to downtown developers." Her reference to giveaways is about plans for a series of sports and arts venues to be built in and around downtown Orlando; her suggestion is that building impressive venues was apparently more important to the city government than addressing the needs of Latinos. With a nod to the public-private partnership, Marquez also acknowledges that it was at least a forward step that Sanz would now have "city clout to hustle grant money from other sources" for the valuable work she was doing.

At some point the city brought Hispanic Achievers into the partnership, which added a business-oriented component to the services offered and a source of conflict with Latino Leadership (Ramos 2005d, 2006b). By 2006 the city had created a coalition that included the Hispanic Chamber, PRFAA, and Trabajando Juntos; Latino Leadership's involvement was greatly reduced, and Hispanic Achievers was out completely (Ramos 2006b). Fomenting conflict among Latinos became an important element in the 2011 Orange County redistricting.

Amid all this, a Puerto Rican law enforcement officer, Orlando Rolón, was named Hispanic affairs adviser to the mayor (Loperena 2007). But by 2008, Rolón was out as well, with the city citing budget cuts in the face of a new anticrime offensive (Pacheco 2008). Rolón said he was puzzled by the move because he knew "the importance and significance of having this role in this community" (in Pacheco 2008). Puerto Rican activists were outraged and complained that there were no Hispanics in the upper levels of the city administration (de la Riva 2009).

Although never as close to the ear of the mayor as Rolón had been, the HOLA office became the Latino community's link to city government. Its offices were eventually relocated to a space it shared with Orlando's Department of Families, Parks, and Recreation and a police substation. Now part of the City of Orlando, HOLA has been placed under the Mayor's Office of Community Affairs and Human Relations, working in coordination with the Mayor's Multicultural Affairs Office.

The aftermath of the 2016 shootings at Orlando's Pulse nightclub offers another example of co-opting resources. Both the City of Orlando and Orange County stepped in quickly to manage the funds that were pouring in from around the country and the world to help survivors and families of the victims. Pushback stopped them from funneling the money to nonprofits that would oversee its distribution and forced a decision to distribute funds directly to those affected. Although most of the shooting victims were Latinos, the process of consolidating several money streams into one largely removed Latinos from the narrative. That almost half the victims were Puerto Rican was not even mentioned. The universalist words "united," "one," and "alliance" are sprinkled around the names of the many well-funded organizations that have emerged from the Pulse tragedy. Even "LGBTQ" disappeared from the name of the LGBTQ Alliance as it became the One Orlando Alliance. A year after the massacre, in the planning for memorial events, an Orlando city commissioner criticized the mayors of the city and county for "pushing their marketing campaign" and neglecting to even mention the impact on the LGBTQ community in their public relations piece (Weiner 2017). These subtle erasures of difference, effected by universalist discourses of sameness, open spaces through which existing power relations are reproduced.

Displacing/replacing Latinos. Closely related to using Latinos as resources to the interests of more powerful others has been the practice of putting Anglos into positions that a Latino had previously managed to obtain. When Orlando Rolón was removed from his position as Hispanic adviser to the mayor and returned to employment with the Orlando Police Department, a non-Latino white man came out of retirement to serve as assistant to the mayor (de la Riva 2009). Likewise, the legal procedures for filling absent seats in local government have challenged Puerto Ricans' and other Latinos' ability to hold onto the hard-won political ground they had gained since the 1990s.

Decisions about how to fill such vacancies rest with the Florida governor and are therefore subject to state-level political interests. When Robert Guevara died in office in 2000, many thought the deceased commissioner's widow should be the one to complete the term in his seat (Padilla 2000c). Mary Johnson lobbied for keeping a Latino in that seat, and Governor Jeb Bush had close relations with many Central Florida Latinos, but Bush selected a non-Latino white man for the position (Cruz 2010:256, *Orlando Sentinel* 2000). The following year, when Mel Martinez stepped down as chair of the Orange County BCC to become the HUD secretary, Governor Bush considered five potential appointees to replace him: three non-Latino white men, one non-Latino black man, and one Latina (Maxwell 2001a). The Latina was Mary Johnson, but Bush appointed Belle Isle resident and Orange County Property Appraiser Richard Crotty, who remained in the position until 2010.

Heading into the 2011 redistricting, these separate acts of displacing and replacing Latinos from positions of power had added up to a point that Puerto Ricans and other Latinos were feeling newly disempowered. In my interview in 2010 with Desmaris she said she felt that the number of area Latinos in places of influence was shrinking rather than expanding. The story of what happened in Johnson's District 2 seat in the city and her District 3 seat in the county demonstrates most if not all of the supposedly color-blind mechanisms that have contributed to the political piece of what Desmaris thought she was seeing.

EAST SIDE STORIES

Despite the glass ceiling that Mary Johnson seems to have hit twice in regard to the Orange County chair position—first in the race against Martinez and then in the appointment to replace Martinez—she remained in local government for twenty-four years. This has been a singular achievement among Hispanics in Central Florida politics. Over the years, her East Side districts in the city and county came to be understood as Latino districts. What became of each of Johnson's seats when she left is a lengthy story of dispossession.

City of Orlando. In 1992 the candidates vying to replace Johnson in Orlando's District 2 were Puerto Rican James Auffant, Cuban American Lou Pendas, and Anglo Betty Wyman. The *Orlando Sentinel* endorsed Auffant (Peach 1992). Wyman won with 51 percent of the vote in a September primary.[27] Despite having Latino challengers in every reelection thereafter, Wyman held onto her seat for sixteen years. The 2000 municipal elections in Orlando were held in conjunction with the presidential primary, which undoubtedly meant that many nonaffiliated voters did not go to the polls. Facing three Latino opponents, Wyman was reelected with only about 35 percent of registered voters participating.[28] Over the years of Wyman's tenure, conditions along Semoran Boulevard deteriorated, and it became known as "heroin alley" (Hudak 2016). The closure of Herndon Nature Park in the 1990s and the roadblocks that Analys witnessed to the community efforts to reopen it in 2002 and 2003 happened under Wyman's watch.

Wyman's reputation for favoring non-Hispanic white seniors in Conway over her Hispanic constituents in East Orlando was no secret. During her final campaign, in 2004, an *Orlando Sentinel* article notes Wyman's neglect of Hispanics and cites Luis Gómez saying, "I've had a law office in this district for 21 years, and she has never once knocked on my door" (in Harris and Pacheco 2004). By the 2004 elections, Latinos' anger at Wyman was strong and the number of Latino voters had continued to grow. The director of the PRFAA office that had been overseeing the Herndon Nature Park project was Luis Pastrana. He decided to run against Wyman. The *Orlando Sentinel* slammed Wyman and endorsed Pastrana (Indigo 2004).

As the city announced its partnership with Latino Leadership and the opening of the HOLA office in her district, Wyman was front and center (Márquez 2004). Luis Pastrana said that it was he who had conceived of the idea for what became the HOLA office after he saw a similar center in Atlanta (Harris and Pacheco 2004). In response to Wyman's sudden interest in Latinos, Evelyn Rivera said, "She announced it before her re-election just to get our votes, but I don't think so" (in Harris and Pacheco 2004). Nonetheless, in a March election that combined the presidential primary with nonpartisan municipal elections, Wyman defeated Pastrana with 64 percent of the vote.[29]

When Wyman finally left office in 2008, two Latino candidates ran against each other to replace her: police officer and Wyman's longtime aide Tony Ortíz and former Johnson aide Belinda Ortíz. In a runoff election, Tony Ortíz narrowly won. At his swearing in, Wyman said that she had long known that he was the one who should replace her (Loperena 2008). The new District 2 representative made cleaning up Semoran Boulevard his signature project (Schlueb 2011, Stokes 2011). By 2009 he had created a Neighborhood Leaders Council and a Business Leaders Council, through which he envisioned "citizens, government, and businesses working together" (Ortíz 2009). As Wyman's handpicked successor and a Puerto Rican with a stated desire to serve the community, Ortíz's election and his work to redevelop an area long neglected by his predecessor is another view of the fine line between opportunity and danger.

Orange County BCC. When Johnson termed out of her District 3 seat on the Orange County BCC in 2004, Puerto Rico–born Mildred Fernández narrowly won the seat in the November general election. Fernández is a Republican but had supported Democrat Al Gore in the 2000 election; in 2004 she supported Republican George Bush (García 2004). In this nonpartisan commission race, she drew support among Latinos from across the political spectrum. One diehard Puerto Rican Democrat told me, "We worked hard for her."

Analys's experience with Fernández, when she sought the commissioner's intervention to protect her neighborhood from the encroachments of new construction, is an example of how some people began to feel that Fernández's links to developers were her priority. With time, her support among Democratic Latinos waned. Many backed her Anglo opponent in 2008.

In 2010 Fernández entered her name in the race to replace outgoing Orange County Mayor Richard Crotty. Fernández was one of five candidates and the only Hispanic. In the wake of media revelations that a lobbyist had held several all-male parties that included elected officials and candidates, Fernández began to criticize the "boys club" and dig in for disclosures of attendees as required by law (Damron 2010). Soon afterward, she was arrested for accepting campaign contributions in a quid pro quo with a developer and suspended from her commission seat (Damron et al. 2010). Her 2011 trial overlapped with the county's redistricting process that same year. By 2012 she was in jail.

To this day the trial and conviction of Mildred Fernández is a painful moment in Orlando Puerto Rican collective memory. Across the political spectrum there has been a feeling that Fernández's public shaming points a finger at all Puerto Ricans. Even her detractors have told me they felt chills up their spines when they first heard of her arrest. Many have expressed deep sorrow that this chance to make a Puerto Rican name in Orange County would end in this shame instead. And there was nagging curiosity about the sequence of events. One Orlando Puerto Rican said to me, "Just before this is preceded by her talking about the all-men's club and this sort of stuff, and I had to wonder. . . . I just kept looking at it and saying, 'OK, is she a victim or a criminal and what's going on here?'"

As the trial went forward in 2011, even some of those who had spoken out against Fernández rallied around her. The courthouse was packed every day. Conversations revolved around "what they are doing to her." "She's *de lo nuestro* [one of us]," I heard, "and the whole thing feels like a slap in the face." Isabel, a Puerto Rican woman with long experience in Central Florida, drew a comparison for me between the Fernández case and earlier resistance to African American political power in Orange County: "African Americans tell me the same thing. When they started to have some power, they started to be jailed by other political factions. History is repeating itself with the Puerto Ricans who are gaining power in Central Florida today like what happened to the African Americans here fifteen to twenty years ago."

In the fallout from Fernández's arrest, Orange County District 3 went without representation for about four months until Governor Charlie Crist appointed an interim commissioner (Damron and Ramos 2010, de la Riva 2010b). Several Hispanics including Mary Johnson were among those considered, but Crist gave the seat to Johnson's non-Latino former assistant instead. Crist had recently left the Republican Party and become an independent. That likely explains why he appointed a fellow independent. Nonetheless, Latino protest was loud. "¿Que hará en la silla hispana?" (What will happen in the Hispanic seat?) was the headline in *La Prensa* (de la Riva 2010b).

In the protected spaces of Latino Orlando, many of these events—and especially the Fernández arrest and pending trial—were discussed amid a growing feeling of displacement and dispossession. As the 2011 redistricting began, many looked to that process for the opportunity to solidify the Orange County BCC seat that had been occupied by a Latina for nearly two decades. Instead, the new lines drawn during the 2011 redistricting process reduced the Latino percentage in District 3 and brought a powerful group of white voters into the district.

Toward the end of 2011 as her trial was set to begin, Mildred Fernández officially resigned. Rick Scott had been elected governor in 2010, and so it fell to him to appoint a permanent replacement for the remainder of Fernández's term. The person he appointed was Mel Martinez's son. He did not live in District 3 and had no prior experience in office (Damron 2011b). The governor's move felt like yet another insult to Latinos in general and to Puerto Ricans in particular.

MAKING HOME IN GOOD TIMES AND BAD

Amid these displacements and the other mechanisms contributing to a collective feeling of dispossession among many Orlando Puerto Ricans and other Latinos, a 2010 event at the Asociación Borinqueña gave physical form to the political losses and highlighted the importance of maintaining the intimate spaces of home for diaspora community formation. The financial troubles that would lead to the organization's bankruptcy were in full swing, and Mildred Fernández had been arrested. Along with other challenges to Puerto Rican and Latino political and physical territory, the Puerto Rican parade was having real troubles staying in the black financially.

To save the cost of paying for the Orlando police, the parade took place on the grounds of the Asociación Borinqueña in September 2010. Voting in the race between Mercado and Cannon was only a few weeks away. Mercado was featured in the parade, and Cannon made his presence known as well. But instead of taking over an Orlando street for the day, the parade did a few turns through the parking lot—visible only to those of us who made a point of attending. It rained throughout much of the event, pushing us into the shelter formed by a small tented area by the front door. Soon after the parade, many left and those remaining went inside. There, in the comforts of home, it felt like a private party. The intimate presence of a Puerto Rican community was enhanced, and the visibility of that community was reduced, as once again the building offered Puerto Ricans an island in Orlando.

Mercado's loss to Cannon was one of several Latino losses in the 2010 midterms. Darren Soto retained his seat in the Florida House, but thirty years after Johnson was elected in 1980 and fifteen years after Joe Pérez's election in Deltona marked the start of a series of Puerto Rican firsts in the 1990s, Soto remained one of only three Latinos, all of them Puerto Rican, ever elected to the Florida legislature from Central Florida. But the rained-out parade and the 2010 midterm elections underscore as well the dialogic relation between the more intimate activities of building trust and mutuality in the inside spaces of home and the more visible and public assertions of belonging physically and politically in Orlando.

Despite Cannon's win, the effort and expense he went to for that win signaled something significant was afoot. Mercado got 40 percent of the vote and won all the Latino precincts she targeted on a fraction of the money that Cannon spent to defend his incumbency. As in the election of Robert Guevara, Mercado presented a palpable challenge to the historically constructed social relations in Florida that have structured who has access to political power and who does not.

Not only did her campaign challenge Tallahassee's racial-ethnic power structure, as an Afro–Puerto Rican and a woman, she also stood out among the few Puerto Ricans who had managed to be elected from Central Florida. As she asserted her right to belong as a Puerto Rican and a citizen, her gender and in-between color served as reminders of the contested history of US citizenship and the rights accorded to it. In another election six years later, Mercado was back and this time won election to the Florida House.

This is something of a political parallel to what I saw in the changing physical landscape of Puerto Rican and Latino Orlando. As much as I saw places disappear with each return visit during my fieldwork, I also saw new places emerge in a persistent claim to belonging. On Easter Sunday in 2018, I was witness to a lively and interactive celebration of the traditional Puerto Rican music and dance called bomba in front of Guavate.[30] Like the rebirth of the Asociación Borinqueña building as Acacia, these new spaces affirm that place-making is an achievement and that like political formation, it is a process that is never complete.

Another example is the island-based tradition of celebrating the end of the Christmas season with the Festival de San Sebastián, which had begun to make a modest showing in Orlando about the time my fieldwork began. I only became aware of it in 2011 when the festival was held at Café d'Antaño. By 2015 or so, San Sebastián was shortened to Sanse and the festival renamed La Sanse Takes Orlando. It is most often simply called La Sanse. The annual event has grown so large that by 2018 it completely took over the extensive Central Florida Fairgrounds for an entire weekend in January. As La Sanse takes Orlando, it is a physical demonstration of the Puerto Rican refrain, "We're not going anywhere."

In the meantime, Café d'Antaño's owner managed to purchase the building just off Colonial and opened a similar space with a new name. For a while, a new cultural center called Hispanos sin Fronteras (Hispanics without Borders) took over the same space in the back of the office park near Executive Airport that has been home to so many different organizations.

A Puerto Rican parade began in Osceola County in 2011, and since Mildred Zapata's death, renewed efforts have revived the parade in Orlando. Four Puerto Ricans, among them Evelyn Rivera and James Auffant, served on the Orange County School Board's redistricting committee in 2011. Central Florida Latino representation in Tallahassee has grown, and Central Florida has sent Puerto Rican Darren Soto to the US Congress. And staking a simultaneous claim to being seen and being at home, with every election cycle, *caravanas* plant a Puerto Rican flag in the streets of Orlando.

PART III

THE CASE OF REDISTRICTING IN ORANGE COUNTY, FLORIDA

CHAPTER 6

DIVIDED BY BEANS

Tensions of Collective Identification

In a March 29 meeting, one week before the 2011 redistricting process was to begin, the Orange County Board of County Commissioners (BCC) met with serious Puerto Rican and Latino opposition to the composition of the county's Redistricting Advisory Committee (RAC). The RAC's assignment was to study Orange County demographics and existing district lines and to develop new maps that balanced the population among the county's six voting districts. Members of the RAC would present map proposals in public hearings, and the advisory committee as a whole would determine what recommendations to make to the BCC. The commissioners would then make the final determination of the geography and demographics of county voting districts for maps that would go into effect in 2012. How the maps were drawn would affect Puerto Ricans' and Latinos' collective strength in choosing their representatives for the next decade.

Redistricting processes for Orlando city, the Orange County School Board, the state legislature, and Florida's congressional districts would also be going on as separate processes in 2011. The dynamics between racial and political gerrymandering had long managed to block Central Florida Latinos' access to political ground. In 2001, Orlando-area Latinos were sidelined during redistricting at every level of state and local representation. As pertains to Orange County, the growth of the Latino population in the 1990s had raised the pressure in 2001 for creating a Latino district on the East Side like the black district on the West Side (Maxwell 2001b). According to one Orange County commissioner in 2011, the commissioners in 2001 had essentially ignored the recommendations from the advisory committee whose members they themselves had appointed (BCC March 29, 2011).[1] The new map that went into effect in 2002 looked very much like the one from 1992. This is how incumbent control happens.

In 2011 Puerto Rican and Latino strategizing for a better outcome was putting racial-ethnic identification over party affiliation for many. Common Latino issues such as a high dropout rate among Latino youth and the ongoing struggle for compliance with Spanish-language requirements in schools and on ballots reached across partisan divides. "Let's get a district," they said, "and then the Republicans and Democrats can duke it out." A bipartisan group, mostly Puerto Rican, formed the Central Florida Redistricting Committee to monitor the process and propose maps at state and local levels. The two Orange County districts with the largest Latino populations in 2011 were District 3 (45 percent) and District 4 (37 percent). District 3 had been represented by a Latina—first Mary Johnson and then Mildred Fernández—from 1992 until 2010, when Fernández was arrested and Governor Crist appointed as the interim District 3 commissioner a non-Latino man, whom I will refer to as Commissioner D3.[2]

Each of the six county commissioners selected two RAC members, and the newly elected county mayor selected three at-large members. The appointments created a committee of eight men and seven women, with a racial-ethnic mix of eight non-Latino white, four non-Latino black, and three Latino members. The three Latinos were Cuban and Nicaraguan. The mayor had appointed a Cuban member. A Nicaraguan appointee was one of those chosen by Commissioner D3. Another Cuban member was appointed by Commissioner D5. Commissioner D4 did not appoint a Latino, choosing instead two non-Latino white committee members. When challenged about her choices given the large percentage of Latinos in her district, Commissioner D4's response was that her priority had been to find a qualified person (Damron and Rivera-Lyles 2011). This supposedly colorblind view of universal human sameness in a meritocracy simultaneously normalized Commissioner D4's perspective and left the impression that District 4 Latinos were not as qualified as the district's non-Latino white residents (Bonilla-Silva 2014, Omi and Winant 2015).

Not only did District 4 not have Latino representation, but there was not a single Puerto Rican on the entire RAC. Many Puerto Ricans were outraged. The RAC's composition had been a central topic of the March 18 National Congress for Puerto Rican Rights meeting, and people were urged to attend the March 29 BCC meeting to speak in protest. BCC meetings are at 9 a.m., making attendance difficult for anyone with a 9-to-5 job. A small group attended. They signed the cards required for speaking during public commentary and used various tactics for asserting the right to be different and to belong.

Wearing the traditional Puerto Rican straw hat called the *pava*, Rico Piccard asserted both his US citizenship and his identification with Puerto

Rico (BCC March 29, 2011). In a show of the politics of worthiness, he talked about his years in Vietnam. Aligning himself with a wider Latino constituency, he said Puerto Ricans "led the way for all other Hispanics to obtain their civil rights." Another speaker was Emilio Pérez, co-chair of the Central Florida Redistricting Committee and president of the Puerto Rican Chamber of Commerce of Central Florida. He commented that only a small group of Hispanics got "board participation, grants, jobs, referrals, and contracts" that the BCC had to offer. "Being Hispanic is kind of tricky," he said, referring to national and cultural diversity among Hispanics. He then asked, "Have any of you ever seen a Hispanic flag?" Finally, in response to a commissioner's earlier remark that the process should not be racial, Pérez offered, "I challenge you to make a selection of only African-American and Puerto Rican citizens and let's see what will happen" (BCC March 29, 2011).

These and other appeals to the BCC did not succeed in getting a Puerto Rican on the RAC. Protesters appeared again the following week to speak during the first RAC meeting, on April 7 at 6 p.m. In that evening meeting and the seventeen that followed, the RAC conducted its business and then took public commentary as the final part of the agenda. On April 7, African American James Q. Mitchell told the RAC members, "If you're really concerned with input from the public, you have to sometimes adopt what the public is telling you." Puerto Rican Daisy Morales said, "I just want to let you know that I am listening. I'm very interested in this issue, and I will be watching. Because that's all we can do—watch." Ecuadorian Trini Quiroz talked about attending every meeting during the previous redistricting and asked, "Are we going to go through the same thing . . . or are we moving forward to include?" (RAC April 7, 2011).

When her turn to speak came, Zoraida Ríos-Andino placed a Puerto Rican flag on the podium in front of her and took her full allotted time to explain to the RAC members all the reasons that a Puerto Rican should be on that committee. As she finished, she looked at the RAC members and said, "Do any of you consider resigning from your position to allow a Puerto Rican to be on this committee?" As they sat in silence and the chairman tried to move on to the next speaker, she continued, "I'm asking the question as a citizen. Would anyone resign to allow a Puerto Rican to be on this committee?" (RAC April 7, 2011).

Needless to say, no one stepped down, but the point is that Ríos-Andino used citizenship in various forms to validate Puerto Rican belonging and to back up her demand that the RAC include specifically Puerto Rican representation among Hispanics. Puerto Ricans fought in every US war, she asserted, including the Revolution on which the United States rests. She used taxes paid by Latinos to underwrite a claim to redistributive rights, and she further stressed Latino economic belonging with reference to Hispanic buying power. Her complaint—the truth of which seems evident in the final maps—was that the county's only concern was in taking care of the Anglo-dominated areas of Conway, Winter Park, and downtown. She claimed affiliation with African Americans, saying she had grown up in a black community during the civil rights movement. Alternating identification as Puerto Rican and as Hispanic, she inserted and asserted in her every word the argument that Puerto Ricans are a visible and deserving community in Orlando. She even set visibility at the Asociación Borinqueña as a measure of belonging when she said she had never seen any of the Hispanic RAC members there.

True to the styles of dust-kicking and diplomacy, not all agreed with these bold tactics. "You can't just go and demand someone resign," one person said to me. I heard concern that "people are raising eyebrows" and that this was "bad for the Puerto Rican image." There was worry that the Latino organizing for local redistricting was coming out of New York and that some of the organizers were Puerto Rican nationalists. There was also talk about the Puerto Ricans who had recently been appointed to the Orange County schools' new Hispanic Advisory Board: "*That's* how we get in there. *This* is the way we get things done." But one person admitted to me that things actually get done in this mix of dust-kicking and diplomacy.

Throughout the months of redistricting, there were undoubtedly quiet, behind-the-scenes efforts to work things out in a manner favorable to Latino voting strength. The point here is to follow the public navigation and negotiation of Puerto Rican and Latino diversity in interaction with local powerholders. Using both challenging and accommodating rhetoric, those attending the public hearings would continue to speak out and eventually offer their own maps. Both dust-kicking and diplomacy were repeatedly countered with claims of universal human sameness that set race and ethnicity aside.

The combined oppositional commentary from the March BCC meeting and the first RAC meeting in April went back and forth in arguments for the importance of a Hispanic district and dismay at Puerto Ricans having been excluded right out of the gate. The shifting claims point to a merry-go-round of identity in which the decision to identify as Puerto Rican, American, Hispanic, or Latino is informed by the territorial claims at stake. The insistence on national-origin identifications among Latinos would give way in future meetings to an emphasis on Hispanics as a whole, but at this initial stage the choice of identifiers was aimed mostly at highlighting Puerto

Ricans' citizenship as evidence that they should have a seat at the table as representatives of all Hispanics.

Throughout my fieldwork I heard Orlando Puerto Ricans reference the idea of a *balde de jueyes* (bucket of crabs) to describe infighting as something unique to Puerto Ricans. Among Cubans, the saying goes, each crab holds out a claw to the other and they help each other out. Among Puerto Ricans, they say, as one crab nears the top of the bucket, another reaches up and pulls that crab back down.[3] In this chapter I take the *balde de jueyes* as an apt metaphor for not only intra–Puerto Rican conflicts but also among Latinos more widely as they struggle—sometimes in concert and sometimes in competition—for equitable opportunities and outcomes in Orlando's social field.[4] As Orlando Latinos interact with each other and with others in Orlando's simultaneously color-blind and multicultural meritocracy, the contrasting images of the *balde de jueyes* and the sleeping giant offer metaphors for thinking through tensions between collective identification and the vectors of difference that could disrupt the mobilization needed to confront the dispossession Latinos experienced during the first decade of the twenty-first century.

The redistricting process offers an opportunity to examine differences of place such as national origin, island or diaspora, and various Orange County spaces as they intertwine with a Latino race-class continuum, with Orlando's historically black-white racial frame, and with Orange County as a supposedly color-blind meritocracy in which economic success is attributed to individual ability rather than structural advantage. As the bases to demands for inclusion, race and class emerge in the commentary, glossed as arguments about national origin, deserving citizenship, and the emergent sleeping giant. In the process, different framings of citizenship relate to different ideas about what constitutes community and what form the relations between communities and the governing body should take.

I will return later to technical and racial-political details of the redistricting process and maps proposed. My purpose here is to point out that by simultaneously promoting Hispanic homogeneity and sowing discord between Puerto Ricans and other Latinos, the social dynamics of the RAC appointments stirred up the *balde de jueyes*. Despite the lack of Latino representation from District 4 and the total absence of Puerto Rican representation anywhere, the Hispanic makeup of the RAC as a whole appeared inclusive. The situation worked to incorporate Latinos as a singular identity group into the process, to render invisible the particulars of a Puerto Rican presence, and to divide Latinos as Puerto Ricans rose in protest. The powerful sleeping giant was both recognized and contained.

Apart from including black and Hispanic men as well as any women at all, the well-connected social composition of the RAC resembled that of the 1971 Citrus Center luncheon (discussed in chapter 2). The RAC affiliations listed online suggest that the representatives for the East Side districts (3, 4, and 5) in particular included prior experience in real estate and development, public relations, and local government. The shape of things in the Orange County government four decades after 1971 stands as testimony to how well the power elite has been able to accommodate the social conflicts of the civil rights movement while still supporting the reproduction of capitalist relations and maintaining a hold on local power (Torres 1995:23).

Because of Puerto Rico's colonial relations to the United States, Puerto Rican studies as a field engages empire in ways that other studies of US racial, social, economic, and political power may not. It may feel to some that drawing parallels between colonial-style relations and how the RAC membership was determined is like trying to push in a thumbtack with a sledgehammer. Yet it remains true that the practice of appointing members of smaller groups to nominative positions of power over the larger group is a time-honored colonial strategy for maintaining power and control. This is a practice of granting privilege to a few with the outcome of containing the power of the whole. The result is a "nesting hierarchy of ethnic identities" that nonetheless are "*interrelated* products of an historically specific confrontation" between dominant and subordinate groups (Comaroff and Comaroff 1992:58). The outcome situates "each group differently in relation to the hegemonic polarity of whiteness and blackness" (De Genova and Ramos-Zayas 2003:175).

RACE, CLASS, AND COLLECTIVE IDENTIFICATION

During the April 7 RAC meeting, one of the Cuban RAC members spoke up to say that she was born in Orlando, was married to a Puerto Rican, and had lived with her husband and children in Puerto Rico for a number of years. This was not the first or last time I heard non–Puerto Rican Latinos in the Orlando area refer to connections with Puerto Rico and/or Puerto Ricans as part of their claim to belonging in Orlando's Latino social field. While it is often true that non–Puerto Rican Latinos in Orlando and elsewhere work to distance themselves from the pejorative colonial-migrant stereotypes about Puerto Ricans, it is also true that non–Puerto Rican *Orlando* Latinos at times work to claim their own belonging by demonstrating their knowledge of and affiliation with things Puerto Rican. Thus, as Puerto Ricans made their claim as citizens, those they sought to replace justified their own appointments by implying, "I'm just like you."

At one point during that April 7 meeting, the Puerto Rican husband of the Cuban RAC member handed in his speaker's card and came to the podium. He said,

> I'll keep it short, I've got one point to make. I'm a Puerto Rican, born and raised in Puerto Rico. I moved to the Central Florida area when I was twelve. . . . This was in 1985, this was in Osceola County. Back then there were five Hispanics. I'm not talking Puerto Ricans, Cubans, Dominicans, it was five Hispanics. We had to stick together. The point I'm trying to make is, yes, first of all, I'm a Puerto Rican, but I'm also an American, and I consider myself first and foremost a Hispanic American. . . . If we bicker amongst each other, and we start going back and forth, guess what? We're going to be outside looking in, and we're going to miss our seat at the table. This is awesome. I mean, the fact that there's three Hispanics on the board? I mean, I call that phenomenal. Twenty years ago, you wouldn't dream of this. (RAC April 7, 2011)

This Puerto Rican man's experience of the merry-go-round of identity was very different from that of the protesters, who were insisting on specifically Puerto Rican representation and saying things like, "If they're going to leave me out of the pie, I won't even get the crumbs." This man was instead happy to be represented at the table in the unitary person of the Hispanics on the RAC. In one short statement he identified as Puerto Rican, Hispanic, American, and finally Hispanic American. The memories from Osceola County in 1985 that informed his perspective differ from those of an older generation whose members remember struggles in other diaspora communities.

In reference to the RAC appointments, I later heard an older-generation Puerto Rican say that he was no longer Hispanic; he was Puerto Rican. In ensuing conversations he considered that perhaps it was OK to be Latino but not Hispanic. For some, the distinction between "Hispanic" and "Latino" lies in whether engagement in the public sphere is through middle-class consumerism or through loud and oppositional politics (Davila 2008:83). Furthermore, with its association with the Spanish language, Hispanic emphasizes the whiteness of European heritage over Africanness and indigeneity. Given that, it is noteworthy that a nationwide study by the Pew Research Center in 2012 found that while just over half of Latinos most often use their country of origin or family heritage to identify themselves to others, those who use the umbrella identifier prefer Hispanic (Taylor 2012).

Some Latino scholars reference unequal relations to whiteness among Latinos and argue against intra-Latino race and class discrimination (Dávila

2008, De Genova 2010, Torres-Saillant 2003). In the dynamics of US white supremacy, color-blind multiculturalism, and neoliberal capitalism, Latinos face the constant risk of being valued for buying power as consumers rather than for political power as citizens (Báez 2014:274). Considering this through the lens of colonial relations highlights how Latino differences may set class-based and racial-ethnic identifications and interests against each other in a *balde de jueyes*.

As they struggle against being seen as colonial migrants rather than as US citizens, Orlando Puerto Ricans and by extension other Latinos regularly confront these race-class predicaments in their choices of racial-ethnic identification. Mérida Rúa (2012:49) has described a tendency among "socially mobile" Puerto Ricans in 1950s Chicago to refer to themselves as "Hispanos" precisely to distance themselves from the stigma of the so-called Puerto Rican problem. In Orlando, Jorge Duany (2011:107) finds that "the relatively large proportion of well-educated [Puerto Rican] professionals and managers" have mostly identified as white and preferred Puerto Rican over Hispanic.[5] While aligning with the Pew study, this finding also speaks to the local reframing of the idea of the Puerto Rican that is under way in Orlando as well as to the awareness of how the particular needs of Puerto Ricans disappear into any unitary identification, whether Hispanic or Latino.

The insistence on a Puerto Rican presence—and the distinction made between Hispanic and Latino—gave voice to the perspective that Puerto Ricans were being displaced in the redistricting process by Hispanics who would likely not have Puerto Rican interests in mind. Examples from Central Florida history of this Puerto Rican invisibility are easy to find. An exhibit featuring local Hispanic artists in the Orange County government building almost left Puerto Rican artists out (Padilla 1999b). In a 2000 political event, the candidates repeatedly left Puerto Ricans out of the Hispanic groups they named until, as reported by María Padilla (2000d), "Puerto Ricans in the audience could stand it no longer, shouting, 'Somos Boricuas!'—'We're Puerto Ricans!'—as if to say, 'We're here. Don't you see us?'"

At the March 29 Orange County BCC meeting when Emilio Pérez talked about the small group of Hispanics favored by the Orange County powers that be, he added that the group was not Puerto Rican and "none of them like us Puerto Ricans." Pérez directed the commissioners to look for the organizations that identify themselves according to their national origins. "You will find," he said, "that most of these organizations are more grassroots, are more respected between the communities" (BCC March 29, 2011).

These shifting identifications do not happen in a Latino vacuum. If I dig deeply enough into one argument or another, I often find amid the tensions in the *balde de jueyes* that arguments stem from competition for resources needed to survive and thrive in Orlando's social field. This is another reflection of colonialist divide-and-conquer practices. Although a variety of Latino organizations in the Orlando area reach to an umbrella term—Hispanic Health Initiatives, Latino Leadership, National Council of La Raza, Mi Familia Vota, and so on—the national origins behind each are well known among politically active Orlando Latinos. Like the appointments to the RAC, decisions about which organization receives what public or private funding as well as about how the money is spent often lie in non-Latino white hands. This is the frustration that Orlando Latino political strategists have experienced when those who are funding advertising buys have been unwilling to listen to local arguments in favor of the radio.

Sometimes funding is funneled through local organizations controlled by non-Latinos who then hire Latinos to do local outreach. When funding does go directly to local Latino organizations and there are overlapping projects such as voter-registration campaigns, competition emerges among differently identified organizations as they compete for funding and territory. In a conversation I had with Yasmín about how to spend get-out-the-vote resources heading into the 2012 elections, she asked, "In the Southwest we talk about the Mexican vote and in Miami we talk about the Cuban vote. Why in Orlando do we not talk about the Puerto Rican vote?"

The view that all social activity takes place in a constantly shifting social field highlights the questions of who does what, to what end, and with what effect on social relations. For instance, Puerto Rican performances of the cultural capital associated with whiteness in Orlando suggest a common claim to the desire to advance the standing of Orlando's Puerto Rican and Latino "community" (Delerme 2017). For some, advancing the community means networking with other Puerto Ricans and Latinos of means to create business opportunities for individual gain and promotion of a particularized, favorable image of Latinos. For others it is about connecting to that network for the purpose of bringing much-needed resources to Puerto Ricans and Latinos who are homeless, unemployed, and/or among the working poor.

The question is, what constitutes the boundaries of community. Who is in and who is out? Does the outcome from any given use of an identity idea or racial-ethnic identification contribute to more evenly distributed or more concentrated social power? I make no effort to assert unspoken intentions behind the actions I observed, but looking at patterns of outcomes gives evidence of effect, intentional or not. It is simply a question of who is hurt and who is helped in the final analysis. Looking to "a viable integrated image of 'the community' by which all subsections of the US Hispanic population can feel adequately represented," Silvio Torres-Saillant (2003:126) argues for the imperative of recognizing "intra-Latino race and class biases." In the *balde de jueyes*, who is helping whom to get out? Because constructions of difference are informed by the larger social field, with its unequal access to power and opportunity, it will be important to ask what is happening outside the bucket that may be raising the temperature inside.

STIRRING UP THE *BALDE DE JUEYES*

A lunchtime conversation at a 2012 community event I attended serves as a joking reference to the intersections of Puerto Rican and Latino race, class, and place with the supposedly color-blind consumerist ethos of Orlando's social field. Everyone at the table was a member of a Latino professional organization. Two men seated next to each other, one Puerto Rican and one Cuban, were exchanging commentaries on the lunchtime program. As a presentation for Goya food products began, the Puerto Rican man chuckled, leaned over, and said to his Cuban friend, "The Latino community is one divided by beans." The Cuban man replied with a sarcastic tone, "A bean is a bean, regardless of color."

Goya sells all kinds of beans to all kinds of Latinos, and the bean metaphor can apply equally to commonality or difference. Marytza Sanz once told a reporter, "The Chileans say *porotos*, the Puerto Ricans say *habichuelas* and the Cubans say *frijoles*—but it all means beans, you know?" (in Kunerth and Brewington 2002). But in this case the Puerto Rican man's remarks stressed difference and seemed to me to mock the commodified homogenization of Latinos. In the rejoinder I heard a rejection of color-blind assumptions of sameness and acknowledgement of intra-Latino racial discrimination.

Along with rejecting Latino homogeneity, the initial comment about division by beans suggested national-origin tensions among Latinos from different places. In Chicago, for instance, Rodríguez Muñiz (2010:249) notes the "pervasive idea of Puerto Rican/Mexican animosity" as he details the workings of a Puerto Rican activist group that used the commonality of colonial relations to draw the two groups together. In Orlando, if there is a pervasive idea of intra-Latino rivalries, it is about Puerto Ricans and Cubans. It is a rivalry formed largely in other places but now playing out in a state where Hispanic has long been synonymous with Cuban. Framed as place of origin, Cuban–Puerto Rican tensions have deep roots crosscut historically by race and class.

Cuba-born Rafael Medina made a veiled reference to tensions among those who socialized at his grocery in the 1970s and 1980s: "We always got along well with everyone, resolving what we could" (PRCF Medina).[6] Among Orlando Puerto Rican memories, there are accusations that the first wave of Cuban refugees to Puerto Rico in the 1960s took what was rightfully Puerto Rican, and resentment that the same continues in Orlando. There is grumbling that the Sociedad Cubana was getting contracts that have kept it afloat while the Asociación Borinqueña struggled against bankruptcy (Domenech 2006). Referring to the back-and-forth ownership of and membership in chambers of commerce, Duany (2011:126) cites "Ernesto," who said with resentment that "Cubans 'took over' the Hispanic Chamber of Commerce in Orlando, so Puerto Ricans had to form their own chamber." Ernesto's resentment toward Cuban power in Florida located the difference in class relations when he said that many Cubans come from "moneyed families."

Puerto Rican public events like the parade and the Noche de San Juan have had to compete with the Orlando Cuban Calle Orange festival that plays on the theme of the famous Calle Ocho in Miami. A frequent critique is that the Puerto Rican parade and festival are open and free but people have to pay to enter Calle Orange. Those offering the complaint are setting profit making from a commodified ethnicity into opposition with the use of visibility as a political strategy. All this paints challenges to Cubans and Puerto Ricans coming together in Orlando in anything like what Rodríguez Muñiz (2010) saw in Chicago between Mexicans and Puerto Ricans.

Despite the Cuban–Puerto Rican tensions in contemporary Orlando, there is ample historical evidence of common cause and collaboration—against Spanish colonial rule in the nineteenth century and against working conditions for cigar makers in the late nineteenth and early twentieth centuries. The relations between the two nationalities were even celebrated in the poem "Cuba y Puerto Rico son de un pájaro las dos alas" (Cuba and Puerto Rico are two wings of the same bird). Much more recently, in 2013, Puerto Rican workers went to Miami from Puerto Rico in support of Cuban workers engaged in a hunger strike (Aranda et al. 2014:154). And in his oral history, Puerto Rican US Air Force pilot José Santana, who flew missions over the waters between Cuba and Florida in the 1960s, talked about a small spit of land from which the Cubans would wave to the US pilots overhead. He spoke of his hope to one day meet one of those Cubans and know that he might have been the one to send aid their way (PRCF Santana).

In Orlando proper, Cuban-owned Medina's grocery is a constant marker in Puerto Rican memories of building community, and in his 2008 oral history Rafael Medina credited Puerto Ricans for his success. That Puerto Rico–born Patricia González Durocher collected clothing and furniture at her home in downtown Orlando for Cuban exiles also speaks to cooperative relations. Duany (2011:126) writes about Puerto Rican children who grew up in Orlando and dated Cubans. There are Cuban–Puerto Rican marriages in Orlando like the couple at the RAC meeting. During my fieldwork there was an annual friendly *trova* competition of improvised recitations between the two groups (de la Riva 2010a). And my field notes have the story of a Puerto Rican woman who spent a good deal of her time and energy "sharing her own experiences of isolation and fear" from her first days in the US states with a recently arrived Cuban woman having a hard time adjusting to her new home.

Referencing Cubans, Puerto Ricans, Mexicans, Chicanos, "and others of Latin American descent," Suzanne Oboler argues that there has long been a sense of community among Latinos. Rivalries, she argues (1995:xv), emerge from differential treatment in the US states: "What is at issue is the different emphasis in U.S. politics on ethnic categories and their changing attributions and the state's distribution and withdrawal of resources on the basis of those terms since the 1960s."

The distinct histories of Puerto Rican and Cuban relations to the United States in the latter half of the twentieth century offer an example of Oboler's generalized observations, an example of stirring up the *balde de jueyes*. Following the Cuban Revolution and at the height of the Cold War, the Cuban Adjustment Act gave Cuban exiles arriving on US shores a leg up, out of the boiling pot, so to speak. This was happening at the same time that Puerto Ricans in New York were struggling against being stereotyped as a problematic group living in a self-perpetuating culture of poverty. Although he framed his comments in terms of Cuban gratitude to Puerto Rico, Rafael Medina asserted that many Cubans became millionaires as exiles in Puerto Rico (PRCF Medina). In the Orlando area, a comparative overview of Cuban, Puerto Rican, and non-Latino white median household incomes indicates that Puerto Ricans' household income in 2017 was somewhat lower than Cubans', about $45,000 to $48,000, respectively, but both were significantly lower than the $64,000 median income for non-Latino white households (US Census Bureau, ACS 2017a). One might think that mutual recognition of this shared reality would awaken a sense of common cause.

Evidence from Richard Foglesong's biography of Mel Martinez offers some explanation for local Cuban–Puerto Rican rivalry (Foglesong 2011:80–89). Although by 1980 Puerto Ricans outnumbered Cubans in the Orlando metro area, the picture of the 1980s to emerge from Foglesong's early twenty-first-century interviews is one of an Orlando Latino elite with very few Puerto Ricans compared to Cubans. Foglesong writes that through the vehicle of Mayor Frederick's Hispanic Advisory Committee, Martinez was able to open the door to a group of Cubans. Although Frederick was a Democrat, the Hispanic Advisory Committee was politically conservative with the exception of the only Puerto Rican among them, James Auffant (Foglesong 2011:84).

Whatever the actual national origin of the various Latinos beginning to make names for themselves in Orlando, it seems clear that a group of well-heeled Cubans represented the face of Hispanic Orlando. Foglesong (2011:83) cites one person who referred to the group as the "Cuban mafia." As the 1980s brought "later-wave Cubans of lower social strata" and "Puerto Ricans migrating from the Commonwealth and New York," disquiet arose among the earlier arrivals that "their efforts to blend into mainstream Anglo culture as upstanding citizens and accomplished business people and professionals, was threatened by the newcomers" (Foglesong 2011:88). This evidence about Cuban–Puerto Rican relations in Orlando weaves together places of origin, intra-Latino differences of racial identification and class relations, the local black-white binary, and the dictates of the area's supposedly color-blind meritocracy. As the Latino population has increased, some have managed to retain honorary white status, while others have been lumped together as a Latino threat, and the difference can turn up the heat in the *balde de jueyes*.

Despite evidence of Cuban–Puerto Rican tensions in the 1980s, I heard a reference to that time in Orlando as "when the Cubans and Puerto Ricans got along." Curious about that, I asked someone else how things had been when she arrived in 1996. She laughed and said, "Better than now." Given historically divergent relations to the United States and the particulars of Orlando's social field, the fact that two of the three Hispanic members of the RAC were from Cuba or of Cuban descent undoubtedly fanned the flames of that rivalry.

Convivencia diaria. The person who laughed about Puerto Rican–Cuban rivalries quickly added that this was really about a small group of people, which seemed to confirm the conclusions I have drawn from Foglesong's evidence about an elite circle. That then leaves the question of how Cubans, Puerto Ricans, and other Latinos relate to each other day to day in their encounters in schools, churches, and groceries where they are just trying to live their lives and get by in a social field where they are often lumped together as a Latino threat. The same person who told me about comforting the Cuban woman who had just arrived also told me how proud she was to help that Cuban woman vote for the first time. She said she herself is proud to be Puerto Rican *and* Latina. In contrast to the umbrella identity created through government, media, and social activism, her collective identification as Latina emerged from commonly lived daily experience. It is the social basis to the politics in rice and beans promoted by Ramos and embraced by Analys. It underlies the kind of emergent solidarity that Rodríguez Muñiz (2010) has observed in Chicago, that Hardy-Fanta (1993) has observed in Boston, and that Rocco (2014) has observed in Los Angeles.

Clearly, this pan-Latino recognition of mutuality is not unique to Orlando. Between the 1920s and 1960s in Grand Rapids, Michigan, Mexicans and Puerto Ricans developed a common identification grounded in daily life activities at work, church, and community social activities (Fernández 2013). Similarly, *convivencia diaria* (daily living together) in Queens, New York, has helped unite Latinas of many different national origins in a common identification born of the relationships that emerge in the "daily-life settings of residence, neighborhood, and workplace" (Ricourt and Danta 2003:10). In Queens, common language, religion, working-class relations, and geographic proximity helped to make an "experiential Latino panethnicity" (24).

In Orlando, none of those elements is clearly present among people who might collectively identify as Hispanic/Latino.[7] There, Latinos live all over the place, although there are concentrations such as the East Side and the cross-county area around Meadow Woods and Buenaventura Lakes. Common meeting places, radio programs, and the internet help bridge the disconnected spaces. And while many identify with the working class, Orlando Latinos lead widely different economic lives. Language abilities and preferences in Orlando vary with generation, birthplace, and migration experience. The assumption of a shared Catholic faith does not apply to Orlando, where Catholic churches have not always welcomed the growing Latino population and where Latinos and especially Puerto Ricans have founded many nondenominational churches.

What is true about Orlando is the unquestionable numeric dominance of Puerto Ricans among those who could make up a Latino community. Despite references to a *balde de jueyes*, Puerto Ricans use their citizenship to offer an opening to wider Latino claims of inclusion. In a very different reference from crabs pulling each other down, longtime Orlando activist Zulma Vélez Estrada said, "When a Puerto Rican rises, all Latinos rise," (100PR_OHP Zulma Vélez Estrada #25).[8]

In an example from Chicago of Puerto Rican citizenship in service to other Latinos as well as of racial-ethnic and class-based tensions that may supersede national origin affiliation, Jillian Báez (2014:279) tells of an undocumented Mexican woman who took sanctuary in a Puerto Rican church in Chicago. Not only was this a case of Puerto Rican–Mexican solidarity, but also the Mexican woman said she felt more supported by her working-class

Puerto Rican neighbors than by Chicago's professional Mexicans. Together with what Foglesong (2011) has suggested about Orlando's Latino elite, the woman's view is evidence against a possible *latinidad* that reaches across the divisions of class relations and racial identifications in Orlando. What is more, even with a common identification as Hispanic/Latino, there is not necessarily an embrace of common political ideologies. In other words, none of the evidence for a pan-Latino mutuality implies a direct move from collective identification to political solidarity.

Nor is it to say that such a move is impossible. Similar to what Antonia Pantoja achieved for Puerto Ricans in New York, a cross-class collaboration emerged in Queens among Latinas of different national origins (Ricourt and Danta 2003). The evidence from Queens describes a path from collective identification to political community forged by combining working-class and middle-class knowledge and resources (150). An illustration in Orlando is that those who are better able to show up and speak out at a BCC meeting are those who have a greater measure of control over their time.

The studies from Queens (Ricourt and Danta 2003) and Boston (Hardy-Fanta 1993) have associated women with grassroots attention to collective reciprocity and men with pursuing the public and private resources needed to sustain political campaigns for social justice. In Orlando I see evidence of women and men engaged in both areas of political organizing. Multiple fronts and activities contribute to Puerto Rican and Latino struggles for social justice in Orlando, painting an image distinct from those of the sleeping giant and the *balde de jueyes*.[9] It is important to remember that many of the early twenty-first-century Latino organizations, even in the neoliberal era of corporatization and professionalization, are led by people who came up in the civil rights struggles of the 1960s and 1970s, with all the knowledge and experience that such a background implies. Memories from that period inform many Orlando Latino political actors.

An incident during the 2010–2011 school year at East River High School in eastern Orange County serves as evidence of Puerto Ricans opening the way for other Latinos through their bilingual skills and citizenship status in a cross-class push for social justice. In the area of East River, the expanding Alafaya Latino population is bumping up against rural areas long dominated by a non-Latino white population. The school made the news as a site of racial tensions when a Puerto Rican boy's jaw was broken in a fight, Latino students were sent home for wearing T-shirts with flags from Latin American countries on them, and a YouTube video showed a Cuban boy being beaten by non-Latino white youths. The high school is in Orange County School

District 1, where Jacqueline Centeno ran for the seat in 2010 and lost in the August primaries to the Anglo incumbent. That same incumbent's ineffectual response to the violence was that she could not watch the YouTube video because it would make her cry.

Frente Unido 436 took up the issue. Its leaders called meetings that brought parents, school board members, police, and the press together in one room. Students and parents said previous friendships between Latino and non-Latino students were now strained, and Evelyn Rivera lamented the missed opportunity when—knowing that "the two groups do not mesh well"—she and others had suggested getting together with church and parent groups when they met with the East River administration prior to the school's opening (Stokes 2010). Apparently, the suggestion had gone unheeded.

In February 2011 I attended a Frente Unido 436 meeting in which angry and anxious parents, some with their children, crowded into a room at the Alafaya branch of the Orange County Library System.[10] They aired their grievances and demanded action. Although attendees were mostly Latino, there were also non-Latino white and black participants. Students, some of whom had transferred out of the school, stated that the Confederate flag had been allowed but not the flags of their families' countries of origin.

A Puerto Rican man spoke for Latinos generally: "We Hispanics have all experienced bad things from guys with Confederate flags—we want to know if our kids have to confront the same things we did as adults?" An African American man rose to say the problem is in the community and had been there for a long time. A Latina asked how the Anglo parents present felt about the situation, and one responded, "My daughter comes home every day and says there's fights. We're concerned." Puerto Ricans offered translations, as some in attendance spoke only English and others only Spanish. Friendly laughter broke out when the bilingual police officer spoke Spanish to an African American man without realizing it.

The outcomes from Frente Unido's efforts included the school's forming an internal student group and bringing in consultants to address racial tensions. By the end of the school year the principal was out. Throughout the process, police claimed that these were not hate crimes and the school board asserted that the situation was being handled. Newspaper blog posts suggested that Latinos were overreacting. But the scene at that meeting revealed a concern about intolerance and white supremacy that reached across Latino, non-Latino white, and non-Latino black participants. Their shared sense of purpose paints a different picture from that of a bucket in which each crab struggles to keep the other down.

FAIRNESS FOR ALL IN MULTICULTURAL NEOLIBERALISM

At the end of the very tense March 29, 2011, BCC meeting that preceded the first RAC meeting on April 7, each of the commissioners took a moment to address the public. Several made a point of identifying the Puerto Ricans and other Latinos they had on their staff or whom they had appointed to an advisory board. For some, however, it seemed that this was the first time they had ever thought about national-origin differences among Orange County Latinos. One commissioner expressed surprise and appreciation at being so informed. There was repeated encouragement to those present to apply for positions on the boards. The word "community" was sprinkled throughout the comments in reference to all of Orange County, to different racial-ethnic groups, and to specific places within the county. Before closing the meeting, the mayor told those who had come to speak that they had made a difference and raised awareness. She promised to do better next time and said, "The community, our Hispanic businesses, our Hispanic members, our Puerto Ricans, our Cubans, our Dominicans, all of us has to know that this is our Orange County. This is our country now. We're citizens" (BCC March 29, 2011).

It has become prevalent in the neoliberal, consumer-oriented social order for individuals to take on a brand, and the mayor's was fairness and inclusivity. When she came into office in 2010, she instituted the now-standard practice of public commentary during meetings, and she made sure that every commissioner had the opportunity to voice opinions. She often spoke out during public commentary to offer her own thoughts on the kind of welcoming and open community that she asserted Orange County to be. The mayor's concern for "our Hispanics," however, sounds strikingly like the concern of the Anglo man who said he was speaking for "conservative Puerto Rican Republicans" during the meeting of the National Congress for Puerto Rican Rights. It suggests paternalistic, or in this case maternalistic, colonial-style relations in which deserving citizens should be trusted by all the rest to look out for everyone's interest. Years later, at the memorial marking one year since the Pulse shootings, when she and the Orlando mayor were criticized for neglecting to mention the actual victims, she used the same language to say there was never an intention to be insensitive to "our cherished LGBTQ and Hispanic populations" (in Weiner 2017).

Although the mayor's words carry extra weight because of her position at the head of Orange County government, she was not alone during the BCC and RAC meetings in using this language of exclusionary inclusion, which gives recognition while still maintaining control firmly in hand. A few weeks into the redistricting, as Spanish-language talk radio was still targeting

Commissioner D4 for not appointing a Latino to the RAC and the *Orlando Sentinel* was still saying she "appeared to show little regard for a community that makes up more than a third of her district," the commissioner attempted to clarify the situation of her RAC appointments: "Had I realized . . . the kind of backlash that I would be getting because I said that, or the kind of backlash I would get because I didn't appoint the right type of person for that board, I would have played the game and tried to fill that quota seat or try to put the right person in there" (in Damron and Rivera-Lyles 2011).

Speaking from a universalist view of human sameness that normalizes the particular perspective of the speaker, Commissioner D4 seemed to assume her own maturity and authority. Her words did little to placate Latinos, who understood perfectly well that in positioning her own neutrality and suggesting that the so-called right kind of person was playing games, she dismissed Latino concerns as inconsequential. In essence, she erased them from the equation.

Try as she might, Commissioner D4 just kept doing and saying things that reinforced the image that she was at best clueless and at worst not interested. During the March 29 meeting, as speakers were giving their public input, she leaned back in her chair with her eyes shut, appearing to be either totally disengaged or perhaps even asleep. *La Prensa* newspaper ran her photo on the front page, and she earned the nickname Sleeping Beauty. By a week later as the redistricting process was beginning on April 7, the RAC appointments and Commissioner D4 had made national news (Van Natta 2011).

At the start of that first RAC meeting, the fifteen RAC members were seated where the six commissioners and the mayor had sat on March 29. Speaking from the podium and stressing how important their task was, the mayor thanked the RAC members for their service. She emphasized that this was about "making sure every citizen in Orange County has a fair voice in our upcoming elections" (RAC April 7, 2011). She invited Commissioner D4, who was in the audience, to speak, and the commissioner began by directing a remark to the Cuban RAC member appointed by Commissioner D5. She said sympathetically, "You're in my chair, and I recently had it altered so it doesn't lean back. So I hope that you're comfortable" (RAC April 7, 2011). Although perhaps intended to make a public, joking reference to her appearing to be asleep at the March 29 meeting, Commissioner D4's choice of tone signaled a familiarity between her and that RAC member. She went on to address the entire RAC, saying she knew most of them personally, naming first her two appointees, and then saying that the mayor's Cuban American appointee was a District 4 resident. Her manner suggested cozy relations with the RAC members as a community of politically and economically influential Orlandoans.

Affinity between the RAC and the BCC was not lost on those who spoke out at the March 29 meeting against the RAC appointments. Although Puerto Ricans' and Latinos' objections had focused on racial-ethnic inclusion and economic citizenship, an Anglo man who lived in District 4 said Commissioner D4's appointment "reeks of political favor" as "political and business appointments" (BCC March 29, 2011). As the various commissioners spoke to defend their appointments, it was only Commissioner D6, the one African American on the BCC, who expressed empathetic understanding of "the voice of this [Puerto Rican] community" as she said that her appointees came "from more of a community action background" (BCC March 29, 2011). Where the other members assured the protesters that the appointees would "do what's best for everyone" or that "everybody's interests are represented," Commissioner D6 emphasized the importance of extending mutuality and protecting rights.

The distinction that Commissioner D6 was drawing between her criteria for appointing RAC members and those of the other commissioners again brings attention to different ideas about what constitutes community, with consequential perspectives on what constitutes a citizen. As framed by the protesters and acknowledged by Commissioner D6, citizenship is collective and participatory; it offers a vehicle for claims to justice and participation in decisions about the distribution of and access to public resources. Countering the protesters' assertion of their right to participate was an emphasis on property and participation rights achieved through building the appropriate social capital. In this latter perspective, the right to participate must be earned; it is contingent on being a deserving citizen.

Further conversation at the April 7 RAC meeting added class relations and economic participation to the competing formulas for deserving citizenship. Ríos-Andino overstayed her time at the podium and the RAC chair attempted to move on to the next speaker. But one of the Cuban RAC members asked for a word and tried to placate Ríos-Andino (RAC April 7, 2011).

RAC MEMBER: May I say something?

RAC CHAIR: Absolutely.

RAC MEMBER: You know, the way we're appointed, we're appointed by the different commissioners. And, you know the commissioner is who makes the decision. Even if we were to resign, that doesn't mean that they would appoint who you want them to appoint. I think that there are three Hispanics in this commission. I agree with you they're not Puerto Ricans—I wish they were—

RÍOS-ANDINO: They're not Puerto Rican, and they're not the majority—

RAC MEMBER: But listen to this. You know, when—

RÍOS-ANDINO: And you're in business, and many of our people are working-class people.

At this point the RAC chair cut in and said he did not want to get "into a point-counterpoint debate" between the two, but the RAC member continued to say she wanted only to offer her help.

RÍOS-ANDINO: All right. Would you be willing to resign? That's what I want.

RAC MEMBER: But if I resign, that doesn't mean you get appointed.

RÍOS-ANDINO: It gives a chance for a Puerto Rican to be on. I bet you if there were no whites on this board, it'd be full of white people complaining, or no blacks. We want to be at the table making decisions. Who's going to get this money? That's our tax money. I pay taxes here. I own a home here. I should have some of that money coming back to my community. And it's not coming back to my community. That's why I'm concerned.

Ríos-Andino showed no sign of confidence that the Hispanic business elite of Orlando would bring much-needed resources to her working-class community. What is not entirely clear is whether "our people" refers only to Puerto Ricans or to working-class Latinos generally. And conversely, "You're in business" could refer to an identity idea about Cubans as a whole or to the race-class relations of the Hispanics represented by the RAC appointments. In any case, it is noteworthy that "our" in this use implies solidarity rather than possession.

Among the protests over the absence of a Puerto Rican on the RAC, this was one of the few exchanges that directly addressed class differences between representatives and represented. In fact, speaking in defense of the selection process during the March 29 meeting, Commissioner D4 said that the Cuban District 4 resident appointed by the mayor deserved appointment because of her deep involvement with Moss Park Elementary School (BCC March 29, 2011). Demographic profiles of that school and community at the time of the redistricting only serve to reinforce the point about RAC members' place among the Orlando elite. Near the Moss Park area a new medical center and medical school were leading the way toward future development of southeast Orange County. US Census Bureau data indicate that in 2010 the two census tracts for that area were well over 70 percent white, inclusive of Latinos and non-Latinos (US Census Bureau 2010). Median household incomes in both tracts were between $70,000 and $80,000 annually; mean household incomes were $94,000 and $110,000 (US Census Bureau 2010; US Census Bureau, ACS 2010). Clearly, the Moss Park area is well removed geographically, socially, and economically from the East Side and from what Simone Delerme (2020) documents in the Kissimmee area.

The story of Orange County's 2011 redistricting offers evidence for pulling apart when the differences among people are expressions of the necessary incompleteness of community formation through which relations form and reform amid vectors of sameness and difference, and when the differences are about something stirring up the *balde de jueyes* to disrupt solidarity in service to the interests of a power elite. That is the tension I find in Orlando, as race, class, national origin, birthplace, and experience as a US minority are all vectors of sameness and difference that Puerto Ricans and other Latinos navigate in their relations with each other and with non-Latino white and black people in the context of Orlando's natural neoliberalism. Whether emerging from shared daily life or promoted by activist organizations, collective identification can and does exist; it is grounded for some in shared language and heritage and for others in the consciousness of a shared history of exploitation and dispossession. One person said to me about Orlando Puerto Ricans, "I don't think the Puerto Rican community is as divided as people think they are. I think they want to make us think that we're a lot more divided. We have our differences in opinion, but the bottom line, I think that there's still a lot of pride in our community."

Alongside acknowledged differences, the situational and strategic use of a homogeneous identity idea of Hispanic or Latino or Puerto Rican is used by different actors to empower and to contain Orlando Puerto Rican and Latino presence and participation. The line between opportunity and danger is apparent in the argument that embracing a pan-ethnic identity may align with "articulations of upward social mobility aspirations" as well as with "cross-class efforts at political mobilization" (De Genova and Ramos-Zayas 2003:19). The distinct outcomes are in some cases greater Latino solidarity and in others greater intra-Latino injustice. Víctor Alvarado's 2008 assessment of difference and community among Puerto Ricans in Central Florida in earlier days spells this out:

> Groups were formed and were divided. OK? This is this group here; this is this group here; and this is this group here. OK? But that's OK too. See,

> everybody thinks because there's division, that it's wrong. That's how cities were formed. That's how governments are formed. That's how everything is formed. Division is good as long as it's communicated and it's shared and it's healthy. But the only time it's not healthy is when they attack each other, because now you're attacking from within. And this is what always hurts. When you're attacked from within. And this is my point. (PRCF Alvarado)

THE ART OF STEPPING SIDEWAYS TO MOVE FORWARD

The responses to the protests over the RAC appointments articulated by the mayor and Commissioner D4 are emblematic of the universalist-particularist tension that is at the core of color-blind multiculturalism and that was evident throughout the Orange County 2011 redistricting process. The exclusion of Puerto Ricans created a particularity at odds with the universalist claim to do what is best for everyone. In this frame it is those "loud Latinos" who appear to be the disrupters; those voicing opposition to the exclusionary inclusion they are experiencing are "playing games." The assumed neutral and more mature stance, as expressed by the mayor, is the one that calls for every citizen to have a fair voice. That what constitutes fairness is not shared equally, however, rings familiar to many Puerto Ricans and other Latinos. About the relations between Latinos and the powers that be in Orange County, Evelyn Rivera said, "They think that by giving us beer, dominoes, *arroz con gandules* and *lechón*, and *baile*, that's what's going to convert us or keep us quiet. They want our votes but keep us quiet at the same time" (100PR_OHP Evelyn Rivera #18).

Maybe the either-or about unity and division—sleeping giant or *balde de jueyes*—is the wrong question. Maybe the thing to ask is what conditions are conspiring to both stir up the bucket *and* keep the giant asleep. Is the frantic activity in the *balde de jueyes* because the temperature in the bucket rises amid practices that open access to social power for a few and close it to most others?

A look at other uses of crab imagery offers another interpretation of the apparent *balde de jueyes* in Latino Orlando. With the term "crab antics," Peter Wilson (1973) directs anthropologists to a framework that acknowledges colonial and postcolonial dialectics of imposed social stratification and reactive responses to the resultant subordination. For Wilson (1973:220–223), "dialectic" means "tensing implicitly toward change," which suggests not merely resistance but the transformative potential for upending the relations of power. He describes his meaning in words that evoke a *balde de jueyes* as he talks about the interrelationship "of action and reaction, of imposition and evasion, of boasting and gossiping, of climbing up and pulling down." And all this frantic activity is about circumventing, undermining, and transforming dominant-subordinate relations.

Puerto Rican scholars often turn to another crab metaphor called *jaibería*. The reference is to a crab's ability to move forward by moving sideways. The movement avoids full-on confrontation when one is faced with a more powerful opponent. *Jaibería* is "an active, low-intensity strategy to obtain the maximum benefits of a situation with the minimum blood spilled" (Grosfoguel et al. 1997:31). Juan Flores (2005:203–204) links these crablike antics to another commonly used Puerto Rican expression, *bregar*, a practice he describes as an evasive response to "contemporary colonial reality."[11] It is about negotiating and slipping among positions (Suárez Findlay 2014:11). Arcadio Díaz Quiñones (2000:20) writes that *bregar* is "another order of knowing, a smooth and subtle method for navigating daily life, where everything is extremely precarious, changeable and violent, as it has been during the 20th century for the Puerto Rican emigrants and is today in the whole of the island territory."[12] It is like "deal with," as when Víctor Alvarado said Puerto Ricans in Orlando need to learn to "deal with what's here."

One element of this practice is the use of shifting identifiers and thus alliances among Puerto Rican, Latino, Hispanic, American, and so on. The RAC anecdote offers an illustration of these "situational ethnic identities" (Padilla 1985:4). "Puerto Rican" was used to contradict the RAC's claim to inclusive representation, but it was also glossed as "Hispanic" when arguing for representation in District 4. It is a case of strategic and situational use of samenesses and differences for particular ends (Rodríguez Muñiz 2010). In Orlando, maybe those who argue "That's how we get things done" are in fact demonstrating "the knack for avoiding fixed and dangerously head-on positions, advancing sideways like the weak but wise crab" (Sommer 1999:3). Evelyn Rivera says, "They think because we're polite that we agree" (in Hobbs 2010b).

As with other political tactics and identity ideas, *jaibería* and *bregar* can be used by anyone to any purpose. And so again, it is important to look to the outcome more than to the action itself. Despite the mayor's claim that the protestors' voices had been heard, that the county "would do better," and that "this is our Orange County," the final outcome in November 2011 was that Districts 3 and 4 both remained well under 50 percent Latino, and the historically Latino District 3 actually diminished in Latino voting power. Following the 2011 redistricting, District 4 emerged as the new place with the greatest percentage of Latino residents.

During redistricting and in the years that followed, Commissioner D4 worked to sidestep any accusation that she was ignoring Latinos. She and her Puerto Rican assistant were more visible in Orlando Puerto Rican and Latino spaces, and she actively worked to meet with those invested in the redistricting process in order to hear their views. Toward the end, her proposal for how to draw the district lines met a brick wall from the other commissioners. To defend her position she emphasized that she had listened to all the hours of public testimony from the meetings, reminding the other commissioners,

> You guys know I've been a target of a lot of that testimony. . . . Remember when they put the picture of me in *La Prensa* saying I was sleeping? I was a target on day one. Also the reason that I started coming and really listening to all that testimony. I will admit wholeheartedly, I should have thrown a wider net. It has been a *learning* experience. (BCC November 15, 2011)

Was Commissioner D4 now waking up or playing a game? That is hard to know, but looking at patterns of outcomes once again gives evidence. In the final deliberations over the maps—in opposition to everyone else on the BCC—it was she who proposed a map that actually increased Latino percentages in District 3, and hers was one of the votes against the map finally selected by the BCC. She spoke up in support of John Quiñones's fight to name the Kissimmee park after the Borinqueneers (Damron and Rivera-Lyles 2011). The annual Three Kings event, which had been hosted by Bill Negrón for more than a decade, became the province of Commissioner D4. In the 2014 elections, following redistricting and with the increased percentage of Latinos in her district, Commissioner D4 handily won reelection in the August primaries against two Latino opponents.

CHAPTER 7

FOUR DISTRICTS FOR AMERICANS

Mapping Community in Orange County

On August 1, 2012, Latino Justice PRLDEF issued a press release titled "Latinos Sue Orange County Florida over Redistricting." The lawsuit was a response to the final outcome of the 2011 Orange County redistricting, which reduced Latino voting power in District 3 and located powerful groups of non-Latino white voters in each of the three East Side districts. The press release explains,

> The suit claims that the Orange County Commission adopted a plan last November that minimized the voting strength of Latinos. This suit asks that the court issue a judgment that the redistricting plan is unlawful and void. The suit further asks that the county be prevented from holding, supervising or certifying any elections under the current redistricting plan. (Latino Justice PRLDEF 2012)

Orange County engaged in various stalling tactics, and it was May 2014 before the case got to federal court in Orlando. In the meantime, the 2012 election—based on the map approved in 2011—took place. No Latinos were elected to the Orange County Board of County Commissioners (BCC) that year. Slightly over a week after the trial began, the presiding federal judge decided against the plaintiffs.[1]

During the trial the county's defense lawyers took the tension between the universal and the particular, which had marked the debates about who was on the Redistricting Advisory Committee (RAC), and turned it on its head. The argument in defense of having left Puerto Ricans off the RAC had rested on a universalist idea that three Hispanics on the RAC meant that Hispanics were very much included, but the county now used differences among Hispanics—especially between Cubans and Puerto Ricans—to argue that in essence there is no Hispanic community in the first place. In brief, the defense used the idea of the *balde de jueyes* to argue that there had been no violation of the Voting Rights Act (VRA) because there was no Latino vote to dilute.

This strategy was evident during my deposition by Orange County's defense team in 2013. Over seven hours of questioning, I was repeatedly asked about Puerto Rican–Cuban rivalry in particular and a general lack of affinity among Latinos from different national origins:

> Are you aware of rivalries between Puerto Ricans and Cubans, those vying for their own leadership within their communities? . . . Are you familiar with tension between Orlando's Hispanic Chambers of Commerce? . . . Would you agree that there are tensions between Puerto Ricans and Cubans? . . . Would you agree that the Puerto Rican Chamber of Commerce was formed because of tensions with the Hispanic having too many Cubans? . . . Do some Puerto Ricans dislike Cubans? . . . Are you aware, based on your research, of animosity between Puerto Ricans and Cubans? . . . In your research, have you explored the individual's perspective about different subgroups of Hispanics? . . . In your research, have you explored how Puerto Ricans feel about Cubans?[2]

Despite the prevalence of the term "community" throughout the redistricting process from people on all sides of every argument, the word was almost entirely absent in the county attorney's questions to me, appearing only in reference to Puerto Ricans and Cubans as isolated groups.

In what follows, I examine the technologies of the mapmaking process that obscured the workings of power through which local racial-ethnic and class hierarchies were reproduced in Orange County's 2011 redistricting and that supported the judge's decision against the lawsuit. Census categories, GIS software applications, and legal precedents that have emerged from challenges to the VRA provided parameters for mapmakers to follow. The importance of keeping what were called "communities of interest" together was foundational to those parameters, but legal precedents disallowing race as a predominant factor in the mapmaking served to remove racial-ethnic identification as constitutive of a community of interest. Non-Latino white residents used supposedly race-neutral language to describe their communities of interest, and the GIS program used census-designated places (CDPs) to identify the geographies of the county's many communities. This left the undesignated space between Azalea Park and Union Park out of consideration. Despite their vociferous participation in public hearings, Puerto

Ricans and other Latinos were essentially silenced and rendered invisible as a community of interest.

I take this chapter's title from the words of a frustrated and angry non-Latino white woman who was among a small group of steady attendees at the public hearings. Amid the pressures to maintain the black district mandated by the VRA on the West Side and create a comparable district for Latinos on the East Side, the woman predicted a new problem to emerge for "Americans" in 2020: "Instead of six county commissioners after the census of 2020, we are going to need eight county commissioners. We're going to need one for the Hispanics, one for the blacks. And by then you're going to need one for the Asians, one for the Muslims, and then you're going to need four for we Americans!" (BCC November 15, 2011).

Echoing the words of the schoolteacher who asked her elected officials to change the laws and keep "these people home in Puerto Rico," the comments to the RAC from the frustrated and angry woman are about racial-ethnic identification and national belonging—about who is deserving of inclusion and who is not. They tie race to place as they suggest an exclusionary form of inclusion for the nonwhite half of Orange County's population.

During the Jim Crow era and before the 1980s, while the Latino population was still too small to be really noticed, invisibility had protected light-skinned Puerto Ricans in Orlando by offering an honorary white racial status. As the number of Latinos grew and non-Latinos began to perceive a Latino threat, Latino invisibility in public-record statistics contributed to their perpetual foreigner status in the local black-white social framing. Now, during the Orange County redistricting, the invisibility of whiteness itself pointed to how power works over time to make what is seen and what is not seen part of "the taken-for-granted foundations of everyday life" (Carter 2010:15).[3]

There is certainly evidence of the conscious use of power by those who have it to overcome Latino pressures for political territory, which in the case of the 2011 redistricting came in the form of a voting district that would allow Latinos a more determinative voice in electing a representative. Other evidence from the protracted redistricting debates suggests that color-blind multiculturalism facilitated a lack of awareness of the benefits of whiteness on the part of many non-Latino white participants as well as on the part of some honorary white Latinos. A 2017 report from the National Academy of Sciences lends weight to this supposition, as it argues that there is a serious misperception in the United States about just how large the race-based wealth gap is (Kraus et al. 2017).[4] I argue that the findings from this national study about misperceptions regarding equality of opportunity according to racial-ethnic identification intensify in the context of Central Florida's long history of privileging an individualist and entrepreneurial meritocracy.

The anthropologist Heath Pearson (2015) has used the words of an Indiana research participant to describe unconscious racial thinking as a kind of not-thinking, a response to place-specific "things that linger." It is an invisibility of the kinds of seemingly innocuous everyday acts—made possible by the simple fact of being white—that make presumably well-intended people into the beneficiaries of more conscious and racially oppressive acts by others (Ramos-Zayas 2001). In redistricting, the reproduction of Orange County's historically embedded racial-ethnic and class hierarchies happened in the dialogic relations between the not-thinking whiteness of some and the deliberate use by others of the race-neutral language of redistricting in the interests of maintaining power.

Redistricting and its legal parameters may seem like a less engaging topic than the excitement of close and contested elections, but in the wake of the 2016 election, the topic of redistricting gained more visibility and traction. The 2020 Census will be in progress by the time this book is published, and the 2021 redistricting process will begin soon afterward. Redistricting talk focuses on state legislatures, but one need look no further than Palm Beach County, Florida, in 2001 and again in 2018 to understand how local-level arrangements of power and technology trickle up to national consequences.[5] In what follows, I first describe the legal, numeric, and technological parameters of the Orange County mapmaking process and then detail how the maps themselves served as vehicles for contesting and reproducing existing power relations. Then I examine how the language available to and selected by participants—white, black, and Latino—informed and was informed by the technology of redistricting, in combination with color-blind multiculturalism. Using the language available, different participants sketched out competing criteria for defining community and determining who qualifies for full inclusion.

EQUAL PROTECTION, RACE, AND REDISTRICTING

According to commentary I heard in my fieldwork, a decision was made during the 2001 redistricting process to include largely non-Latino white Baldwin Park in District 3. Baldwin Park is the upscale development built during the 1990s on the former Naval Training Center land, and the 2001 RAC apparently recommended putting it in District 5. The BCC ignored that recommendation, with the consequence that District 3 was blocked from becoming more than one-third Latino in 2001 (BCC March 29, 2011).

A decade later, as the 2011 process was set to begin, Puerto Ricans and other Orange County Latinos were prepared to take the county to court if the events of the 2001 redistricting should happen again. Thus, concerns about creating a map that could stand up in court if challenged were central to the Orange County process in 2011. It fell to the assistant county attorney to explain the many legal directives and precedents of redistricting to the members of the RAC. Early on in the process, she gave a PowerPoint presentation titled "Creating Districts That Withstand Legal Challenges." As she presented a checklist to guide the RAC's deliberations, she said, "Now, your handy-dandy legal checklist. . . . These are the rules that you're going to need to follow when you draw your districts in order to make sure that they are legally sound. And this list of principles is basically known as your traditional districting principles" (RAC May 25, 2011).[6]

The first two items on the list were "Equal Population" and "Compliance with the Voting Rights Act." They reference federal requirements reaching back to the 1960s that established legal protections for voters to further the Fourteenth and Fifteenth Amendments to the US Constitution.[7] The four remaining items on the list were as follows:

- Compactness and Contiguity
- Preservation of Political Boundaries
- Preservation of Communities of Interest
- Partisan and Incumbent Interests

The principles on this checklist are the product of a series of court cases that followed a 1986 US Supreme Court decision in *Thornburg v. Gingles* that a North Carolina map made it almost impossible for black voters to elect representatives of their choice.[8] That decision also required that majority-minority districts be created if possible in order to protect the choices of those voters (MacManus et al. 2015:188).[9] One measure of what determines the possibility of drawing such a district is related to whether the minority group is geographically compact enough to form a district. The Supreme Court has not ranked the items on the checklist in terms of priorities, and in the racial-ethnic geography of Orange County, this factor became significant.

In the wake of the 1990–1992 redistricting cycle around the United States, several cases by white plaintiffs made their way to a US Supreme Court that now included Reagan appointees noted for giving the court a conservative turn (Buchman 2003:53). In 5–4 decisions across several cases, the Supreme Court shifted to a color-blind interpretation of the Fourteenth Amendment's equal protection clause and decided that drawing districts based predominantly on race violated that clause.[10] Writing in 2003, Jeremy Buchman (2003:51) describes the impact of the 1990s decisions: "Today, cases involving the Voting Rights Act increasingly are brought not by racial and language minorities seeking relief from dilutionary majoritarian political processes, but by white plaintiffs brandishing the rhetoric of color-blindness and raising equal protection claims." Although the lawsuit against Orange County *was* brought by Latinos seeking relief from vote dilution, the power of color-blind rhetoric was in evidence throughout the Orange County 2011 redistricting.

By contrast, race was explicitly part of determining the contours of the county's historically black District 6 in order that it remain a majority-minority district. In another 5–4 decision in 2009, just before the 2010-2012 redistricting cycle, the US Supreme Court set a requirement in *Bartlett v. Strickland* that minority protections only be extended if the minority group constituted more than 50 percent of a district's voting-age population (Liptak 2009). Thus, despite the frequent reminder that race was not to be a determining factor, RAC members were instructed not to let District 6 fall below that 50 percent benchmark.

In brief, this series of court decisions produced contradictions between the VRA mandate for minority protections and subsequent decisions that race may not be the determining factor in drawing a district. Although legal discussions of this contradiction continue, what the Orange County attorney presented to the RAC is what has become standard redistricting practice. The legal checklist, devoid as it may be of a clear ranking of priorities, now holds sway over racial gerrymandering. Race is thus at once central to redistricting in accord with the VRA and only one issue among many—if even that—of the traditional districting principles. At one point, a RAC member said, "I know we're not supposed to consider ethnicity within these numbers, but that's like disregarding the elephant in the room" (RAC September 21, 2011).

The language and technology of redistricting. One of the factors identified in the PowerPoint presentation that could lead to a legal complaint was if the new map divided a community of interest. In the confusing space between VRA protections and the subsequent ruling that race cannot be a primary factor, the idea of a community of interest remained in need of clarification. The attorney's presentation made explicit that a community of interest is something that "extends beyond race." To expand on that, she added, "Are you looking at a rural settlement, are you looking at an urban area? Are you looking at an industrial area versus a tourist corridor? Are you looking at a group of people that have the same economic class?" (RAC May 25, 2011). Along with these color-blind references to social and economic criteria for determining a community of interest, the GIS technology further facilitated identifying communities of interest in geographic terms as neighborhoods, subdivisions, municipalities, and CDPs. Thus, as RAC members and people from the public worked with the county's GIS team to propose maps, the ability to identify a community of interest was affected by the software's ability to map it.[11]

Other items on the list easily link into the larger idea of a community of interest and contribute to turning its definition from racial-ethnic to political. Existing political boundaries such as for municipalities offer a point of common identification, and partisan interests also suggest a cohesive community of like-minded individuals. The attorney discussed partisan and incumbent interests during her presentation as related to the "core" of a district, saying that the voters of a district have elected a commissioner and should not be displaced from that commissioner if at all possible. In fact, the Orange County Charter requires that a commissioner live in his or her district, and for this reason, the RAC was directed to draw lines with that in mind. Relating the idea of a political core to comfort and belonging, the attorney asserted, "You don't want to put people into a place that they don't consider is home" (RAC May 25, 2011).

When framed this way, the checklist can be collapsed into what redistricting literature often calls the three Cs of redistricting: compactness, contiguity, and community of interest. The attorney's presentation used a series of Supreme Court decisions regarding specific maps to illustrate compactness and contiguity. Using legal language from the decisions, she explained that legally defensible districts must not have "snakelike" or "dramatically irregular shapes," but then she added that there is no constitutional mandate for what "the regularity of district shape" might look like. She pointed out that a district could be considered racially gerrymandered without being oddly shaped. With head-spinning arguments like these, it is hard to imagine being a member of the RAC or of the Orange County public endeavoring to correctly participate in redistricting.

Given the complexity of the process, the attorney's legal expertise carried a great deal of weight. Members of the RAC and later the BCC turned to her for clarification as they sought to comply with the checklist. In answer, she repeatedly brought either explicit or implicit attention to the ambiguously racial-ethnic issue of mapping an East Side district that would allow Latino voters to elect representatives of their choosing. In this way, the RAC members quietly received the message that an East Side Latino majority-minority district was unlikely to be in accordance with the "handy-dandy legal checklist."

Districts 3 and 4, with their large Latino populations, became the example to explain that it is illegal to "pack" a single district with minorities if a second minority district could be created. Creating a majority-minority Latino district by combining Districts 3 and 4, she asserted, would reduce Latinos' ability to influence the vote from two districts to one.[12] The existing District 3 also became an example of an effective minority district, between 30 and 49 percent, that has a high enough percentage of minority voters to allow them to elect their preferred candidates. The attorney explained further that an influence district is one in which the minority group is able to align with others to influence the outcome (RAC May 25, 2011).

The message that emerged from the attorney's presentation and became a mantra during RAC discussions avoided the ambiguities at issue in the legal debates and made it clear that race may not be the primary consideration when drawing districts, even districts that complied with the other traditional districting practices. In one meeting (RAC August 31, 2011), the attorney referred to traditional districting principles as "race-neutral," and several times during meetings she reminded mapmakers who struggled to increase the Latino percentage in District 3 that doing so could not be their primary goal. When one of the proposed maps created a majority-minority Latino District 3, the attorney spoke up to say that precisely because the public had demanded a Latino district, the fact of creating one could make the map subject to court scrutiny (RAC July 6, 2011).

Because the US Census Bureau considers "Hispanic or Latino" to be an ethnicity and not a race, opponents of creating a Latino district could deflect the assumption that there should be a Latino district on the East Side, comparable to the black district on the West Side. Demographic data provided to the RAC included percentages of white, black, Asian, and other in the total population of each district.[13] Hispanic percentages were then an additional piece of data so that the RAC would have that information as well. When first RAC members and later others observing the process questioned why the percentages for white, black, Asian, other, and Hispanic gave totals greater than 100, they would be reminded that Hispanic is not a race. One confused RAC member questioned the total over 100 percent and asked to confirm that Hispanic is not a "minority-designated class." Without mentioning the 1975 extension of VRA protections to language minorities, the attorney replied, "No, Hispanic is actually an ethnicity. It's not considered a race under the Census" (RAC June 22, 2011).

In brief, together with the census and GIS technology, the legal checklist provided a set of concepts that appeared measurable, depoliticized, and largely race-neutral. Together, they also resulted in prioritizing older neighborhoods over newly emerging developments in unincorporated Orange County where many Latinos live. Although there may be a CDP called Chickasaw by 2020, during the 2011 redistricting the heavily Latino space between the Azalea Park and Union Park CDPs had no geographic designation in the census. All of this combined in the 2011 Orange County redistricting to support arguments for not creating a Latino district in Orange County, especially not in District 3.

MAKING MAPS IN 2011

Over the course of the summer of 2011, the fifteen RAC members appointed by the BCC, as well as members of the public, drew maps that proposed distinct plans for dividing the Orange County population into six single-member voting districts that would elect representatives to the BCC until another redistricting process in 2021 would produce a new map for 2022. The county's attorney evaluated each map using the legal checklist to point out issues in any given map that could be challenged in court. There was also time at each meeting for public input on the various maps presented. At the end of the process in September, RAC members were to sort through all of that and forward a recommendation to the BCC. The BCC would then take the RAC recommendation and finalize the 2012–2022 map in November.

Among the maps in the 2011 process, all of those drawn by members of the public offered significantly different arrangements of the districts. Each public map challenged the existing lines and sought to transform power relations in Orange County by creating radically different voting districts that could diversify the BCC—not only in terms of racial-ethnic makeup but also in terms of rural and urban orientation. Most of the maps drawn by RAC members maintained the basic contours of 1992 and 2002, moving small blocks of voters from one district to another to arrive at an acceptable balance of the population. In the simplest terms, arguments for one map or another in 2011 boiled down to a tug of war between those suggesting some transformative change and those arguing that simple tweaking would be enough.

The 2011 Orange County districts had been in effect since 2002 (map 7.1). In order to understand what follows, it is important to note in the 2002–2012 map that there is an east-west split with Districts 1, 2, and 6 on the west and Districts 3, 4, and 5 on the east.[14] Each of the six districts includes parts of Orlando city, but the smaller and more densely populated Districts 3 and 6 include more of the urban core. The outer districts (1, 2, 4, and 5) sprawl westward or eastward to include unincorporated areas of rural

Orange County. At the start of the 2011 redistricting process, District 6 had a majority-minority black voting-age population of almost 56 percent, and District 3 fit the description of an effective Latino district, with 41 percent. District 4 needed to lose a significant number of people because economic development projects and new housing in the southeastern sector of the district meant that the population had grown considerably since 2001. The part of District 4 that juts up between Districts 3 and 6 in map 7.1 is the Conway Chain of Lakes area encompassing Belle Isle, Edgewood, Conway, and Pine Castle. The Conway area is something of a white island between east and west. The political power of the Conway area was clearly evident and duly noted during the 2011 mapping process. In the end, residents of the Conway area successfully argued that they were a deserving community of interest, and they got what they wanted at the expense of a majority-minority Latino district.

Mapping power. Each map proposal from a RAC member received a number, and the member would spell out his or her rationale for the lines drawn. A letter would be attached to the new version as a map received tweaks in response to input from the attorney, other RAC members, and the public. For instance, RAC Proposal 12 was followed by 12a and 12b. RAC Proposal 12b (map 7.2) was submitted by one of the Latino members on the committee, and it was eventually forwarded to the BCC. In that map, the Conway Chain of Lakes area was moved into District 3, and an eastern part of District 3 was divided between Districts 4 and 5. The result reduced District 3 from about 41 percent Latinos of voting age to about 33 percent and increased District 4's proportion to about 39 percent Latino voting age.

Map proposals submitted by members of the public were given letters (map A, B, and so on). There were five public proposals, four of which substantially increased the Latino population numbers in District 3. The reality of Orange County Latinos living all over the place presented a challenge to drawing a compact and contiguous map with a majority-minority Latino community in one district. One public map succeeded but was quickly disqualified by the attorney because the lines for District 3 did not include Commissioner D3's home. An objection was raised that Commissioner D3 had been appointed, not elected, but it was clear the proposed map was never going to get past the RAC selection process. It was therefore revised, but including the commissioner's residence brought the Latino voting-age percentage below 50 percent of the total. None of the iterations that kept Commissioner D3 in the district managed to get the Latino voting-age population up to 50 percent.

While they were at the Orange County offices downtown to use the GIS software and draw maps, activists for black and Latino voting rights recognized their common interests and formed a multiracial alliance. Their Public Proposal E (map 7.3) was one of the maps forwarded on to the BCC and thus figured in the 2014 trial against the county.

Public Proposal E extended District 3 southward to include Southchase and Meadow Woods, which brought the Latino voting-age population to 49 percent, and it maintained District 6 as a majority-minority district with more than 56 percent black voting-age population. The most transformative aspect of this map was not that it solidified black and Latino voting power but that it sought to restrain non-Latino white domination of the BCC. To do that, it redesigned District 5, grouping together the neighborhoods that surrounded the Conway Chain of Lakes with the downtown business district of Orlando and the bedroom communities to the north that reach toward and include affluent Winter Park. Historically these areas had been distributed among Districts 3, 4, and 5. Doug Head presented Public Proposal E to the RAC, explaining that this map grouped the neighborhoods from Conway through Winter Park into a single district because more than other areas of the county, they represented a "community of interest." He went on to describe why, saying that until 2010,

> every single one of Orange County's chairmen or mayors has come from these privileged and established communities. Over the twenty years of the Charter Government . . . this proposed district . . . elected and occupied County Commission seats for a combined total of 54 years. This might be truly characterized as the "corridor of power." (RAC June 22, 2011)

The point was that this "corridor of power" had historically controlled elections for the Orange County BCC since the county had initiated single-member districts. Apparently, Commissioner D3 lived in that corridor of power, because the odd-shaped finger jutting into District 5 from District 3 was what was needed to accommodate Commissioner D3's residence.

During a few rounds of the selection process that moved recommendations on to the BCC in September, RAC members each selected a specified number of preferred maps to send to the BCC. The maps with the most votes went into the next round. The goal was to move a single map forward to the commission. Public Proposal E was the only public map that survived the first round of cuts. When it was eliminated in the next round, the public outcry was intense. In response, the groups that had formed an alliance and presented Public Proposal E formalized their status and became the Black-Latino-Puerto Rican Alliance for Justice. Protests even came from people who did not support the proposal but considered it important to keep

MAP 7.1. Orange County voting districts, 2002–2012

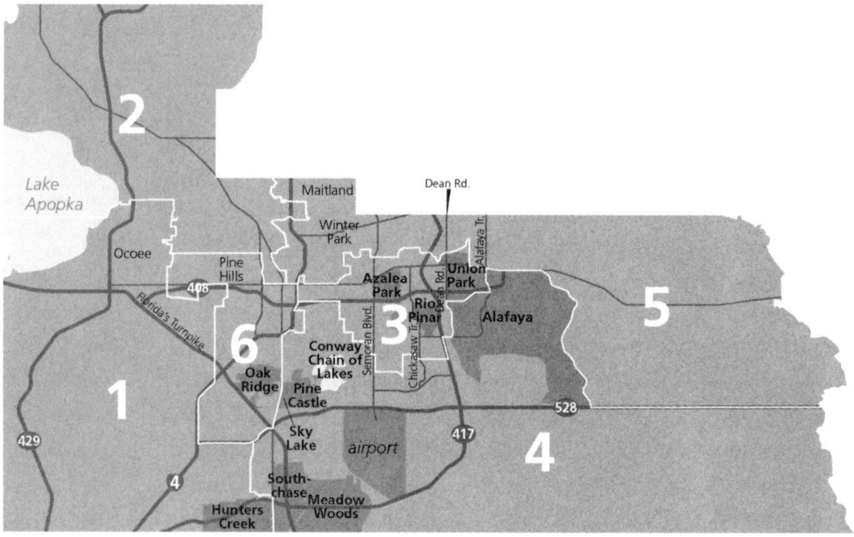

Districts 1, 2, and 6 are on the western side and 3, 4, and 5 on the eastern side. Districts 3 and 6 are the urban core, and Districts 1, 2, 4, and 5 sprawl out into more rural areas. The Conway Chain of Lakes portion of District 4 separates Districts 3 and 6. Map by Chicago CartoGraphics.

MAP 7.2. RAC Proposal 12b

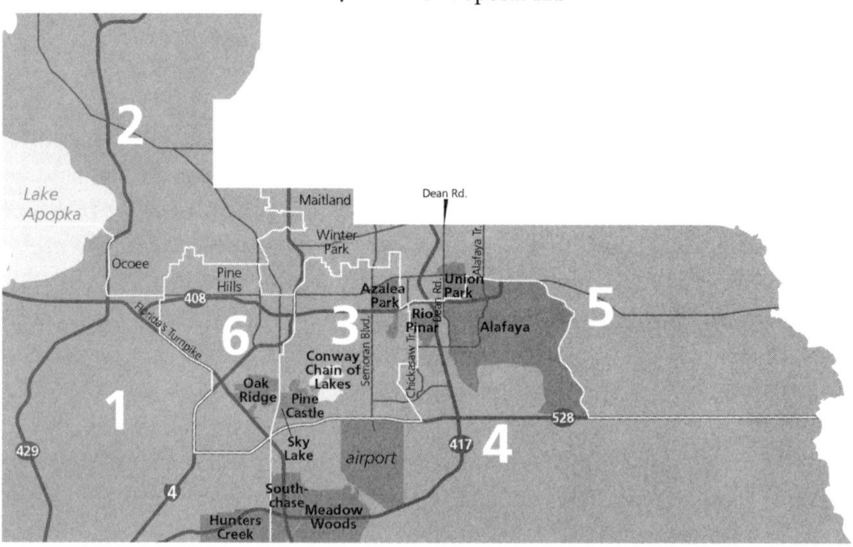

The Conway Chain of Lakes is moved into District 3; the eastern part of District 3 is now split between Districts 4 and 5; Union Park is now out of District 3; and Rio Pinar and part of Chickasaw Trail are moved into District 4. Map by Chicago CartoGraphics.

MAP 7.3. Public Proposal E

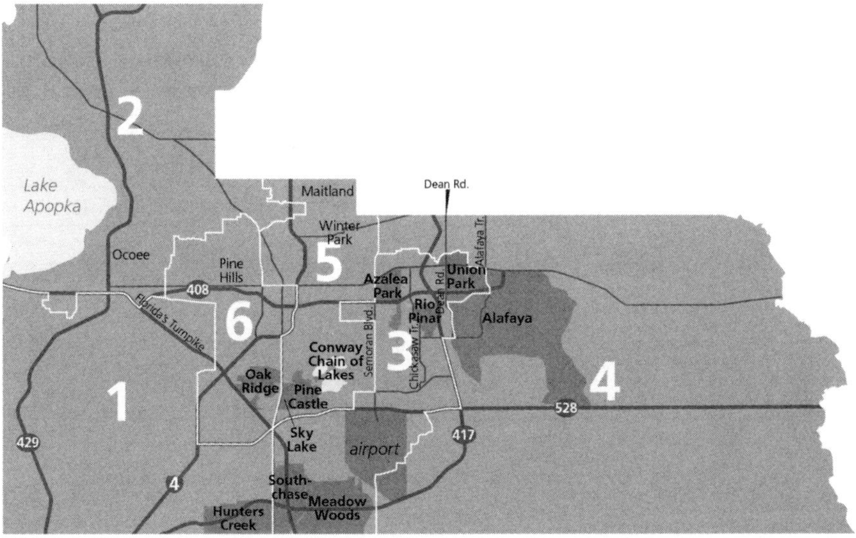

District 3 is extended south to include Southchase and Meadow Woods; District 4 is now an eastern Orange County district; and District 5 has been dramatically redrawn and now includes the Conway Chain of Lakes. The thumb jutting off to the west of District 3 is where the commissioner lived. Map by Chicago CartoGraphics.

MAP 7.4. Mayor's Map M-3, adopted by Orange County Board of County Commissioners in November 2011

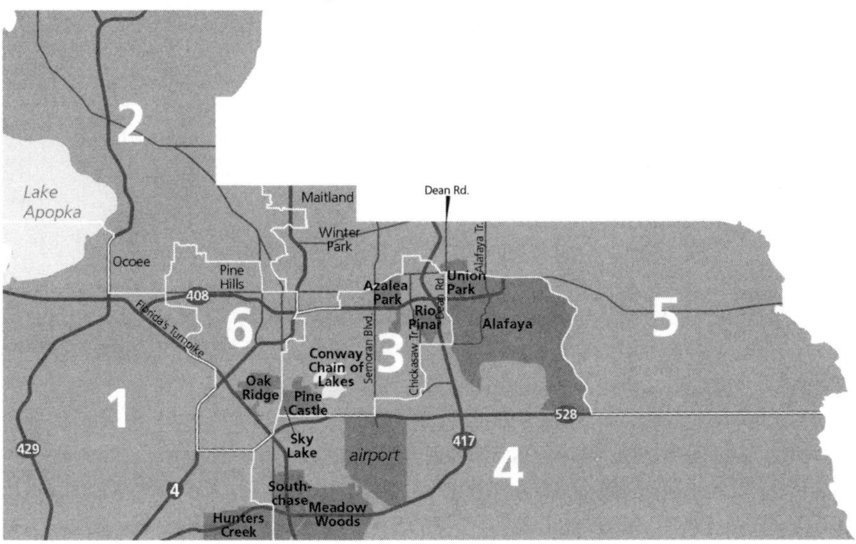

The Conway Chain of Lakes is in District 3; Union Park has been moved out of District 3 and split (65/35 percent) between Districts 4 and 5; and Dean Road is now the dividing line between Districts 3 and 4. Map by Chicago CartoGraphics.

TABLE 7.1. Comparison of RAC Map 12b, Public Map E, and Map M-3 using the legal checklist

Legal checklist criteria	RAC Map 12b	Public Map E	Mayor's Map M-3
Equal population by deviation	7.51	2.43	7.51
VRA compliance, voting-age population			
District 3	32.79	49.30	38.26
District 4	38.75	25.29	39.95
District 6	50.04	56.24	52.17
Three Cs			
Compactness, contiguity	Lesser	Greater	Lesser
Communities of interest per GIS	Split 4	Split 5	Split 4

Note: Information came from maps as they were presented during the redistricting process. Each map was followed by statistics that measured deviation and district populations.

[a]The voting-age population for VRA compliance in Districts 3 and 4 was Latino and in District 6 was black.

a publicly generated map in the mix. By the following week during a meeting that lasted past midnight, Public Proposal E was back under consideration; maps 12b and E were forwarded to the BCC.

A comparison of RAC Proposal 12b and Public Proposal E using the legal checklist the attorney presented to the RAC gives the advantage to Public Proposal E (table 7.1). "Equal population" means that each of the six districts would have as close as possible to the same number of residents. A maximum deviation of 10 percent from the ideal of an exact balance was allowed. At 2.43 percent deviation, Public Proposal E was by far more compliant than RAC Proposal 12b at 7.51 percent, but 12b was still within the legal limit. Both maps maintained District 6 as a majority-minority district in accordance with the VRA. Given the need to accommodate Commissioner D3's residence, neither map made District 3 a majority-minority district, but Public Proposal E's percentage is close enough to assume it would get there within a year or so rather than the decade or more that would be needed in RAC Proposal 12b. In 12b it is in District 4, with a commissioner for whom they did not vote, that a Latino majority would likely come about more quickly.

With regard to the three Cs, the districts in Public Proposal E are visibly more compact and contiguous than in RAC Proposal 12b, in which oddly shaped Districts 4 and 5 snake around District 3. During public commentary, an engineer actually came up with a mathematical formula that proved E to be measurably more compact than 12b (BCC November 15, 2011). Another point of comparison was the degree to which a map divided communities of interest between two or more districts, with the scoring done according to CDPs and municipalities. Moving all or part of a community to a new district meant removing people from the jurisdiction of the commissioner for whom they had voted, and this is one point where competing priorities for defining a community of interest became contentious.

Both maps kept the powerful Conway Chain of Lakes together in one district, but Public Proposal E put the Conway area in District 5 along with the rest of the corridor of power. In order to do so and maintain the black and Latino percentages, Public Proposal E split four communities that had been together before and split a fifth more than it had been before. RAC Proposal 12b split only four communities—three of which were split already but now more so. RAC Proposal 12b would thus seem to have the edge over Public Proposal E in regards to dividing communities, but 12b moved Union Park and most of the unnamed area between Union Park and Azalea Park entirely out of District 3 and into District 5. Because it was removed in its entirety, the Union Park CDP was not considered to have been split, and the division of the unnamed area around Goldenrod did not count. The attorney's directive that the mapmakers not put people "into a place that they don't consider is home" did not apply to this division of the East Side. In brief, the East Side did not receive the same consideration as the older, more GIS-friendly communities.

In the struggle between visions for the arrangement of Orange County voting districts, these two maps outline distinct racial-ethnic and class-based relations of power for the county. The black and Latino alliance that emerged from this process is important to consider.[15] By 2011 the shifting demographics of Orange County meant that a black and Latino alliance presented a serious challenge to long-standing power relations. At the September meeting where an effort was made to eliminate Public Proposal E, one of the founders of the Black-Latino-Puerto Rican Alliance for Justice, Trini Quiroz, said, "It is clear to me that on occasion, minority communities know how to stick together and recognize that when one is threatened, all are threatened" (RAC September 14, 2011). Later in November during BCC deliberations over the final map, an African American activist defended separate majority-minority districts for black and Latino voters:

> I don't want the minority communities to fight among themselves because we deserve to have two minority-majority districts. If you got 27 percent Hispanic and you got 23 percent African Americans, by God, that's almost half the population of Orange County. Why aren't we having representation

> and why are we having to fight? The bottom line is, change is hard. People don't want to change. That doesn't mean that gives them the right to stay the same way. (BCC November 15, 2011)

In defense of map E's more transformative district lines, a member of the public told the BCC, "I don't think we can tweak our way to justice here" (BCC November 29, 2011).

Deciding the 2012–2022 map. The final map selected by the mayor and the BCC on November 29 (map 7.4) evolved from RAC Proposal 12b. This was the mayor's Map M-3, which would go into effect in 2012. Map M-3 had the same deviation to equal population as 12b, but in addition to the communities split in 12b, Map M-3 removed Union Park from District 3 and split it between Districts 4 and 5. In other words, by the end of the process, none of the three Cs was considered for Latinos. The District 3 area that had previously held a relatively compact Latino community from Azalea Park through Union Park—and the largest concentration of Puerto Ricans in the county—was now divided among Districts 3, 4, and 5. Dean Road, at the geographic center of Analys's world, was the new dividing line between Districts 3 and 4.

One other map warrants mention here because it demonstrates an odd commonality of purpose between those working for a majority-minority Latino district and Commissioner D4, who had begun the redistricting process by angering Latinos for not appointing any to the RAC.[16] At the November 15 BCC meeting, when the BCC took up the task of determining the final map, Commissioner D4 submitted a map proposal that kept the Conway Chain of Lakes together in District 3 and broke up the East Side, but it also increased the Latino voting-age percentage of District 3 from 41 to almost 44 percent by extending District 3 south to include Meadow Woods, Sky Lake, and Southchase. In her interest to create a unified East Orange District 4 that would guarantee representation from that more rural part of the county, her map—with more compact districts and a transformed District 5—looked more like the public maps than the RAC maps. She prefaced her presentation to the BCC by saying that her staff had been told there was no way it would get approval (BCC November 15, 2011). It did not. Two weeks later in a 4–3 decision, Map M-3 was selected by the BCC.

When looked at from the legal checklist in table 7.1, Map M-3 is in a good position to withstand a court challenge despite the odd shapes of Districts 4 and 5. District 6's black voting-age percentage is reduced but remains within the requirements of the VRA and later court rulings. Districts 3 and 4 each had close to 40 percent Latino voting-age population, which made for two effective Latino districts that would likely soon be over 40 percent.

In the end, then, creating a map that could withstand a legal challenge without disrupting existing power relations in Orange County took precedence over strict adherence to the legal checklist. This process was facilitated by the greater ability of some participants to apply the language and technologies of redistricting to their definitions of community and to benefit from a depoliticized, universalist discourse that assumes equal standing in a meritocracy. Arguments for and against maintaining, displacing, or breaking up communities of interest became entangled with the technologies of redistricting. Together, these technologies more often than not facilitated a depoliticized appearance of looking beyond particularized racial-ethnic interests to a color-blind universalist claim of serving all of Orange County in the interest of fairness.

LANGUAGE AND FORMS OF POWER

The hours and hours of debate at the RAC meetings and later those of the BCC reveal patterns of discourse that align with divergent interests in tweaking or transforming existing power relations in Orange County. Among those speaking out at the meetings, perspectives about who is deserving of what divided largely along racial-ethnic lines. Because the thorniest issue was the shape of District 3, this most often pointed to divergent perspectives between Latino and non-Latino white participants.

The West Side had its share of controversy, but the final debates came down to the shape of District 3 on the East Side. The combined need for District 4 to lose population and the persistent demand from residents in the Conway area to stay together had the consequence of reducing the District 3 Latino population. As one commissioner put it, "There's no way to put the Conway chain in without diluting District 3. And it comes down to that" (BCC November 29, 2011).

To say that debates divided along racial-ethnic lines is not to say that there was solid unanimity within each racially and ethnically identified group. More accurately, the language used to argue the worthiness of one claim or another related to opinions about tweaking or transforming the county's political districts and, with that, maintaining or upending social hierarchies and political control. At the hearings, some Latinos spoke out against setting Latinos apart in a specific district identified as theirs, and both non-Latino white and non-Latino black speakers supported a Latino district.[17] Like the majority of non-Latino white speakers who spoke at the meetings, the Latinos in opposition to creating a Latino district generally used color-blind language to appeal to human sameness. Differences in Latino racial identifications and class relations also surfaced in objections to referencing Latinos as "poor" or "a minority."[18]

Because speakers at the public hearings were asked to state their addresses, the zip codes represented in one argument or another offer racial-ethnic and income comparisons. Among those speaking in support of a Latino district, the zip codes most often indicated the East Side. Those speaking against often had zip codes in areas with high percentages of white residents, including both non-Latinos and Latinos who select white on the US Census race question. For instance, two Latinos who expressed opposition to a majority-minority district were both living in an area that was identified in the 2010 Census as 77 percent white, inclusive of both Anglos and Latinos. The median household income was $82,500 at the time, and the mean household income was just under $94,000 (US Census Bureau, ACS 2010). Like Moss Park, these areas are a good distance—geographically and socioeconomically—from the more densely populated Latino areas on the East Side and in the cross-county area to the south.

Among those arguing for a Latino district, there was disagreement across party affiliations over the question of whether two districts of 40 percent Latino population or one majority-minority district would better serve Latinos in Orange County. The Latino RAC member who submitted RAC Proposal 12b, which left Districts 3 and 4 respectively at 33 and 39 percent, contended that two influential districts were preferable to a single district of more than 50 percent (RAC September 7, 2011). Given the 2009 Supreme Court decision in *Bartlett v. Strickland*, however, the only legal avenue available if Latinos were ignored and their votes were diluted was to argue that a district with over 50 percent voting-age Latino population had been possible. Despite divergent ideas about the percentages, there was a collective recognition that Latinos as a community of interest may not receive any attention at all.

An exchange that happened as Doug Head was explaining the rationale for District 5's radical changes lays bare the degree to which the reproduction of existing racial-ethnic and class relations is obfuscated by discourses and practices of color-blind and multicultural meritocracy, in which whiteness is normalized even as it obscures racial-ethnic political and economic inequalities. Describing the communities that make up what he called the "corridor of power," Head said,

> A strong community of interest exists in the communities. These communities are characterized [by] . . . heavily white populations, wealth, lakes, big old trees, homeownership, large lots and large homes owned

> by residents, intense community engagement, historically high-quality schools, low home turnover compared with other areas, a sense of historic entitlement and obligation to participate, very high voter participation and civic involvement. (RAC June 22, 2011)

Then he added with just a touch of irony in his voice, "It's time for this area of uniform opinion and lifestyle to select one voice, one true voice and to speak strongly for the historic urban neighborhoods which are represented." When questioned by a confused Hispanic RAC member, Head continued somewhat tongue-in-cheek to further explain that the residents of the proposed District 5 deserved a district, but not three.

His point was that it was time to disrupt the white elite grip on power, but the RAC member replied, "I guess I'm still missing the point." The anecdote offers evidence of how the privileges that accrue to the powerful can disappear into the belief that privileges are themselves earned through individual merit. For this light-skinned and well-connected Hispanic RAC member, sitting among others who were well-situated in Orlando's political and economic fields, that Orlando's political relations had been in the hands of a small elite group for decades was apparently not problematic.

Managing difference in a melting pot. In the competing pressures to keep the Conway Chain of Lakes together and to increase the percentage of voting-age Latinos in District 3, the directive that race could not be the primary criterion gave the discursive advantage to the Conway-area residents as they argued that environmental concerns for their lakes required being unified under one commissioner. Non-Latino white speakers—members of the RAC and BCC as well as members of the public—generally found race-neutral ways to press their arguments and only mentioned race or ethnicity overtly to express a universalist belief in the commonality of all humans. An example is evident in the testimony from a Pine Castle resident who gave a softer version of the message delivered by the frustrated and angry woman earlier: "I kind of feel a little disturbed when I hear you saying that you want a Spanish community or a this community or a that community. . . . We used to call ourselves the melting pot. I like that. I prefer that" (RAC May 25, 2011). This language describes a world in which all individuals are presumed to have the same opportunities and resources. It is there in the *Orlando Sentinel*'s New Orlando series and in the Orange County mayor's words when she first greeted the RAC members and told them that their process was about fairness for every citizen. It surfaced again in the public testimony of another Pine Castle resident who implied a preference for the melting pot and said, "We are a united Orange County. We are all citizens. We all require equal representation" (RAC August 3, 2011). This is what Rosa and Bonilla (2017:205) refer to as a "cosmetic diversity" that works to absorb difference into existing institutions rather than looking to transform racial-ethnic and class hierarchies in the interests of social justice.

By subsuming all into a harmonious whole, this view of diversity pushes against particularist demands by one group or another for recognition as different and deserving. In the response to protests over the RAC appointments at the March 29 BCC meeting, the particularist argument from a subordinate group—in this case Puerto Ricans—was construed by others as disrupting their universalist "we are one" perspective (Bonilla-Silva 2014). This in turn supports the argument that those in power—whose behavior is not disruptive—are the ones who deserve to represent others. If the universalist view is more deserving, then the opinions of the individuals who embrace that perspective must carry more weight. In this way, cosmetic diversity becomes a vehicle for creating and maintaining exclusionary inclusion in a social field operating through colonial-style rule.

Thus, while non-Latino white speakers argued for the worthiness of their particular community using race-neutral language that welcomed everyone, Latinos who pointed to the exclusionary inclusion assigned to their particular racial-ethnic identification were disruptive. These are examples of a tension between the universal and the particular that supports the claims of the already powerful and contributes to the reproduction of existing power relations in Orlando's color-blind and multicultural natural neoliberalism. In Ana Yolanda Ramos-Zayas's words, "The power to ignore race, when white is the race, is a privilege, a social advantage" (2001:76). Such power and privilege remained unspoken and to many apparently invisible in the redistricting process.

The view that those voicing opposition to the status quo were the disrupters also contributed to commentary from non-Latino white members of the public that suggested an affinity and even intimacy with those in power. Beyond the testimony from the Conway area, non-Latino white speakers from elsewhere in the county assumed the deserving authority of their own perspectives and began their testimony to the BCC with expressions of empathy for what the RAC members had had to endure. Without necessarily mentioning Latino petitions for a district per se, the implication was clear. One person told the commissioners that what the RAC had had to go through was "ridiculous." And with veiled reference to the threat of a lawsuit if a Latino district was overlooked, this speaker then introduced a petition for her community as the more deserving one by saying, "We're a diverse community. We're a united community. We would like to try to stay that way. . . . We would appreciate your consideration first, just because we're nice people and don't threaten anyone" (BCC November 15, 2011).

In the context of cosmetic diversity and universalist assumptions that individual actors operate on a level playing field, the concepts of consensus and competition offered further support to non-Latino white claims that they were deserving of whatever petition they were presenting. The idea of a simultaneously color-blind and multicultural community operating as a meritocracy moves easily into the assumption that all reasonable people agree and that there is a consensus about what is best for all. The problem is, of course, that the assumption that there is consensus among unequal participants presents the likely conundrum that dissent has simply been silenced or not even heard in the first place because those in dissent must not be reasonable people (Pineda 2014:3).[19]

The value of competition was another argument against forming a Latino district. The reasoning, again based on the apparent assumption of an even playing field for all, was that diversifying the districts would result in greater competition among candidates, which would in turn yield better representation. The problem with this in the real world is that promoting a cosmetic diversity by spreading Latino voices among multiple districts may well produce a BCC with no Latino voice at all if no district manages to elect a Latino. This condition reflects the 1960s strategy for maintaining white control in the wake of the VRA by shifting to at-large elections (Buchman 2003:46).

An example can be found in the words of a non-Latino white speaker who saw Latino influence in multiple districts as more important than a Latino majority in a single district because the former promoted competition. Her comments also pull together the threads I have been pulling apart in this discussion. Presenting her own stance as authoritative, she made her argument for competition and then turned back to a universalist discourse that was inclusive of everyone—as long as they speak English:

> I cannot support—and speaking only for myself—cannot support a minority-majority district. . . . I've concluded that I feel that the districts of influence are better for all of the people of Orange County. Districts of influence promote competitive races. . . . The people that throw their hats in a race know they have to be competitive and have the interest of all people of their district in their heart in order to win that race. . . . We have responsibilities as American citizens. We have the responsibility to unite under our flag, the United States of America. We have the responsibility to learn the language that unites this country so that we can all work together and not be divided. (RAC August 3, 2011)

Another theme that those arguing against transformative change used as proof of their merits was their long history in Orange County. The Latino RAC member who drew RAC Proposal 12b talked about family in the area since the 1970s and recounted swimming in the lakes around Conway (RAC September 7, 2011). Residents from the Conway Chain of Lakes area, including several from Pine Castle, repeatedly used references to their families' long histories in Orange County to introduce their petitions to first the RAC and later the BCC. And they were not alone. Objections from non-Latino white residents to a Latino district came from all corners of the county. The woman who said the county would soon need four districts for Americans was from District 1. She introduced each of her many petitions by saying that her family had been there since the late 1800s, and she peppered her comments with recollections of Orlando that few others shared. Objecting to the transformative details of Public Proposal E, another speaker from the largely white eastern edge of District 5 argued, "It's just the changes are too radical. You're taking away Orange County's history" (RAC August 31, 2011).

History was also a factor in the defense of the West Side's District 6 as a majority-minority black district, but the inviolability of that history was apparently less certain than that of the Conway Chain of Lakes area. RAC members showed concern about the VRA-sanctioned, historically black district dropping below 50 percent black voting-age population. And in a review of the legal checklist for drawing districts, the assistant county attorney reminded the RAC about the legal problems such a drop could bring. She affirmed that if a majority-minority district is possible while respecting the districting principles, it should be drawn. Then she added her own interpretation of the intent of the VRA:

> If the population in District 6 has changed to the point where you can't draw a district that has 50 percent or more black voting-age population and have equal population, compact contiguous districts, where you're keeping your communities of interest together, your political boundaries together, you're not displacing people unnecessarily and your incumbents are still in place, then I don't think the intent of the law is to tell you that you have to continue to stay at that number just because that's where it's been for twenty-plus years. (RAC July 6, 2011)

In keeping with the dictate that race not be the determining factor, the attorney projected forward to a time when such protections would disappear completely and that particular historical precedent would no longer be relevant.

Co-opting language and talking back. During the protracted public debate over the worthiness of the Latino claim to a district, Latinos and their allies co-opted the language of the opposition and fashioned it into arguments in support of their territorial and political claims. Trini Quiroz used Florida history as she addressed the RAC to inform everyone that Spanish settlements in Florida predated the existence of the United States. Ponce de León was in Florida before the Mayflower, she said (RAC August 3, 2011). Quiroz also criticized the attorney for playing "the race card" to say that race could not be a primary reason for drawing a district when Hispanic is not a race but rather an ethnicity (RAC July 20, 2011). With this, she reclaimed a Hispanic community of interest. Doug Head used history to argue that the powerful bloc of non-Latino white voters in the corridor of power deserved a district, and he used the value of competition to argue that they should be grouped into a single district rather than three.

As the terms describing communities of interest increasingly relied on history, CDPs, and the race-neutral service needs of the lake area, Latinos introduced other terms. "Community of interest also includes language," said Tony Suárez, and he used race-neutral framing to argue further that communities of interest form around reading the same newspapers, going to the same churches, and shopping at the same stores. It is "too simplistic" to just say "we're all Americans," he told the BCC. Returning to the constitutional mandate for equal representation and mentioning specifically Pine Castle and Conway, he also argued that the Hispanic community is "just as equal" (BCC November 15, 2011).

Various other Latino speakers also took up a universalist view of membership in the human race or commonality as Americans but used it to demand a particularist regard for and inclusion of Latinos. In contrast to assuming consensus, this demand for the right to be different and to belong would allow—indeed require—a transformation from white normativity to the messiness of difference as the underlying rubric of institutional life.[20] Reacting to one of the maps that reduced the Latino percentage in District 3, Bill Negrón told the commissioners, "It just does not make any sense." Negrón had been among those arguing that two 40 percent districts were preferable to one majority-minority district, but that did not mean it was acceptable to reduce the Latino percentage in District 3. In defense of his position he picked up on the argument about commonalities as Americans and argued for the particular needs of Latinos, saying, "I just want to mention that our pledge to our nation says 'one God, one nation under God, indivisible with liberty and justice for all'" (BCC November 15, 2011).

During the county commission deliberations over the relative merits of RAC Proposal 12b and Public Proposal E, the mayor repeatedly used history against the idea of a Latino district because District 3 had had Latino representation in the persons of Mary Johnson and Mildred Fernández without a Latino majority. She also pointed out that Mel Martinez had been elected countywide when Latinos were under 20 percent of the county population.

These arguments were countered by Commissioner D6, the same commissioner who had spoken up in March in support of Puerto Ricans who were protesting the appointments to the RAC. This time, Commissioner D6 spoke to oppose the changes being imposed on District 3, and she specifically objected to how drastically District 3 was being changed to accommodate the Conway Chain of Lakes. Without mentioning race as she talked about the power of the Conway area, she argued that not only was this map changing District 3, but it was doing so by bringing into the district "strong political communities." Countering the mayor's claims about Latino wins without a majority, she argued that they had not done so with these other powerful communities in the district. Her concern was that "you still won't have a Hispanic serving this district, because of what you brought to the district" (BCC Sunshine November 22, 2011).[21]

Turning language to the purpose of power. By 10 p.m. on November 15, the commissioners had been unable to reach agreement on a map, and so an unofficial meeting was scheduled for November 22 in order to officially adopt a final map on November 29. It was during the November 22 meeting that the mayor first offered her map. In her presentation, she used District 3's history of electing Latinos as an argument for increasing the District 4 Latino population even as her map decreased the District 3 percentage (BCC Sunshine November 22, 2011). As the mayor pressed her case, at least one commissioner seemed swayed by her arguments. Having originally said that Commissioner D6's concerns about bringing the powerful Conway Chain of Lakes into District 3 were "exactly on point," he now said that with the tweaks in the mayor's map, "a Hispanic that lives in the Conway area and is used to the Conway area and has been a part of the Conway area could easily get elected" (BCC Sunshine November 22, 2011). That this particular Hispanic would likely be from an elite living in a less densely Latino area seems hardly worth mentioning. Earlier in the process, Trini Quiroz had drawn attention to precisely that, arguing that electing a Hispanic who belonged "to a certain circle" and who would not address Latino needs was in effect disenfranchising "the grassroots in the community" (RAC July 20, 2011).

The November 22 meeting also included an extended exchange between Commissioner D4 and the attorney about displacement versus compactness, and this became a key argument about tweaking versus transformative change. Displacement, which refers to the numbers of people removed from the district in which they had voted since the last redistricting, had been part of the conversation throughout the process in terms of how many communities of interest were newly split up on any given map. Commissioner D4, who was interested in creating an East Orange district that would by definition displace much of the former District 5, asked, "Is minimum displacement a requirement or a preference? And how do you define core?" (BCC Sunshine November 22, 2011). The attorney's response connected displacement to maintaining the core of the prior district so that voters can stay with the commissioner for whom they voted.

Ironically, when one of the first maps drawn had removed heavily Latino Union Park from District 3, the attorney had warned that this could be a problem because "Union Park was the core of District 3 before" (RAC July 6, 2011). By the time the full RAC process was complete and the BCC was deliberating which final map to adopt, that particular idea of a core seemed to have fallen off everyone's radar. The map finally adopted had taken this former core of the East Side Latino community out of District 3 and divided it between Districts 4 and 5.

The attorney's reiteration of the political definition for a district's core clearly leads to a foregone conclusion that district lines will never be more than tweaked every ten years, so Commissioner D4 asked the obvious question of how it would ever be possible to fix a poorly drawn district. The attorney's explanation now used the equal protection clause of the Fourteenth Amendment to draw a distinction between necessary displacement to meet requirements for equal population and "extreme displacement" that would not hold up in court (BCC Sunshine November 22, 2011).

This response left Commissioner D4's question unanswered, and she now asked about how the courts weigh displacement versus "snakelike districts." In her response to this next question, the attorney gave a clear priority to compactness—and therefore to avoiding snakelike districts—but then added that "displacement will bring up lawsuits faster than compactness will" (BCC Sunshine November 22, 2011).

A week later, at the November 29 meeting, as some commissioners continued to emphasize the validity of Commissioner D6's argument in support of a Latino District 3, the mayor grew increasingly emphatic in her opposition. To explain her opposition to Public Proposal E, she argued that it packed

Latinos into District 3 and diluted the Latino vote in District 4, which she said was "blatantly illegal" (BCC November 29, 2011). Instead of considering displacement as one issue among many, the mayor cited her concerns about being challenged in court and gave displacement a priority over everything else on the checklist. Asserting her own authority to determine priorities, she said,

> Compactness is one of the criteria that we're supposed to look at. It is not the prevailing, all-determining factor. And a lot of the testimony I've heard today would suggest that compactness, that's it. Other testimony would suggest that there's something in the law that says Hispanics must have a 50 percent . . . district. There's nothing in any law that says that either. I want to be clear about what we're supposed to do. We're supposed to look at the totality of the issue. We're supposed to look at compactness as one of the issues. Displacement is a legitimate issue for us to consider. (BCC November 29, 2011)

The vote to adopt Map M-3 took place after another fifteen minutes or so of discussion during which compactness, displacement, history, and legal parameters all seemed to shift in the mayor's favor. Following the vote, the mayor thanked the members of the public for their passion and participation. She then talked about the importance of setting aside differences and getting to consensus: "At the end of the day, the only way we can reach consensus is if we all set aside those issues that we differ on and come to consensus. I appreciate that, and we look forward to working together with the entire community as we move forward" (BCC November 29, 2011). It is not clear what differences the 4-3 vote for the mayor's Map M-3 was setting aside; Commissioners D4, D5, and D6 voted against it. If this is consensus, it is a consensus that silences dissent and reproduces the status quo.

As the BCC deliberations stretched across the month of November and Public Proposal E was eliminated from consideration, the reaction in the press was strong. "¡Pa' fuera los latinos!" (Latinos out!) read a headline in a Spanish-language paper with the smiling face of the mayor just below it (Jiménez 2011). After the final vote for the mayor's Map M-3, the first line of the story in the *Orlando Sentinel* was "Orange County leaders adopted new political boundaries Tuesday that weaken minority voting power in its historically black and Hispanic districts" (Damron 2011a). The article quoted David Rucker, the African American cofounder of the Black-Latino-Puerto Rican Alliance for Justice, as saying that the BCC "did everything the white folks wanted. We're going backward, to Jim Crow."

"PEOPLE WERE SAYING, 'YES, WE ARE WITH YOU'"

The lawsuit against Orange County for drawing a district map that "minimized the voting strength of Latinos" used Section 2 of the VRA. To win a Section 2 argument, there are three measurable criteria to be met. The first is that the minority group must be large enough to form a majority in a geographically concentrated area. The other two are that the members of the minority group must vote along the same lines and that their vote, if not protected, is usually blocked by the majority.[22]

Along with these conditions, other, more qualitative measures such as patterns of political discrimination make up the "totality of circumstances." The mayor may have had this in mind when she argued for displacement over compactness by saying that they were "supposed to look at the totality of the issue." But the totality of circumstances in regard to Section 2 is not about compactness and displacement. It is about a history of discrimination that has impeded the minority group's democratic participation. It asks questions like whether elected officials are responding to the needs of the minority group and whether racial appeals are made in campaign advertising.

Nonetheless, the trial never got to the totality of circumstances because the judge determined that the measurable criteria had not been met in *Ríos-Andino v. Orange County*.[23] This decision turned on two issues. The first was a court precedent requiring not just voting-age population but citizen voting-age population despite the inability to get that count from the census and the lack of attention to citizen voting-age data during the redistricting process. The second was the fact that District 3 had elected Mildred Fernández, even though that had happened before moving the Conway area into District 3. Expert testimony for the defense broke Latinos' residence patterns up in relation to their national origin groups and focused on Cubans. Along with defense arguments that denied the existence of a compact and politically cohesive Latino community, the county's trial lawyer argued that Orange County's non-Latino white population was only 45 percent of the total. Therefore, the argument went, they were not a majority and could not vote as a bloc against Latino candidates. In this way the defense used its own version of *jaibería* and stepped sideways around concerns about the power of the non-Latino white vote in any given district.

By the time the case was tried in Orlando's US District Court in 2014, the 2012 elections were long over. The report prepared for the plaintiffs that analyzed polarized non-Latino and Latino voting thus included data from the 2012 election. That year the August primary ballot had candidates for Orange County District 3, which on the new map now included a reduced

Latino percentage as well as the powerful Conway Chain of Lakes area. The report's analysis concluded that one of the candidates in that race, Michael Aviles, was the Latino-preferred candidate, but Aviles received only 11 percent of the vote in the primary, which eliminated him from the November general election. The result of the five-way primary race for District 3 commissioner in August was a tie between Commissioner D3 and an Anglo from the Conway Chain of Lakes area. With the race then between two non-Latinos, an article in the *Orlando Sentinel* referred to the "historically Hispanic commission seat" to say that a "nearly two-decade streak of an elected Hispanic in the seat will end" (Damron and Roth 2012).

Commissioner D3 had strong support among some Latinos in his district, but he also had serious opposition from others because he had voted for Map M-3 and against Public Proposal E. His opponent had support from the Conway area (Damron 2012). Commissioner D3's Conway challenger won in an election so close that it was a week before the results were known. Ironically, his victory drew on the combined votes from disaffected Latinos and the very communities that had blocked their way to a majority-minority district.

While this and other elections were being examined during the trial, I was remembering the less measurable parts of the 2012 election season, like the conversations I had and those I overheard while I waited for Rafael to vote on election night. And the Puerto Rican–style jingle that played on the radio. And political bumper stickers using Puerto Rican phrases. I thought also about the geography of Analys's day and how I regularly traversed what were now Districts 3, 4, and 5 in the course of a day's fieldwork on the Latino East Side.

Evidence of that community emerges from the voices in the 2012 oral history collection I conducted just after the 2012 elections. Following her emphatic statement about how voting counts people in, Wanda Ramos continued by describing a *caravana* from that election:

> We did do an event that was a caravan that we did the last week of early voting. It was amazing to see the reaction of people in the street . . . for people to see a caravan of supporters going down the street in our cars, with our flags, the American flags and the things that we put in our cars . . . and the music, we had music and it was interesting to see the reaction, the welcoming reaction, the smiles, the people were honking also their horns, saying, "yes, we are with you," their thumbs up. It was amazing, really amazing and that put energy into the community when they saw us. (PRPPCE Ramos)

I remember that *caravana.* Puerto Rican politicians—pro-statehood and pro-Commonwealth—joined us. We left from the Bravo supermarket and went down Semoran past the *lechonera* where Barack Obama had stopped that summer. We wove our way through the neighborhoods on either side of the road and ended up at the business park where Ana G. Mendez University is because there was also an early voting center at the library there. We had live music with us, and the musicians stayed and played a long time. It would be hard to deny that this was a community of interest.

CONCLUSION

Navigating Ambiguity in the Interests of Community

A few months before the federal trial against Orange County began in 2014, East Side residents woke up one day to find that a mural depicting Roberto Clemente at the Azalea Park Little League ballfield had been painted over in black (Salazar 2015). Clemente is a beloved figure among Puerto Ricans for his athletic skill, his triumph over the double discrimination he faced in US baseball as black and Latino, and his generosity toward those in need. His death while on a humanitarian mission to Nicaragua in 1972 was honored in Puerto Rico by three days of mourning (*New York Times* 1973). Commenting on the Puerto Rican response to the defacement of the mural, an *Orlando Sentinel* columnist wrote that it was, "for many of the Puerto Ricans who've made the east Orange community home, almost like watching their hero die a second tragic death" (Owens 2014).

There was never news about who was responsible for the vandalism, and the question of who would be responsible for helping to repair the destruction only pointed to the confused relationship of the ballfield to any given public entity with budgeting for its upkeep. The field—on the west side of Semoran between Colonial Drive and the 408—lies in the city's District 2 and the county's District 3, but it is actually on Orange County Public Schools property next to the Azalea Park Elementary School. The school district does not own the building that held the mural, nor does it maintain the field (Salazar and Damron 2014).

The mural had been there since 2011, when Little League coach Earl Lugo, a Puerto Rican man from the Bronx, brought a well-known muralist, Héctor Nazario, to Orlando to paint it (Palm 2011). This was part of a community effort to clean up the ballfield and give Azalea Park's children a role model. It was reported that in reaction to the mural's destruction, Lugo's pained emotion was evident as he said, "Our kids, they go to fancy parks to play in the city, but we've got this mural. . . . It would make us stand out. It would make us proud" (in Salazar and Damron 2014).

Neglect of the ballfield had gone hand in hand with the neglect of Azalea Park in general under Commissioner Wyman's tenure during the 1990s and first years of the twenty-first century, when the area gained a reputation for drugs and crime. In what seems a tongue-in-cheek reference to the Disney-esque façade around Orlando, Latino Leadership President Marytza Sanz is quoted as saying, "What you see coming out of the airport is beautiful, but as you get to Pershing it vanishes as if by magic" (in Piccard 2007).[1] Every few years, it seems, there was a new effort to improve conditions. It was a constant uphill struggle with limited resources available to help.

When the mural was blacked over, community response was strong. Lugo again reached out to bring his friends from New York. They painted on scaffolds while a community party with grilled food and music took over the park for the day. The event is touted in the *Orlando Sentinel* as having unified the community: "The repainting of Clemente's image brought a crowd to the youth fields that pledged to fix the fences, add water fountains and improve the bathrooms. Lugo said several businesses helped and the '$20 here and there' paid for the event" (Hudak 2014). Next to the new Clemente image, words from Clemente himself offer a message about the importance of counting oneself in: "If you have an opportunity to make things better and you don't, then you are wasting your time on earth."

Around the same time, there was also a public outcry from Orlando's West Side about another ballfield that the city administration had just announced was to be torn down (Schlueb 2014). Tinker Field, where Jackie Robinson played and Martin Luther King Jr. spoke, had also fallen into disrepair as public moneys went to other, more lucrative projects. The final straw came with plans to renovate the Citrus Bowl football stadium next to Tinker Field, which would significantly encroach on the baseball field. Renovation of the Citrus Bowl was part of a plan to build state-of-the-art venues to draw visitors and their dollars to downtown Orlando. More than one of these had needed to repurpose a piece of Orlando's historically black community in service to the city's emergent twenty-first-century color-blind multiculturalism. These venues were also the target of Marquez's sarcasm (2004) when she lamented that there was not $60,000 in the city's budget to pay for the HOLA office.

In a plea to save Tinker Field, a member of the Orlando City Council addressed his fellow commissioners and stressed the importance of the field to his community:

FIGURE C.1. Repainted mural depicting Roberto Clemente at the Azalea Park Little League ballfield, 2017. Photo by the author.

> I see it as a museum and as a living, breathing document right now, in the city of Orlando. Yet, we are not taking an advantage of it. The hardest part for me to understand is, "Why not?" . . . I'm seeing black businesses being displaced. . . . Now, I see Tinker Field, knocking down the buildings, putting some land out there. I don't see economic development in the black community. I don't see that at all.[2]

As he continued to speak, he criticized decisions made "for profit that benefits the city and definitely not the black community." In reference to the East Side ballfield, he said, "Clemente is back . . . the community rose up and the artist decided that he would restore that picture . . . and it meant a lot." After politely listening to hours of such commentary, the City Council moved ahead and voted to demolish the West Side ballfield in 2015. The former Citrus Bowl is now Camping World Stadium, which looms over a newly designated Tinker Field History Plaza (Gillespie 2018a).

The stories of these two ballfields are about place-making in twenty-first-century Orlando and about what is seen and unseen in the process. Both stories set a boundary around history and memory that reflects an exclusionary inclusion in Orlando's social order.[3] They are reminders that place is something at once abstract, physical, and political. On the West Side, a piece of black history in Orlando was contained in a memorialized plaza rather than being rebuilt to offer continuity to that memory through contemporary use. In East Orlando, covering over Roberto Clemente's image was literally and symbolically a challenge to Puerto Rican and Latino claims to any territory at all in Orlando, memorialized or otherwise. The columnist Darryl Owens (2014) suggests links between the defaced mural, the poverty of the area, and the community's lack of political power when he describes Azalea Park as a place "bitten hard by the subprime-mortgage snake oil" and then goes on to describe "a community where muttering for increased political clout to match changing demographics has become a full-throated scream." As 2015 was beginning, an article in *El Sentinel* began its look back over 2014 with the devastating news about the destruction of the mural and continued with descriptions of hard times for the Casa de Puerto Rico and Hispanos sin Fronteras and the pending bankruptcy of the Asociación Borinqueña (Salazar 2015).

The upkeep for the Azalea Park ballfield that began around the time that the mural was first painted had been part of a planned makeover of the Semoran corridor "from a strip of rusty, sometimes dilapidated and abandoned businesses to a prosperous, community-focused gateway from the Orlando International Airport to downtown Orlando" (Stokes 2011). In contrast to the construction of the large downtown and West Side projects promoting the image of Orlando as an emergent urban center, the East Side redevelopment model follows the more intimate Main Street USA prototype. Locally and nationally, the Main Street program focuses on historic spaces and emphasizes small-business economic development as the foundation to creating a nostalgic small-town feeling in twenty-first-century consumer-oriented, multicultural spaces. The Gateway Orlando website describes the Semoran corridor as "a virtual melting pot district experiencing an urban revival."[4] This echoes descriptions of neoliberal redevelopment in other southern spaces such as Nashville, where "the diversity of the city street—once routinely condemned as a scene of danger, disorder and alienation—is now re-imagined as an urban amenity for a new class of 'cosmopolitan' consumers" (Lloyd 2011:115). Although the most visible changes are in the area heading north on Semoran from the airport and few reach beyond Curry Ford Road, a speaker at a 2017 news event celebrating the new name of Semoran as Gateway Orlando highlighted Oh! Que Bueno restaurant, which is actually much closer to downtown (map 5.1).[5]

Reductions in crime and improved conditions are a welcome change, but this redevelopment plan fits so well into the Orlando area's color-blind, multicultural consumerist ethos that it raises questions about who will benefit and who will be hurt. What will happen if a new class of cosmopolitan consumers begins to frequent the sidewalks of Azalea Park? To what degree will this project have the consequence of displacing the Puerto Ricans and other Latinos who have come to call Azalea Park home? How long will it be before property taxes climb too high for current residents of Azalea Park to sustain? And where will they go if so?

At the heart of these questions lies the reflection on what constitutes a community, who is deserving of membership, and who deserves to represent others. The questions point again to the relation between place-making and collective identification. In Orlando's natural neoliberalism, nested as it is in intersecting global and local histories that have brought new populations and new power struggles to the area, the reproduction of whiteness as the unseen measure of normalcy incorporates the changing face of Orlando into a further reproduction of capitalist and colonial-style relations of power. It is a case in which the meanings assigned to being seen or unseen in the tension between the universal and the particular are about the process of particularization itself (Flores 2005:202).

The story of the Clemente mural and redevelopment of Semoran Boulevard reflect outright erasures of Puerto Rican and Latino presence in Orlando as well as more subtle processes of absorbing difference into a single homogenized representation. Together the two ballfields offer parallels to how the new district maps in Orange County made both black and Latino Orlandoans a little less visible in a supposedly color-blind and multicultural social field. This is the quandary that Orlando Puerto Ricans and other Latinos face as they navigate the local in their efforts to assert the right to be different and to belong.

In the insistence on community exhibited in the rebirth of the mural, there is an implicit question about how race and class will inform the image of the City Beautiful that will be written on the landscape and how that image will correspond to decisions about whether public resources go to build stadiums or to clean up ballfields and pursue community development in ways that do not displace people from their homes and neighborhoods. As we saw in the decisions about the Orange County map, the answer lies in simply observing who is in and who is out once the lines are drawn. Responding to different political memories, some charge straight ahead and make themselves as visible as possible, and others step sideways in order to move forward. And all of this activity demonstrates that the ambiguity of "ongoing contingency" simultaneously marks and makes political formations, which are themselves never complete (Beltrán 2010:159).

MAKING THINGS BETTER UNDER CONDITIONS NOT OF ONE'S MAKING

On election night 2012 as I raced to find Rafael and get him to the polls, I felt deeply the attention that had been focused for months on Florida in general and Orlando in particular. As it turned out, the 2012 presidential race was decided without the count from Florida, which was not completed until the next day. We joked in Orlando that Miami had gone to bed. Nonetheless, in its demographics and politics, Florida and in particular Orlando offer insights into broader questions about social, political, and economic relations in the United States (McKee 2015:xiii).

In this book I have brought an ethnographic and anthropological approach to a political question of how Puerto Ricans and other Latinos arriving in Orlando from many places have drawn on their divergent experiences of race and class to navigate the encounter with this new place. Orlando is an increasingly diverse Sunbelt city with a sociopolitical past written in white and black where late twentieth-century neoliberalism has encountered an already-present foundation of entrepreneurial and individualist pathways to capitalist accumulation. My approach has been to look out from this one locale with a perspective that engages with the messiness of difference rather than setting difference aside as the exception to the rule. And this messiness of difference informs and is informed by intersecting histories and contradictory relations of power.

Through these lenses, a move can be seen from Puerto Ricans' and Latinos' invisibility in Orlando to an emergent hypervisibility and the resulting struggles for the right to be different and to belong by creating visibility on their own terms. The stirrings of that sleeping Puerto Rican and Latino giant have provoked reactions both loud and subtle that have contributed to producing and reproducing colonial-style forms of exclusionary inclusion. I have used metaphors like the merry-go-round of identity and the *balde de jueyes* to facilitate a focus on process and not product in community formation. Orlando Puerto Rican and Latino political community formation engages a fine line between the opportunity to create visibility and the danger of being co-opted into a universalist agenda that manages to simultaneously recognize difference and absorb it into the reproduction of hierarchical political and economic relations.

Navigating the lines between opportunity and danger can make for ambiguous signals about what any particular action by any particular individual might say about how such an action nourishes or contains the potentially transformative power of a Latino politics in Orlando. As Puerto Ricans and other Latinos navigate the tensions between opportunity and danger in an effort to upend race- and class-based stereotypes about the Puerto Rican problem and a Latino threat, ambivalence about racial identification apart from whiteness and identification as a professional migration are among the tactics used. How this will play out in the *balde de jueyes*—and what outcomes may result from newly energized political efforts to awaken a sleeping giant—remain to be seen. It will always be important to ask how any given identity idea is used and with what effect on social relations. In any given situation, are the differences among people part of the ongoing incompleteness of politics as a verb, or are the interests of others stirring up the *balde de jueyes* for their own advantage?

This is the context in which Puerto Rican political identifications and practices are being reworked in one twenty-first-century Sunbelt diaspora space. The Orlando findings may or may not ring true for Puerto Rican and Latino political identifications and practices in other nontraditional destinations. But it is my hope that my insistence on attention to time and place and my efforts to examine data from multiple dimensions will provoke comparative studies of other places.

On a return to Orlando in 2016, I asked an Orlando Puerto Rican woman who had given this project a good deal of her time and attention over the years what message she wanted readers to take from this book. "Puerto Ricans are here and they stood their ground," she told me. "And that we are represented. We are participating. We have integrated. But we stood our ground. Whatever ideology we are from, but we stood our ground. We defended what we are all about." She continued to talk about the wealth of experience and knowledge that Puerto Ricans bring with them wherever they go. She talked about sharing rather than imposing sociocultural perspectives with others. In closing, she said, "And I hope that this nation is gracious enough to see all the goodness that we bring. So, yes, uniquely, all of us have given a way, or a style, to stand our ground and say, 'Here we are.'"

EPILOGUE

"Things Will Be Different Now"

After the 2014 trial I returned to New York to get serious about writing, and it was early 2015 before I could get back to Orlando. On that return I sensed a new political energy that I now understand as another turning point in the history of Puerto Rican Orlando. Now when I listen to a 2015 oral history by Zulma Vélez Estrada, I smile at how she pinpointed the moment of that energy shift. Vélez Estrada's memories of Orlando Puerto Rican and Latino politics stretch back to 1991. When asked in 2015 how she saw things in Central Florida for Puerto Ricans at the time of the recording, Vélez Estrada answered,

> These 25 years have been 25 years of a lot of struggle but a lot of satisfactions. But there is still a long way to go. . . . Our Puerto Rican community has always shown that it's a propeller of civil rights, it's a propeller of creating opportunities for all Latinos. . . . We are in the propitious moment. A path has been created. (100PR_OHP Zulma Vélez Estrada #25)[1]

She looked forward to what future generations would be able to do because of those decades of struggle. She could not have known just how much events in Puerto Rico were about to conspire to solidify Orlando's place in the Puerto Rican diaspora and the Puerto Rican and by extension Latino place in Orlando.

A few months after that oral history was recorded, the Puerto Rican governor declared Puerto Rico's $72 billion debt unpayable. The smoke and mirrors that had been concealing the depth of the problem behind the Wall Street bonds being issued to Puerto Rico for decades came to an abrupt end, and the bondholders wanted all of their money back. Puerto Rico's colonial relation with the United States both precipitated the economic crisis and blocked pathways to resolutions that had been open to US states and municipalities in financial trouble. US rule in Puerto Rico also made it difficult if not impossible to pursue international justice avenues open to countries whose governments accrued debts that had not benefited the people. Within a year the US Congress passed the Puerto Rico Oversight, Management, and Economic Stability Act (PROMESA) and established a Fiscal Oversight and Management Control Board. In another reminder of the parallels between neoliberal and colonial-style rule, the control board imposed austerity measures and worked to privatize government services in Puerto Rico in much the same way that the impositions of structural adjustment programs ushered in market-based social policies throughout Latin America in earlier decades.

Increasing numbers of Puerto Ricans began moving to the US states in 2015, and a translocal organizing effort from island and diaspora began to emerge. As the primary destination for those leaving the island, Orlando was the early center of the organizing effort. That autumn, in the room at Acacia that held the Díaz mural *En mi viejo San Juan*, several hundred Puerto Ricans from very different places gathered to consider together how diaspora Puerto Ricans with supposedly full citizenship rights could use their mainland status to push for justice on the island. Despite efforts by the organizers to keep the divisiveness of Puerto Rican status politics out of the proceedings, political tensions erupted repeatedly in a display of the *balde de jueyes*. Nevertheless, organizing in resistance to Wall Street and in negotiations with the US Congress did happen. By summer 2016, as President Obama signed the PROMESA bill, a nonpartisan alliance called the National Puerto Rican Agenda was forming.

During the 2016 election season, national eyes once again turned to Florida and its growing Latino population, but as in 2012, Florida's outcome was not as decisive as predicted. In all the coverage of Donald Trump's win, an interesting local outcome in Central Florida escaped national attention: Orlando-area Puerto Rican representation in local, state, and federal government increased. Darren Soto left the Florida Senate and became the first US congressman from Florida of Puerto Rican descent. New York Puerto Rican Victor Torres moved from the Florida House to the Florida Senate, and Central Floridians sent five Puerto Ricans of different backgrounds and political affiliations to the Florida House. In Orange County, despite continued Anglo representation in heavily Latino Districts 3 and 4, 2016 brought to largely Anglo District 5 a new commissioner of Puerto Rican heritage. Emily Bonilla ran and won on an environmental platform in a district in which only about 15 percent of registered voters were Latino.

In fall 2017, Hurricanes Irma and Maria drew a new dividing line between then and now in Puerto Rico.[2] A description of Puerto Rico in the 1930s and 1940s, written in the 1970s, is strikingly appropriate for describing the impact of the hurricanes on top of the already churning economic storm:

> The depth of the economic crisis, the level of misery and despair, as well as the pitiful inadequacy and heavy handedness of the emergency relief machinery added to the harshness of the strife. But at the root of the matter was a wrenching turnover of internal class forces and an attempt to impose newly fashioned forms of colonial control. (History Task Force 1979:118)[3]

The federal response to the devastation that followed Hurricane Maria left no doubt that Puerto Rico is no longer as useful to the United States as it was in the twentieth century and that at least some see it as a burden instead (Cabán 2018). No subtle analysis is necessary. The image of the US president tossing rolls of paper towels into the crowd on his only visit to the devastated island has become part of a national collective memory. In the face of evidence coming from Puerto Rico about the ingenious and creative ways that people were dealing with the situation in front of them by working together to get by as best they could, Donald Trump's comment that Puerto Ricans want everything done for them mirrors an uncritical, knee-jerk adoption of the culture-of-poverty stereotype that has so plagued Puerto Ricans since the term was coined in the 1960s (Common Dreams 2017, Rucker and O'Keefe 2017). Insult followed injury for this US territory when the 2017 tax reform bill that passed just months after Hurricane Maria treated Puerto Rico as a foreign country while leaving in place laws requiring Puerto Rico to use US shippers. The actions in 2017 epitomize Puerto Rico's status as "foreign in a domestic sense" (Burnett and Marshall 2001).

If the economic crisis had gone a long way to opening islanders' eyes to the potential collective power of the diaspora, Hurricane Maria left no doubt. In the face of unresponsive governments both *acá* and *allá*, diaspora Puerto Ricans used the skills of the wise crab and stepped sideways to circumvent the combined US and Puerto Rican government roadblocks. Puerto Ricans throughout the diaspora pulled out every stop to get things into the hands of their families in Puerto Rico.

In Orlando, the Acacia building quickly became a collection center, managed by a hastily constructed coalition of organizations using the acronym CASA.[4] In an oral history interview, CASA's organizer Jimmy Torres Vélez (2018) recalled that the first bag of rice to arrive was from a Cuban family who said Puerto Ricans had been good to them. As the relief effort grew, he

FIGURE E.1. Pallets in Orange County warehouse being prepared for shipment to Puerto Rico, 2018. Photo by the author.

said, a young, unemployed African American man took two buses every day to come and volunteer. More and more donations came in the days following the storm. It soon became clear that Acacia could only be a temporary collection space. "We filled the place, then we filled the inside of the building, then we filled the patio, then we used the parking lot," said Torres Vélez. "It was exhausting." Commissioner Bonilla managed to find an empty warehouse for the relief efforts.

A major challenge was going to be housing. In contrast to the good prices on new homes that had spurred Puerto Rican relocation to Orlando decades before, in the wake of the recession Orlando was in a housing crisis even before hurricane evacuees began to arrive in 2017. As the Central Florida population had grown, developers set out their own definitions of what constitutes community by concentrating on building profitable and pricey condos beyond the reach of workers in Orlando's service economy. This problem was compounded by the state's continual sweeps of funds from a trust dedicated to affordable housing into the general fund to cover budget shortfalls (Klas 2017). About a year and a half after the 2017 hurricane season, the *Orlando Sentinel* reported that the Puerto Ricans who had gone to

Miami did not face the degree of difficulty experienced by those who went to Orlando (Padró Ocasio 2019).

As Puerto Rican evacuees arrived in greater numbers, a row of Kissimmee hotels—already known as temporary housing for those unable to muster what it takes to secure an apartment—became home to many Puerto Rican evacuees receiving Federal Emergency Management Agency (FEMA) vouchers.[5] A newly emerging organization, Vamos4PR Orlando, took up the housing issue, organized the evacuees in the hotels, protested outside the FEMA offices, and appeared before the Orange County Board of County Commissioners (BCC) petitioning for support (BCC February 20, 2018).

In addition to deflecting responsibility and directing petitioners to the state government, the BCC stressed using the nonprofit sector. Seven months after Hurricane Maria there were still six hundred families living in hotels. FEMA was setting an end to the vouchers, and Vamos4PR Orlando members again came to address the BCC. Using individual testimony to illustrate a collective problem, the activists explained the convoluted system of background checks in which landlords charged applicants, kept the money, and then told them there was no housing. Several had found jobs but could not get enough money together to pay the rent deposits required, and the repeatedly failed background checks ate up what little reserves they had. As the group patiently unpeeled the onion of red tape and discrimination, the mayor gasped audibly as the full picture became clear (BCC April 24, 2018). At the start of the issue back in October, as the extent of the crisis was just beginning to dawn on the non–Puerto Ricans in Orlando, she had wondered out loud who would live in a hotel room for a week when they knew they could be here for months. Now she had the answer (BCC October 3, 2017).

On a more positive note, as the University of Central Florida worked to accommodate an influx of Puerto Rican students, a new, politically active Puerto Rican Student Association emerged. And in 2018, the university finally created a Puerto Rico Research Hub, something that had long been strikingly absent in Orlando. At a student association meeting, one of the newly arrived Puerto Rican students seemed to know that not all Orlandoans were happy about this turn of events. She asked one of the presenters, "What are you going to do to address the issue of people who don't want us here?" The presenter was someone I had known casually for years. Usually very soft-spoken in public venues, he responded in anger about how little Orlandoans know about Puerto Rico and Puerto Ricans in the US states. His words echoed those of Puerto Ricans in Orlando from the 1980s.

One change, at least, was that Puerto Rican Orlando got on the local political radar like never before in 2017 and 2018. The attention began almost immediately as scores of evacuees began to arrive in Orlando from Puerto Rico. As potential voters despite the trauma they were still living, Florida Puerto Ricans were targeted as a resource by the two major parties. In sharp contrast to treatment of earlier arrivals, these newcomers found a temporary, government-sponsored welcome center at the Orlando airport offering them orientation. Among other services there, they could obtain driver's licenses and check in with health care providers for their prescriptions.[6]

With Georgia and Florida coming close to electing African American governors for the first time in 2018, news coverage after that year's midterm elections spoke of the changing politics of the South, and Central Florida made national headlines for voting Democratic. Once again, though, Republican control of the US Senate in 2018 was determined before results from the tight Senate race in Florida were announced. And once again, what drew less, if any, national attention in 2018 were very local results that opened the question of whether the process of Puerto Rican and Latino political community formation is finally bearing fruit in Orange County.

The midterm elections brought two more Latinas to join Emily Bonilla on the BCC, and for the first time an African American was elected as Orange County mayor. With the exception of the mayor, all members of the 2018 BCC were women, and the three Latina commissioners drew on the diverse places of origin among Orlando Latinos. Of the two Puerto Ricans, Bonilla is from the diaspora, and the commissioner elected in 2018 for District 4, Maribel Cordero, is from the island. The third Latina on the 2018 BCC, Mayra Uribe for District 3, is of Colombian and Argentine heritage, and she was born and raised in Orange County. Uribe's childhood memories about walking for Mary I. Johnson's campaign counter Latino invisibility and give historic legitimacy to the Orlando Latino claim to both physical and political territory. In the 2011 redistricting debate over the merits of creating multiple districts with significant Latino voting-age population versus one district with a solid Latino majority, both sides can argue that they were right.

At an informational meeting I attended in 2013 about the Voting Rights Act, Latino Justice PRLDEF president Juan Cartagena substituted "the right to vote" into Roberto Clemente's phrase about "the opportunity to make things better," saying to those gathered at the meeting, "If you have the right to vote and you're not voting . . . you're wasting your time on earth." Five years later in 2018, with the sea changes and activism that had happened in between, one quarter of Orange County registered voters were Latino going into the midterms; in Districts 3 and 4, Latinos were respectively 39 percent and 41 percent. In the November midterms that brought two more Latinas onto the BCC, Latino turnout counted for 30 percent of District 3 and 35 percent of District 4.[7] In a conversation with an Orlando Puerto Rican activist soon after the election, I heard, "Things will be different now because we showed up."

Although it took nearly a decade after the 2011 redistricting, the results of the 2018 elections meant that Latino representation on the BCC was solid, at least for the time being. The 2020 election year, as this book is published, brings new challenges to two of the three Latinas on the 2018 BCC just months before the beginning of the 2021 redistricting process. One thing is certain. The aftermath of Hurricane Maria has brought thousands more Puerto Rican newcomers to Orlando—some for the first time, others with prior diaspora experience in the US North—and they bring their own ideas about racial-ethnic identifications and class relations as well as their own memories of place. The confusing forms of exclusionary inclusion they will undoubtedly experience in their new home may conflict or coalesce with the experiences they bring from other places. Voter-registration efforts will target them. It is again a situation of opportunity and danger in which it may take the skills of the wise crab to avoid participation in programs and projects whose secondary gains bring profits to the already privileged rather than securing equitable relations for Puerto Ricans and other Latinos in Orlando's social field.

APPENDIX

Oral History Collections and Orange County Board of County Commissioners Proceedings

ORAL HISTORY COLLECTIONS

PRCF—Puerto Ricans in Central Florida 1940s to 1980s: A History (2008–2009)

Copyright holder is the University of Central Florida (UCF). The born-digital project is housed at the Orange County Regional History Center (http://www.thehistorycenter.org/resources/library-archives/) and the Center for Puerto Rican Studies Library and Archives, Hunter College, CUNY (https://centropr.hunter.cuny.edu/library). In-text citations include PRCF and the name assigned to each interview as listed below in parentheses after the participant's name.

The PRCF project was conducted under the auspices of the UCF Digital Ethnography Lab directed by Natalie Underberg-Goode and the UCF Department of Anthropology, with generous in-kind support from UCF's Center for Research and Education in Arts, Technology, and Entertainment (CREATE), directed by Stella Sung. Funding for the collection and public programming was from the Florida Humanities Council, supplemented by a Research Exchange grant from the Center for Puerto Rican Studies at Hunter College, CUNY. Interviewers were Emilia Blackwell, Alia Diab, Lisa Cruz, Megan Douglass, Julio Firpo, Russell Moore, Cyndia Morales Muñiz, Patricia Silver, Cheney Swedlow, Natalie Underberg-Goode, and Keisha Wiel. Many participants contributed photographs and other documents. A DVD accompanies the collection with digital stories from Lilly Carasquillo, the Kennedy Space Center engineers, Ernesto Peña Roque, and Amaury Díaz. The Orange County Regional History Center in Orlando, the Osceola County Public Library in Kissimmee, and the Winter Park Library donated space and skills to the public exhibits.

Project Participants

Project participants are listed below, followed by the name assigned to the interview in the collection. Several interviews include multiple participants.

Alexander, Sheila (González Durocher)
Alvarado, Víctor (Alvarado)
Auffant, James (Auffant)
Auffant, Lillian (Auffant)
Brown, Roy Sr. (Brown)
Bursian, Henry (Bursian)
Caldero, Ana (Caldero)
Carrasquillo, Marilia "Lilly" (Carrasquillo)
Casanova de Toro, Dora (Casanova de Toro)
Ciceraro, Elaine (Ciceraro)
Coll Cermeño, Margarita (Coll Cermeño)
Conville, Nilda (Conville)
DaCosta, Miriam (DaCosta)
Dávila, Carmen (Dávila)
Dávila, Victor (Dávila)
De Arrigoitia, Enrique "Hank" (De Arrigoitia)
De Arrigoitia, Tere (De Arrigoitia)
Delgado, Luis (Delgado)
Díaz, Amaury (A. Díaz)
Díaz, Victor (V. Díaz)
Enseñat, Edel (Enseñat)
Franceschini, Betsy (Franceschini)
Gamache, Paul (Gamache)
Gambaro, Charles (Gambaro)
García, Luisa (García)
Gelpi, Rafael (Gelpi)
Ghigliotty, Isabel, photos with notes (Ghigliotty)
Gómez, Haydée (H. and L. Gómez)
Gómez, Ivette (I. Gómez)
Gómez, Luis (H. and L. Gómez)
González, Ana (A. González)
González, Darío González (D. González)
González Durocher, Patricia (González Durocher)
Heinzman, Edward (Heinzman)
Hernández, John (Hernández)
Jiménez Miranda, Benjamin (Jiménez Miranda)
Johnson, Mary I. (Johnson)
Lee, Raquel (Lee)
LeGrand, Delores (LeGrand)
LeGrand, José (LeGrand)
Medina, Rafael (Medina)
Mercado, Elsa (Mercado)
Mercado, Fabian (Mercado)
Milligan, Yvonne (Milligan)
Moctezuma, Luis (Moctezuma)
Pagán Hill, Eva (Pagán Hill)
Peña Roque, Ernesto (Peña Roque)
Pérez, José (Pérez)
Plasencia, René (Plasencia)
Rivera, Gerardo (G. Rivera)
Rivera, Juan Pedro (J. P. Rivera)
Rivera, Roberto (R. Rivera)
Rodríguez, Miguel (Rodríguez)
Rojas, Judith Magali (Rojas)
Rosado, Lina (L. and P. Rosado)
Rosado, Pedro (L. and P. Rosado)
Rosado, Rafael (R. and Y. Rosado)
Rosado, Yolanda (R. and Y. Rosado)
Rubert, Reina (Rubert)
Santana, José (Santana)
Seale Collazo, James (Seale Collazo)

Serrano, Waldemar (Serrano)
Smith, Linda (González Durocher)
Soto, Heriberto (Soto)
Soto Toro, Félix (Soto Toro)
Soto Torres, Gilbert (Soto Torres)
Torres, Angel Luis (A. L. Torres)
Torres, Eugene (E. Torres)
Valarino, Lizette (Valarino)
Vélez, Carmen (Vélez)
Vélez, Glenn (Vélez)
Vélez, Monserrate (Vélez)
Wentz, Ana (González Durocher)
Zapata, Mildred (Zapata)

CFPRO—Cultural Foundations of Puerto Rican Orlando (2012)

Copyright holder is the Center for Puerto Rican Studies, Hunter College, CUNY. The born-digital project is housed at the Orange County Regional History Center (http://www.thehistorycenter.org/resources/library-archives/) and the Center for Puerto Rican Studies Library and Archives, Hunter College, CUNY (https://centropr.hunter.cuny.edu/library). In-text citations include CFPRO and the name assigned to each interview as listed below in parentheses after the participant's name.

Support for the project came from the Center for Puerto Rican Studies Library and Archives Historical Preservation and Research Partnership Program at Hunter College, CUNY. The project was conducted by Puerto Rican community volunteers from Orlando, Florida: Elsa and Hector De Jesús, Clara Quiñones, Zoraida Ríos-Andino, Jean Ruiz Sandor, and Nancy Torres. New York–based research assistants were Rachel Torres Zamora and Sarah Molinari. Technical assistance was provided by Ricardo Rodríguez.

Project Participants

ASOCIACIÓN BORINQUEÑA (AB)

Alancastro, Yahaira (Alancastro-AB)
Balderas, Carolina (Balderas-AB)
Capristán, Gonzalo (Capristán-AB)
Cordero, Henry (Cordero-AB)
De Jesús, Heriberto (De Jesús-AB)
Díaz, Juan (Díaz-AB)
Estrella, Julia (Estrella-AB)
Franceschini, Betsy (Franceschini-AB)
González, Darío (González-AB)
Lanzó, Miguel (Lanzó-AB)
López, Leila (L. López-AB)
López, Magali (M. López-AB)
Mirabal, Elsie (Mirabal-AB)
Piccard, Elias "Rico" (Piccard-AB)
Ríos-Andino, Zoraida (Ríos-Andino-AB)
Rodríguez, Felicita (Rodríguez-AB)
Ubiñas, Palmira (Ubiñas-AB)

CASA DE PUERTO RICO

Birriel, Rafael (Birriel-CPR)
Bracero, Joseph (Bracero-CPR)
Calcaño, Victor (Calcaño-CPR)
Carmona, María (Carmona-CPR)
Centeno, Jacqueline (Centeno-CPR)
Estrada, Juanita (Estrada-CPR)
González, Darío (González-CPR)
Lanzó, Miguel (Lanzó-CPR)
Lugo, Angel (Lugo-CPR)
Marrero, Sylvia (Marrero-CPR)
Piccard, Elias "Rico" (Piccard-CPR)
Ríos-Andino, Zoraida (Ríos-Andino-CPR)
Rodríguez, Felicita (Rodríguez-CPR)
Rolón, Efrén (Rolón-CPR)
Ruiz Sandor, Jean (Ruiz Sandor-CPR)
Sánchez, María Judith (Sánchez-CPR)
Santiago, Gladys (Santiago-CPR)
Torres, Cynthia (C. Torres-CPR)
Torres, Gloria (G. Torres-CPR)
Vargas, Monserrate (Vargas-CPR)

PRPPCE—Puerto Rican Political Participation and Civic Engagement in Central Florida (2012)

Copyright holder is the Center for Puerto Rican Studies, Hunter College, CUNY. The DVD collection of this born-digital project is housed at the Center for Puerto Rican Studies Library and Archives, Hunter College, CUNY (https://centropr.hunter.cuny.edu/library). In-text citations include PRPPCE and the name assigned to each interview as listed below in parentheses after the participant's name. The Orlando-based research assistant was Janice Stiglich.

Project Participants

Cerrud, Euribades (Cerrud)
de la Riva, Roxana (de la Riva)
Franceschini, Betsy (Franceschini)
Freytes, Dennis (Freytes)
González, Ana (González)
La Luz, José (La Luz)
López, Dulyn (López and Paniagua)
Mercado, Josephine (Mercado)
Ortíz, Antonio (Ortíz)
Padilla, María (Padilla)
Paniagua, Blanca (López and Paniagua)
Piccard, Elias "Rico" (Piccard)
Ramírez, Alicia (Ramírez)
Ramírez, Samuel (Ramírez)
Ramos, Wanda (Ramos)
Ríos-Andino, Zoraida (Ríos-Andino)
Rodríguez, Felicita (F. Rodríguez)
Rodríguez, Vivian (V. Rodríguez)
Suárez, Anthony (Suárez)
Torres, Carmen (Torres)
Velázquez, Denise (Velázquez)

100PR_OHP—100 Puerto Ricans Oral History Project (2013-)

Copyright holder is the Center for Puerto Rican Studies (Centro), Hunter College, CUNY. Centro initiated this ongoing project in 2013 in recognition of the fortieth anniversary of the Center for Puerto Rican Studies. The nationwide collection of Puerto Rican leaders around the diaspora includes interviews with Orlando Puerto Ricans. The entire collection is available at https://centropr.hunter.cuny.edu/digitalarchive/index.php/Detail/collections/154. The interviews are alphabetized by first name, and until about 2018 they were divided into numbered segments. In-text citations include 100PR_OHP, the first and last name of the participant, and the segment number.

ORANGE COUNTY BOARD OF COUNTY COMMISSIONERS PROCEEDINGS

Florida's Sunshine laws require that all records of government business be accessible by the public. The regularly scheduled official meetings of the Orange County Board of County Commissioners (BCC) are video recorded and available through a link on the Orange County website (http://netapps.ocfl.net/Mod/meetings/1). In-text citations identify the recordings as (BCC + meeting date).

The proceedings of unofficial meetings, posted as Sunshine Meetings, are available at the "Sunshine Minutes" page at the Orange County Comptroller's website (https://www.occompt.com/clerk-of-the-bcc/sunshine-minutes/). In-text citations identify the recordings as (BCC Sunshine + meeting date).

Video recordings of the 2011 Orange County BCC redistricting meetings are available at "2011 Redistricting Advisory Committee Meetings" on the Orange County Government website (http://www.ocfl.net/OpenGovernment/OrangeTVVisionTV/VideoArchiveBefore2014/2011RedistrictingAdvisoryCommitteeMeetings.aspx#.XR-BSnt7lfg). In-text citations identify the recordings as (RAC + meeting date).

NOTES

INTRODUCTION. RACE, CLASS, PLACE, AND POLITICS IN A NEW PUERTO RICAN DIASPORA

1. Except in the cases of historically identifiable individuals and citations taken from the media or publicly archived oral histories, I use pseudonyms in order to protect ethnographic confidentiality.
2. Florida's key role in national elections became clear in 2000 when a manual recount tipped the election to George W. Bush over Al Gore. Similar to Rafael's experience in 2012, Florida had conducted a voter purge in 2000.
3. The term "Latinx," although accompanied by some controversy, was taking hold in Orlando in the wake of the Pulse shooting and as I was writing this book. For a discussion and critique of the term, see Rodríguez 2017. "Latino," "Latina," and "Hispanic" were the terms most used in the interviews and conversations at the time of my fieldwork; for that reason I use those terms in this book to refer to people with ancestry from Spanish-speaking places. In accordance with Suzanne Oboler's (1995:4) observation that "Latino" is a more inclusive, grassroots term and "Hispanic" is an imposed term chosen by the Census Bureau, I have most often used "Latino" or "Latina." Also in keeping with the usage during my fieldwork, I most often use "Latino" for the collective term. Since Oboler wrote those words in 1995, the US Census Bureau has adopted "Hispanic or Latino."
4. Puerto Ricans became US citizens in 1917.
5. The Orange County Charter is a local-level constitution created in 1986. The charter is reviewed every four years, and the public votes on changes to it.
6. See Vargas-Ramos 2014:280 for a discussion of Puerto Rican voters in Florida in 2012.
7. Affigne et al. 2014, Barreto 2007, Barreto et al. 2008, Cruz et al. 2007–2008, de la Garza and DeSipio 2005, Espino et al. 2007, García Bedolla 2009. See also Pew Research Center (http://www.pewresearch.org) on Latino political participation year by year and Latino Decisions (http://www.latinodecisions.com) on Latino politics and public opinion.
8. Jorge Duany (2011:108–109) notes with surprise that there has been no social science study of Puerto Rican politics in Orlando. For other qualitative studies of

Puerto Rican political activity in diaspora, see Cruz 1998, 2010; Dávila 2004; De Genova and Ramos-Zayas 2003; Ramos-Zayas 2003; Sánchez 2007; Thomas 2010; Torres and Velázquez 1998. See also *Puerto Rican Politics in the United States*, the 2003 special issue of *Centro Journal* (vol. 15, no. 1).

9. De Genova and Ramos-Zayas 2003; Duany 2002, 2011; Pérez 2004; Rúa 2012.
10. For examination of media images of Latinos and the relation of those images to membership in US society, see Báez 2018; Dávila 2008, 2012; Rodríguez 1997.
11. For example, see Marrow 2009, 2011; Massey 2008. Literature on new destinations has been largely developed by sociologists, historians, and geographers, and rarely entails a book-length monograph of one community. With notable exceptions (Delerme 2020, Duany 2011, Griffith 2008, Striffler 2007, Torres 2020) anthropologists have not often taken new destinations as their field sites.
12. Ansley and Shefner 2009, Bankston 2007, Cobb 2005, Frederickson 2011, Guerrero 2017, Lippard and Gallagher 2011, Mantero 2008, Mohl 2008, Odem 2010, Odem and Lacy 2009, Smith 1998, Smith and Furuseth 2006.
13. It is important to note the symbiotic relationship between North and South (Crespino 2011, Lassiter and Crespino 2010). Lorrin Thomas's 2009 account of Puerto Rican invisibility in the US racial binary in New York in the 1930s is a richly detailed example from the North.
14. Luis Martínez-Fernández (2010:45–46) asserts that in the 2008 presidential elections, the Central Florida Puerto Rican vote effectively neutralized the South Florida Cuban vote.
15. For a history of Florida's growth from backwater to Sunbelt destination, see Mormino 2005.
16. For cultural memory and the reproduction of racial hierarchies in the South, see Hoelscher 2003.
17. Acharya et al. (2018) argue that a predictive factor in contemporary voting patterns in the South is the southern soil that supported cotton plantations. They name Florida as the exception because of its indigenous population and the absence of cotton plantations. Thus, it is noteworthy that Orlando was a cotton plantation.
18. Often understood as a political expression of hostility toward organized labor, "right to work" refers to legislation prohibiting the practice of requiring union membership in an organized workplace. Together with Arkansas, Florida was the first state to pass right-to-work legislation, in 1944 (Shermer 2011:40).
19. For discussion of transnationalism and bifocality as Puerto Rican points of reference, see Aranda 2007b, Duany 2011, Meléndez 2017, Vargas-Ramos 2015. For an examination of transnational ties embedded in local experience, see Pérez 2004.
20. The Pulse massacre happened during Latin Night at this gay club. More than one hundred people were wounded or killed by a gunman. For a photo essay from Orlando in the immediate aftermath of the Pulse massacre, see Torres 2016.
21. Chavez 2013, De Genova 2006, Duany 2011, Lowe 1996, Rocco 2014, Rosaldo 1997, Tuan 2001.

22. For discussion of whiteness and blackness in Puerto Rico and white privilege among US Latinos, see Duany 2002; Godreau 2002, 2008, 2015; Haslip-Viera 2018; Jiménez-Muñoz 2002; Lloréns 2014, 2018; Rivero 2005; Thomas 2009.
23. See, for instance, Acosta-Belén and Santiago 2018; Aranda 2007b, 2008; Glasser 1995; Padilla 1987; Pérez 2004; Ramos-Zayas 2003; Rúa 2012; Sánchez Korrol 1994; Toro-Morn 1995, 2005; Whalen 2001; Whalen and Vázquez-Hernández 2005. For challenges that the Orlando case offers to traditional migration theories, see Silver and Vélez 2017.
24. Writing about middle-class diaspora Puerto Ricans has been limited but significant. See Aranda 2007a, 2008; Delerme 2017; Duany 2011; Vaquera et al. 2014.
25. See Ramos-Zayas 2001 on Latino constructions of "ladders of whiteness" in Chicago.
26. López and Espiritu (1990) offer a strong argument about pan-ethnic identification as a structural, rather than cultural, outcome. They point to religion and language as unifying cultural factors, and to race and class as causes of friction for pan-ethnic identification. Their analysis centers on organizational identification, however, which circumvents the question of the degree to which Latinos actually adopt the structurally available pan-ethnic category.
27. Arlene Dávila (2008:17) cites Alcoff 2005 and Goldberg 1993 to argue that the term unveils Latino experiences of racialization.
28. For this narrative in internet chatter about the Orlando area, see Delerme 2013b, 2020.
29. Padilla (1985:60–61) also found this practice among Puerto Ricans in Chicago.
30. *Clara* refers to his wife's light skin color. *Trigueño* refers to a color somewhere between white and black.
31. PRCF refers to the 2008–2009 oral history collection "Puerto Ricans in Central Florida 1940s to 1980s: A History" identified in the appendix. Participants in this collection are cited in text using PRCF and the name assigned to their interviews as listed in the appendix.
32. See McConnell 2011 for Latinos in the US South. See also the 2010 special issue of *Latino Studies* (vol. 10, no. 1–2).
33. See also Aranda and Rebollo-Gil 2004 for Puerto Ricans as "sandwiched" minorities lacking a feeling of belonging.
34. For analysis of citizenship and constructions of difference in Chicago, see Ramos-Zayas 2003, De Genova and Ramos-Zayas 2003. See Pérez 2015 on Latino citizenship and belonging.
35. Bhambra and Margree 2010, Brubaker and Cooper 2000, Gregory 1998, Young 1997.
36. For collective memory, see Halbwachs 1992, Olick et al. 2011, Radstone and Schwarz 2010, Ricoeur 2000, Rossington and Whitehead 2007.
37. Cole 2001, Hobsbawm and Ranger 1983, Nora 1989, Ricoeur 2000.
38. This law allows a person in a public space to shoot if feeling threatened. Trayvon Martin's death in 2012 called national attention to the law, but he was not its first casualty.

39. The project was supported by the Center for Puerto Rican Studies (Centro), Hunter College, CUNY. The 2007 report "Stories from Puerto Rican Orlando: Documenting a Migration in Progress" is available at Centro's Library and Archives. Several interviews were conducted by Naomi González.
40. See the appendix for information on the several oral history collections described and their citation styles.
41. Irma Olmedo (1997) also conducted oral histories with her own family, many of whom now live in Orlando.
42. Literature on voter distribution in electoral politics at times uses both terms, and some distinguishes between them. In Orlando in 2011, the term used by the Orange County Board of County Commissioners (BCC) was "redistricting," and so that is the term I use in this book.

CHAPTER 1. BETWEEN BLACK AND WHITE

1. There are many *lechoneras* in the Orlando area. They are informal counter-serve eating places offering up traditional Puerto Rican foods. The name comes from *lechón*, which is pork slow-roasted on a spit.
2. For histories of black Orlando, see Altensee 2014, 2016; Brotemarkle 2005; Washington 1977.
3. Feld and Basso 1996, Gordillo 2004, Gupta and Ferguson 1997, Gray 1999, Price 2012.
4. Brown 2005, Gregory 1998, Hartigan 1999, Price 2012.
5. The US Census Bureau includes both foreign-born and US-born in the count for any national-origin group. This is perhaps the place to mention Polk County, adjacent to Osceola's western border. The 1960s development Poinciana straddles the Osceola and Polk County line and is now about 50 percent Latino. Polk County is distinct among the counties of Central Florida because the Mexican population is close in number to the Puerto Rican population, and together they make up about 75 percent of Polk County Latinos (US Census Bureau, ACS 2017b).
6. Duany (forthcoming) explores potential consequences of Hurricane Maria for the Puerto Rican diaspora in Florida.
7. For Azalea Park, see Padilla 1999a. For Landstar in Buenaventura Lakes, see Delerme 2014, 2020.
8. In 2010, the Buenaventura CDP was 70 percent Latino, and 64 percent of Latinos were Puerto Rican (US Census Bureau, ACS 2010).
9. See Duany 2002 on circular migration.
10. Although others may have been born in Puerto Rico, it is safe to read the birthplace data from the assumption that those born in Puerto Rico are overwhelmingly people who identify as Puerto Rican. The ongoing economic crisis in Puerto Rico that has driven Puerto Ricans to the Orlando area intensified after Hurricane Maria in 2017 to the point that it is likely birthplace numbers have shifted to favor Puerto Rico. But it is also true that many arriving from Puerto Rico still have diaspora experience. It will be a time before this settles out.
11. See Schein 2006 on race and cultural landscapes.

12. Haslip-Viera 2018, I. López 2005, Martínez-Echazábal 1998, Rodríguez 2000, Safa 1998.
13. The chapter in Duany 2002 is "Neither White nor Black: The Representation of Racial Identity among Puerto Ricans on the Island and in the US Mainland." See also West-Durán 2005. See García 2018; Godreau 2002, 2008, 2015; Jiménez-Muñoz 2002; Lloréns 2014, 2018; Rivero 2005; Torres 1998 on how blackness is marginalized in Puerto Rico.
14. Childs et al. 2011; Findlay 2012; Godreau 2008, 2015; Leeman 2018.
15. See Tafoya 2004 for "some other race" in the 2000 Census. See also Leeman 2018.
16. See Ramos-Zayas 2003 on race, class, place, and politics in Chicago.
17. For more on material conditions in this part of the Orlando area, see Delerme 2020.
18. Because Sky Lake is relatively small, there are no data for its Puerto Rican population. For consistency, I use "Hispanic or Latino" data for this section.
19. The management employment category clusters together economic and cultural capital under the heading "management, business, science, and arts occupations." Education data are for the population twenty-five years of age and older. Employment and other economic data are for the population sixteen years of age and older.
20. See also Padilla 1985:64.
21. See Cruz 2010 on obstacles confronting Osceola County's Hispanic electorate.
22. United States v. Osceola, Fl, 474 F. Supp. 2d 1254 (M.D. Fla. 2006). Single-member districts divide the larger political entity into smaller districts, each with a dedicated elected official.
23. In 2012 Ramírez was elected Osceola County clerk of court.
24. Data retrieved from the Orange County Supervisor of Elections website (https://www.ocfelections.com/Public%20Records/2018%20Elections/2018%20Elections.htm).
25. For statistics on Florida Latino voters in the 2016 elections, see the political opinion research center Latino Decisions (http://www.latinovote2016.com/app/#puerto_rican-fl-all).
26. Although this changed by at least 2016, Puerto Ricans have pointed out to me that Latinos who were elected used Anglicized political names. The point is borne out in this list of firsts.

CHAPTER 2. HIDDEN HISTORIES IN THE NEW ORLANDO

1. In her account of the African American Great Migration from South to North in the 1930s, Isabel Wilkerson (2010) selected the life stories of four people to ground the larger history. One of these was a man from Lake County in Central Florida.
2. See also Bonilla-Silva 2014, Omi and Winant 2015.
3. "Neoliberalism" describes the policies and practices that came to dominate US and global political economies during and beyond the 1980s, when Ronald Reagan was president of the United States and Margaret Thatcher was prime

minister of the United Kingdom. For a comprehensive understanding of neoliberalism, see Collins et al. 2008, Harvey 2005.

4. Duany (2011) and Flores (2000) also argue convincingly that Puerto Rican migration history offers insights into wider Latino experience. See Harvey 2003 on neoliberalism as a form of imperial control.
5. See, for instance, Acosta-Belén and Santiago 2018, Cruz 1998, Meléndez 2017, Padilla 1958, Padilla 1987, Pérez 2004, Sánchez Korrol 1994, Thomas 2010, Whalen 2001, Whalen and Vázquez-Hernández 2005.
6. *Downes v. Bidwell*, 182 U.S. 244 (1901). See also Burnett and Marshall 2001, Sparrow 2006.
7. For more than this brief overview of tax code practices and Puerto Rico's long history as a US colony, see Ayala and Bernabe 2007, Baver 1993, Cabán 1999, Dietz 2003, Picó 2006, Trías Monge 1997.
8. See also Pérez 2004.
9. See also Ayala and Bernabe 2007:206, Briggs 2002, Cruz 2003:157, Thomas 2010, Whalen 2009.
10. Washington, DC, has similar nonvoting representation in Congress.
11. See Thomas 2010 on New York Puerto Ricans' relations to the Democratic and Republican Parties during this time.
12. For discussion of this period of time in Puerto Rican diaspora politics, see Ayala and Bernabe 2007, Barreneche et al. 2012, Jennings 1977, Thomas 2010.
13. Mérida Rúa (2012:50) writes that Chicago Puerto Ricans at this time were "marginalized by two seemingly contrary tendencies—welfare dependency on the one hand, and radical terrorism on the other—a near fatal coupling of images, both essentially false, but nevertheless effective in shaping Chicagoans' sense of who their Puerto Rican neighbors were." For similar processes in other US cities where Puerto Ricans were locating, see Cruz 1998 and Whalen 2001.
14. For discussion of Puerto Rican organizations in the mid-twentieth century, see Ayala and Bernabe 2007, History Task Force 1979, Pantoja 2002, Sánchez 1994, Sánchez Korrol 1994, Thomas 2010.
15. For black-brown activism, see Behnken 2016. In Philadelphia, see Whalen 2001. In New York, see also Lee 2014.
16. Lee 2014, Sánchez 2007, Thomas 2010, Torres and Velázquez 1998.
17. See Laó 1995 on the New York Young Lords and their eventual transformation into the Puerto Rican Revolutionary Workers Organization.
18. See also *Oral History and Puerto Rican Women*, the 1988 special issue of *Oral History Review* (vol. 16, no. 2).
19. See Ramos-Zayas 2003 on islander-mainlander tensions in Chicago and Findlay 2009 on return-migrant navigations of these tensions in Puerto Rico.
20. Translated by the author.
21. Sonia Sotomayor is a diaspora-born Puerto Rican justice on the US Supreme Court. PRPPCE refers to the 2012 oral history collection Puerto Rican Political Participation and Civic Engagement in Central Florida, identified in the appendix. Participants in this collection are cited in text using PRPPCE and the name assigned to their interviews as listed in the appendix.

22. In keeping with arguments against seeing the South as an exception, it is noteworthy that Nixon and Reagan both "honed their conservative platforms in the segregated suburbs of postwar California" (Lassiter and Crespino 2010:6).
23. Perlstein (2009) explains the recovery of the audio recording of the Atwater interview. A link to the full interview is embedded in the article. For a book-length analysis of this "rearticulation of racial ideology," see Omi and Winant 2015.
24. Aranda and Rebollo-Gil 2004, Antrosio 2005, Bonilla-Silva 2014, Dávila 2008, Gregory 1994, Holland et al. 2007, MacLean 2010, Nickerson and Dochuk 2011, Omi and Winant 2105, Winders and Smith 2010. Lassiter (2006:275) argues that the southern strategy was a failure that was nonetheless countered by "the political success of the color-blind suburban strategies." See Aranda et al. 2009 on "color-blind" Miami.
25. See also Shermer 2011.
26. For more on the commodification of ethnicity, see Báez 2018; Comaroff and Comaroff 2009; Dávila 2008, 2012; Rodríguez 1997.
27. Di Leonardo 2008, Freeman 2007, Giroux 2008, Ong 1999, Ramos-Zayas 2012.
28. See also Goldberg 2009 on "racial neoliberalism."
29. See also Omi and Winant 2015.
30. Special districts, sometimes called "authorities," are a feature of many state systems. Usually run by boards appointed by the cities or counties where they are located, they have responsibility for particular functions of public administration such as water supply, highway maintenance, and so on, and they can collect and disburse funds without city or county supervision (MacManus et al. 2015:341–343). Two special districts in the Orlando area include the Orlando Expressway Authority, formed in 1963, and the Orlando Airport Authority, formed in 1975. Both were formed using a model similar to that of the Orlando Utilities Commission and are run by gubernatorial appointees (Foglesong 2001:88).
31. See Foglesong 2001 on the powers held by Reedy Creek Improvement District. See also Bezdecny 2015.
32. See Dávila 2008 on whiteness and normativity among Latinos. See Delerme 2013b on multiculturalism and the normalization of whiteness specific to the Orlando area.
33. For archived data on Orange County voter registration back to 1928, see the Orange County Supervisor of Elections page at http://www.ocfelections.com/Public%20Records/Stats/oldstatshtmlformat.pdf.
34. See Deslatte 2010 for a brief overview of the historical intersections of partisan and racial politics in Florida state redistricting. In a 5-4 decision in 2019 the US Supreme Court decided that it does not have jurisdiction over partisan gerrymandering.
35. Freytes has given oral histories to the 2012 PRPPCE and the 100PR_OHP collections. See the appendix.
36. Serrano's oral history is in the PRCF collection. See the appendix.

CHAPTER 3. "YOU DON'T LOOK PUERTO RICAN"

1. *Boricua* is a term often used by Puerto Ricans to identify themselves. It comes from the Taíno name for the island, Borikén.
2. Farmworker records from the Migration Division are part of an invaluable resource in the archives of the Center for Puerto Rican Studies titled "Offices of the Government of Puerto Rico in the United States (OGPRUS)."
3. Born in Puerto Rico, Ferré was the first Hispanic mayor of Miami, serving from 1973 through 1985. Prior to that, in 1967, he became the first Puerto Rican to be elected to the Florida legislature.
4. See Delerme 2013b, 2014 on developers targeting Puerto Ricans and other Latinos for land sales in the 1980s.
5. This chapter builds on data presented and arguments made in Silver 2016.
6. Besides Mary I. Johnson, the other woman on the council was Pam Schwartz, who had been elected the previous month. The first black Orlandoan elected to the city council was Arthur "Pappy" Kennedy in 1973 (McEvoy 1973).
7. The information about Mary I. Johnson comes from her oral history in the PRCF collection and box 1, Mary I. Johnson Papers, Orange County Regional History Center Archives, Orlando (http://www.thehistorycenter.org/resources/library-archives/).
8. Translated by the author.
9. Translated by the author.
10. Luis and Haydée Gómez offer another memory about this first location in their 2008 oral history (PRCF H. and L. Gómez).
11. See Bardach 2015 on immigration policies for Cubans prior to 2015.
12. In 1998 Universal Studios bought Wet 'n Wild; the annual festival continued until about 2010.
13. A 1991 *Orlando Sentinel* article makes a similar point (Gallagher 1991c).
14. See Cruz 2010:259 for an example from Osceola County.
15. Latinos were not the only ones arriving in Orlando. African American and white people from the North were also coming to Orlando. Orlando's Vietnamese population had been growing since 1975. Although still a small percentage compared to Latinos or even just Puerto Ricans, there is a visible Vietnamese presence along Colonial Drive in Orlando city.
16. See Ramos-Zayas 2003:124 on this dynamic in Chicago.
17. In her 2008 oral history, Elaine Ciceraro tells an even earlier story of coming to university in Orlando to study journalism in 1973 (PRCF Ciceraro).
18. Foglesong (2011:87) references a Cuban-American Club formed in the late 1970s.
19. El Barrio is the name given to East Harlem in New York City.
20. Translated by the author.
21. See Delerme 2013b, 2014 on language and racialization in the Orlando area.
22. A diaspora-born Puerto Rican who speaks only English even told me people thought her accent from the northeastern United States was a Spanish accent.
23. Marcos Feldman's 2011 study of the historically Puerto Rican neighborhood in Miami's Wynwood includes oral histories from Miami Puerto Ricans who came in the 1950s and 1960s. See also Cabrera Pérez 2018.

24. Translated by the author.
25. Translated by the author.
26. This history is also discussed in Firpo 2012:105–108.
27. Juan Pedro Rivera's 2008 oral history includes a reading of the 1982 press release detailing the merger of the two chambers (PRCF J.P. Rivera).
28. Translated by the author.
29. See also Ramos-Zayas 2004.
30. The 1947 California case was Méndez v. Westminster.
31. Rúa (2012:50) describes a similar process of collective consciousness among Puerto Ricans emerging in response to racial prejudice in mid-twentieth-century Chicago.

CHAPTER 4. ENOUGH IS ENOUGH

1. For more on this episode of Puerto Rican Orlando history, see Martínez-Fernández 2010:49.
2. Rocco (2014:xxv) uses the term "exclusionary inclusion" to describe the contradiction between "the principles of equality and justice for all" and the reality of systemic exclusion. Venator-Santiago (2013, 2015) uses the related term "inclusive exclusion." See also Aranda et al. 2009.
3. T. H. Marshall's 1950 classic text *Citizenship and Social Class* is generally recognized as the starting point for literature on citizenship that has followed the postwar emergence of a global world system. For a discussion of Marshall's legacy and neoliberal citizenship formations, see Crouch et al. 2001, Rocco 2014. For Latinos and citizenship, see especially Báez 2018, Flores and Benmayor 1997, Oboler 2006, Rocco 2014, Rosaldo 1997. For a study of Orlando Puerto Rican attitudes toward citizenship, see Valle 2019.
4. Alcoff 2007; Beltrán 2010; García Bedolla 2009; Padilla 1985, 1987; Rocco 2014; Torres 1995; Young 2000a. Portes and Rumbaut (2001) and Torres (2006) refer to "reactive ethnicity."
5. The citation to 100PR_OHP refers to the 100 Puerto Ricans Oral History Project conducted by the Center for Puerto Rican Studies, Hunter College, CUNY. For information on the collection and citations, see the appendix.
6. Translated by the author.
7. Translated by the author. "Carpeta roja" refers to FBI files on Puerto Ricans suspected of revolutionary activity.
8. Translated by the author.
9. See Padilla 1985, 1987; Pérez 2004; Ramos-Zayas 2003; Rúa 2012 on Puerto Rican Chicago.
10. Translated by the author.
11. President Obama commuted López Rivera's sentence in 2017.
12. Aponte-Parés 1995, Flores 2000, Martinez 2010, Sciorra and Cooper 1990.
13. On the *Intersections* program, WMFE Orlando, February 27, 2008.
14. For a more in-depth exploration of this family's political views and activities, see Silver 2017.
15. See Cruz 1998 on racial-ethnic awareness and political action in Hartford, Connecticut.

16. Translated by the author.
17. Curtis 1996; Curtis and Leusner 1996a,b; Leusner 1996; Leusner and Curtis 1996. Some say the articles were part of an effort to discredit President Clinton and get Florida to go Republican in the November 1996 elections, and it is true that a Florida congressman had been criticizing Clinton for not doing enough to stop the flow of drugs into the state (Mathers and Curtis 1996). Whether or not this was another example of US political party manipulation of Latinos to the party's own ends, the impact on Orlando Puerto Ricans was by all accounts devastating. For perspectives on the impact, see Barreto 1996, Decker 1996, Ramírez 1996.
18. See also Delerme 2020.
19. Translated by the author.
20. Translated by the author. I have translated Piccard's use of the root word *luchar* as first "fight" and then "struggle." Both meanings are contained in the Spanish.
21. "¡Arriba los de abajo!" is associated with Puerto Rican activism of the 1960s and 1970s in Puerto Rico and the diaspora. It is a call for social justice for the oppressed.
22. Translated by the author.
23. For instance, see Jackson 1996.
24. See Ramos-Zayas 2004 on the racialization of Puerto Rican spaces and framing of Puerto Ricans as "delinquent" citizens.
25. The testimony is in the May 25, 2011, recording in the video archive "2011 Redistricting Advisory Committee Meetings" on the Orange County Government website. Video recordings of the 2011 RAC meetings are available on the web page listed in the appendix. In-text citations identify the recordings as (RAC + meeting date).
26. Radio has been complemented, of course, in the twenty-first century by social media. During my fieldwork, *Orlando Sentinel* reporter Victor Ramos hosted the *Hispanosphere* blog. With the anonymity of the blog platform, the site became a contentious one. See Delerme 2013b, 2014, 2017 for postings from the blog.
27. Translated by the author.
28. Translated by the author.
29. Descriptions and quotes are taken from my field notes.
30. Translated by the author.
31. Translated by the author.
32. From notes and interviews, I believe that the founders of the league were Víctor Alvarado, Darío González, Evelyn Rivera, and Miguel Ruiz.
33. For examples of the Koch brothers' actions in Florida, see Deslatte 2012, Hundley 2011.
34. Translated by the author.
35. Carter (2010) references the "blood debt" owed to soldiers in colonial situations.
36. For analysis of Puerto Rican participation in the US military and its impact on political developments in Puerto Rico, see Franqui 2018. Franqui (2017) addresses Puerto Rican military service and middle-class status. See also Avilés-Santiago 2014.

37. For an examination of the "politics of citizenship" between Mexicans and Puerto Ricans in Chicago, see De Genova and Ramos-Zayas 2003.
38. Translated by the author.
39. The DACA program was started by President Obama in 2012. Following the 2016 election of Donald Trump, a tug of war ensued between the White House and the courts over whether the program would continue.

CHAPTER 5. "THIS BUILDING IS OUR ISLAND"

1. Translated by the author.
2. In analysis of a similar process among Japanese residents in Los Angeles, Jenks (2008:234) draws on Nora 1989 to define *lieux de memoire* (sites of memory) as "the historically significant physical locations and associated cultural traditions around which a sense of shared identity is constructed."
3. CFPRO refers to the 2012 Cultural Foundations of Puerto Rican Orlando oral history collection as identified in the appendix. Interviews are identified by CFPRO and the name of the participant followed by an abbreviation for the cultural organization, AB for the Asociación Borinqueña and CPR for the Casa de Puerto Rico.
4. Translated by the author. *Bacalaítos* and *alcapurrias* refer to traditional Puerto Rican foods that the organizers sold at events to earn money for buying land and building the building.
5. Translated by the author.
6. Delerme (2020) has analyzed the impact on housing in Buenaventura Lakes.
7. Translated by the author.
8. See Delerme 2020 on Puerto Rican visibility in Buenaventura Lakes.
9. Concepción Torres (2008) makes a similar statement about Puerto Rican businesses and homes in the Orlando area.
10. This may be changing. At a home I passed for years in downtown Orlando, a huge Puerto Rican flag suddenly appeared hanging from the porch in the aftermath of Hurricane Maria.
11. The PRCF oral history collection includes an interview with Judith Magali Rojas. From notes and interviews, I believe that other early leaders of the Centro de Cultura Puertorriqueña included Magín López, Eric Jiménez, Mike Rivera, and Manny Cintrón.
12. El Jibarito expanded to this second location from the success of its first restaurant in Kissimmee.
13. See Eichenberger 2004 on Puerto Ricans in southeastern US Latino churches. See Fernández 2013 on the role of the Catholic Church in building relations among Latinos in the mid-twentieth-century Midwest. See López-Sanders 2012 for Latino incorporation into southern churches.
14. Delgado (1988b) describes the Latino response to a Catholic church discontinuing its Spanish mass.
15. "About," National Latino Evangelical Coalition Facebook page, https://www.facebook.com/nalec.org/.
16. For this notion of trust Rocco draws on Vélez-Ibañez 1983.

17. To maintain confidentiality, the pseudonym Analys Cruz represents a composite person. The map of her daily life and the concerns she expresses are drawn from those of real people. Her political trajectory and actions are inspired by real people and situated in newspaper reports and other data I have collected over the years.
18. Rocco (2014) finds networks of trust and mutuality to be foundational to collective action among Latinos.
19. The at-large member of the BCC was county chair until the title was changed to mayor as an amendment to the county charter.
20. See Foglesong 2011:80-100 on Martinez's Orange County pathway into national politics.
21. Data retrieved from the Orange County Supervisor of Elections website (https://www.ocfelections.com/Public%20Records/2010%20Elections/2010%20%20Elections.htm).
22. Data retrieved from the Orange County Supervisor of Elections website (https://www.ocfelections.com/Public%20Records/2012%20Election%20Results/2012%20Election%20Results.htm).
23. Data retrieved from the Orange County Supervisor of Elections website (https://www.ocfelections.com/Public%20Records/2012%20Election%20Results/2012%20Election%20Results.htm).
24. League of United Latin American Citizens (LULAC) et al. v. State Board of Education Consent Decree, United States District Court for the Southern District of Florida, August 14, 1990 (http://www.fldoe.org/academics/eng-language-learners/consent-decree.stml).
25. For information on the Florida Senate districts in 2002, see the Florida Senate web page "Redistricting, Plan: FL2002_SEN" (https://www.flsenate.gov/Session/Redistricting/Plan/fl2002_sen).
26. By 2006, a lawsuit against Osceola County resulted in a return to single-member districts (Cruz 2010:270).
27. Data retrieved from the Orange County Supervisor of Elections website (http://www.ocfelections.com/Public%20Records/Results/Election%20Results/1992-98-99-00%20Results/1992%20Results/1992_countywide_election_results.htm).
28. Data retrieved from the Orange County Supervisor of Elections website (http://www.ocfelections.com/Public%20Records/Results/Election%20Results/ppp_2000/Cont100.htm).
29. Data retrieved from the Orange County Supervisor of Elections website (https://www.ocfelections.com/Public%20Records/Results/2004%20PPP%20Muni%20Results/Orl%20Dist%202_4_6.pdf).
30. Bomba is an Afro–Puerto Rican tradition performed as an exchange between the rhythm of a barrel drum and the dancer.

CHAPTER 6. DIVIDED BY BEANS

1. Video recordings of the BCC meetings are available in the archives of the BCC website as listed in the appendix. In-text citations identify the recordings as (BCC + meeting date).

2. The BCC in 2011 had five non-Latino white commissioners, one African American commissioner, and a non-Latino white mayor. Rather than names, I use district numbers to connect the commissioners to the districts they represent—Commissioner D1, D2, and so forth. The mayor will simply be called the mayor. The purpose here is to examine the intersections of place with racial-identifications, class-based relations, and the use of universalist-particularist discourse in the reproduction of power relations, not to identify individual commissioners, none of whom were still on the commission by 2019 due to term limits or election losses.
3. The metaphor of crabs in a bucket is not unique to Puerto Ricans. It has widespread usage among others living in colonial relations to white people, including African Americans, Caribbean peoples, and Native Americans.
4. In his study of middle-class Puerto Ricans in Orlando, Jorge Duany (2011:125) cites Raúl, who felt that Hispanics in Orlando tended to go in different directions and "cut each other's heads."
5. The chapter in Duany 2011 is "The Orlando Ricans: Overlapping Identity Discourses Among Middle-Class Puerto Rican Immigrants."
6. Translated by the author.
7. Boston is more similar to Orlando in Hardy-Fanta's 1993 study of Latino/a political community formations there.
8. Translated by the author.
9. For a gendered analysis of Orlando Latino activism, see Torres 2020.
10. Descriptions and quotes are taken from my field notes.
11. See Findlay-Suárez 2014:11–13 on the nuances of *bregar* as "a central political and cultural practice in Puerto Rican history."
12. Translated by the author.

CHAPTER 7. FOUR DISTRICTS FOR AMERICANS

1. Ríos-Andino v. Orange County 51 F.Supp.3d 1215 (M.D. Fla. 2014).
2. Deposition of Patricia L. Silver, Ríos-Andino v. Orange County, Case #6:12-CV-1188-ORL-22-KRS, October 10, 2013.
3. See Dinzey-Flores 2013, 2017 on whiteness and racial invisibility.
4. The study, conducted after the 2016 elections, surveyed white and black participants. Although both groups underestimated the gap, white perceptions of economic equality were further removed from the reality enumerated in the census data. For media coverage of the report, see Badger 2017.
5. Palm Beach County was at the heart of the contested 2001 presidential election and of the 2018 Florida elections for the governorship and the US Senate.
6. For a historical explanation of traditional redistricting principles, see Buchman 2003.
7. The Fourteenth Amendment extends equal protection to voters, and the Fifteenth Amendment guarantees that voters may not be disenfranchised because of their race.
8. Thornburg v. Gingles, 478 U.S. 30 (1986), Justia Opinion Summary and Annotations, Justia US Supreme Court, n.d., https://supreme.justia.com/cases/federal/us/478/30/.

9. There are various opinions on whether this was an actual court mandate.
10. Scholars still debate whether this inverted the intent of the VRA (Arrington 2010:9–10). See Buchman 2003 on the legal history that has led to contemporary interpretations of the VRA.
11. See Arrington 2010:3–5 on GIS systems and redistricting.
12. Arrington (2010:11) argues that the intent of the VRA was to provide an "equal opportunity to elect and not influence."
13. The categories are designated in US Census Bureau terms.
14. District 6 would appear to be out of numeric order. Although I do not have a documented explanation, I take this to be because Orange County had five at-large districts until the late 1980s and early 1990s. With the switch to six single-member districts, District 6 became a majority-minority black district.
15. In truth, my participant observation did not see much black-Latino interaction. That some efforts were being made was apparent from time to time, as in the spring of 2012 when a black and Latino group headed to Sanford for protests after the shooting of Trayvon Martin. In his 2008 oral history, James Auffant said that it was African Americans who first reached out to help Puerto Ricans as they were arriving in Orlando in the 1970s (PRCF Auffant).
16. Unfortunately, it was not possible to include an image of this map. The important point, however, is the affinity between Commissioner D4's map and the public maps.
17. Public testimony also included a mixed racial-ethnic representation from Occupy Orlando, which was happening at the same time. Those speakers listed their address as the downtown park where the Occupy Movement was grounded. They tied their arguments for a Latino district as required by the VRA into a class critique of the 1 percent, which they said was overseeing the redistricting process. Whether or not RAC and BCC members were actually among the 1 percent, most of the maps they presented maintained the county's established power relations.
18. Mora (2014:156–157) describes class-based differences in Latino images used according to distinct political and economic goals.
19. See also Beltrán 2010, Reyes 2010, Rocco 2014.
20. Rocco (2014:203) posits this as the basis to his concept of "associative citizenship."
21. An audio recording of an unofficial November 22, 2011, meeting is available at the Orange County Comptroller's website, as listed in the appendix. In-text citations identify the recording as (BCC Sunshine + meeting date).
22. For a detailed discussion of Section 2, see Buchman 2003.
23. Ríos-Andino v. Orange County 51 F.Supp.3d 1215 (M.D. Fla. 2014).

CONCLUSION. NAVIGATING AMBIGUITY IN THE INTERESTS OF COMMUNITY

1. Translated by the author. Pershing Avenue crosses Semoran just north of Conway Lake, which implies redevelopment up to the Conway area and no farther.
2. Orlando City Council meetings are available on YouTube via a link at the council's webpage (http://www.cityoforlando.net/council/watch/). On YouTube this meeting is titled "March 9, 2015 Orlando City Council Meeting."

3. Jenks (2008:234) discusses a similar process of contemporary narratives drawing boundaries around a collective identity in the Los Angeles "Little Tokyo" neighborhood.
4. "Gateway Orlando," Orlando Main Street, n.d., https://www.orlandomainstreets.com/districts/gateway-orlando/.
5. "Semoran Corridor to Be Renamed GateWay Orlando," ClickOrlando, March 23, 2017, https://www.clickorlando.com/news/semoran-corridor-rebranding-as-gateway-orlando.

EPILOGUE. "THINGS WILL BE DIFFERENT NOW"

1. Translated by the author.
2. See Padilla and Rosado 2020 for accounts from Hurricane Maria survivors in Orlando.
3. See Klein 2018 for discussion of the contemporary struggle against disaster capitalists for the future of Puerto Rico.
4. CASA is the acronym for Coordinadora de Apoyo, Solidaridad y Ayuda (Coordinating Group of Support and Solidarity).
5. The 2017 film *The Florida Project* is set in one of these hotels. Also see González Guittar 2012.
6. For discussion of the welcome center from the perspective of someone helping to assess health care needs, see Rudner 2019.
7. Data retrieved from the Orange County Supervisor of Elections website (https://www.ocfelections.com/Public%20Records/2018%20Elections/2018%20Elections.htm).

REFERENCES

Abbey-Lambertz, Kate. 2016. "NPR Reporter Squashes Question about 'Vetting' Puerto Ricans." *Huffington Post*, December 29. https://www.huffpost.com.

Acharya, Avidit, Matthew Blackwell, and Maya Sen. 2018. *Deep Roots: How Slavery Still Shapes Southern Politics*. Princeton: Princeton University Press.

Acosta-Belén, Edna, and Carlos E. Santiago. 2018. *Puerto Ricans in the United States: A Contemporary Portrait*. 2nd ed. Boulder, CO: Lynne Rienner.

Affigne, Tony, Evelyn Hu-DeHart, and Marion Orr, eds. 2014. *Latino Politics en Ciencia Política: The Search for Latino Identity and Racial Consciousness*. New York: New York University Press.

Alcoff, Linda Martín. 2000. "Is Latina/o Identity a Racial Identity?" In *Hispanics/ Latinos in the United States*, edited by Jorge J. E. Gracia and Pablo De Grieff, 23–44. New York: Routledge.

———. 2005. *Visible Identities: Race, Gender, and the Self*. New York: Oxford University Press.

———. 2007. "Fraser on Redistribution, Recognition, and Identity." *European Journal of Political Theory* 6(3):255–265. https://doi.org/10.1177/1474885107077305.

Alcoff, Linda Martín, Michael Hames-García, Satya P. Mohanty, and Paula M. L. Moya, eds. 2006. *Identity Politics Reconsidered*. New York: Palgrave Macmillan.

Alden, Robert. 1960. "Advertising: Studies Aid Clients—Analysis of Puerto Rico Finds a Big Potential There." *New York Times*, November 20. http://nytimes.com.

Altensee, Fred. 2014. *The Orlando, Florida, Civil Rights Movement: A Case Study in Cooperation and Communication, 1951–1971*. Cocoa, FL: Murfeus.

———. 2016. *Recollections of the Orlando, Florida, Civil Rights Movement*. Cocoa, FL: Jammin!

Anderson, Benedict. 1991. *Imagined Communities: Reflections on the Origin and Spread of Nationalism*. Rev. ed. New York: Verso.

Ansley, Fran, and Jon Shefner. 2009. *Global Connections and Local Receptions: New Latino Immigration to the Southeastern United States*. Knoxville: University of Tennessee Press.

Antrosio, Jason. 2005. "Disappearing Act: Race and the Neoliberal State." *Social Analysis* 49(2):199–204.

Aponte-Parés, Luis. 1995. "What's Yellow and White and Has Land All around It? Appropriating Place in Puerto Rican *Barrios*." *Centro Journal* 7(1):8–19.

Aranda, Elizabeth. 2007a. "Struggles for Incorporation among the Puerto Rican Middle Class." *Sociological Quarterly* 48:199–228.

———. 2007b. *Emotional Bridges to Puerto Rico: Migration, Return Migration, and the Struggles of Incorporation*. Lanham: Rowman and Littlefield.

———. 2008. "Class Backgrounds, Modes of Incorporation, and Puerto Ricans' Pathways into the Transnational Professional Workforce." *American Behavioral Scientist* 52(3):426–456.

Aranda, Elizabeth M., and Guillermo Rebollo-Gil. 2004. "Ethnoracism and the 'Sandwiched' Minorities." *American Behavioral Scientist* 47(7):910–927.

Aranda, Elizabeth M., Rosa E. Chang, and Elena Sabogal. 2009. "Racializing Miami: Immigrant Latinos and the Colorblind Racism in the Global City." In *How the United States Racializes Latinos: White Hegemony and Its Consequences*, edited by José A. Cobas, Jorge Duany, and Joe R. Feagin, 149–165. Boulder, CO: Paradigm.

Aranda, Elizabeth M., Sallie Hughes, and Elena Sabogal. 2014. *Making a Life in Multiethnic Miami: Immigration and the Rise of a Global City*. Boulder, CO: Lynne Rienner.

Archer, Kevin, and Kris Bezdecny. 2009. "Searching for a New Brand: Reimagining a More Diverse Orlando." *Southeastern Geographer* 49(2):185–199.

Arrellano, Gustavo. 2012. "Why Do Mexicans Look Down on Chicanos?" *Ask a Mexican*. Blog. *Dallas Observer*, March 22. http://www.dallasobserver.com/news/why-do-mexicans-look-down-on-chicanos-6424880.

Arrington, Theodore S. 2010. "Redistricting in the U.S.: A Review of Scholarship and Plan for Future Research." *The Forum* 8(2). https://doi.org/10.2202/1540-8884.1351.

Avilés-Santiago, Manuel. 2014. *Puerto Rican Soldiers and Second-Class Citizenship*. New York: Palgrave Macmillan.

Ayala, César J., and Rafael Bernabe. 2007. *Puerto Rico in the American Century: A History Since 1898*. Chapel Hill: University of North Carolina Press.

Bacon, Eve. 1977. *Orlando: A Centennial History*. 2 vols. Chuluota, FL: Mickler House.

Badger, Emily. 2017. "Whites Have Huge Wealth Edge over Blacks (but Don't Know It)." *New York Times*, September 18.

Báez, Jillian. 2014. "Latina/o Audiences as Citizens: Bridging Culture, Media, and Politics." In *Contemporary Latina/o Media: Production, Circulation, Politics*, edited by Arlene Dávila and Yeidy M. Rivero, 267–284. New York: New York University Press.

———. 2018. *In Search of Belonging: Latinas, Media, and Citizenship*. Champaign: University of Illinois Press.

Banks, Adelle M. 1990. "Churches Serve Needs of Hispanics." *Orlando Sentinel*, Orange Extra edition, August 12.

Bankston, Carl L. III. 2007. "New People in the New South: An Overview of Southern Immigration." *Southern Cultures* 13(4):24–44.

Bardach, Anne Louise. 2015. "Why Are Cubans So Special?" Opinion. *New York Times*, January 30. https://www.nytimes.com.

Barreneche, Gabriel Ignacio, Jane Lombardi, and Héctor Ramos-Flores. 2012. "A New Destination for 'The Flying Bus'? The Implications of Orlando-Rican Migration for Luis Rafael Sánchez's 'La guagua aérea.'" *Hispania* 95(1):14–23.

Barreto, Matt A. 2007. "¡Sí, Se Puede! Latino Candidates and the Mobilization of Latino Voters." *American Political Science Review* 101(3):425–441.

Barreto, Matt A., Luis R. Fraga, Sylvia Manzano, Valerie Martinez-Ebers, and Gary M. Segura. 2008. "'Should They Dance with the One Who Brung 'Em? Latinos and the 2008 Presidential Election." *PS: Political Science and Politics* 41(4):753–760.

Barreto, Matt A., Sylvia Manzano, Ricardo Ramírez, and Kathy Rim. 2009. "Mobilization, Participation, and Solidaridad: Latino Participation in the 2006 Immigration Protest Rallies." *Urban Affairs Review* 44(5):736–764.

Barreto, Wanda. 1996. "Don't Stereotype Puerto Ricans." Letter to the editor. *Orlando Sentinel*, October 20.

Baver, Sherrie L. 1993. *The Political Economy of Colonialism: The State and Industrialization in Puerto Rico*. Westport, CT: Praeger.

Beatty, Robert L. 2002. "Legacy to the People: Community and the Orange County Regional History Center." Master's thesis, Department of History, University of Central Florida.

Behnken, Brian D. 2016. "African American and Latino/a Activism(s) and Relations: An Introduction." In *Civil Rights and Beyond: African American and Latino/a Activism in the Twentieth-Century United States*, edited by Brian D. Behnken, 1–19. Athens: University of Georgia Press.

Beltrán, Cristina. 2010. *The Trouble with Unity: Latino Politics and the Creation of Identity*. Oxford, England: Oxford University Press.

Bezdecny, Kris. 2015. "Imagineering Uneven Geographic Development in Central Florida." *Geographical Review* 105(3):325–343.

Bhambra, Gurminder K., and Victoria Margree. 2010. "Identity Politics and the Need for a 'Tomorrow.'" *Economic and Political Weekly*, April 10–16, 59–66.

Bonilla-Silva, Eduardo. 2004. "From Bi-Racial to Tri-Racial: Towards a New System of Racial Stratification in the USA." *Ethnic and Racial Studies* 27(6):931–950.

———. 2014. *Racism without Racists: Color-Blind Racism and the Persistence of Racial Inequality in America*. 4th ed. New York: Rowman and Littlefield.

Bonner, Tanya. 1996. "'Bob' Guevara's Win Is Talk of BVL—Hispanic Residents Say They Are Glad Finally to Have Sympathetic Voice in Local Government." *Orlando Sentinel*, Osceola edition, November 8.

Bousquet, Steve. 2014. "Florida Gov. Rick Scott's 2012 Voter Purge Violated Federal Law, Court Rules." *Tampa Bay Times*, April 1. https://www.tampabay.com.

Brewington, Kelly. 2002. "Groups Will Help Votes Be Counted." *Orlando Sentinel*, October 31.

———. 2003a. "A City Divided by City Lines—Orlando's Municipal Boundaries Snake over 286 Miles." *Orlando Sentinel*, February 20.

———. 2003b. "Pine Hills Fights Stigma—United Effort Is Key to Change, Activists Say." *Orlando Sentinel*, October 12.

Brewington, Kelly, and Walter Pacheco. 2002. "Hispanic Residents in Uproar over Delay of Park's Opening." *Orlando Sentinel*, May 11.

Briggs, Laura. 2002. "*La Vida*, Moynihan, and Other Libels: Migration, Social Science, and the Making of the Puerto Rican Welfare Queen." *Centro Journal* 14(1):75–101.

Brotemarkle, Benjamin D. 2005. *Crossing Division Street: An Oral History of the African-American Community in Orlando*. Cocoa: Florida Historical Society Press.

Brown, Jacqueline Nassy. 2005. *Dropping Anchor, Setting Sail: Geographies of Race in Black Liverpool*. Princeton, NJ: Princeton University Press.

Brown, Matthew Hay. 2002. "At a Crossroads—Fifty Years Ago, Puerto Rico Became a U.S. Commonwealth and Embarked on a Path of Political Transition and Economic Ascension." *Orlando Sentinel*, July 21.

Brubaker, Rogers, and Frederick Cooper. 2000. "Beyond 'Identity.'" *Theory and Society* 29(1):1–47.

Buchman, Jeremy. 2003. *Drawing Lines in Quicksand: Courts, Legislatures, and Redistricting*. New York: Peter Lang.

Burnett, Christina Duffy, and Burke Marshall, eds. 2001. *Foreign in a Domestic Sense: Puerto Rico, American Expansion, and the Constitution*. Durham, NC: Duke University Press.

Cabán, Pedro A. 1999. *Constructing a Colonial People: Puerto Rico and the United States, 1898–1932*. Boulder, CO: Westview.

———. 2018. "PROMESA, Puerto Rico, and the American Empire." *Latino Studies* 16(2):161–184.

Cabranes, José A. 1978. "Citizenship and the American Empire: Notes on the Legislative History of the United States Citizenship of Puerto Ricans." *University of Pennsylvania Law Review* 127(2):391–492.

Cabrera Pérez, Nydia Milagros. 2018. "In Their Own Voices: Evolution, Identity, and Contributions of the Puerto Rican Community to Miami-Dade, Florida from 1940 to Modern Times." PhD diss., Centro de Estudios Avanzados de Puerto Rico y el Caribe.

Carter, Donald Martin. 2010. *Navigating the African Diaspora: The Anthropology of Invisibility*. Minneapolis: University of Minnesota Press.

Chavez, Leo R. 2013. *Latino Threat: Constructing Immigrants, Citizens, and the Nation*. 2nd ed. Stanford, CA: Stanford University Press.

Childs, Jennifer Hunter, Rodney Terry, and Nathan Jurgenson. 2011. "Measuring Race and Hispanic Origin: Cognitive Test Findings Searching for 'Truth.'" *Bulletin de Méthodologie Sociologique* 3:26–42. https://doi.org/10.1177/0759106311408874.

Cobas, José A., Jorge Duany, and Joe R. Feagin, eds. 2009. *How the United States Racializes Latinos: White Hegemony and Its Consequences*. Boulder, CO: Paradigm.

Cobb, James C. 2005. *Globalization and the American South*. Athens: University of Georgia Press.

———. 2011. *The South and America since World War II*. New York: Oxford University Press.

Colburn, David R. 2007. *From Yellow Dog Democrats to Red State Republicans: Florida and Its Politics since 1940*. Gainesville: University Press of Florida.

Colburn, David R., and Lance deHaven-Smith. 1999. *Government in the Sunshine State: Florida since Statehood*. Gainesville: University Press of Florida.

Cole, Jennifer. 2001. *Forget Colonialism? Sacrifice and the Art of Memory in Madagascar*. Berkeley: University of California Press.

Collins, Jane L., Micaela Di Leonardo, and Brett Williams. 2008. *New Landscapes of Inequality: Neoliberalism and the Erosion of Democracy in America*. Santa Fe, NM: School for Advanced Research.

Comaroff, John L., and Jean Comaroff. 1992. *Ethnography and the Historical Imagination*. Boulder, CO: Westview.

——. 2009. *Ethnicity, Inc.* Chicago: University of Chicago Press.

Comas, Martin E. 2002. "Pine Castle District Isn't End of Debate." *Orlando Sentinel*, November 17. https://orlandosentinel.com.

Common Dreams. 2017. "In 'Disgusting' Attack, Trump Blames Puerto Rico; Says FEMA Can't Stay Forever." *Common Dreams*, October 12. https://www.commondreams.org.

Concepción Torres, Ramón Luis. 2008. "Puerto Rican Migration, Settlement Patterns, and Assimilation in the Orlando MSA." Master's thesis, State University of New York, Binghamton.

Confino, Alon. 1997. "Collective Memory and Cultural History: Problems of Method." *American Historical Review* 102(5):1386–1403.

Crespino, Joseph. 2011. "Strom Thurmond's Sunbelt: Rethinking Regional Politics and the Rise of the Right." In *Sunbelt Rising: The Politics of Place, Space, and Region*, edited by Michelle Nickerson and Darren Dochuk, 58–81. Philadelphia: University of Pennsylvania Press.

——. 2012. *Strom Thurmond's America*. New York: Hill and Wang.

Crouch, Colin, Klaus Eder, and Damian Tambini. 2001. "Introduction: Dilemmas of Citizenship." In *Citizenship, Markets, and the State*, edited by Crouch et al. Oxford, England: Oxford University Press.

Cruz, José E. 1998. *Identity and Power: Puerto Rican Politics and the Challenge of Ethnicity*. Philadelphia: Temple University Press.

——. 2003. "Unfulfilled Promise: Puerto Rican Politics and Poverty." *Centro Journal* 15(1):152–175.

——. 2010. "Barriers to Political Participation of Puerto Ricans and Hispanics in Osceola County, Florida: 1991–2007." *Centro Journal* 22(1):243–285.

Cruz, José E., Cecilia Ferradino, and Sally Friedman. 2007–2008. "Latino Voting in the 2004 Election: The Case of New York." *Latino(a) Research Review* 6(3):7–36.

Curtis, Henry Pierson. 1996. "Addiction Rate Runs 4 Times Higher than Florida's—Counselors Look at Puerto Rico's Heroin Abuse Statistics and Say They Reflect a Crisis Situation." *Orlando Sentinel*, October 27.

Curtis, Henry Pierson, and Jim Leusner. 1996a. "San Juan Dumps Drug Dealers Here: Local Authorities Not Told of Relocations by Puerto Rico Witness Protection Program." *Orlando Sentinel*, October 11.

——. 1996b. "An Island under Siege." *Orlando Sentinel*, October 27.

Damron, David. 2010. "Men-Only Parties for Leaders Continue to Prompt Backlash." *Orlando Sentinel*, April 18.

———. 2011a. "Orange Approves Districts That Dilute Minority Clout, May Spark Legal Fight." *Orlando Sentinel*, November 30.

———. 2011b. "Mel Martinez's Son Replaces Fernandez." *Orlando Sentinel*, December 13.

———. 2012. "Hispanics, Partisans Helped Clarke Upset Damiani to Win Orange Seat." *Orlando Sentinel*, November 17.

Damron, David, and Jeannette Rivera-Lyles. 2011. "'Backlash' Grows over Puerto Ricans' Exclusion." *Orlando Sentinel*, April 26.

Damron, David, and Lauren Roth. 2012. "Runoff to Decide Commission Seat." *Orlando Sentinel*, August 15.

Damron, David, and Victor Manuel Ramos. 2010. "Crist Picks Damiani to Replace Suspended Orange Commissioner Fernandez." *Orlando Sentinel*, August 7.

Damron, David, Victor Manuel Ramos, and Walter Pacheco. 2010. "Fernández Is Ready for Fight." *Orlando Sentinel*, May 5.

Dávila, Arlene M. 1997. *Sponsored Identities: Cultural Politics in Puerto Rico*. Philadelphia: Temple University Press.

———. 2001. *Latinos, Inc.: The Marketing and Making of a People*. Berkeley: University of California Press.

———. 2004. *Barrio Dreams: Puerto Ricans, Latinos, and the Neoliberal City*. Berkeley: University of California Press.

———. 2008. *Latino Spin: Public Image and the Whitewashing of Race*. New York: New York University Press.

De Genova, Nicholas, ed. 2006. *Racial Transformations: Latinos and Asians Remaking the United States*. Durham, NC: University of North Carolina Press.

———. 2010. "'White' Puerto Rican Migrants, the Mexican Colony, 'Americanization,' and Latino History." In *Latino Urban Ethnography and the Work of Elena Padilla*, edited by Mérida M. Rúa, 157–177. Urbana: University of Illinois Press.

De Genova, Nicholas, and Ana Yolanda Ramos-Zayas. 2003. *Latino Crossings: Mexicans, Puerto Ricans, and the Politics of Race*. New York: Routledge.

de la Garza, Rodolfo O., and Louis DeSipio. 2005. *Muted Voices: Latinos and the 2000 Elections*. Lanham, MD: Rowman and Littlefield.

de la Riva, Roxana. 2009. "Reclaman a Orlando falta de contacto hispano." *La Prensa*, March 26-April 1.

———. 2010a. "Exitoso encuentro entre Cuba y Puerto Rico." *El Sentinel*, February 11–17, 21.

———. 2010b. "Luigi Damiani reemplaza a Mildred Fernández—¿Qué hará en la silla hispana?" *La Prensa*, August 12.

———. 2010c. "Seguros Multiples inicia su retiro." *La Prensa*, December 16–22.

Decker, Twila. 1996. "Group Slams Coverage, Promotes Local March—Puerto Rican Leaders Urge the Community to Join an Anti-Drug March in Orlando—on Nov. 3." *Orlando Sentinel*, October 18.

Delerme, Simone. 2011. "Latinization of Space and the Memorialization of the Borinqueneers." *Anthropology News* 52(6):7, 12.

———. 2013a. "The Latinization of Orlando: Race, Class, and the Politics of Place." PhD diss., Rutgers University.

——. 2013b. "The Latinization of Orlando: Language, Whiteness, and the Politics of Place." *Centro Journal* 25(2):60–95.

——. 2014. "'Puerto Ricans Live Free': Race, Language, and Orlando's Contested Soundscape." *Southern Spaces*, March 24. https://southernspaces.org.

——. 2017. "Reflections on Cultural Capital and Orlando's Puerto Rican and Latino 'Elite.'" *Centro Journal* 29(3):74–96.

——. 2020. *Latino Orlando: Suburban Transformation and Racial Conflict.* Gainesville: University Press of Florida.

Delgado, Dora. 1988a. "Hispanic Community Is Growing." *Orlando Sentinel*, April 7.

——. 1988b. "Fight to Restore Spanish Mass Frustrates Hispanics." *Orlando Sentinel*, April 10.

Delgado, Pura. 2017. "Puerto Rican: Artiles' Racial Remarks Reopen Old Wounds." *Orlando Sentinel*, May 5. https://orlandosentinel.com.

Deslatte, Aaron. 2010. "Shifting Population Spurs Battle." *Orlando Sentinel*, July 6.

——. 2012. "Merit-Retention Fight Brings out the Politics on Both Sides." *Orlando Sentinel*, September 30.

Díaz Quiñones, Arcadio. 1993. *La memoria rota.* 2nd ed. San Juan: Huracán.

——. 2000. *El arte de bregar: Ensayos.* San Juan: Callejón.

Dietz, James L. 2003. *Puerto Rico: Negotiating Development and Change.* Boulder, CO: Lynne Rienner.

Di Leonardo, Micaela. 2008. "The Neoliberalization of Minds, Space, and Bodies: Rising Global Inequality and the Shifting American Public Sphere." In *New Landscapes of Inequality*, edited by Jane L. Collins, Micaela Di Leonardo, and Brett Williams, 191–208. Santa Fe, NM: School for Advanced Research.

Dinzey-Flores, Zaire. 2013. *Locked In, Locked Out: Gated Communities in a Puerto Rican City.* Philadelphia: University of Pennsylvania Press.

——. 2017. "Spatially Polarized Landscapes and a New Approach to Urban Inequality." *Latin American Research Review* 52(2):241–252.

Domenech, Sarah. 2006. "Cae el telón en centro boricua." *El Nuevo Día Orlando*, June 20.

Duany, Jorge. 2002. *The Puerto Rican Nation on the Move: Identities on the Island and in the United States.* Chapel Hill: University of North Carolina Press.

——. 2003. "Puerto Rican, Hispanic, or Latino? Recent Debates on National and Pan-Ethnic Identities." *Centro Journal* 15(2):256–267.

——. 2011. *Blurred Borders: Transnational Migration between the Hispanic Caribbean and the United States.* Chapel Hill: University of North Carolina Press.

——. Forthcoming. "'May God Take Me to Orlando': The Puerto Rican Exodus to Florida before and after Hurricane Maria." In *Caribbean Migrations: The Legacies of Colonialism*, edited by Anke Birkenmaier. New Brunswick, NJ: Rutgers University Press.

Duany, Jorge, and Félix V. Matos-Rodríguez. 2006. *Puerto Ricans in Orlando and Central Florida.* New York: Center for Puerto Rican Studies, Hunter College, City University of New York.

Duany, Jorge, and Patricia Silver. 2010. "The 'Puertoricanization' of Florida: Historical Background and Current Status: Introduction." *Centro Journal* 22(1):4–31.

Dye, Thomas R. 1998. *Politics in Florida*. Upper Saddle River, NJ: Prentice Hall.

Eichenberger, Susan E. 2004. "'Where Two or More Are Gathered': The Inclusion of Puerto Ricans in Multiethnic Latino Parishes in Southeastern United States." PhD diss., University of Florida.

Epele, Maria E. 2010. "Memory, Forgetting, and Economic Crisis: Drug Use and Social Fragmentation in an Argentine Shantytown." *Medical Anthropology Quarterly* 24(1):22–41.

Espino, Rodolfo, David L. Leal, and Kenneth J. Meier, eds. 2007. *Latino Politics: Identity, Mobilization, and Representation*. Charlottesville: University of Virginia Press.

Fairbanks, Robert P., and Richard Lloyd. 2011. "Critical Ethnography and the Neoliberal City: The US Example." *Ethnography* 12(1):3–11.

Feigenbaum, Nancy. 1996. "Puerto Ricans Feel Stereotypes' Sting—Most Hispanics Who Move Here Have Good Incomes and Educations, but Often—That's Not the Perception." *Orlando Sentinel*, October 27.

Feld, Steven, and Keith H. Basso. 1996. *Senses of Place*. Santa Fe, NM: School of American Research.

Feldman, Marcos. 2011. "The Role of Neighborhood Organizations in the Production of Gentrifiable Urban Space: The Case of Wynwood, Miami's Puerto Rican Barrio." PhD diss., Florida International University.

Fernández, Delia. 2013. "Becoming Latino: Mexican and Puerto Rican Community Formation in Grand Rapids, Michigan, 1926–1964." *Michigan Historical Review* 39(1):71–100.

Fernández, Lilia. 2012. *Brown in the Windy City: Mexicans and Puerto Ricans in Postwar Chicago*. Chicago: University of Chicago Press.

Ferré, Maurice. 2010. "Legacy Series: Welcome to Florida at Centro A Conversation with Maurice A. Ferre, the Former Mayor of Miami." Interview by Carlos Vargas-Ramos. September 28. New York: Center for Puerto Rican Studies, Hunter College, City University of New York. https://centropr.hunter.cuny.edu/events-news/events/legacy-series-welcome-florida-centro-conversation-maurice-ferre-former-mayor.

Findlay, Eileen J. 2009. "Portable Roots: Latin New Yorker Community Building and the Meanings of Women's Return Migration in San Juan, Puerto Rico, 1960–2000." *Caribbean Studies* 37(2):3–43.

——. 2012. "Slipping and Sliding: The Many Meanings of Race in Life Histories of New York Puerto Rican Return Migrants in San Juan." *Centro Journal* 24(1): 20–43.

Firpo, Julio. 2012. "Forming a Puerto Rican Identity in Orlando: The Puerto Rican Migration to Central Florida, 1960–2000." Master's thesis, University of Central Florida.

Flores, Juan. 1993. *Divided Borders: Essays on Puerto Rican Identity*. Houston: Arte Público.

——. 2000. *From Bomba to Hip-Hop: Puerto Rican Culture and Latino Identity*. New York: Columbia University Press.

——. 2005. "Reclaiming Left Baggage: Some Early Sources for Minority Studies." *Cultural Critique* 59(Winter):187–206.

Flores, William V., and Rina Benmayor, eds. 1997. *Latino Cultural Citizenship: Claiming Identity, Space, and Rights*. Boston: Beacon.

Foglesong, Richard E. 2001. *Married to the Mouse: Walt Disney World and Orlando*. New Haven, CT: Yale University Press.

———. 2011. *Immigrant Prince: Mel Martinez and the American Dream*. Gainesville: University Press of Florida.

Franqui-Rivera, Harry. 2017. "Migration and the Military Service: a Pathway to the Middle Class." In *State of Puerto Ricans 2017*, edited by Edwin Meléndez and Carlos Vargas-Ramos, 33–42. New York: Centro Press.

———. 2018. *Soldiers of the Nation: Military Service and Modern Puerto Rico, 1868-1952*. Lincoln, NE: University of Nebraska Press.

Fraser, Nancy, Dahl Hanne Marlene, Stoltz Pauline, and Willig Rasmus. 2004. "Recognition, Redistribution, and Representation in Capitalist Global Society: An Interview with Nancy Fraser." *Acta Sociologica* 47(4):374–382.

Frederickson, Mary E. 2011. *Looking South: Race, Gender, and the Transformation of Labor from Reconstruction to Globalization*. Gainesville: University Press of Florida.

Freeman, Carla. 2007. "The 'Reputation' of Neoliberalism." *American Ethnologist* 34(2):252–267.

Freytes, Dennis. 2007. "A Salute to All Veterans, Especially the 'Borinqueneers'." Editorial. *Orlando Sentinel*, November 9.

Gallagher, Kirsten. 1991a. "Hispanics Counting on Numbers for Clout." *Orlando Sentinel*, March 17, A1.

———. 1991b. "Home but Not Alone—Most Blacks Still Live in Black Neighborhoods." *Orlando Sentinel*, May 19.

———. 1991c. "Middle-Class Hispanics Break 'Barrio' Stereotypes." *Orlando Sentinel*, June 16.

García, Jason. 2004. "Political Parties Play Key Roles in Nonpartisan Races." *Orlando Sentinel*, October 25.

García, John A. 2012. *Latino Politics in America: Community, Culture, and Interests*. 2nd ed. Lanham, MD: Rowman and Littlefield.

García, William. 2018. "White Privilege and the Effacement of Blackness: Puerto Rico and Its Diaspora in the Early 21st Century." In *White Latino Privilege: Caribbean Latino Perspectives in the Second Decade of the 21st Century*, edited by Gabriel Haslip-Viera, 73–89. New York: Latino Studies Press.

García Bedolla, Lisa. 2009. *Latino Politics*. 2nd ed. Cambridge, England: Polity.

García Colón, Ismael. 2006. "Notes on the Role of Oral History in Puerto Rican Studies: Its Applications for the Puerto Ricans in Central Florida Oral History Project," unpublished report.

Geertz, Clifford. 1996. Afterword in *Senses of Place*, edited by Steven Feld and Keith H. Basso. Santa Fe, NM: School of American.

Ghani, Ashraf. 1995. "Writing a History of Power: An Examination of Eric R. Wolf's Anthropological Quest." In *Articulating Hidden Histories: Exploring the Influence of Eric R. Wolf*, edited by Jane Schneider and Rayna Rapp, 31–48. Berkeley: University of California Press.

Gillespie, Ryan. 2018a. "Orlando's Tinker Field History Plaza Memorializes Civil Rights and Baseball." *Orlando Sentinel*, May 3.

———. 2018b. "Orlando Rolón Sworn in as OPD Chief, Becomes First Latino to Hold Rank." *Orlando Sentinel*, October 29.

Giroux, Henry A. 2008. "Beyond the Biopolitics of Disposability: Rethinking Neoliberalism in the New Gilded Age." *Social Identities* 14(5):587–620. https://doi.org/10.1080/13504630802343432.

Glasser, Ruth. 1995. *My Music Is My Flag: Puerto Rican Musicians and Their New York Communities, 1917–1940*. Berkeley: University of California Press.

Gledhill, John. 2007. "Neoliberalism." In *A Companion to the Anthropology of Politics*, edited by David Nugent and Joan Vincent, 332–348. Oxford, England: Blackwell.

Godreau, Isar P. 2002. "Changing Space, Making Race: Distance, Nostalgia, and the Folklorization of Blackness in Puerto Rico." *Identities* 9(3):281–304.

———. 2008. "Slippery Semantics: Race Talk and Everyday Uses of Racial Terminology in Puerto Rico." *Centro Journal* 20(2):5–33.

———. 2015. *Scripts of Blackness: Race, Cultural Nationalism, and U.S. Colonialism in Puerto Rico*. Urbana: University of Illinois Press.

Goldberg, David Theo. 1993. *Racist Culture: Philosophy and the Politics of Meaning*. Cambridge, England: Blackwell.

———. 2009. *The Threat of Race: Reflections on Racial Neoliberalism*. Oxford, England: Wiley-Blackwell.

González, Juan. 2000. *Harvest of Empire: A History of Latinos in America*. New York: Penguin.

González Guittar, Stephanie. 2012. "This Is Just Temporary: A Study of Extended Stay Motel Residents in Central Florida." PhD diss., University of Central Florida.

Gordillo, Gastón R. 2004. *Landscape of Devils: Tensions of Place and Memory in the Argentinean Chaco*. Durham, NC: Duke University Press.

Gray, John. 1999. "Open Spaces and Dwelling Places: Being at Home on Hill Farms in the Scottish Borders." *American Ethnologist* 26(2):440–460.

Gregory, Steven. 1994. "Race, Identity, and Political Activism: The Shifting Contours of the African American Public Sphere." *Public Culture* 7(1):147–164.

———. 1998. *Black Corona: Race and the Politics of Place in an Urban Community*. Princeton, NJ: Princeton University Press.

Griffin, Michael. 1991. "Orange OKs New Districts—A Commissioner Finds Himself in Another District as Boundaries Shift, but He'll Get to Keep His Seat." *Orlando Sentinel*, December 19.

Griffith, David. 2008. "New Midwesterners, New Southerners: Immigration Experiences in Four Rural American Settings." In *New Faces in New Places: The Changing Geography of American Immigration*, edited by Douglas S. Massey, 179–210. New York: Russell Sage Foundation.

Grosfoguel, Ramón, and Chloe S. Goeras. 2000. "'Coloniality of Power' and Racial Dynamics: Notes toward a Reinterpretation of Latino Caribbeans in New York City." *Identities: Global Studies in Culture and Power* 7(1):85–125.

Grosfoguel, Ramón, Frances Negrón-Muntaner, and Chloé S. Goeras. 1997. "Beyond Nationalist and Colonialist Discourses: The *Jaiba* Politics of the Puerto Rican

Ethno-Nation." In *Puerto Rican Jam: Rethinking Colonialism and Nationalism*, edited by Frances Muntaner Negrón, 1–36. Minneapolis: University of Minnesota Press.

Guerrero, Perla M. 2017. *Nuevo South: Latinas/os, Asians, and the Remaking of Place.* Austin: University of Texas Press.

Gupta, Akhil, and James Ferguson. 1997. "Culture, Power, Place: Ethnography at the End of an Era." In *Culture, Power, Place: Explorations in Critical Anthropology*, edited by Akhil Gupta and James Ferguson, 1–29. Durham: Duke University Press.

Gupta, Akhil, David Nugent, and Shreyas Sreenath. 2015. "State, Corruption, Postcoloniality: A Conversation with Akhil Gupta on the 20th Anniversary of 'Blurred Boundaries.'" *American Ethnologist* 42(4):581–591.

Guzmán, Lydia. 2005. "Lección de odio imparte maestra." *El Nuevo Día Orlando*, August 17.

Guzmán, Pablo "Yoruba." 1980. "Puerto Rican Barrio Politics in the United States." In *Historical Perspectives on Puerto Rican Survival in the United States*, edited by Clara E. Rodríguez and Virginia Sánchez Korrol, 143–151. Princeton, NJ: Marcus Wiener.

Halbwachs, Maurice. 1992. *On Collective Memory*. Chicago: University of Chicago Press.

Hale, Charles R. 2005. "Neoliberal Multiculturalism: The Remaking of Cultural Rights and Racial Dominance in Central America." *Political and Legal Anthropology Review* 28(1):10–28.

Hardy-Fanta, Carol. 1993. *Latino Politics, Latina Politics: Gender, Culture, and Political Participation in Boston*. Philadelphia: Temple University Press.

Harris, Melissa, and Walter Pacheco. 2004. "Newcomer Challenges City Hall Veteran: Betty Wyman Has Had Her Orlando Council Seat for 12 Years; Now Luis Pastrana Wants It." *Orlando Sentinel*, Orange, February 19.

Hartigan, John. 1999. *Racial Situations: Class Predicaments of Whiteness in Detroit.* Princeton, NJ: Princeton University Press.

Harvey, David. 2003. *The New Imperialism*. Oxford, England: Oxford University Press.

———. 2005. *A Brief History of Neoliberalism*. Oxford, England: Oxford University Press.

Harvey, David L., and Michael Reed. 1992. "Paradigms of Poverty: A Critical Assessment of Contemporary Perspectives." *International Journal of Politics, Culture, and Society* 6(2):269–297.

Haslip-Viera, Gabriel. 2018. "White Privilege and the Ideology of White Supremacy in the Spanish-Speaking Caribbean, Its Diaspora, and Latin America, 1492-Present." In *White Latino Privilege: Caribbean Latino Perspectives in the Second Decade of the 21st Century*, edited by Gabriel Haslip-Viera, 9–72. New York: Latino Studies.

Head, Doug. 2012. "The Secret of Power: Trends in Hispanic Voting." Presentation, Frente Unido 436 community seminar. Ana G. Mendez University, Orlando, FL, January 2012.

Hernández, Pedro Juan. 2012. "The Evolution of Centro's Archives of the Puerto Rican Diaspora, 1973–2012." Albany, NY: Puerto Rican Studies Association.

Herzfeld, Michael. 2015. "Anthropology and the Inchoate Intimacies of Power." *American Ethnologist* 42(1):18–32.

Hinton, William Dean. 2001. "No Man's Land." *Orlando Weekly*, August 30. https://www.orlandoweekly.com.

History Task Force, Center for Puerto Rican Studies. 1979. *Labor Migration under Capitalism: The Puerto Rican Experience*. New York: Monthly Review Press.

Hobbs, Erika. 2009a. "Orange Botched School Closures." *Orlando Sentinel*, April 8.

———. 2009b. "District Scrambles to Fill Bi-Racial Committee Posts." *Orlando Sentinel*, April 9.

———. 2009c. "Biracial-Panel Gaffe May Keep Feds' Oversight." *Orlando Sentinel*, April 26.

———. 2010a. "No Other Option, Orange Says—Parents Fight Plan to Cut Bilingual Program." *Orlando Sentinel*, March 27.

———. 2010b. "Hispanic Leaders, Parents Rally for Bilingual Classes." *Orlando Sentinel*, May 8.

Hobsbawm, Eric, and Terence Ranger, eds. 1983. *The Invention of Tradition*. Cambridge, England: Cambridge University Press.

Hoelscher, Steven. 2003. "Making Place, Making Race: Performances of Whiteness in the Jim Crow South." *Annals of the Association of American Geographers* 93(3):657–686.

Hoffman, Odile. 2002. "Collective Memory and Ethnic Identities in the Colombian Pacific." *Journal of Latin American Anthropology* 7(2):118–139.

Holland, Dorothy, Donald Nonini, Catherine Lutz, Lesley Bartlett, Marla Frederick-McGlathery, Thaddeus Guldbrandsen, and Enrique Murillo, eds. 2007. *Local Democracy under Seige: Activism, Public Interest, and Private Politics*. New York: New York University Press.

Holloway, Pippa. 2008. *Other Souths: Diversity and Difference in the U.S. South, Reconstruction to Present*. Athens: University of Georgia Press.

Horvitz, Lori. 2001a. "Districting Plan Draws Ire." *Orlando Sentinel*, May 22.

———. 2001b. "English Barrier Riles Parents to Action." *Orlando Sentinel*, July 1.

Hudak, Stephen. 2014. "Clemente Is Back—Azalea Park Is Thrilled." *Orlando Sentinel*, March 16.

———. 2016. "Azalea Park Fed Up with the 'Heroin Alley' Label." *Orlando Sentinel*, January 11.

Hundley, Kris. 2011. "Billionaire's Cash to FSU Comes with Strings." *Orlando Sentinel*, May 12.

Indigo. 2004. "Orlando Council Endorsements—Our Position: Patty Sheehan and Ernest Page Deserve Re-Election. Betty Wyman Does Not." *Orlando Sentinel*, March 2.

Jackson, Jerry. 1996. "Hispanic Marchers: No to Drugs, Yes to Unity." *Orlando Sentinel*, November 4.

Jenks, Hillary. 2008. "Urban Space, Ethnic Community, and National Belonging: The Political Landscape of Memory in Little Tokyo." *GeoJournal* 73(3):231–244.

Jennings, James. 1977. *Puerto Rican Politics in New York City*. Washington, DC: University Press of America.

Jiménez, Angel. 1990. "Parada Puertorriqueña." *La Prensa*, May 31-June 6, 1.
Jiménez, Marina. 2011. "¡Pa' fuera los latinos!" *Tu Nuevo Amanecer*, November 23–December 6.
Jiménez-Muñoz, Gladys M. 2002. "The Blackface of 'Puerto Rican Whites': Race and Representation in Postwar Puerto Rico." *Latino(a) Research Review* 5(1):99–117.
Johnson, Julie. 1984. "Orange Aims Voter Drive at Hispanics." *Orlando Sentinel*, January 10.
Joshi, Khyati Y., and Jigna Desai, eds. 2013. *Asian Americans in Dixie: Race and Migration in the South*. Chicago: University of Illinois Press.
Kassab, Beth. 2001. "Perez Turns to Democrats for Help—Slipping GOP Support in Nonpartisan Deltona Mayoral Race Prompts Party Switch." *Orlando Sentinel*, Volusia, September 21.
Klas, Mary Ellen. 2017. "Where Did $1.3 Billion for Affordable Housing Go? Florida Legislature Took It." *Miami Herald*, March 31.
Klein, Naomi. 2018. *The Battle for Paradise: Puerto Rico Takes On the Disaster Capitalists*. Chicago: Haymarket Books.
Koenig, John. 1997. "Hispanic Bakery Tinkers with Recipe to Tempt a Broader Market." *Orlando Sentinel*, November 3, 5.
Kraus, Michael W., Julian M. Rucker, and Jennifer A. Richeson. 2017. "Americans Misperceive Racial Economic Equality." *Proceedings of the National Academy of Sciences* 114(39):10324–10331.
Kunerth, Jeff. 1976. "Some Orange School Budget Rises Forced Upon System, Officials Say." *Sentinel Star*, August 5.
———. 2006a. "17 Houses in Pine Hills: A Story of Race in Orlando." *Orlando Sentinel*, October 1.
———. 2006b. "Blacks Move in, Move Up." *Orlando Sentinel*, October 2.
———. 2008a. "They Taught Schools a Lesson in Equality." *Orlando Sentinel*, February 24.
———. 2008b. "Parks Offer Islands of Tranquility." *Orlando Sentinel*, May 28.
———. 2012. "Churches Reflect Sharp Change in Azalea Park Demographics." *Orlando Sentinel*, September 8.
Kunerth, Jeff, and Dan Tracy. 2005. "The New Orlando: The Faces and Stories of the People Who Work at the Citrus Center in Downtown Orlando Show How Central Florida Has Changed in the Past 35 Years." *Orlando Sentinel*, December 4.
Kunerth, Jeff, and Kelly Brewington. 2002. "Hispanic Migration Soars, Diversifies, in Central Florida." *Orlando Sentinel*, April 24.
Laó, Augustín. 1995. "Resources of Hope: Imagining the Young Lords and the Politics of Memory." *Centro Journal* 7(1):34–49.
Lassiter, Matthew D. 2006. *The Silent Majority: Suburban Politics in the Sunbelt South*. Princeton: Princeton University Press.
Lassiter, Matthew D., and Joseph Crespino, eds. 2010. *The Myth of Southern Exceptionalism*. New York: Oxford University Press.
Latino Justice PRLDEF. 2012. "Latinos Sue Orange County Florida over Redistricting." Press Release, August 1. New York.

Lee, Sonia Song-Ha. 2014. *Building a Latino Civil Rights Movement: Puerto Ricans, African Americans, and the Pursuit of Racial Justice in New York City*. Durham: University of North Carolina Press.

Leeman, Jennifer. 2018. "Becoming Hispanic: The negotiation of ethnoracial identity in US Census interviews." *Latino Studies* 16(4):432–460.

Lemongello, Steven. 2017. "Neighborhood 'Enclaves' Caught in Middle of Annexation March." *Orlando Sentinel*, May 20.

Leusner, Jim. 1996. "Heroin Suspects Rearrested—A Jailed Associate Talked to Police, Describing How the Men Ran an International Drug Ring with Ties to Orlando." *Orlando Sentinel*, October 12.

Leusner, Jim, and Henry Pierson Curtis. 1996. "Heroin Flow Has Orlando in a Crisis—Pipeline of Drugs Brings San Juan's Problems Here." *Orlando Sentinel*, October 6.

Lewis, Oscar. 1966. *La Vida: A Puerto Rican Family in the Culture of Poverty—San Juan and New York*. New York: Random House.

Lippard, Cameron D., and Charles A. Gallagher, eds. 2011. *Being Brown in Dixie: Race, Ethnicity, and Latino Immigration in the New South*. Boulder, CO: First Forum.

Liptak, Adam. 2009. "Justices, 5–4, Set Limit on Sweep of Voting Law." *New York Times*, March 9.

Lloréns, Hilda. 2014. *Imaging the Great Puerto Rican Family: Framing Nation, Race, and Gender during the American Century*. New York: Lexington.

———. 2018. "Identity Practices: Racial Passing, Gender, and Racial Purity in Puerto Rico." *Afro-Hispanic Review* 37(1):27–49.

Lloyd, Richard. 2011. "East Nashville Skyline." *Ethnography* 12(1):114–145.

Loperena, Italis. 2007. "Reconociendo a la comunidad hispana." *La Prensa*, December 6–12.

———. 2008. "Juramenta Tony Ortiz." *La Prensa*, May 8–14.

López, David, and Yen Espiritu. 1990. "Panethnicity in the United States: A Theoretical Framework." *Ethnic and Racial Studies* 13(2):198–224.

López, Edrik. 2005. "Nuyorican Spaces: Mapping Identity in a Poetic Geography." *Centro Journal* 17(5):203–219.

López, Ian Haney. 2005. "Race on the 2010 Census: Hispanics and the Shrinking White Majority." *Daedalus* 134(1):42–52.

López-Sanders, Laura. 2012. "Bible Belt Immigrants: Latino Religious Incorporation in New Immigrant Destinations." *Latino Studies* 10(1–2):128–154.

Lowe, Lisa. 1996. *Immigrant Acts: On Asian American Cultural Politics*. Durham, NC: Duke University Press.

Lush, Tamara. 2004. "Both Parties Chase State's Elusive Puerto Rican Vote." *St. Petersburg Times*, October 29. https://www.tampabay.com.

MacLean, Nancy. 2008. "Southern Dominance in Borrowed Language: The Regional Origins of American Neoliberalism." In *New Landscapes of Inequality: Neoliberalism and the Erosion of Democracy in America*, edited by Jane Collins, Micaela di Leonardo, and Brett Williams, 21–38. Santa Fe, NM: School for Advanced Research.

———. 2010. "Neo-Confederacy versus the New Deal: The Regional Utopia of the Modern American Right." In *The Myth of Southern Exceptionalism*, edited by Matthew D. Lassiter and Joseph Crespino, 308–329. New York: Oxford University Press.

MacManus, Susan, Aubrey Jewett, David J. Bonanza, and Thomas R. Dye. 2015. *Politics in Florida*. 4th ed. Sarasota, FL: Peppertree.

Manson, Steven, Jonathan Schroeder, David Van Riper, and Steven Ruggles. 2018. IPUMS National Historical Geographic Information System: Version 13.0. Database. Minneapolis: University of Minnesota. http://doi.org/10.18128/D050.V13.0.

Mantero, José María. 2008. *Latinos and the U.S. South*. Westport, CT: Praeger.

Marquez, Myriam. 1996a. "Puerto Rican Tale of Two Cities: Prominent Banker, Ostracized Boy." *Orlando Sentinel*, October 21.

———. 1996b. "Election of Osceola's 1st Hispanic Commissioner Carries Sad Irony." *Orlando Sentinel*, November 18.

———. 2000. "There's No Room for Mediocrity." *Orlando Sentinel*, December 20.

———. 2001. "On Redistricting, Hispanics Must Be Loud and Clear." *Orlando Sentinel*, June 11.

———. 2004. "Hola, City Hall, Are You Serious about Hispanics?" *Orlando Sentinel*, Febraury 18.

———. 2005. "Hispanic Kids Lose in Money Shell Game." *Orlando Sentinel*, April 5.

Marrow, Helen. 2009. "New Immigrant Destinations and the American Colour Line." *Ethnic and Racial Studies* 32(6):1037–1057.

———. 2011. *New Destination Dreaming: Immigration, Race, and Legal Status in the Rural American South*. Stanford, CA: Stanford University Press.

Marsh Kennerley, Catherine. 2003. "Cultural Negotiations: Puerto Rican Intellectuals in a State-Sponsored Community Education Project, 1948–1968." *Harvard Educational Review* 73(3):416–448.

Marshall, T. H. 1950. *Citizenship and Social Class and Other Essays*. London: Pluto.

Martínez, Angel. 2018. Interview by Patricia Silver. February 27, Orlando. Digital recording. Florida Folklife Program. State Archives of Florida, Tallahassee. https://dos.myflorida.com/historical/preservation/florida-folklife-program/.

Martinez, Miranda J. 2010. *Power at the Roots: Gentrification, Community Gardens, and the Puerto Ricans of the Lower East Side*. Lanham, MD: Lexington.

Martínez-Echazábal, Lourdes. 1998. "'Mestizaje' and the Discourse of National/Cultural Identity in Latin America, 1845–1959." *Latin American Perspectives* 25(3):21–42.

Martínez-Fernández, Luis. 2006. "When R-E-S-P-E-C-T Is Spelled Respeto—Warning: Failure to Understand Hispanic Culture May Be Hazardous." Editorial. *Orlando Sentinel*, March 9.

———. 2010. "La diaspora en la frontera: Retos y oportunidades para el estudio del Orlando Puertorriqueño." *Centro Journal* 22(1):32–55.

Massey, Doreen. 1994. *Space, Place, and Gender*. Cambridge, England: Polity.

Massey, Douglas S., ed. 2008. *New Faces in New Places: The Changing Geography of American Immigration*. New York: Russell Sage Foundation.

Mathers, Sandra. 2002. "Residents Told They'll Get Park." *Orlando Sentinel*, November 22.

Mathers, Sandra, and Henry Pierson Curtis. 1996. "McCollum Criticizes Clinton Drug War—Florida's GOP Congressmen Accused the President of Shifting Money away from the Fight to Block Drugs Flowing from Puerto Rico." *Orlando Sentinel*, September 27.

Maxwell, Scott. 1998a. "Johnson Quits 'Big-Money Race'—Rival Camps Seemed Shocked at her Late-Breaking Decision to Leave the High-Spending Contest to Lead Orange County." *Orlando Sentinel*, July 3.

———. 1998b. "Johnson Makes Decision Easier for Hispanic Voters." *Orlando Sentinel*, July 5.

———. 2001a. "5 Make Bush List to Replace Martínez." *Orlando Sentinel*, January 5.

———. 2001b. "Redistricting Will Slice Up Orange." *Orlando Sentinel*, April 25.

McConnell, Eileen Diaz. 2011. "Racialized Histories and Contemporary Population Dynamics in the New South." In *Being Brown in Dixie: Race, Ethnicity, and Latino Immigration in the New South*, edited by Cameron D. Lippard and Charles A. Gallagher, 77–98. Boulder, CO: First Forum.

McCormick, Jennifer, and César J. Ayala. 2007. "Felícita 'La Prieta' Méndez (1916–1998) and the End of Latino School Segregation in California." *Centro Journal* 19(2):12–35.

McDonald, Steve, ed. 2004. *2003–2004 Florida Annual Policy Survey Report*. Tallahassee: 2004 Survey Research Laboratory, College of Social Sciences, Florida State University.

McEvoy, George. 1973. "Victorious Arthur 'Pappy' Kennedy: The Black Man Who Beat the Odds." *Orlando Sentinel*, January 14.

McGranahan, Carole. 2010. *Arrested Histories: Tibet, the CIA, and Memories of a Forgotten War*. Durham, NC: Duke University Press.

McKay, Rich. 2000. "U.S. Agents Look into Voters' Complaints." *Orlando Sentinel*, December 5.

McKee, Seth C., ed. 2015. *Jigsaw Puzzle Politics in the Sunshine State*. Gainesville: University Press of Florida.

Meléndez, Edgardo. 2003. "Puerto Rican Politics in the United States: Examination of Major Perspectives and Theories." *Centro Journal* 15(1):9–39.

———. 2017. *Sponsored Migration: The State and Puerto Rican Postwar Migration to the United States*. Columbus, OH: Ohio State University Press.

Mohl, Raymond A. 2008. "Globalization, Latinization, and the Nuevo New South." In *Other Souths: Diversity and Difference in the U.S. South, Reconstruction to Present*, edited by Pippa Holloway, 408–422. Athens: University of Georgia Press.

Molina, Carlos. 2005. "Exigen disculpa pública." *El Nuevo Día Orlando*, August 18.

Montalvo, Iza. 2012. "El 'pavaso' de Alan Grayson." *La Prensa*, August 7.

Montanez, Lillyana. 1996. "Hispanic Community Integrating." *Orlando Sentinel*, Orange Extra 3, November 6.

———. 1998. "Puerto Rican Native Joins Bush Transition Team." *Orlando Sentinel*, December 25.

Mora, G. Cristina. 2014. *Making Hispanics: How Activists, Bureaucrats & Media Constructed a New American*. Chicago: University of Chicago Press.

Morales, Iris. 1998. "¡PALANTE, SIEMPRE PALANTE! The Young Lords." In *The Puerto Rican Movement: Voices from the Diaspora*, edited by Andrés Torres, 210–227. Philadelphia: Temple University Press.

Mormino, Gary Ross. 2005. *Land of Sunshine, State of Dreams: A Social History of Modern Florida*. Gainesville: University Press of Florida.

Morris, Allen, and Joan Perry Morris. 2014. *Florida Handbook 2013–2014*. Edited by Office of the Clerk. Tallahassee: Florida House of Representatives.

Needham, Andrew. 2011. "Sunbelt Imperialism: Boosters, Navajos, and Energy Development in the Metropolitan Southwest." In *Sunbelt Rising: The Politics of Place, Space, and Region*, edited by Michelle Nickerson and Darren Dochuk, 240–264. Philadelphia: University of Pennsylvania Press.

Negroni, Germán. 1960. "Boricuas en Miami: Han logrado una rápida asimilación a sociedad." *El Mundo*, July 28.

Newman, Joe. 2006. "Making Their Mark: Developers Adjust Strategies as 'Millennials' Are Poised to Shape Future of Central Florida." *Orlando Sentinel*, April 17.

Newman, JoNel. 2006. *Voting Rights in Florida: 1982–2006: A Report of RenewtheVRA.org*. Protect Voting Rights. http://www.protectcivilrights.org/pdf/voting/FloridaVRA.pdf.

———. 2007. "Ensuring that Florida's Language Minorities Have Access to the Ballot." *Stetson Law Review* 36:329–364.

New York Times. 1973. "Clemente, Pirates' Star, Dies in Crash of Plane Carrying Aid to Nicaragua." January 2. https://timesmachine.nytimes.com.

Nichols, John. 2014. "When the Republicans Really Were the Party of Lincoln." *The Nation*, July 2.

Nickerson, Michelle, and Darren Dochuk, eds. 2011. *Sunbelt Rising: The Politics of Place, Space, and Region*. Philadelphia: University of Pennsylvania Press.

Nolin, Robert. 1998. "The 'True' Running Mates—Anne Mackay And Columba Bush Hold Their Own." *Orlando Sentinel*, October 30. https://orlandosentinel.com.

Nora, Pierre. 1989. "Between Memory and History: *Les lieux de mémoire*." *Representations*, 26:7–24.

Oboler, Suzanne. 1995. *Ethnic Labels, Latino Lives: Identity and the Politics of (Re) Presentation in the United States*. Minneapolis: University of Minnesota Press.

———, ed. 2006. *Latinos and Citizenship: The Dilemma of Belonging*. New York: Palgrave Macmillan.

———. 2014. Foreword to *Transforming Citizenship: Democracy, Membership, and Belonging in Latino Communities*, edited by Raymond A. Rocco. East Lansing: Michigan State University Press.

Odem, Mary E. 2010. "Latin American Immigration and the New Multi-Ethnic South." In *The Myth of Southern Exceptionalism*, edited by Matthew D. Lassiter and Joseph Crespino, 234–260. New York: Oxford University Press.

Odem, Mary E., and Elaine Cantrell Lacy. 2009. *Latino Immigrants and the Transformation of the U.S. South*. Athens: University of Georgia Press.

Olick, Jeffrey K., Vered Vinitzky-Seroussi, and Daniel Levy, eds. 2011. *The Collective Memory Reader*. New York: Oxford University Press.

Olmedo, Irma. 1997. "Voices of Our Past: Using Oral History to Explore Funds of Knowledge within a Puerto Rican Family." *Anthropology and Education Quarterly* 28(4):550–573.

Omi, Michael, and Howard Winant. 2015. *Racial Formation in the United States*. New York: Routledge.

Ong, Aihwa. 1999. *Flexible Citizenship: The Cultural Logics of Transnationality*. Durham, NC: Duke University Press.

Orlando Sentinel. 1988. "Good Move for Airport Park." Editorial, July 18.

———. 1990. "Teacher of the Year." Orange South, June 17.

———. 2000. "Appointment List Shapes Up." *Orlando Sentinel*, Osceola, April 29.

Ortiz, Tony. 2009. "Commentary." *East Orlando Sun*, October 15–November 11.

Osorio, Carla. 2005. "Mantener calma piden a comunidad." *El Nuevo Día Orlando*, August 18.

Owens, Darryl E. 2014. "Defaced Clemente Mural Has Revealed Portrait of Neglect." *Orlando Sentinel*, March 3.

Pacheco, Walter. 2003. "Hispanic Parents Find FOCUS for School Issues—Meetings Bridge Communication Gap." *Orlando Sentinel*, Orange, May 11.

———. 2004. "Hispanic Kids Are New Faces of Segregation." *Orlando Sentinel*, May 15.

———. 2008. "Orlando shuffles police roles." *Orlando Sentinel*, November 11.

Padilla, Elena. 1958. *Up from Puerto Rico*. New York: Columbia University Press.

Padilla, Félix. 1985. *Latino Ethnic Consciousness: The Case of Mexican Americans and Puerto Ricans in Chicago*. Notre Dame: University of Notre Dame Press.

———. 1987. *Puerto Rican Chicago*. Notre Dame: University of Notre Dame Press.

Padilla, María. 1998. "The Cultural Divide of Puerto Ricans—Islanders and Mainlanders Can Feel Apart." *Orlando Sentinel*, October 27.

———. 1999a. "Hispanics Bloom in Neigborhood." *Orlando Sentinel*, June 13.

———. 1999b. "Art Canvass Averts Public Disaster—'Hispanic' Exhibit Didn't Include Work of Puerto Ricans." *Orlando Sentinel*, October 9.

———. 2000a. "Treasured Tradition." *Orlando Sentinel*, Orange Extra, January 2.

———. 2000b. "Hispanic Voters Lodge Complaints in Orange." *Orlando Sentinel*, November 11.

———. 2000c. "Hispanics Lose Public Offices—Several Central Florida Candidates Lost Their Bids for Election in Tuesday's Vote." *Orlando Sentinel*, Orange Extra, November 12.

———. 2000d. "To Get Ahead, We Have to Get Along." *Orlando Sentinel*, December 13.

———. 2001. "Hispanics Could Get a Seat at the Table." *Orlando Sentinel*, May 23.

Padilla, María, and Nancy Rosado. 2020. *Tossed By the Wind*. Gainesville: University Press of Florida.

Padró Ocasio, Bianca. 2019. "Puerto Ricans Who Fled to Orlando after Hurricane Maria Struggled More Than Those in South Florida, Study Finds." *Orlando Sentinel*, February 2.

Palm, Matthew J. 2011. "Graffiti Artist to Brighten Kids' Field." *Orlando Sentinel*, September 1.

Pantoja, Antonia. 2002. *Memoir of a Visionary: Antonia Pantoja*. Houston: Arte Público.

Patrizio, Ron. 1990. "Fiesta Celebrates Puerto Rican Life." *Orlando Sentinel*, May 25.

Peach. 1992. "Auffant—An Effective Voice." Editorial. *Orlando Sentinel*, August 19.

Pedicini, Sandra. 2005. "Orlando Celebrates Puerto Rico." *Orlando Sentinel*, October 3.

Pérez, Gina M. 2004. *The Near Northwest Side Story: Migration, Displacement, and Puerto Rican Families*. Berkeley: University of California Press.

——. 2015. *Citizen, Student, Soldier: Latina/o Youth, JROTC, and the American Dream*. New York: New York University Press.

Pérez, Nélida. 2009. "Two Reading Rooms and the Librarian's Office: The Evolution of the Centro Library and Archives." *Centro Journal* 21(1):199–218.

Perlstein, Rick. 2009. "Exclusive: Lee Atwater's Infamous 1981 Interview on the Southern Strategy." *The Nation*, November 13. https://www.thenation.com/article/exclusive-lee-atwaters-infamous-1981-interview-southern-strategy/.

Piccard, Elias Rico. 2007. "Reportero Comunitario: Rico Informa." *El Nuevo Día*, March 13.

Picó, Fernando. 2006. *History of Puerto Rico: A Panorama of its People*. Princeton, NJ: Markus Wiener.

Pineda, Erin. 2014. "Enacting Democracy: Deliberation, Agonism, and the Empty Place of Political Action." Paper presented at the Western Political Science Association Annual Meeting, Seattle, March.

Pinsky, Mark I., and Jeannette Rivera-Lyles. 2008. "Hispanic Evangelicals Join as Potent Political Force." *Orlando Sentinel*, May 6.

PIR-SIPA. 2012. *The Pulse of the Latino Voter: The US and Florida*. Miami: Department of Politics and International Relations and Steven J. Green School of International and Public Affairs (PIR-SIPA), Florida International University. http://news.fiu.edu/wp-content/uploads/The-Pulse-of-the-Latino-Voter.pdf.

Portelli, Alessandro. 1991. *The Death of Luigi Trastulli, and Other Stories: Form and Meaning in Oral History*. Albany, NY: SUNY Press.

Porter, David D. 2003. "The Truth about Central Florida's Racial History." *Orlando Sentinel*, August 10.

Powers, Scott. 2012. "Congressional Race Could Pit Political Party, Ethnic Identity." *Orlando Sentinel*, March 30. https://orlandosentinel.com.

Price, Patricia. 2012. "Race and Ethnicity: Latino/a Immigrants and Emerging Geographies of Race and Place in the USA." *Progress in Human Geography* 36(6):800–809.

Radstone, Susannah, and Bill Schwarz. 2010. *Memory: Histories, Theories, Debates*. New York: Fordham University Press.

Raffaeta, Roberta, and Cameron Duff. 2013. "Putting Belonging into Place: Place, Experience, and Sense of Belonging among Ecuadorian Migrants in an Italian Alpine Region." *City and Society* 25(3):328–347.

Ramos, Victor Manuel. 2005a. "Central Florida Top Region for Puerto Ricans." *Orlando Sentinel*, March 4.

——. 2005b. "Hispanics Hit Voting Hurdles." *Orlando Sentinel*, July 23.

———. 2005c. "Tensions Mount over Hispanics—An Orange County Teacher's Letter Sparks Debate over Their Role in Central Florida." *Orlando Sentinel*, August 29. https://orlandosentinel.com.

———. 2005d. "Alliance Frays between City, Latino Group." *Orlando Sentinel*, December 22.

———. 2006a. "Between 2 Worlds; Puerto Ricans remember roots as they sink new ones." *Orlando Sentinel*, February 5.

———. 2006b. "City Extends Outreach Program—Orlando Mayor Buddy Dyer Plans to Increase Services Provided by the Hispanic Office of Local Assistance." *Orlando Sentinel*, March 28.

———. 2006c. "Too Little, Too Late? Some Activists and Experts Say the 2 Leading Gubernatorial Candidates Have Failed to Adequately Reach out to and Develop Rapport with Central Florida Hispanic Candidates." *Orlando Sentinel*, October 28.

———. 2008. "Candidates Pay Little Attention to State's Hispanics." *Orlando Sentinel*, January 23.

———. 2009a. "'To Join Biracial Panel, Choose Race,' Orange Tells Hispanics." *Orlando Sentinel*, April 24.

———. 2009b. "Businesses Aim To Spruce Up Ailing Stretch of S.R. 436." *Orlando Sentinel*, October 22.

Ramos-Zayas, Ana Y. 2001. "All This Is Turning White Now: Latino Constructions of 'White Culture' and Whiteness in Chicago." *Centro Journal* 13(2):73–95.

———. 2003. *National Performances: The Politics of Class, Race, and Space in Puerto Rican Chicago*. Chicago: University of Chicago Press.

———. 2004. "Delinquent Citizenship, National Performances: Racialization, Surveillance, and the Politics of 'Worthiness' in Puerto Rican Chicago." *Latino Studies* 2:26–44.

———. 2012. *Street Therapists: Race, Affect, and Neoliberal Personhood in Latino Newark*. Chicago: University of Chicago Press.

Republican Party. 1968. Republican Party Platform of 1968. At American Presidency Project, John Woolley and Gerhard Peters, University of California Santa Barbara. https://www.presidency.ucsb.edu/node/273407.

Reyes, G. Mitchell. 2010. "Memory and Alterity: The Case for an Analytic of Difference." *Philosophy and Rhetoric* 43(3):222–252.

Reyes, Luis. 2006. "The Aspira Consent Decree: A Thirtieth-Anniversary Retrospective of Bilingual Education in New York City." *Harvard Educational Review* 76:369–400.

Ricoeur, Paul. 2000. *Memory, History, Forgetting*. Chicago: University of Chicago Press.

Ricourt, Milagros, and Ruby Danta. 2003. *Hispanas de Queens: Latino Panethnicity in a New York City Neighborhood*. Ithaca, NY: Cornell University Press.

Rivera, Raquel Z. 2007. "Will the 'Real' Puerto Rican Culture Please Stand Up? Thoughts on Cultural Nationalism." In *None of the Above: Puerto Ricans in the Global Era*, edited by Frances Negrón-Muntaner, 219–233. New York: Palgrave Macmillan.

Rivero, Yeidy M. 2005. *Tuning Out Blackness: Race and Nation in the History of Puerto Rican Television*. Durham, NC: Duke University Press.

Rocco, Raymond. 2006. "Transforming Citizenship: Membership, Strategies of Containment, and the Public Sphere in Latino Communities." In *Latinos and Citizenship: The Dilemma of Belonging*, edited by Suzanne Oboler, 301–327. New York: Palgrave Macmillan.

———. 2010. "The Structuring of Latino Politics: Neoliberalism and Incorporation." *NACLA Report on the Americas* 43(6):40–43.

———. 2014. *Transforming Citizenship: Democracy, Membership, and Belonging in Latino Communities*. East Lansing: Michigan State University Press.

Rodríguez, Clara E. 1979. "Economic Factors Affecting Puerto Ricans in New York." In *Labor Migration under Capitalism*, History Task Force, Centro de Estudios Puertorriqueños, 197–221. New York: Monthly Review Press.

———. 1994. "Challenging Racial Hegemony: Puerto Ricans in the United States." In *Race*, edited by Steven Gregory and Roger Sanjek, 131–145. New Brunswick, NJ: Rutgers University Press.

———, ed. 1997. *Latin Looks: Images of Latinas and Latinos in the U.S. Media*. Boulder, CO: Westview.

———. 2000. *Changing Race: Latinos, the Census, and the History of Ethnicity in the United States*. New York: New York University Press.

Rodríguez, Richard T. 2017. "X Marks the Spot." *Cultural Dynamics* 29(3): 202–213.

Rodríguez Muñiz, Michael. 2010. "Grappling with *Latinidad*: Puerto Rican Activism in Chicago's Pro-Immigrant Rights Movement." In *¡Marcha! Latino Chicago and the Immigrant Rights Movement*, edited by Amalia Pallares and Nilda Flores-González, 237–258. Urbana: University of Illinois Press.

Rosa, Jonathan, and Yarimar Bonilla. 2017. "Deprovincializing Trump, Decolonizing Diversity, and Unsettling Anthropology." *American Ethnologist* 44(2):201–208.

Rosado, Nancy. 2018. Interview by Patricia Silver. May 21, Orlando. Digital recording. In the author's possession.

Rosaldo, Renato. 1997. "Cultural Citizenship, Inequality, and Multiculturalism." In *Latino Cultural Citizenship: Claiming Identity, Space, and Rights*, edited by William V. Flores and Rina Benmayor, 27–53. Boston: Beacon.

Roseberry, William. 1989. *Anthropologies and Histories: Essays in Culture, History, and Political Economy*. New Brunswick, NJ: Rutgers University Press.

———. 1995. "The Cultural History of Peasants." In *Articulating Hidden Histories: Exploring the Influence of Eric R. Wolf*, edited by Jane Schneider and Rayna Rapp, 51–66. Berkeley: University of California Press.

Rossington, Michael, and Anne Whitehead. 2007. *Theories of Memory: A Reader*. Baltimore, MD: Johns Hopkins University Press.

Roth, Lauren. 2013. "Lost in Translation." *Orlando Sentinel*, May 26.

Rúa, Mérida M. 2012. *A Grounded Identidad: Making New Lives in Chicago's Puerto Rican Neighborhoods*. New York: Oxford University Press.

Rucker, Philip, and Ed O'Keefe. 2017. "Trump Threatens to Abandon Puerto Rico Recovery Effort." *Washington Post*, October 12.

Rumbaut, Rubén G. 2009. "Pigments of Our Imagination: On the Racialization and Racial Identities of 'Hispanics' and 'Latinos.'" In *How the United States Racializes*

Latinos: White Hegemony and Its Consequences, edited by José A. Cobas, Jorge Duany, and Joe R. Feagin, 15–36. Boulder, CO: Paradigm.

Sabulis, Thomas. 1981. "Mid-Florida Gets More of a Latin Accent." *Orlando Sentinel*, May 3.

Safa, Helen. 1998. "Introduction: Race and National Identity in the Americas." *Latin American Perspectives* 25(3):3–20.

Salazar, Carolina. 2015. "Lo bueno y lo malo del 2014—Organizaciones latinas terminaron el año sin sedes pero con ganas de trabajar." *El Sentinel*, January 3.

Salazar, Carolina, and David Damron. 2014. "Roberto Clemente Mural Painted over in Azalea Park: Little Leaguers, Hispanic Community Upset." *Orlando Sentinel*, February 12.

Sánchez, José Ramón. 1994. "Puerto Ricans and the Door of Participation in U.S. Politics." In *Handbook of Hispanic Cultures in the United States: Sociology*, edited by Félix Padilla, 110–132. Houston: Arte Público.

———. 1996. "Puerto Rican Politics in New York: Beyond 'Secondhand' Theory." In *Latinos in New York: Communities in Transition*, edited by Gabriel Haslip-Viera and Sherrie L. Baver, 259–301. Notre Dame: University of Notre Dame Press.

———. 2007. *Boricua Power: A Political History of Puerto Ricans in the United States*. New York: New York University Press.

Sánchez, Luis. 2009. *The New Puerto Rico? Identity, Hybridity, and Transnationalism within the Puerto Rican Diaspora in Orlando, Florida*. Saarbrücken, Germany: VDM Verlag Dr. Müller.

Sánchez Korrol, Virginia E. 1994. *From Colonia to Community: The History of Puerto Ricans in New York City*. Berkeley: University of California Press.

Santa Ana, Otto. 2002. *Brown Tide Rising: Metaphors of Latinos in Contemporary American Public Discourse*. Austin: University of Texas Press.

Santos-Berry, Laura. 1981. "Latin Presence Grows in Orlando." *Orlando Sentinel*, December 13.

Schein, Richard H., ed. 2006. *Landscape and Race in the United States*. New York: Routledge.

Schlueb, Mark. 2001. "Minorities Worry about Redrawn Districts—Black Councilman Ernest Page Said City Council's Action 'Sent a Seething Message.'" *Orlando Sentinel*, October 1.

———. 2011. "Gateway Role Seen for Semoran." *Orlando Sentinel*, September 25.

———. 2012. "Face-Lift Starts on Shabby Stretch of Semoran." *Orlando Sentinel*, November 28.

———. 2014. "'20s Tinker Field to Be Leveled, Rebuilt Nearby." *Orlando Sentinel*, January 29.

Schneider, Jane, and Rayna Rapp. 1995. *Articulating Hidden Histories: Exploring the Influence of Eric R. Wolf*. Berkeley: University of California Press.

Sciorra, Joseph, and Martha Cooper. 1990. "'I Feel Like I'm in My Country': Puerto Rican Casitas in New York City." *Drama Review* 34(4):156–168.

Shankar, Shalini. 2015. *Advertising Diversity: Ad Agencies and the Creation of Asian-American Consumers*. Durham, NC: Duke University Press.

Shanklin, Mary. 2005. "Letter triggers Spirited Debate—The Orange County School Board Backs the Superintendent's Suspension of a Teacher." *Orlando Sentinel*, August 24. https://orlandosentinel.com.

———. 2011. "Home Slump Pummels Minorities." *Orlando Sentinel*, September 25. https://orlandosentinel.com.

Shanklin, Mary, and Charles Minshew. 2016. "Puerto Rican community branches out in Central Florida." *Orlando Sentinel*, December 8. https://orlandosentinel.com.

Shell-Weiss, Melanie. 2009. *Coming to Miami: A Social History*. Gainesville: University Press of Florida.

Shenot, Christine. 2000. "Hispanics, Blacks Give Details of Problems They Faced at the Polls." *Orlando Sentinel*, November 12.

Shermer, Elizabeth Tandy. 2011. "Sunbelt Boosterism: Industrial Recruitment, Economic Development, and Growth Politics in the Developing South." In *Sunbelt Rising: The Politics of Place, Space, and Region*, edited by Michelle Nickerson and Darren Dochuk, 31–57. Philadelphia: University of Pennsylvania Press.

Silva, Mark. 2001. "Jeb Bush Pursues Orlando Hispanics." *Orlando Sentinel*, August 24. https://orlandosentinel.com.

Silver, Patricia. 2010. "'Culture Is More than Bingo and Salsa': Making Puertorriqueñidad in Central Florida." *Centro Journal* 22(1):57–83.

———. 2015. "Remembering *Abuela*: Memory, Authenticity, and Place in Puerto Rican Orlando." *Latino Studies* 13(3):376–401.

———. 2016. "'You Don't Look Puerto Rican': Collective Memory and Community in Orlando." *Memory Studies* 9(4):405–412.

———. 2017. "Sunshine Politics: Puerto Rican Memory and the Political in New Destinations." *Centro Journal* 29(2):4–37.

Silver, Patricia, and William Vélez. 2017. "'Let Me Go Check Out Florida': Rethinking Puerto Rican Diaspora." *Centro Journal* 29(3):98–125.

Smith, Barbara Ellen. 1998. "The Postmodern South: Racial Transformations and the Global Economy." In *Cultural Diversity in the U.S. South: Anthropological Contributions to a Region in Transition*, edited by Carole E. Hill and Patricia D. Beaver. Athens: University of Georgia Press.

Smith, Heather A., and Owen J. Furuseth. 2006. *Latinos in the New South: Transformations of Place*. Burlington, VT: Ashgate.

Sommer, Doris. 1999. *Proceed with Caution, When Engaged by Minority Writing in the Americas*. Cambridge, MA: Harvard University Press.

Sparrow, Bartholomew H. *The* Insular Cases *and the Emergence of American Empire*. Lawrence: University Press of Kansas.

Spear, Kevin. 1998. "Johnson Joins Race for County Chairman." *Orlando Sentinel*, April 22.

Steinman, Jon. 2001. "Lines for Districts Draw Fire." *Orlando Sentinel*, September 4.

Stokes, Megan. 2010. "Racial Tensions High." *East Orlando Sun*, December 10.

———. 2011. "Semoran Makeover." *East Orlando Sun*, January 7.

Stratton, Jim. 2004. "Early Voters Flock to Polls; Floridians Endure Lines, Some Glitches." *Orlando Sentinel*, October 19.

Stratton, Jim, and Victor Manuel Ramos. 2006. "At Least 20,000 Rally in Orlando—Supporters of Immigrant Rights Fill Streets." *Orlando Sentinel*, May 2.

Striffler, Steve. 2007. "Neither Here nor There: Mexican Immigrant Workers and the Search for Home." *American Ethnologist* 34(4):674–688.

Stutzman, Rene. 1994. "'Everyone' Targeting Hispanics." *Orlando Sentinel*, Central Florida Business, January 17.

Suárez Findlay, Eileen J. 2014. *We Are Left without a Father Here: Masculinity, Domesticity, and Migration in Postwar Puerto Rico*. Durham, NC: Duke University Press.

Swift, Mike. 2002. "Central Florida: A New Promised Land." *Hartford Courant*, reprinted in *Orlando Sentinel*, July 21.

Tafoya, Sonya. 2004. "Shades of Belonging." Washington, DC: Pew Research Center.

Tauber, Steven. 2005. "African Americans in the Contemporary Florida Legislature." In *Politics in the New South: Representation of African Americans in Southern State Legislatures*, edited by Charles E. Menifield and Stephen D. Shaffer, 43–72. Albany: SUNY Press.

Taylor, Paul. 2012. "When Labels Don't Fit: Hispanics and Their Views of Identity." Washington, DC: Pew Research Center.

Thomas, Lorrin. 2009. "Resisting the Racial Binary? Puerto Ricans' Encounter with Race in Depression-Era New York City." *Centro Journal* 21(1):5–35.

———. 2010. *Puerto Rican Citizen: History and Political Identity in Twentieth-Century New York City*. Chicago: University of Chicago Press.

Thomas, Lorrin, and Aldo A. Lauria Santiago. 2019. *Rethinking the Struggle for Puerto Rican Rights*. New York: Routledge.

Toro-Morn, Maura I. 1995. "Gender, Class, Family, and Migration: Puerto Rican Women in Chicago." *Gender and Society* 9(6):712–726.

———. 2005. "Boricuas en Chicago: Gender and Class in the Migration and Settlement of Puerto Ricans." In *The Puerto Rican Diaspora: Historical Perspectives*, edited by Carmen Teresa Whalen and Víctor Vázquez-Hernández, 128–150. Philadelphia: Temple University Press.

Torres, Andrés. 1995. *Between Melting Pot and Mosaic: African Americans and Puerto Ricans in the New York Political Economy*. Philadelphia: Temple University Press.

———, ed. 2006. *Latinos in New England*. Philadelphia: Temple University Press.

Torres, Andrés, and José E. Velázquez, eds. 1998. *The Puerto Rican Movement: Voices from the Diaspora*. Philadelphia: Temple University Press.

Torres, Arlene. 1998. "La Gran Familia Puertorriqueña 'Ej Prieta de Beldá' (The Great Puerto Rican Family is Really Really Black)." In *Blackness in Latin America and the Caribbean: Social Dynamic and Cultural Transformations*, edited by Arlene Torres and Norman E. Whitten Jr., 285–306. Bloomington: Indiana University Press.

Torres, Julie. 2016. "Mourning in Orlando." *Anthropology News* 57(11):e103–e119.

———. 2020. "In Times of 'Crisis': Puerto Rican Activism, Gender, and Belonging in Orlando." PhD diss., University of Illinois Urbana-Champaign.

Torres-Saillant, Silvio. 2003. "Inventing the Race: Latinos and the Ethnoracial Pentagon." *Latino Studies* 1:123–151.

———. 2009. "Problematic Paradigms: Racial Diversity and Corporate Identity in the Latino Community." In *Latinos: Remaking America*, edited by Marcelo M.

Suárez-Orozco and Mariela M. Páez, 435–455. Rev. ed. Berkeley: University of California Press.

Torres Vélez, Jimmy. 2018. Interview by Patricia Silver. May 15, Orlando. Digital recording. In the author's possession.

Tracy, Dan. 1990. "Minority Candidates Aim to Break Barriers." *Orlando Sentinel*, September 2.

Trías Monge, José. 1997. *Puerto Rico: The Trials of the Oldest Colony in the World*. New Haven, CT: Yale University Press.

Trouillot, Michel-Rolph. 1995. *Silencing the Past: Power and the Production of History*. Boston: Beacon.

Tuan, Mia. 2001. *Forever Foreigners or Honorary Whites? The Asian Ethnic Experience Today*. New Brunswick, NJ: Rutgers University Press.

Unmuth, Katherine Leal. 2002. "More Puerto Ricans Make County Home." *Orlando Sentinel*, April 24.

US Census Bureau. 1960–2010. Decennial Census. Washington, DC.

US Census Bureau, ACS (American Community Survey). 2010. 5-Year Estimates. Washington, DC.

———. 2015. 5-Year Estimates. Washington, DC.

———. 2017a. 1-Year Estimates. Washington, DC.

———. 2017b. 5-Year Estimates. Washington, DC.

Valle, Ariana. 2019. "Race and the Empire-State: Puerto Ricans' Unequal U.S. Citizenship." *Sociology of Race and Ethnicity* 5(1):26–40.

Van Natta, Don Jr. 2011. "Latinos Rise in Numbers, Not in Influence." *New York Times*, April 8.

Vaquera, Elizabeth, Elizabeth Aranda, and Roberto G. Gonzales. 2014. "Patterns of Incorporation of Latinos in Old and New Destinations: From Invisible to Hypervisible." *American Behavioral Scientist* 58(14):1823–1833.

Vargas-Ramos, Carlos. 2014. "Puerto Rican Political and Civic Engagement in the United States." In *Puerto Ricans at the Dawn of the New Millennium*, edited by Edwin Meléndez and Carlos Vargas-Ramos, 260–283. New York: Center for Puerto Rican Studies, Hunter College, City University of New York.

———. 2015. "Puerto Ricans and Transnationalism: A Critical Empirical Assessment." *Centro Journal* 28(2):4–49.

Vázquez-Hernández, Víctor. 2015. "The Boricua Triangle: Tampa, Miami, and Orlando; A Historical Overview of the Development of a Transnational Puerto Rican Diaspora in Florida." *FCH Annals: Journal of the Florida Conference of Historians* 22:155–169.

Vélez-Ibañez, Carlos G. 1983. *Rituals of Marginality: Politics, Process, and Culture Change in Urban Central Mexico, 1969–1974*. Berkeley: University of California Press.

Venator-Santiago, Charles R. 2013. "Extending Citizenship to Puerto Rico: Three Traditions of Inclusive Exclusion." *Centro Journal* 25(1):50–75.

———. 2015. *Puerto Rico and the Origins of US Global Empire: The Disembodied Shade*. Oxford, England: Routledge.

Villarreal, Luz. 1994. "Butler, 4 Foes, Run on Her Record." *Orlando Sentinel*, Orange Extra, August 21.

Wadsworth, Charlie. 1981. "Hush Puppies." *Sentinel Star*, January 12.

Washington, John Thomas. 1977. "Power in the Black Subcommunity of Orlando." PhD diss., University of Florida.

Weiner, Jeff. 2017. "Sheehan: City Tone-Deaf with LGBTQ Omission." *Orlando Sentinel*, March 29.

Weise, Julie. 2012. "Dispatches from the 'Viejo' New South: Historicizing Recent Latino Migrations." *Latino Studies* 10(1–2):41–59.

West-Durán, Alan. 2005. "Puerto Rico: The Pleasures and Traumas of Race." *Centro Journal* 17(1):47–69.

Whalen, Carmen Teresa. 1998. "Bridging Homeland and Barrio Politics: The Young Lords in Philadelphia." In *The Puerto Rican Movement: Voices from the Diaspora*, edited by Andrés Torres, 107–123. Philadelphia: Temple University Press.

———. 2001. *From Puerto Rico to Philadelphia: Puerto Rican Workers and Postwar Economies*. Philadelphia: Temple University Press.

———. 2009. "Radical Contexts: Puerto Rican Politics in the 1960s and 1970s and the Center for Puerto Rican Studies." *Centro Journal* 21(2):221–255.

Whalen, Carmen Teresa, and Víctor Vázquez-Hernández, eds. 2005. *The Puerto Rican Diaspora: Historical Perspectives*. Philadelphia: Temple University Press.

Wilkerson, Isabel. 2010. *The Warmth of Other Suns: The Epic Story of America's Great Migration*. New York: Random House.

Wilson, Peter J. 1973. *Crab Antics: A Caribbean Case Study of the Conflict between Reputation and Respectability*. Prospect Heights, IL: Waveland.

Winders, Jamie, and Barbara Ellen Smith. 2010. "New Pasts: Historicizing Immigration, Race, and Place in the South." *Southern Spaces*, November 4.

Wolf, Eric. 1982. *Europe and the People without History*. Berkeley: University of California Press.

Young, Iris Marion. 1997. "Difference as a Resource for Democratic Communication." In *Deliberative Democracy: Essays on Reason and Politics*, edited by James Bohman and William Rehg. Cambridge, MA: MIT Press.

———. 2000a. *Inclusion and Democracy*. Oxford: Oxford University Press.

———. 2000b. "Structure, Difference, and Hispanic/Latino Claims of Justice." In *Hispanics/Latinos in the United States: Ethnicity, Race, and Rights*, edited by Jorge J. E. Gracia and Pablo De Grieff, 147–165. New York: Routledge.

Yow, Valerie Raleigh. 2005. *Recording Oral History: A Guide for the Humanities and Social Sciences*. Walnut Creek, CA: Alta Mira.

Ziffer, Randy. 1980. News article. *Orlando Sentinel Star*, October 8. In box 1, Mary I. Johnson Papers, Orange County Regional History Center Archives, Orlando. http://www.thehistorycenter.org/resources/library-archives.

Zukin, Sharon. 1991. *Landscapes of Power: From Detroit to Disney World*. Berkeley: University of California Press.

INDEX

Note: page numbers in *italics* refer to maps.